Economic Globalization and Governance

Luís Brites Pereira · Maria Eugénia Mata ·
Miguel Rocha de Sousa
Editors

Economic Globalization and Governance

Essays in Honor of Jorge Braga de Macedo

Springer

Editors
Luís Brites Pereira
Nova School of Business and Economics
Universidade Nova de Lisboa
Carcavelos, Portugal

Maria Eugénia Mata
Nova School of Business and Economics
Universidade Nova de Lisboa
Carcavelos, Portugal

Miguel Rocha de Sousa
Department of Economics,
CICP, CEFAGE
University of Évora
Évora, Portugal

ISBN 978-3-030-53264-2 ISBN 978-3-030-53265-9 (eBook)
https://doi.org/10.1007/978-3-030-53265-9

This Springer imprint is published by the registered company Springer Nature Switzerland AG
The registered company address is: Gewerbestrasse 11, 6330 Cham, Switzerland

To our families and friends, present in body or spirit. Our lives are richer for your presence. Our hearts are fuller for your love.

Foreword

Jorge Braga de Macedo: The Great Bridge-Builder

I first met Jorge Braga de Macedo under fairly odd circumstances: he was, at the time, serving in Portugal's military, while I, a mere 23 years old, was consulting for the Bank of Portugal.

Jorge's story, as I understand it, was that he had interrupted his graduate education at Yale to do his required military service, which began in Angola and finished with a stint as an army journalist. It was in that capacity that he found himself interviewing a group of MIT graduate students who ended up spending the summer of 1976 at the Bank. One of that group, by the way, was the late Miguel Beleza, who would later serve as Portugal's finance minister, among other things.

A little over a year later, Jorge was back at Yale—and I had just arrived at the same place as a newly minted assistant professor. We have been friends ever since, over a tumultuous era that spanned the global economic crisis following the 1979 oil shock, Portugal's 1986 entry into the European Union (EU), the 2008–2013 financial and Euro crisis, and Portugal's recent, gratifying economic recovery.

What strikes me now is that Jorge's journeys of the mid-1970s, from Portugal to Yale, back to Portugal, and then back to Yale again, prefigured the shape of his professional life. His research, teaching, and public service have added up to an impressive career. However, he has always been more than that resume implies. For he has been a bridge between Portugal, a small nation that when we met had just joined the ranks of Western democracies, and the West's intellectual and political core.

I've known a number of excellent economists from small countries who did their graduate work at core-country universities, and I've noticed that all of them face a kind of tension that's literally foreign to those of us with monocultural backgrounds.

On the one side, there are the opportunities and satisfactions that come from being a player in the core, whether that means Anglo-Saxon academia, global institutions like the International Monetary Fund or the European Commission and other EU institutions. Quite a few economists I know have built their careers entirely away from their home countries—which is O.K.!

On the other side, however, there's the chance to play an important role in one's nation of origin, and I know a number of economists who finished their education in America or Britain, then pursued academic and/or policy careers at home—which is also O.K.!

What's fairly rare is for an economist to keep a firm grip on both sides of the divide—to manage, in effect, to remain a valuable resource both in the big city and in his or her home village. (Apologies to anyone who considers that an insult to Portugal, which it isn't. Remember, I'm from New York.) And Jorge is a prime example of someone who has managed that feat.

As an academic, Jorge, who taught at Princeton for six years, has remained part of the international economics nomenklatura—people who are part of that circuit know what I'm talking about. He authored or co-authored influential papers on exchange rates and international finance and remains to this day a regular participant in key academic gatherings like the National Bureau of Economic Research's summer institute. He has always stayed in close touch with cutting-edge research.

Yet, he has also been a powerful force in economics education in Portugal itself, having a deep influence on multiple cohorts of students—some of them represented in this volume.

Jorge is also one of those people—a fairly small group, actually, even in my country—who have moved back and forth between academia and public service. And here too, he has managed to play an important role both abroad and at home—perhaps most notably at the European Commission and with a stint as finance minister and a more behind-the-scenes role as economic adviser.

There's a reason few people are able to play multiple roles the way Jorge has: it requires a special set of personal attributes. Obviously, you have to be smart, energetic, and intellectually curious, which already cuts the applicant pool way down. But you also have to combine flexibility with the kind of good humor that lets you ride out the occasional nastiness that pops up in all the environments that I've mentioned. And yes, that includes academia, where, as the old saying goes, the fights are especially vicious because the stakes are so small.

Luckily, Jorge is one of the most balanced, good-humored people I know. His students and colleagues obviously love him. I feel honored to call him a friend, and I hope people will see this volume as the heartfelt tribute it is.

New York, United States Paul Krugman

Testimonials

A Singular Academic and Generous Person

Luís Campos e Cunha

Nova School of Business and Economics, Universidade Nova de Lisboa, Carcavelos, Portugal
e-mail: lccunha@novasbe.pt

Jorge Braga de Macedo leaves no one indifferent. And this is a compliment. Jorge is a delightful person but can be hard-edged as well. Jorge is a man of passion with all the attributes that come with that condition.

He is an academic with a craving need of publishing; Jorge is a politician with a strong and feverish attachment to the centrist party in Portugal, and is able and eager to intervene in the media as a columnist or as a commentator on television; he also is a professional and worked in relevant organizations, both at the international and domestic levels.

Jorge, after a non-start in medicine, really started his education with a degree in Law at the *Universidade de Lisboa*. Later, he turned to Yale for a Master program in (economic) international relations and, much later, finished his Ph.D. in economics. In the meantime, Jorge was drafted and served the Portuguese army in Angola and this had an important impact on him, until today.

Jorge, as an academic, has an impressive record of well over 300 publications in international journals, books chapters, and books. His main interests are international economics, development, namely related with the African economies, and European affairs.

This engagement with Africa is what he brought from his military service in Angola and he has reinforced that interest during the last two decades. This African "disease" is common to many that, during the times of the empire, were drafted and served in one of the Portuguese African colonies. Due to that interest, he was appointed as President of the Tropical Research Institute in Lisbon.

He has taught in a countless number of Schools: *Universidade de Luanda*, *Universidade Católica Portuguesa*, Princeton University, *Universidade Nova de Lisboa, Science Po* in Paris…

Jorge has a strong interest in social intervention as a complement to his academic career. As an active member of the *Partido Social Democrata*, he was finance minister (1991–1993) and adviser to several prime ministers. He also participated actively in numerous election campaigns. This is also the trigger for his media intervention, both in newspapers and on television.

Jorge was at the European Commission as Director for National Economies. He is a member of NBER and CEPR and he also belongs to the *Academia das Ciências* where he is a very active member. As a Member of the Portuguese Parliament, he chaired the Commission of European Affairs.

I have met Jorge, in 1975, as my professor at the Catholic University in Lisbon, still during my undergraduate studies. He was a shock to all students. He was young, fresh, and different from all other faculty, and he loved to be in that role. I am not sure about what we learned, but we got the idea there was another world in economics and in academia. That was very important.

Later, as a colleague at the Nova School of Business and Economics, I witnessed his pleasure in helping students and young faculty with his immense international network. He also engaged actively with his colleagues, so much so that everyday work and professional interactions often gave rise to genuine comradery over the years. I am thinking in particular about the Pinto Barbosa twins (António and Manuel), Fernando Brito Soares and Paulo Barcia, also known as the briscola group. I am sure several others could also be associated with this Festschrift in honor of Jorge. Indeed, no one can ever claim that Jorge refused to lend a helping hand when asked. He is a very generous person. Not in money issues, his parsimonious way of spending is well established, and I am being very polite!

On this score, I owe Jorge friendship and solidarity in important moments of my life. Even without asking for it, Jorge was also always there with a word of comfort or with a helping hand. A very generous person, indeed!

A Perspective from the Overseas Historical Archive

Ana Canas

Arquivo Histórico Ultramarino, Lisbon, Portugal
e-mail: ana.martins@ahu.dglab.gov.pt

The Overseas Historical Archive (AHU—*Arquivo Histórico Ultramarino*) contributed decisively to the life of the Tropical Research Institute (IICT—*Instituto de Investigação Científica Tropical*), which was presided by Prof. Jorge Braga de

Macedo from December 2003 until its extinction at the end of August 2015.[1] I had an opportunity to witness this fact directly, and often intensely, when I accepted the challenge to become the AHU's new director in July 2005. I took over from Conceição Casanova who, like me, had come over from the *Torre do Tombo* National Archive.

During this period, the AHU's open public access policy allowed for the dissemination of a wide variety of research outputs, not only of those related to AHU's scientific disciplines (such as the archival, information and conservation sciences) but also those of the IICT, notably history. More important, however, was the decision to link the AHU's archives together with the IICT's own historical and scientific archives, thereby ensuring their connection and greater public visibility. This decision addressed the urgent need to register, preserve, and make available the archival materials originating from different departments within the IICT. Up till then, these materials had often been in very disparate locations, only accessible to a selected few or even nobody at all, as the linkages to the original creators and source locations diminished over time.

The decision to grant universal access to the whole of the archives was significant and directly attributable to the importance and recognition that this objective was afforded by the IICT's presidency. Rather than one specific moment in time, this decision was materialized in an ongoing succession of actions and initiatives, including formal deliberations by relevant institutional bodies.[2] This profound change was witnessed by various visitors coming from many different organizations, such as the diplomatic missions based in Lisbon, the United Nations Educational, Scientific and Cultural Organization (UNESCO), the Royal Museum for Central Africa, and especially the Community of Portuguese-speaking Nations (CPLP—*Comunidade dos Países de Língua Portuguesa*), as well as CPLP member states, of course. Indeed, the fact that the IICT's heritage, including its archives, was seen as a shared cultural legacy of all CPLP member states, and not just that of Portugal, meant that the AHU had increased sense of responsibility when it came to fulfilling its mission, going over and beyond the production and dissemination of scientific and technical outputs.

In practice, this concern implied that the IICT's scientific research, also pursued in collaboration with universities, sought to foster mutual knowledge and

[1]The AHU was tasked with preserving and accessing the records pertaining to Portugal's Colonial periods. Many of the records stretch from the end of the sixteenth until the twentieth century, and originate from such diverse countries as Angola, Brazil, Cape Verde, Guinea Bissau, India, Macao, Mozambique, Sao Tome and Principe and East Timor, among others. The Tropical Research Institute, meanwhile, was established in 1883 (as the Cartography Commission) and its mission was to promote Tropical Knowledge through interdisciplinary research of relevance to Portuguese-speaking countries. Another of its objectives was to grant these countries access to IICT's vast historic and scientific archives.

[2]Specifically, the Presidency (broadened to include departmental heads), Steering Committee and Monitoring Unit (which included the Directorate General of the Book, Archives & Libraries, Ministry of Culture, as well as the Ministry of Science, Technology and Higher Education, which was responsible for the IICT's political oversight).

understanding between persons, communities, and countries, which implied paying attention to the archival heritage. To be sure, it was not always easy to breach the then prevailing institutional and scientific barriers in response to the President's recurrent call for the AHU to become organizationally more open and integrated in order to contribute more actively toward the IICT's mission. This difficulty was felt more keenly at times, especially during the constant and necessary process of external and self-assessment. Although results were mixed, this course of action was certainly worthwhile when it came to changing mindsets and ensuring openness to collaboration, which is still evident today after the AHU's incorporation into the Ministry of Culture's Directorate General of the Book, Archives and Libraries (DGLAB—*Direção Geral do Livro, Arquivos e Bibliotecas*) at the end of August 2015.[3]

While the deepening of the AHU's integration in the IICT addressed the issue of its then relative isolation, this could not come at the cost of reducing the AHU's public notoriety, however, which is still relatively high. Other issues remained to be resolved, as is to be expected under the circumstances. Some of these would prove to be increasingly limiting, such as the reduction in personnel and funding, which the 2008 financial crisis made worse. The uncertainty regarding the IICT's role, as an autonomous institution, in contributing toward Portugal's international development policy through its Tropical Knowledge, was also unhelpful.

Notwithstanding, the AHU and its users benefited greatly from Prof. Jorge Braga de Macedo's determination to endow the IICT with a clear mission and unified operational structure, comprising the archival heritage, and often in the face of misconceptions and misunderstandings, especially regarding the demanding need to constantly monitor and evaluate performance. In this process, the AHU also relied on the contribution of new researchers, mostly young, who were funded through fellowships granted by the Portuguese Agency for Science and Technology (FCT—*Fundação para a Ciência e Tecnologia*). Indeed, their contribution was to become increasingly significant, as they forged fruitful working relationships with existing researchers and technicians. In particular, they monitored the documentation repositories, mitigated the damage caused by various pests, and also prepared and digitized most of the AHU's photographic collections in order to place these online at the Digital Tropical Science Archive (ACTD—*Arquivo Científico Tropical Digital*).[4] A significant part of the catalog of the IICTs' library collections was also made available in this manner, in an initiative funded by the FCT.

The AHU's scope of work extended to include other projects involving external institutions, namely the description of the defunct Overseas Ministry Archives (*Fundação Calouste Gulbenkian*), records-based research (FCT), matters of pure archival processing (ADAI Program—*IberArchivos*, with the support of DGLAB), and also commemorative events (such as the Centenary of the Portuguese Republic). In a similar vein, the improved identification and study of various other

[3]As of the same date, the University of Lisbon incorporated the IICT's other departments upon the latter's extinction.

[4]The reader will find the archive at the following website: actd.iict.pt.

archival sources was also undertaken. These sources included: the various departments of Portugal's Overseas Ministry, as well as of its Overseas Council (with respect to the countries of Angola, Cape Verde, Guinea Bissau and Sao Tome and Principe); the Cartography Commission and the Public Works (which in this case also included Mozambique); the territories controlled by Portugal in India (Goa), China (Macao) and in the Pacific (East Timor); the military expeditions in Angola and Mozambique during World War I; and, the private collection donated by Francisco Mantero which mostly had to do with Sao Tome and Principe.

All these initiatives, as well as conservation efforts and public access policy, reflected the fulfillment of the IICT's commitment to grant access to its archives, which came to include those of the AHU, as already described. This commitment was undertaken during the CPLP Ministers of Science and Technology meeting in Rio de Janeiro in 2003. Indeed, it was never forgotten by Prof. Braga de Macedo as it underpinned the impetus and organizational changes that the AHU would go on to implement under his leadership.

At the same, and notwithstanding the lack of physical space, the AHU also housed documentation that had been widely dispersed within the Overseas Ministry, as well as some coming from defunct IICT departments. In these cases, conservation and public access remained paramount concerns. This was amply demonstrated in the case of the Dembos Archives, which were to be inscribed in the UNESCO's World Registry jointly by Angola and Portugal. The improvement in physical storage capacity and repositories' integrity resumed the incipient but incomplete effort that had been initiated by Prof. Mariano Gago during his tenure as Minister of Science and Technology during 1995–2002. While insufficient in scope, resuming this effort nonetheless allowed the AHU to address the serious risks that its archives faced, as well as the building that housed them.

In this regard, Prof. Braga de Macedo understood that making the AHU archives more visible and accessible for external use would justify the increased allocation of resources needed to keep, process, and disseminate their content. This concern underpinned the AHU's public initiatives, which Prof. Braga de Macedo always supported and participated in at times. He also encouraged the free and frank of ideas around this topic, in open debates. The "Science in the Tropics" initiative, which comprised numerous conferences in the AHU's Brazil Hall with a highly diversified set of speakers, moderators, and audiences, exemplified the increased collaboration *modus operandi* adopted within the IICT. The knowledge that was shared during these events, which included showing selected historical records, breathed new life into the old archives, thereby increasing their value for all.

Other diverse initiatives were also undertaken at the AHU, transcending both the time and space in which they took place, in terms of topics and audience. Indeed, these initiatives may still inspire renewed efforts at affecting the senses of belonging and responsibility with respect to the future use of the AHU's archives. In January 2006, the conference on Preventative and Emergency Plans for Museums, Libraries and Archives, set the tone for the appreciation by the public, still relevant today, of the Pompeii Hall's splendor. It should be said that the walls of this iconic AHU hall are covered with Dutch tiles dating from the beginning of the XVIII century. The tiles themselves depict the European ports comprising the international trade routes going past Portugal, which stretched all the way to Istanbul. One month later, upon the launch of the book *Jorge Borges de Macedo: Saber Continuar*,[5] the presence of the then Minister of State and Foreign Affairs, Prof. Diogo Freitas do Amaral, lent institutional importance to the AHU and also to the work of the historian being honored. This was particularly fitting as the historian had often consulted the AHU's archives in his endeavor to reconstruct the past, in keeping with his indispensable spirit of critical thinking. In that same year, the AHU celebrated its 75th anniversary in a series of concerts,[6] which also served to consolidate the objective of preserving and broadening the access to the AHU's archives. In 2007, Perrine Canavaggio (International Archives Council) and Jay Levenson (Director of the International Program of the New York Museum of Modern Art and Commissioner of the "Encompassing the Globe" exhibition) opened the International Seminar of Lusophone Memories, entitled "The Departure of the Royal Court to Brazil." This seminar was associated with the VIII Meeting of the Luso-Brazilian Commission for the Safeguarding and Dissemination of Documental Patrimony (COLUSO), as well as the IV Meeting of the Forum of Portuguese-language Archives.

In 2012, the Pompeii Hall and other locales within the AHU witnessed the International Colloquium "Science in the Tropics: Perceptions from the Past, Perspectives for the Future." This event was complemented by the Exhibition "Scientific Travels and Missions, 1883–2010," which was housed in the Tropical Botanical Garden. Professor Braga de Macedo was deeply involved in the conference's organization, as was the late Jean-Pierre Contzen, a keen observer and external evaluator of the system of Science and Technology in Portugal. The event's main takeaway was that the IICT could play an important role in ensuring S&T collaboration with CPLP countries, given the grounding that the IICT's historical and scientific archives could provide for this endeavor, especially as the AHU's archival heritage is shared across CPLP countries.

The management of the IICT's heritage and knowledge was changed after August 2015 when other institutions (academic and governmental) took over this responsibility. To be sure, the passage of the IICT's legacy at that time undoubtedly also reflected the past actions of many different people across time, belonging to different generations. Those individuals responsible for decision-making would have had to deal with numerous uncertainties, institutional inertias while also needing to acquire an existential sense of mission, which may not have been that clear to them at first. During his time as IICT president, Jorge Braga de Macedo showed that not only was he fully aware of the legacy he inherited from those who

[5]Jorge Borges de Macedo was a distinguished Portuguese historian and pedagogue, and also the father of Prof. Braga de Macedo. The book's title refers to his insight that it is important to know how to carry on in life (*saber continuar*, in Portuguese) by adapting past values and then projecting them into future actions.

[6]Following efforts in the preceding decade, the AHU was established in 1931 in order to safe-guard the historical records of Portuguese colonial administration, as these had been largely neglected.

preceded him but also that he knew how to continue this legacy, by helping to recover, produce, and disseminate the "Tropical Knowledge" of relevance for the socio-economic development of Portuguese-speaking countries, which entailed also using the AHU's archival heritage. This truly is the testament he now bequeaths to those who need to move this legacy forward, under new institutional arrangements, and for the new times that lie ahead!

A Biologist with an Interest in Economics

Rui Malhó

Faculdade de Ciências, Universidade de Lisboa, Lisbon, Portugal
e-mail: rmmalho@ciencias.ulisboa.pt

First Impressions In 1990, I had just finished my graduate degree in Biology and started my Ph.D. at Lisbon University. Thanks to the European structural funds, scientific research in Portugal was about to leave behind a "lag phase," which is a term used in biology to describe the first steps of microorganisms' growth curves. During the lag phase, growth is slow and the population prepares metabolically for fast exponential growth. That next step is obviously dependent not only on the population but on the exogenous supply of energy (be it is food or other resources).

For scientific research, the required energy boost was funding. In the second half of the nineteen eighties, the Portuguese Agency for Science and Technology (FCT), under the presidency of José Mariano Gago, prepared and launched a mobilizing program that intersected with other funding projects aimed at the training of human resources and the development of needed infrastructures. So while Portuguese research was entering the "log phase," I started to grow as a scientist and develop my own notion of how science and technology could and should be used to drive modern societies in general, and Portugal in particular.

It was in this context that I first came across with Jorge Braga de Macedo. In 1991, he was appointed finance minister of the XII Constitutional Government of Portugal under the third electoral mandate of Prime Minister Aníbal Cavaco Silva. In biological processes as in politics, turn-over is important and that XII government experienced great social tension and friction notwithstanding its parliamentary majority. And, needless to say, finance ministers are not usually the most popular members of government! So from a personal (and younger) perspective, my impression of Jorge Braga de Macedo was far from positive. A government that was not driven by knowledge and innovation, and that was investing mostly in physical infrastructure, could certainly not receive my support! From the distance of time, however, and knowing now significantly more about the complexities of governance and Portugal's development at the end of the twentieth century, I concede this was a shallow evaluation. It was nevertheless the impression that prevailed for about a decade and a half until I personally met Jorge Braga de Macedo, as an academic fellow.

The Academia Network In 2007, I was honored to be elected as Corresponding Member of the Lisbon Academy of Sciences (*Academia das Ciências de Lisboa*). The Academy is organized along two main sections—Sciences and Letters—which run separate sessions. So, it is not often that biologists or chemists meet their fellows from law or economics. This is unfortunate as one can argue that economy and finance are as close to law and politics, as to mathematics and applied sciences or, for that matter, to biological sciences. My career path took me from basic plant molecular and cell biology to an interest in agricultural biotechnology with all its applications and implications. Topics ranging from genetic engineering and crop improvement to sustainability and biodiversity intersect easily with food production and distribution, agricultural policies, sovereignty and economic value. During this path, I came across the works of economists like Amartya Sen (particularly focusing on poverty and famine) and Dominic Moran (the value of biodiversity). Indeed, I always refer my students to them, emphasizing that advances in science and technology should be accompanied by comprehensive analysis of philosophical, ethical, and societal aspects.

In one of the rare occasions where academic fellows from both sections meet, I was introduced to Prof. Jorge Braga de Macedo as "a Biologist with an interest in Economics." I vividly remember that the feedback was a very genuine, enthusiastic one, as only someone can have when one really enjoys his work. During the conversation that followed—and the several others after that—I confess it was difficult to maintain that first impression of the finance minister. I was now discussing and exchanging ideas with a person endowed with very broad interests and culture, who could listen and argue, who was highly motivated, particularly open to discussing inter- and multidisciplinary activities, and often disarmingly informal. Soon, I was being recruited to assist with several collaborative projects together with other academic fellows, both from the Sciences and Letters sections, some of which are still ongoing.

The "Writing to Queens" Project The first decade of this century witnessed the subprime crisis and the emergence of an intense debate as to why it had not been predicted. The reasons were diverse, ranging from poor regulation to a cognitive bias, from the misinterpretation of mathematical models to ethical misconceptions. This lead to our first collaboration that resulted in the publication of the book "Writing to Queens while Crises Proceed," edited by Jorge Braga de Macedo. Through him, and thanks to this project, I got to know brilliant colleagues like Rui Vilela Mendes, José F. Santos, Renato Flores and Jean-Pierre Contzen. Through them, I got to know the outstanding works of Parag Khanna and Daniel Kahneman. And as a result, I became more aware of a topic that eventually led me to the writings of Mariana Mazzucato and Thomas Piketty. This, in turn, led to more stimulating discussions with Jorge Braga de Macedo (as one can easily deduce!).

Throughout this collaboration, I had the chance to present and discuss my biological perspective of why dynamics systems oscillate, why stochastic failure happens even in homeostatic processes, how these can be mitigated through data sharing, and the advantages and drawbacks of doing so. In short, I thought of the economy as a complex system, in much the same way we can think of a neuronal network. In such systems, a signal may trigger responses whose intensity and dispersion depend not only on the initial stimulus but also on the local environment where it is perceived and its homeostatic condition. Such an analogy has several implications, namely three that are quite significant for society:

(1) Reliable absolute predictions are impossible so errors will eventually arise, no matter how robust our models are. Dealing with error is a challenge, particularly in topics relating to societal well-being;
(2) No system can experience constant growth so fluctuations must be considered. All dynamic processes deviate from equilibrium experiencing oscillations, more or less regular, more or less intense. Interdependence and data sharing might prevent large changes and help governance but that relies on cooperation, not on competition;
(3) No system functions independently of its environment so external conditions must always be considered. It is therefore important to define, with the maximum possible accuracy, our "location" in the system (geopolitical region), interaction networks (privileged partners), specific characteristics (language, history), and resources (goods and humans). Without this, there is a risk (or perhaps a temptation) of importing well-succeeded models, tailored to specific circumstances, but whose transposition will prove ineffectual or even counter-productive.

This perspective, which I entitled a "cell biologist's *naïve* approach," was discussed in some sessions organized by Jorge at the Academy of Sciences and one, in particular, gathered Manuel Jacinto Nunes, José da Silva Lopes and Paul Krugman into the discussion. It is not easy to describe the adrenaline rush that I experienced during that session.

The Tropical Man Another project that I can relate to strongly concerns the involvement of Jorge Braga de Macedo as former President of the Tropical Research Institute (IICT—*Instituto de Investigação Científica Tropical*). A significant part of the mission of this former state laboratory was to study and help preserve the biodiversity of African countries that have Portuguese as their official language (PALOP). Since I hosted in my research group several members from PALOP countries, this generated further collaborations such as the organization of scientific meetings (e.g. *Ciência nos Trópicos: Olhares sobre o Passado, Perspectivas de Futuro; Tropical em Moçambique: História, Memória e Ciência*); the evaluation of IICT members, joint communications (*XXIII Encontro da Associação das Universidades de Língua Portuguesa*) and participation in the TropikMan Ph.D. management program. In all the activities where I participated, I can testify to the commitment demonstrated by Jorge in promoting initiatives aimed at sharing knowledge and contributing towards the development of these countries. Again, this contrasts with the popular and preconceived idea that politicians afford the common good a low priority in their list of objectives. And, I can also testify his interest in a topic so relevant to our country: Given a shared language, Portugal is in a privileged position to help PALOP countries to develop, promote, and study their ethno-botanical potential.

It's Complex! Like in a cell signaling process, a cascade of network events in 2018 led me to participate in the *Encontros da Arrábida* about Complexity, together with Jorge. The underlying theme was "Perspectives, Speculations and Utopias." The meeting was very fruitful, and we were asked to organize the 2019 edition, which we did under the theme "Complexity 4.0: Models and Global Policies." We discussed the impact of the digital revolution on the environment, economy, labor, and society in general. How to manage information networks that respect individuality and privacy? How to determine the real value of goods and products ensuring manufacturing sustainability and associated processes? How can artificial intelligence help us manage resources and combat climate change? What policies are needed to reconcile automation, labor, and migratory flows? I think this initiative reflects our common belief that bold and innovative ideas should translate into real improvements of governance and policies for the benefit of society. Clearly my first impressions of Jorge Braga de Macedo have changed, and very much for the better!

Jorge Braga de Macedo: A Personal Tribute

James K. Galbraith

Lyndon B. Johnson School of Public Affairs, The University of Texas at Austin, TX, USA
e-mail: galbraith@mail.utexas.edu

I first met Jorge Braga de Macedo a week or two after the start of term at Yale, at the Cowles Foundation, fall of 1976. I had come in from a year on the staff of the Banking Committee, US House of Representatives—it was still permitted, back then, for people with policy interests and some experience to pursue graduate degrees in economics. Jorge was returning from a stint in the military or so I understood at the time. I asked him if he'd been a member of the MFA (an organization of lower-ranking, politically left-leaning officers in the Portuguese Armed Forces that was responsible for instigating the Carnation Revolution of 1974). He hadn't but was surprised that anyone in so distant and provincial a spot had heard of it. We were friends from then on.

Yale in those days, at the dawn of the new classical era, was a peculiar place whose geography I only faintly understood. The top-tier students, in advanced micro-theory, introduced to us as stars, would disappear into academic obscurity. Supposedly, second-tier types would go to the major international institutions, notably the Fund and the Bank. A far fringe—Barry Eichengreen, Nancy Birdsall, myself—were there for other reasons. In my case, the degree seemed necessary for the coming policy wars. And there were the Mexicans, esoteric enthusiasts of CGE models. Some of them would have big, then-unsuspected careers. Many years later at a 60th birthday festschrift conference for Joe Stiglitz, I found myself sitting next to another common friend and classmate, listening to Robert Solow read a highly congenial paper entitled "Dumb and Dumber in Macroeconomics." I remarked to him that I had always thought if one could only close eyes and ears for thirty years, this sort of thing would disappear. He agreed, "it was a good time to enter public service." It was Ernesto Zedillo.

Among the faculty, Jim Tobin seemed in absolute control and yet, in the larger scheme of the higher economics, on the intellectual defensive. Even more so, a periphery of senior Institutionalists, simulation pioneers and applied econometricians—Lloyd Reynolds, Joe Peck, Guy Orcutt, Richard Ruggles—would leave few traces on the next generation. An evolutionary economics, spearheaded by Dick Nelson and Sidney Winter—later my very-tolerant thesis chair—seemed to me somehow not-quite-authentic. I recall writing to them that perhaps their approach had too much Lamarck and too little Darwin. Paul Krugman was in his debut teaching year, talking up increasing returns to scale. The other rising lights were in finance, in capital asset pricing, and in international monetary economics.

In some ways, Jorge was the quintessential Yale economist-graduate-student of our generation. Working with Pentti Kouri at the dawn of Pentti's career on a Tobin-Brainard "pitfalls" model of the foreign exchange markets, pioneering multi-country data analysis with the primitive computers of that day, open to, and yet not entirely sold on, the rational-expectations, representative-agent worldview. I do recall him coming back from a Robert Lucas visiting seminar that I did not bother to attend with a pithy verdict: "an exercise in exogeneity." As I did not then figure Pentti for the leading advocate of Keynesian doctrine in Finland's central banking history—nor for one of the great speculators ever to emerge from academic economics—so I did not figure Jorge, a serious young scholar, far more diligent than myself, for a future minister of finance.

Then and later, Jorge's good standing in the academic mainstream, and my skeptical view of it, have been a deep source of our bond. Once, building on an inside joke between us, I managed to get the Yale computer to print a bogus error message "failure to grasp—type HELP GRSPFL for Help" at the top of one of his printouts: The induced perplexity was momentary but delightful. But when my father came to talk at Yale, Jorge made him cringe—something rarely seen—by reminding him of the inelegant coinage, "technostructure." Game, set, match. Only one of many over the years.

And Jorge did enter public service, in Portugal, at the OECD and also at the IMF, where he served on a commission of inquiry following the disgrace of the Fund's decision-making toward Greece in 2010—a difficult and honorable assignment. Likewise, his long service as President of the Tropical Research Institute in Lisbon. In this way, he has kept a balance between his intellectual and academic diversions and his deeper sense of self, as his father's son, as a Portuguese, as a European and as a citizen of the world.

A scholarly volume is not the ideal place for remarks on a friendship that despite its academic origins is largely personal and sympathetic, stretching over a half century and family interaction covering three generations, ourselves, our wives, our parents, and our children. However, these comments would not be complete without mentioning Jorge's presence through the deepest and most important moments in my life, the joyful and generous hospitality from him and from Luiza on every visit to Lisbon and the Apples Beach in Sintra, from my first honeymoon in 1979 onward, and also on occasions in Paris, and our frequent meetings in Cambridge, Austin and especially in Vermont, where—as he knows—he has a hilltop farmhouse waiting whenever wanted in the summer months. No one ever had a better friend!

Introduction

Abstract Nowadays, the pressures for further global and regional integration exist parallel to growing nationalist demands. The benefits of globalization coexist with frustration at intra-national divides and growing inequality. How to reconcile these opposing forces are placing greater and greater demands on political leaders, and on the economists who advise them. We need Renaissance Economists who can engage with the full range of the global demands recognizing potential trade-offs. We are fortunate in this volume to be honoring and recognizing the contribution of just such an economist.

The Renaissance Economist

We are living in uncertain times. Fact versus fiction are increasingly contested. The pressures for further global and regional integration exist parallel to growing nationalist demands. The benefits of globalization, which has seen hundreds of millions of people lifted out of extreme poverty and some evidence of international convergence in terms of economic development, coexist with frustration at intra-national divides and growing inequality. How to reconcile these opposing forces are placing greater and greater demands on political leaders, and on the economists who advise them. And yet, perhaps we are less equipped to deal with these demands. Economists are increasingly self-isolating and becoming technical modelers and, as a result, are more and more removed from the complexities of the real political economy. We are in need of Renaissance Economists who can engage with the full range of the global demands recognizing potential trade-offs. Policymakers seldom have the choice of option A and are often frustrated by economists not being able to recognize this fact and providing a suite of practical options. We are fortunate in this volume to be honoring and recognizing the contribution of just such a Renaissance Economist.

Jorge Braga de Macedo's work reflects the full range of expertise required in such a world. Few of us can claim to be such a polymath. This is reflected in the scope of his work which this volume attempts to capture. But it is more than this—

his work also reflects a diversity of methodological approaches which are fit for purpose. And then there is the practice which has seen him not only engage in these discussions as an academic but also as a policymaker. As minister of finance, for example, he signed the Maastricht Treaty of the European Union in 1992 on behalf of Portugal, a pivotal moment in European and Portuguese history.

The book is divided into three parts which loosely mirror his contributions over five decades. Each editor introduces one part and together they provide a brief curriculum and detailed list of publications in the appendix.

Part I is structured around economic history and history of thought. As Luciano Amaral reminds us in the opening chapter, Jorge Braga de Macedo's incursions into the realm of economic history, while rare, have been very fruitful. Indeed, understanding present and future challenges requires us to make sense of the past and we are often the poorer for not fully investing the resources into the domains of economic history. The contributions in this part reflect the value of doing so. To mention just one such example, the chapter by Barry Eichengreen provides a useful analysis and comparison of the nineteenth-century classical gold standard and the euro. It reflects important similarities and differences but also provides lessons for the way forward even though "the gold standard operated in a simpler political setting, one in which mass participation in electoral politics was the exception to the rule."

Part II examines macroeconomic theory and practice with a focus on open economy macroeconomics. This approach is suited to Europe more generally, and Portugal more specifically, as it has implications for long run economic growth and development. The chapters convey the importance of his work both as an academic and as a policymaker. This ranges from discussions on the contributions of Krugman and Macedo (1979) as regards understanding Portugal as a small open economy, to the debt crisis and the push for austerity more recently, the challenges of European integration, and directions for the Euro.

Part III looks at five contributions related to international political economy, and two complementary ones from law and sociology, in keeping with the honoree's interdisciplinary research bent. Indeed, the chapters reflect the breadth of Jorge Braga de Macedo's interests including chapters on international cooperation in the age of populism, constitutional issues and intergenerational equity, international migration, and analyses of areas where multilateral cooperation is necessary, such as climate change, international corporate taxation and sustainable development.

In an era of increasing volatility, uncertainty, and complexity, we need Renaissance Economists more than ever. This volume shows why that is the case and pays tribute to just such a person.

John M. Luiz
University of Sussex Business School
Brighton, UK
e-mail: J.M.Luiz@sussex.ac.uk

Contents

Contributors

Gonçalo de Almeida Ribeiro Católica School of Law, Universidade Católica Portuguesa, Lisbon, Portugal

David Amaglobeli Fiscal Affairs Department, International Monetary Fund, Washington D.C., USA

Luciano Amaral Nova School of Business and Economics, Universidade Nova de Lisboa, Carcavelos, Portugal

António S. Pinto Barbosa Nova School of Business and Economics, Universidade Nova de Lisboa, Carcavelos, Portugal

Cátia Batista Nova School of Business and Economics, Universidade Nova de Lisboa, Carcavelos, Portugal

Annette Bongardt CICP – Research Center in Political Science, Universidade de Évora, Évora, Portugal

Michael D. Bordo Department of Economics, Rutgers University, New Brunswick, NJ, USA

José Luís Cardoso Instituto de Ciências Sociais, Universidade de Lisboa, Lisboa, Portugal

Barry Eichengreen University of California, Berkeley, CA, USA

Miguel Faria-e-Castro Federal Reserve Bank of St. Louis, St. Louis, MO, USA

Marc Flandreau Department of History, University of Pennsylvania College, Philadelphia, PA, USA

Jeffry Frieden Department of Government, Harvard University, Cambridge, MA, USA

Vítor Gaspar Fiscal Affairs Department, International Monetary Fund, Washington D.C., USA

Paul De Grauwe London School of Economics and Political Science, London, UK

António Castro Henriques Faculdade de Economia, Universidade do Porto, Porto, Portugal

Yuemei Ji School of Slavonic & East European Studies, University College London, London, UK

Paul Krugman City University of New York, New York City, NY, USA

Jorge De La Barre Department of Sociology and Methodology of Social Sciences, Universidade Federal Fluminense, São Domingos, Niterói, RJ, Brazil

Miguel Lebre de Freitas Universidade de Aveiro and NIPE, Aveiro, Portugal

Pedro S. Martins School of Business and Management, Queen Mary University of London, London, UK

Luís Catela Nunes Nova School of Business and Economics, Universidade Nova de Lisboa, Carcavelos, Portugal

Alfredo Marvão Pereira Department of Economics, College of William and Mary, Williamsburg, VA, USA

Rui Manuel Pereira Department of Economics, College of William and Mary, Williamsburg, VA, USA

Jaime Reis Instituto de Ciências Sociais, Universidade de Lisboa, Lisbon, Portugal

Julia Seither Department of Economics, University of Chicago, Chicago, IL, USA

Aníbal Cavaco Silva Gabinete do Sacramento, Convento do Sacramento, Lisbon, Portugal

Francisco Torres Católica Lisbon School of Business & Economics, Universidade Católica Portuguesa, Lisbon, Portugal

Pedro C. Vicente Nova School of Business and Economics, Universidade Nova de Lisboa, Carcavelos, Portugal

Jürgen von Hagen Department of Economics, University of Bonn, Bonn, Germany

Economic History

Jorge Braga de Macedo contributed to international monetary economics in several ways, and his analytical conclusions have been detailed in empirical studies of presentday national economies as well as in monetary history. Indeed, this part is almost exclusively devoted to economic history, unlike Part II, where European economic issues and their implications for Portugal are discussed, and Part III, which gathers contributions of relevance to international political economy, including two from law and sociology.

The contributions presented here are heartfelt expressions of admiration and gratitude to the honoree. They result from far-ranging partnerships in academic life, scientific sociability, and personal proximity, in different geographical windows and timings.

In the first contribution, Luciano Amaral discusses four of the honoree's pioneering articles and shows how these contributed to our current knowledge of three fundamental Portuguese economic issues, namely: economic growth, openness and connection with other European economies between the 1960s and 1980s.

Jaime Reis, in the second one, uses primary material from the Bank of Portugal's archive to show how it departed from Bagehot's archetype of the central bank as lender of last resort in the first banking crisis of the early 1920s. He concludes that a lack of awareness of his paradigm was not the reason for the policy option of the Bank of Portugal.

In the third, Marc Flandreau, who led the international finance team at Sciences-Po where the honoree taught in the 2000's, presents a loan contract signed on 27 September 1823 between the Portuguese Minister of Finance and Goldschmidt, and offers an economic, historical and political meditation on the bond that was not tied with Rothschild. The failure of Goldschmidt in 1826, and Portugal's default in 1828, tarnished the Crown's reputation with consequences lasting well after the Portuguese Civil War ended in 1834. It is apposite to remark that the honoree's first publication fifty years ago, as well as his most recent, address precisely the issue of Portugal's financial reputation (see Appendix for the publications).

In the fourth contribution, António Castro Henriques, the honoree's nephew and godson, sees the thirteenth century as the first era of constitutional experiences in

Europe, in the form of limits to the fiscal prerogatives of the State. In Portugal, this monetary constitution took the form of a contract to prevent the use of the kings' minting rights as a hidden tax. Nominal interest rates comparable to those of German-speaking city-states suggest that the commitment enforced by the *Cortes* until 1369 was credible.

Next, José Luís Cardoso, also an uncle of the previous author, frames the context for the previous four contributions by considering simultaneously two domains of historiography: economic history and the history of economics. Authors who seek to describe facts and circumstances of economic relevance, in order to establish evolutionary trends, should thus complement those who seek analytical forms or doctrinal frameworks aimed at explaining observed economic changes.[1]

The sixth and seventh contributions, also by friends and coauthors of the honoree, provide an international angle with Bretton Woods and the euro, which spills over into Part II. Michael Bordo argues that expansionary fiscal and monetary policies led to rising U.S. inflation since 1965, which in turn was the key to growing international imbalances culminating in the collapse of the fixed exchange rate system in 1973. For political and doctrinal reasons, this was not directly addressed on 15 August 1971, when Nixon closed the US gold window, and imposed a 10% surcharge on all imports and a ninety-day wage price freeze—at the urging of Fed Chairman Arthur Burns. Instead of confessing to mistaken US policies, the president blamed the rest of the world. The differences between the imbalances of the 1960s and 1970s—relatively stable monetary policy and floating exchange rates—go along with similarities—especially fiscal policy and the use of tariff protection as a strategic tool.

Barry Eichengreen, who famously lent class notes to his late coming classmate, brings Part I to a close by comparing the classical gold standard and the euro. This was also the topic of a conference they decided to hold at the *Arrábida* convent in 1994, which was published by the Bank of Portugal in a volume co-edited with Jaime Reis. Needless to say, the argument is heavily based on recent research. Although the two regimes were vaunted as engines of convergence, these sputtered and fiscal discipline was erratic though both were seen as delivering it. The difference is that, unlike Eurozone membership, the gold standard was always a contingent monetary regime. Also, during the gold standard, mass participation in electoral politics was exceptional. From the European and Portuguese perspective, there is a political economy argument for those two differences, as discussed in Part II.

Maria Eugénia Mata

[1] It should be no surprise that his work on the founder of the Nova School of Business and Economics, Alfredo de Sousa, coauthored with the editor and Jorge Braga de Macedo, joins dozens of "Eulogies and Memories (mostly) of Economists" written by the honoree. These began in a now extinct journal of the Catholic University, which he helped to launch with Cavaco Silva, Jacinto Nunes and Girão, continuing in the Working Papers series with A. M. Pinto Barbosa, Jorge Braga de Macedo's predecessor in the 18L chair at the Lisbon Academy of Science, including Cardoso himself, whom he received in chair 15L following Jacinto's passing away.

Jorge Braga de Macedo as an Economic Historian: The Transition of the Portuguese Economy from the Authoritarian to the Democratic Period (1960–1979)

Luciano Amaral

Abstract Despite not being an economic historian, Jorge Braga de Macedo has delved into economic history, with very favorable results. This is illustrated in the current chapter, which analyzes Braga de Macedo's contribution to the understanding of the Portuguese economy's transition from authoritarianism to democracy. To be sure, Braga de Macedo's analysis has not only enriched our understanding of the transition period itself but also that of the authoritarian and democratic periods. This chapter discusses four of Braga de Macedo's pioneering articles and shows how these contributed to our current knowledge of three fundamental Portuguese economic issues, namely: economic growth, openness and connection with other European economies between the 1960s and 1980s.

Keywords Economic growth and development · Economic history · Economic transition · Europe · Portugal

1 Introduction

Jorge Braga de Macedo is not an economic historian but has sometimes crossed the line in order to fish in the waters of history. Some historical aspects of monetary regimes and of fiscal policy have received his attention, although not necessarily in an autonomous fashion: Historical examples were mostly used as instruments to understand current situations. In this paper, I will not deal with those works where history was used by Braga de Macedo in a more explicit manner but rather with other works where he used economic history as an intrinsic part of his economic argument. I believe this is most visible in the works Braga de Macedo dedicated to the study of the economic transition from the *Estado Novo* period to that of the current democratic regime.[1]

[1]The *Estado Novo* (New State) refers to the authoritarian, corporatist and statist period of rule in Portugal during 1933–1974.

L. Amaral (✉)
Nova School of Business and Economics, Universidade Nova de Lisboa, Carcavelos, Portugal
e-mail: lamaral@novasbe.pt

L. Brites Pereira et al. (eds.), *Economic Globalization and Governance*,
https://doi.org/10.1007/978-3-030-53265-9_1

I am thinking particularly of four works: One is "The Economic Consequences of the April 25th Revolution," written together with Paul Krugman and published in a book coordinated by Braga de Macedo himself and Simon Serfaty (cf. Braga de Macedo and Serfaty 1981); another work is "Portugal and Europe: the Channels of Structural Interdependence", published in the same book. Both of these articles should be read together with another one, published close to thirty years later, where historical reasoning is combined with memory impressions: "Economic Advice and Regime Change in Portugal," published in a book edited by Francesco Franco (cf. Franco 2008). The final element of this tetralogy is a long working paper of the *Faculdade de Economia* of the *Universidade Nova de Lisboa* focusing on trade policy in Portugal, which he published together with Cristina Corado and Manuel Lopes Porto: "The Timing and Sequence of Trade Liberalization Policies: Portugal 1948–1986" (Braga de Macedo et al. 1988).

These works approached the Portuguese economy of the *Estado Novo* and of the transition to democracy in a pioneering way that is still illuminating today. The basis of Braga de Macedo's interpretation was to show the positive behavior of the Portuguese economy during the *Estado Novo*, contrary to the conventional wisdom of the time. The changing conditions after 1973–1974 were, consequently, seen as a crisis rather than the closing of a dark period and the beginning of a new one of relentless prosperity. Consequently, the new conditions had to be approached with care if the Portuguese economy was to become viable in a democratic regime willing to develop an expensive Welfare State: Not everything was possible, especially under circumstances that were much more restrictive than during the *Estado Novo* period. The other major element of Braga de Macedo's interpretation was equally innovative: He showed that the Portuguese economy became increasingly connected with the European one during the *Estado Novo* period, again contrary to the conventional wisdom of the day, which saw the Portuguese authoritarian regime as an isolationist one. What is more, he showed how the period of transition to democracy, on the contrary, reintroduced forms of protectionism that had been on the wane in the previous years. This view was particularly important to understand the integration of the Portuguese economy in the European Economic Community, which was then starting, following the 1977 accession request.

1.1 A Specific Shock

The starting point of Braga de Macedo's approach to the Portuguese economy in this period was that "the Portuguese economy was subject to a unique combination of shocks" between 1973 and 1976 (Braga de Macedo and Krugman 1981, p. 57): the 1973 oil shock, which was common to all economies of the world; a labor shock, resulting from the interruption of emigration to Europe and, mostly, from the arrival of a vast mass of white settlers in 1975 and 1976, who were fleeing the Portuguese African colonies as these were becoming independent; and finally, a political shock resulting from a revolution in 1974–1975 that radically changed the institutional framework of the economy, in a mainly socialist direction at first.

This compound shock had various consequences. The most important of which were to: (1) make real wages in Portugal move away from what Braga de Macedo and Krugman (1981) called the "warranted" real wage and (2) make potential output also move away from its "warranted" level. These warranted levels were, in their own words, the only levels of the two variables that "are consistent with equilibrium in both the labor and foreign exchange markets" (Braga de Macedo and Krugman 1981, p. 60). By means of a very simple model, Braga de Macedo and Krugman showed that the Portuguese economy passed from an extremely tight labor market (with an unemployment rate of 2%), as well as a current account surplus in 1973, into a totally different situation. Wages exploded in 1974 right when the most violent effects of the oil shock were being felt, while at the same time emigration to Europe ground to a halt and about 600,000 white settlers from Africa arrived in Portugal. The wage explosion would always move real wages away from the warranted wage level but, thanks to the interruption of the emigration flow and the return of the white settlers, that level also changed, making the mismatch between it and the actual level particularly serious. At the same time, the new labor abundance also increased potential output. However, the wage explosion and a vast nationalization program of the assets of business groups, in the wake of the political revolution, ensured that actual output also moved considerably away from potential output. The consequence of all of this was a balance of payment crisis of quite large proportions. Figure 1 shows the impact of real wage growth on unit labor cost (ULC) in comparison with similar economies; Table 1 shows the collapse of GDP per capita in 1974 and 1975,

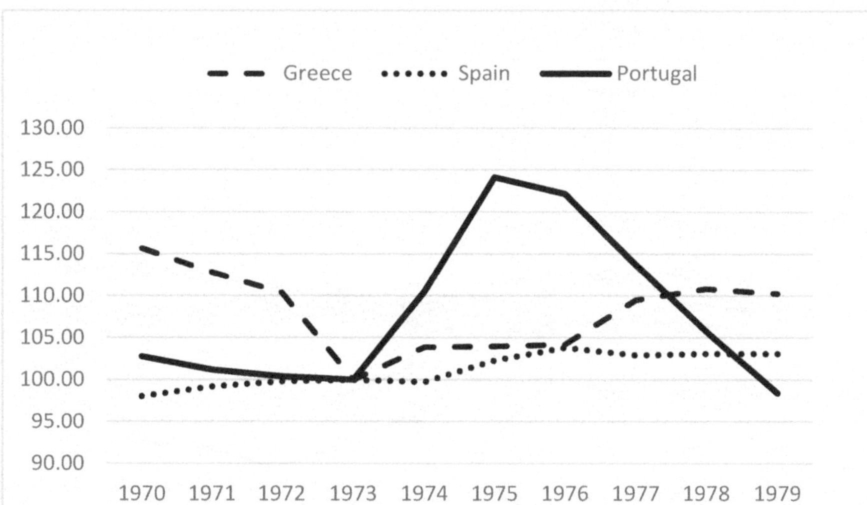

Fig. 1 Real unit labor costs, 1973 = 100 (*Source* AMECO)

Table 1 GDP per capita, Portugal, 1970–1980, annual growth rates (*Source* Amaral 2009)

1970	9.21
1971	11.07
1972	10.29
1973	4.87
1974	0.24
1975	−9.18
1976	−0.24
1977	7.18
1978	5.43
1979	6.71
1980	4.44

especially the latter; Fig. 2 shows the balance of payment crisis, as expressed by the behavior of the current account.

What followed next was an attempt to correct the earlier effects: In 1976–1977, “under pressure from wage controls, devaluations, and the overhang unemployed,

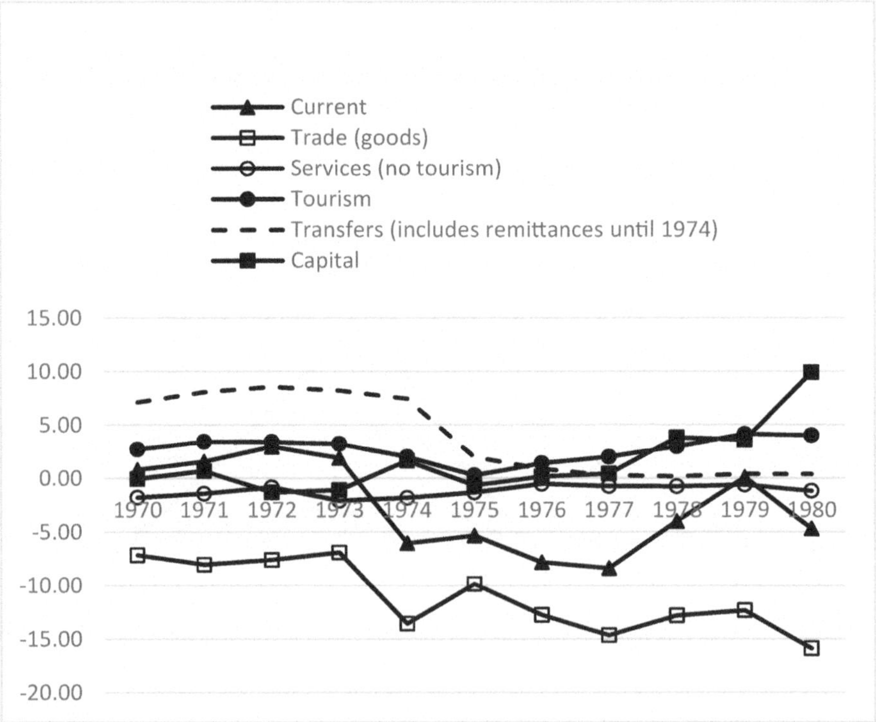

Fig. 2 Balance of payments, Portugal, 1970–1980, %GDP (*Source* Pinheiro 1997)

real wages fell. But an explosion of credit produced rapid growth in output. The effect of output expansion was enough to worsen the external balance in spite of the decline in real wages" (Braga de Macedo and Krugman 1981, pp. 61–63). This describes a series of measures taken by the initial democratic governments to cap wages, raise administered prices and depreciate the Portuguese Escudo. Then, in 1978, following the signing of a standby arrangement with the International Monetary Fund (IMF), "real wages continued to decline; but this was now accompanied by tightened credit, producing slower growth" (Braga de Macedo and Krugman 1981, p. 63). Thanks to the movement in both wages and output, external balance was finally reached. This is again visible in Fig. 1 (real wages), Table 1 (output) and Fig. 2 (balance of payments).

This interpretation was based in a way of looking at the Portuguese economy that was new at the time. In those days, the behavior of the economy during the *Estado Novo* period was normally seen as an unmitigated disaster, while what happened next was an inevitable evolution to correct it. Braga de Macedo and Krugman (1981) explained, however, that the Portuguese economy during the *Estado Novo* had been, instead, a mitigated success, and that the path followed after the revolution was not sustainable. This interpretation was illuminating both for the understanding of the economy during the *Estado Novo* period and for the understanding of the economy in the first years of democracy.

Braga de Macedo and Krugman (1981, pp. 54–53) described the Portuguese economy on the eve of democracy as follows: "in 1973 Portugal's economy was fairly typical of the group of middle-income nations sometimes referred to as newly industrializing countries or "NICs". These countries were able to achieve rapid economic growth during the 1960s and early 1970s via increased trade, exploiting their relatively abundant supplies of semiskilled industrial workers in textbook fashion: exporting labor-intensive manufactured goods, and also exporting labor directly in the form of emigrant workers. Portugal, with its 700,000 emigrant workers, relied more than most NICs on direct export of labor, but substantial exports of textiles, electronic components, and other labor-intensive manufactures had also emerged by the early 70 s". This description of the Portuguese economy in the last decades of the *Estado Novo* period is very valuable from the point of view of an economic historian: First, it places the Portuguese case in an international context; second, it helps to better understand the difficulties of the Portuguese economy from 1974 onward. As Braga de Macedo and Krugman (1981, p. 70) wrote, "what makes the Portuguese experience unique are the developments in the labor market", thanks "to the unusually high proportion of its population working outside the country." This is what explains the vast population movements in the second half of the 1970s and why real wage changes were so strongly felt. Braga de Macedo and Krugman's (1981, p. 85) conclusion was extremely important to understand the correcting measures that were taken after the revolutionary excesses: "what can be learned from Portugal's experience? Perhaps the main lesson is in the 'narrow limits of the possible' when one tries to redistribute income in a market economy. The allocative effects of disequilibrium real wages, manifesting themselves in a critical balance of payment problem, forced governments with pro-worker sympathies to engineer a steep decline in workers' standard of living".

Braga de Macedo (2008) gives further perspective to this picture by providing some inside knowledge on how political decisions about the economy were taken in Portugal from 1976 onward, especially regarding the role played by a group of mostly young economists that came then from MIT to advise Portuguese politicians and officials (such as the Governor of the Bank of Portugal). Braga de Macedo (2008) notes how this advice was instrumental in shifting decision-making away both from the then prevalent socialist-leaning tendencies of Portuguese officials but also from the old *Estado Novo* mind-set, especially regarding the depreciation of the exchange rate in order to address the international payment crisis. In his own words, "economic advice from the MIT group provided a policy framework for macroeconomic stabilization and accompanying structural measures" (Braga de Macedo 2008, pp. 201–202). The MIT group was a very impressive gathering of economic talent: Andrew Abel, Jeffrey Frankel, Raymond Hill and Paul Krugman, together with the Portuguese economist Luís Miguel Beleza, then finishing his PhD at MIT. As noted by Braga de Macedo (2008), this group was responsible for a radical overhaul of economic counseling in Portugal, leading to the adoption of policies that turned out to be quite effective in dealing with the economic crisis from the transition of one political regime to another.

1.2 A Progressively Europeanized Economy

Another major economic history contribution by Braga de Macedo from the same period allowed to place the Portuguese economy in both the *Estado Novo* period and the transition to democracy within the European context. Again, the perspective was pioneering: At a time when most interpretations pointed to the *Estado Novo* regime as being a closed one in international economic terms (following the famous Salazar motto: "proudly alone"), Braga de Macedo (1981) showed the contrary, i.e., the growing integration of the Portuguese economy with Europe during that period. What is more, he showed how the period of transition to democracy, on the contrary, reintroduced forms of protectionism that had been disappearing in the previous years, thus helping to frame the issue in a totally different perspective.

Braga de Macedo (1981) shows the various dimensions of the Portuguese economy's growing integration into the European one during the *Estado Novo* period: in agriculture, industry, foreign investment and labor (i.e., emigrants, with the corresponding return in terms of remittances). But the major concern of this paper is to note how the new protectionist changes introduced after 1974 created difficulties for the prospective joining of the European Economic Community (EEC), to which the Portuguese authorities applied in 1977.

This piece is to be read together with Braga de Macedo et al. (1988), where the long-run efforts of Portuguese authorities to integrate the Portuguese economy in the liberalization of international economic relations in Europe are described in detail. Although the authors stress that "trade policy in Portugal had involved a very gradual liberalization because it reflects an ambiguous commitment to free trade as a development strategy on the part of the Portuguese authorities" (Braga de Macedo et al. 1988, p. 7), they also show that the commitment was unequivocal: Portugal joined the Organisation of European Economic Co-operation (OEEC) in 1948, the European Free Trade Association (EFTA) since its inception in 1959, and signed a free trade agreement with the EEC in 1972 (Braga de Macedo et al. 1988, p. 7). This growing openness is shown by both the evolution of the share of foreign trade in GDP (Fig. 3) and the level of tariffs on imports (Fig. 4).

Braga de Macedo et al. (1988) show that the ambiguity of the *Estado Novo* authorities with respect to free trade was revealed by a very progressive lifting of barriers until 1970. But they also show that in the regime's very final years (1970–1974), much of that ambiguity was eliminated, so that, in their opinion, the government "came close to a credible commitment to trade liberalization" (Braga de Macedo et al. 1988, p. 7). On the contrary, the early revolutionary authorities reverted much of that commitment by introducing a series of protectionist measures, such as a surcharge on imports and an actual quota regime for various goods. This reversal of openness is shown in Fig. 3, where a decline of the share of foreign trade over GDP is noticeable, and in Fig. 4, where the importance of tariffs over imports is seen spiking in 1975 and 1976.

But Braga de Macedo's (1981) main concern was to assess how the recent evolution of the Portuguese economy would square with EEC integration and warn against certain expectations held by Portuguese politicians over the effects of that membership: "whereas Portugal can probably expect to receive some real development resources from the Community, it is quite mistaken to believe that the economic

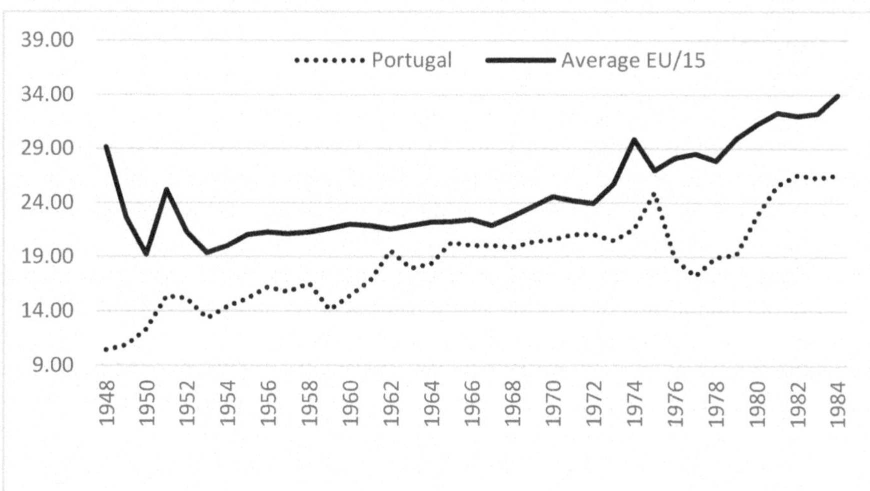

Fig. 3 Openness, Portugal and average European countries, 1948–1985, exports and imports % GDP: [(exports+imports)/2]/GDP (*Sources* EU.-15—AMECO; Portugal—Pinheiro 1997)

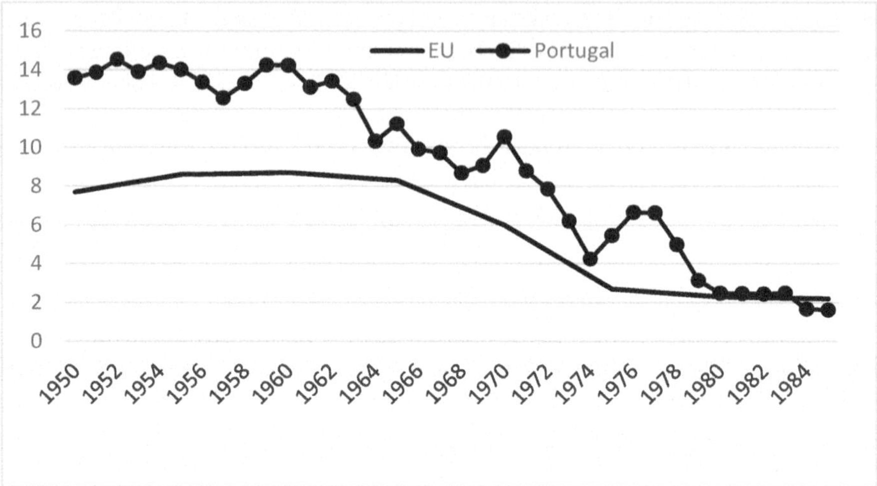

Fig. 4 Average tariffs % of imports, Portugal and European countries, 1950–1985 (*Sources* EEC—adapted from Dür 2008; Portugal—Fontoura and Valério 2001)

consequences of joining the EEC will be the financing by the Community of the remains of 'Portuguese democratic socialism'. [...] Structural interdependence alone is not likely to support the process of autonomous economic development which is essential for European integration not to lead to national disintegration" (Braga de Macedo 1981, p. 191). This is, still today, a very insightful idea.

2 Conclusion

Jorge Braga de Macedo's incursions into the realm of economic history have been rare but very fruitful. I have shown in this paper how he has opened avenues of understanding of the Portuguese economy in the *Estado Novo* period and during the transition to democracy that were new at the time of writing (almost 40 years ago) and are still very valuable today. His main contributions to economic history were to show the good performance of the Portuguese economy in the *Estado Novo* period as well as its increasing integration in the European economy. This has allowed him to put the transformation of the Portuguese economy in the revolutionary and democratic period of the second half of the 1970s into perspective. Much to the shame of Portuguese economic historians, very few of them have improved much over these, already distant, contributions by Braga de Macedo. Hopefully, the baton of his innovative spirit will be taken up by future generations of Portuguese economic historians.

References

Amaral L (2009) New series of Portuguese population and employment, 1950–2007: implications for GDP per capita and labor productivity. . Análise Social XLIV 193:767–791

AMECO (various) Available online. https://www.ec.europa.eu/info/business-economy-euro/indicators-statistics/economic-databases/macro-economic-database-ameco/ameco-database_en. Accessed on 29 March 2020

Braga de Macedo J (1981) Portugal and Europe: the channels of structural interdependence. In: Braga de Macedo J, Saferty S (eds) Portugal since the revolution: economic and political perspectives. Westview Press, Boulder, Colorado

Braga de Macedo J (2008) Economic advice and regime change in Portugal. In: Franco F (ed) Challenges ahead for the Portuguese economy. Imprensa de Ciências Sociais, Lisbon

Braga de Macedo J, Krugman P (1981) The economic consequences of the April 25th revolution. In: Braga de Macedo J, Saferty S (eds) Portugal since the revolution: economic and political perspectives. Westview Press, Boulder, Colorado

Braga de Macedo J, Corado C, Porto ML (1988) The timing and sequence of trade liberalization policies: Portugal 1948–1986. In: Working paper Faculdade de Economia da Universidade Nova de Lisboa, No. 114

Braga de Macedo J, Sefarty S (1981) Portugal since the revolution: economic and political perspectives. Westview Press, Boulder, Colorado

Dür A (2008) Bargaining power and trade liberalization: European external trade policies in the 1960s. Eur J Int Rel 14(4):645–669

Fontoura AP, Valério N (2001) Relações económicas externas. In: Valério N (ed) Estatísticas Históricas Portuguesas. INE, Lisbon, pp 713–739

Franco F (ed) (2008) Challenges ahead for the Portuguese economy. Imprensa de Ciências Sociais, Lisbon

Pinheiro M (ed) (1997) Séries Longas para a Economia Portuguesa, Pós-II Guerra Mundial, Vol. I Séries Estatísticas. Banco de Portugal, Lisbon

Bagehot for "Followers": How Did the Bank of Portugal Manage the First Post World War I Crisis?

Jaime Reis

Abstract The lender of last resort (LLR) function is a form of micro-management employed by central banks, usually in cooperation with or under the direction of governments, either to mitigate banking panics, or to prevent them from occurring. This paper considers the employment of the LLR function in Portugal during the early post World War I years. It is based on primary material in the Bank of Portugal's archive. Using a detailed account of the first banking crisis of the early 1920s, this study shows that the Bank of Portugal did not conform to Bagehot's archetype and explains why the departure from this model was unavoidable. It concludes that a lack of awareness of his paradigm was not the reason for the policy option of the Bank of Portugal.

Keywords Bagehot archetype · Lender of last resort · Monetary regimes · Portugal · Post world war I

1 Introduction

The Lender of Last Resort (LLR) function has been, historically, a form of micro-management employed by central banks, usually in cooperation with or under the direction of government: Its aim is to mitigate banking panics or prevent them from occurring. It involves providing liquidity to the financial system when the latter has to face an intense demand for high-powered money which threatens not only the survival of banking institutions, but also a "contagion effect" among them (Bordo 1990). Along with the goals of maintaining the internal and external stability of the currency, it is one of the oldest and most important functions of central banks. Indeed, it is one of the main criteria used by historians for establishing when, in the course of their gradual evolution, privileged national banks of issue are deemed to have achieved this status (Capie et al. 1994).

J. Reis (✉)
Instituto de Ciências Sociais, Universidade de Lisboa, Lisbon, Portugal
e-mail: jaime.reis@ics.ul.pt

L. Brites Pereira et al. (eds.), *Economic Globalization and Governance*,
https://doi.org/10.1007/978-3-030-53265-9_2

The study of this function has generated a considerable literature and remains to this day a subject of enormous interest for economists, historians and policy makers. To a large extent, this is justified by the present-day relevance of interventions of this kind carried out by central banks to ensure domestic financial stability, in conjunction with their more recently acquired regulatory and supervisory functions. In recent times, it has been motivated also by the fear that the LLR function may have been used excessively, and even wrongly, over the last few years (Kindleberger 2007). Its attraction also derives from its pertinence for issues of international financial stability, in particular for discussions regarding the possibility and effectiveness of global institutions empowered as LLRs (Fischer 1999).

The events of the last few decades and public and political concern over the behavior of the world's financial system have thus continually justified the study of this topic. Within this field, there is a strongly held belief that the LLR function has a strong continuity, with deep roots in the past and a long-term record of reasonable success in keeping systemic stability. This has led to the emergence of a sub-field focusing on the historical aspects of this role of central banks and of claims that "a thorough and clear understanding of this function and its important implications can be best obtained by reviewing its historical development, as well as by recognizing the different monetary regimes under which these important authors developed their interpretations" (Humphrey and Keleher 1983, pp. 8–9).

Several themes have come to the fore as a result. Traces of intervention of this kind go back as far as two hundred years, but in a modern form may be dated at the earliest from the mid-nineteenth century, at least in Britain and France (Bignon et al. 2012).[1] During the world crisis of 1857, LLR interventions materialized in many economically more advanced countries as a result of joint action by governments and central banks. In subsequent crises, however, "the focus shifted from governments to proto central banks" (Grossman and Rockoff 2015, p. 16). By 1900, in a number of European countries, the latter had assumed more or less openly this responsibility although nowhere was this formally recognized in their charters or constitutive laws.[2] The accumulation of the necessary know-how for carrying this out, and a definition of a doctrine for what should be correct LLR behavior in the face of panics, meanwhile, have been growing apace and been internalized among central bankers. Over time, several consequences of its application have been also vigorously debated. Among them are the degree of central bank autonomy in its exercise, the problems of moral hazard it raises, and the difficulty in harmonizing the traditional commercial activity of proto-central banks and the public nature of their role (Humphrey and Keleher 1983).

Although the historical study of LLR episodes has been well served, much remains to be done. Most of what is known and debated in this domain illustrates the experience of two countries—the US and Great Britain—and two periods—the era of

[1] For Belgium, see Buyst and Maes (2008).

[2] Capie et al. (1994), Appendix B, contains a wealth of information concerning the chronology of the historical spread of the LLR function.

the classical gold standard and the crisis of 1929–1931.[3] A large number of other situations of interest in this respect have been ignored or studied in less depth, such as, in particular, the LLR in countries with less developed financial systems; the LLR during panic episodes occurring under conditions of currency inconvertibility; the LLR in economies beleaguered by severe problems of public finance. In all of these, it is expectable that the contours of such interventions would be different from those of "core", well behaved economies.

The present study aims at correcting some of the imbalances in our present knowledge. It considers the employment of the LLR function in Portugal just after the Great War, a country then with a small and fragile banking system, at a time when its currency was inconvertible and its public finances were in a perilous state. A wealth of original primary material in the Bank of Portugal (BP)'s archive enables us to take this analysis beyond the mere scrutiny of published documents and statistics to which many studies have been confined.

The paper is divided into four sections. Following this introduction, the second describes the Portuguese financial system as it emerged from the war and provides a brief retrospect of the BP's earlier history, including of its pre-war experience as an informal LLR. The third presents an account of the Portuguese banking crisis of 1920–1921. It shows that the BP intervened strongly to restore normality but did not conform to the Bagehotian model of a LLR. It explains why it was so hard for the Bank to do otherwise although lack of awareness of the paradigm certainly played no part in this option. The fourth section concludes.

2 The Portuguese Post-War Financial System

The period from the end of the Great War to the mid-1920s is an inviting one for the study of LLR functions in Europe. It was unusually turbulent from the economic, political and social points of view. Numerous countries experienced severe banking crises and, as a result, there was ample call for official assistance to banks in difficulties. For example, the manner in which this was done spelt significant differences, during the ensuing period, between systemic stability or instability. As Feinstein et al. (1995a, b, pp. 20–21) have claimed, "banks were more likely to fail in countries where […] the central bank was unwilling or unable to act as a swift lender-of-last resort".

Three other aspects enhance the interest of these years. One is that in the immediate post-war the advantages of independence from political interference for central banks were a strong theme of public discussion. It was stressed by international conferences in Brussels (1920) and Genoa (1922) to which Portugal was a party, and this created a favorable climate for a more vigorous LLR activity (League of Nations 1920; Fink 1984). This was counteracted, however, by a second feature of contemporary debate,

[3] There is good information, however, on the 1920s LLR's of Italy and Spain. See Toniolo (1990, 1995), Guarini and Toniolo (1993) and Betrán et al. (2012). For the nineteenth century, there is valuable information and analysis in Bignon et al. (2012) and Buyst and Maes (2008).

namely a growing regulatory propensity of governments inherited from the war. This impinged on banking as it did on other economic fields and usually involved trying to deprive central banks of some of their erstwhile autonomy. The tension between these opposing strands of policy is not only worthy of scrutiny in itself but is a valuable clue in the history of how ideas about central banking developed in the inter-war period. The third aspect is that the early 1920s provided the venue for a further policy clash, between the goal of monetary stability, achieved through deflation; and that of securing the stability of financial institutions, which might require inflationary injections of high-powered money as part of LLR interventions. Both aims had dramatic social and political implications, and neither could be given up easily in favor of the other. They were ultimately reconciled but not without severe political struggles which must be borne in mind in examining the evolution of the LLR function during the 1920s.

Portugal came out of the war as one of the countries which suffered acute inflation (price increases of around 2,500% during 1914–1924), exchange rate instability (which went from 7.9 to 134 Portuguese escudos to the British pound, £), and large public deficits, which were heavily monetized with the help of the central bank's printing press.[4] On the other hand, it managed a strong macroeconomic recovery from 1918 to 1924, with an annual overall growth rate of GDP of 4.2% at constant prices and vigorous surges in sectors like food and beverages, wood, paper and cork, chemicals and non-metallic minerals (Batista et al. 1997). Starting in 1924–1925, a harsh deflationary program brought inflation to a halt, putting an end to the plunge of the exchange rate and causing a stabilization of the money supply (Branco 1950).

The banking system comprised a fluctuating population of some 25 corporations and a much larger but not exactly known number of unincorporated banking houses. The latter were mostly small but included a few very large ones too, most of which were incorporated during the 1920s. Business opportunities seem to have been promising though often speculative and risky. This was reflected in the number of bank start-ups, incorporations and closures, as well as in terms of the size and robustness of this sector. Between 1918 and 1926, seventeen joint stock banks were founded but thirteen disappeared.[5] By 1926, total nominal banking assets had risen by 2,800% compared to 1914, but in real terms only by 28%. Meanwhile, total credit to the non-financial private sector at fixed prices had shrunk to a mere 41% of the initial figure, while real capital, in the same interval, had contracted by half (Lumbralles 1926). The ratio of capital to total assets had dropped to 42% of its 1914 level.

The fragility of banks in the early 1920s is revealed by two indicators. On average, they had become much smaller in real terms, which made them less trusted by the public; and they were a good deal more leveraged than before the War and therefore more vulnerable. Poor management and malpractice were undoubtedly

[4]Belgium, Finland, Italy, Spain, Bulgaria and Greece were also in this group. See Feinstein et al. (1995a, b).

[5]See Reis et al. (1995) and Valério et al. (2006). There are small differences between the data used by these authors.

a problem in some cases, but not one which was crucial to the overall picture.[6] Much graver and more pervasive problems were caused by inflation. Chief among these was the erosion of bank capital. This was compounded by the opposition of shareholders to reinforcing the capital account of institutions they did not trust, either by new subscriptions or by cutting dividends. A second difficulty was posed by the growing propensity of banks to become universal by investing heavily in speculative long-term assets as a hedge against the slide in the value of short-term credits. Several of them fell into the liquidity trap of having long-term credits that were more than three times their long-term liabilities, and then found it hard to extricate themselves (Lumbralles 1926). Lastly, inflation and currency depreciation encouraged speculation in foreign exchange, a good refuge from the erosion of asset values but one which entailed entering a heady market where risks were considerable and turnover had to be especially quick. Lack of scale, skill or luck could be fatal, as happened with banks like the small *Banco Economia Portuguesa.* This was wiped out when it delayed repayment of a debt of £100,000 until it had exceeded its entire nominal capital stock during an interval in which currency devalued by 1,200% (Reis et al. 1995).

At the end of the War, the BP was still what it had always been: a joint stock commercial bank, which was privately owned and governed, though under the tutelage of the government, with whom it had to share its profits. The latter also appointed its governing officer.[7] It was chartered to perform several of the functions of a central bank, without, however, being designated as such.[8] It had the national monopoly of note issuing in Portugal, acted as treasurer and banker to the government and, as such, was obliged to keep branches in all district capitals of the country.

The Bank performed two further essential duties for such institutions, albeit informally. Starting in the 1860s and until the end of the gold standard in 1891, it assumed a strong commitment to ensure the stability of the currency. It often intervened with its own resources in the exchange market to prevent "excessive" deviation from par, in which it was aided by a certain degree of help from the Treasury (Esteves et al. 2009; Reis 2007). After the onset of inconvertibility, it relinquished this obligation but took up a strenuous defense of monetary orthodoxy, struggling always to hold the line against the persistent pressures of governments to monetize public deficits.

Its second quasi central bank function was, again informally, that of lender of last resort to the Portuguese banking system. In the aftermath of Portugal's first serious banking panic, in 1876, when it joined forces with the government to save

[6]Only two well documented failures caused by improper or even illicit behavior have been identified, namely the *Banco Industrial Português*, in 1925, and the *Banco Angola e Metrópole*, in 1926.

[7]In addition, a secretary-general was appointed by the government and sat on all meetings of the board, without a vote. His function was to inform the authorities of what went on and to inform the Bank in turn about the government's views concerning board decisions.

[8]This would only happen in 1931. See Banco de Portugal (1946b), vol. VI. Even in 1931, the preambles, respectively, of the monetary reform and banking reform laws of that year made it clear that it was thought impossible for the BP to become, overnight and by legislative fiat, a true central bank. Rather, it was expected that eventually it would develop in that direction, but only gradually and under state guidance. See Mata and Valério (1982).

Table 1 Financial and monetary indicators for Portugal, 1914–1925 (*Source* Branco 1950)

	1	2	3	4	5
	Notes in circulation	Government debt to BP	Price index	Authorized 'commercial' note issue	Ratio 2:4
1914	87	38	100	–	–
1918	229	173	635	100	1,7
1919	305	260	528	100	2,6
1920	472	360	1205	115	3,1
1921	653	588	1430	115	5,1
1922	852	716	1640	140	5,1
1923	1235	1041	2486	160	6,5
1924	1603	1351	3183	195	6,9
1925	1684	1444	2557	195	7,4

Notes: Values in 000s of contos except for the price index which is equal to 100 in 1914; the authorized commercial note issue did not exist in 1914. One conto equals 1,000 escudos

a number of institutions, it described itself as "the supreme dispenser of credit, the banking establishment to which other banks and serious houses turn in moments of anguish" (…).[9] Thereafter and until 1891, we find evidence of occasional assistance being given to individual banks in trouble. However, in 1891, in the aftermath of the Barings crisis, it pooled efforts with the government once again, to save and reconstruct the banking system. Subsequently and until World War I, assistance to troubled banks was undertaken systematically though always discretely and on a one-by-one basis (Branco 1950; Reis 1999).[10]

During all these years, the Bank maintained that its primary goal was the public interest, although privately it also recognized that systemic instability, particularly when it affected large banks, like itself, was not in its own interest either. In the years after 1914, three important changes affected its ability to carry out its emerging LLR duty. The first was the massive expansion of the note issue in response to the desperate needs of governments facing war-time and post-war rocketing expenditures, while being reluctant to increase taxes to meet them. By 1925, the state's nominal debt to the Bank had reached a level more than seventeen times what it had been in 1914, while the total note issue had climbed to a figure nineteen times its pre-war level. Prices shot up as a consequence and were twenty-five times higher than at the start of the War (see Table 1). The second change was shaped by the contract of 1918

[9]The BP published a report in August 1876 describing these efforts and calling for its status as a special bank to be reinforced so that it might undertake this function more regularly and effectively. This request was not heeded until the crisis of 1929–1931. The BP could not have been more precocious as a LLR given that it was not until the 1870s that the system gained a reasonable dimension and required centralized intervention in moments of stress.

[10]Between 1873 and 1887, a number of troubled banks were discretely assisted by the BP. In some cases, the sums employed were significant.

between the BP and the state, which established new rules for the note issue. This was to be divided into two parts, which were thought of as separate but were constituted by identical notes. One would be used for satisfying the loans demanded from the BP by the state. In practice, these increases could not be refused. The other was to be employed by the Bank for its lending operations in the commercial market and was severely limited in size, in the belief that inflationary pressures would thus be attenuated. As shown in Table 1, a consequence of this divergence in motivations was an enormous difference between the size of the two issues. The proportion of the one for government borrowing relative to that for "commercial" purposes rose between 1918 and 1925 from 1.7:1 to almost 7.4:1.[11] A growing stranglehold was thus imposed on the Bank's autonomy to use the faculty to issue in order to finance its traditional commercial functions.

The third alteration was the pronounced decline of the BP's position vis-à-vis the financial system. During the 1920s, it remained still the largest bank in the country, with assets which were about equal to those of all other banks put together. However, as a result of being caught in the scissors of inflation and of the constraint on the amount available for discounts and advances, the credits it could provide to the economy dropped from 32% of those of all other financial institutions, in 1914, to 16%, in 1925. Its capacity to influence the credit market and the behavior of other banks was thus seriously diminished. In a document produced by the ministry of finance in 1931, the Bank was described as "a weak institution, which is not equipped to carry out the functions committed to it […] and which lacks the resources needed to serve the country's economy and regulate its capital market" (Banco de Portugal 1946b, VI: 28).

3 The Bank of Portugal and Bagehot's LLR Model

Much of the debate surrounding the LLR has had to do with the varying circumstances in which the need for it arises and how this function should be correctly exercised. The starting point for this is fairly consensual. The need for a LLR arises in a fractional banking system when there is a loss of confidence in some or all banks which leads the public to rush to convert deposits into high powered money.[12] A run on one or more banks may spread to the entire system and cause the risk of an asset sell-off by them spreading throughout the market.[13] The consequences are a sharp contraction of credit as loans are called in, a collapse of the money supply, and widespread insolvency among enterprises (Humphrey and Keleher 1983). The central bank then

[11] The dual issue continued until 1931, by which time the official thinking of the ministry of finance had evolved in the direction of this being an "incomprehensible arrangement" (Banco de Portugal, 1946b, VI: 12).

[12] Bordo (1990) organizes the causes of bank failures into two categories: internal (poor management, dishonesty) and external (changes in relative prices).

[13] The causes of contagion are much debated. One of the issues is whether the public is able during a panic to distinguish between solvent and insolvent banks. See Gorton (1985).

acts as the ultimate guarantor of deposit-to-currency convertibility and this should therefore prevent or stop the run on the banks. It is a short-run stabilization function which to be of use in the long-run must not only avert instability, but also ensure that when the bank sector returns to equilibrium, it will not be plagued by the recurrence of systemic problems.

The classical statement of the correct procedures to be followed by the LLR was originally spelt out by Walter Bagehot (1873/2006). It was based on the experience of several banking crises in England prior to that date. In every study on this topic ever since, it has been reiterated, clarified and reinterpreted, with the alterations required by supervening changes in the nature of modern financial systems. The advent of open market operations and of inter-bank money markets, for example, have been some of the causes of such modifications.

The model incorporates four rules.[14] The first is that the LLR must lend freely and without delay to all banks in need of it. To this end it must have the freedom to create high powered money, i.e. be a central bank. The second is that it must always be prepared to lend at a high rate in order to discourage borrowing from it by banks which are not in trouble. In normal times, this will dissuade banks from taking excessive risks. The third norm is that the LLR has to make it clear to the market that it will always act, should the need arise. Not to do so will cause uncertainty and increase the propensity to panic. Lastly, the LLR must only lend on "good" collateral. This necessity arises because it serves as a guide to whether a bank in difficulty is nevertheless solvent or not. At the same time, it provides an incentive, under normal circumstances, for banks to handle only good collateral, which will serve them, when in difficulty if they need to go to the LLR for help.[15] Bagehot did not consider the possibility of individual bail-outs and perhaps for this reasons did not discuss the risk for the LLR of encouraging moral hazard.[16]

This section concentrates on the Portuguese banking crisis of 1920–1921. The main evidence consists of the minutes of the Bank's *Conselho Geral* (CG), which met normally once a month but in difficult times did so more frequently. It was the highest executive instance of the Bank and combined the members of the executive board, which looked after daily business (*Conselho de Administração*—CA), and those of the supervisory board (*Conselho Fiscal*—CF), which monitored the institution on behalf of the shareholders. The CG had the last word in all important internal matters

[14]Bagehot's (1873/2006) recommendations have been organized in the literature in various ways. This is due to the fact that Bagehot himself did not lay them out as a body of rules but dispersed them about the text of his chapter VII on "A More Exact Account of the Mode in Which the Bank of England Has Discharged Its Duty of Retaining a Good Bank Reserve, and of Administering It Effectually". The present organization follows Bordo (1990) and Fischer (1999). Bignon et al. (2012, p. 581) limit theirs to three principles: free lending, good collateral and penal rates.

[15]A matter of debate is whether the central bank should lend only to solvent banks, assuming that it can identify them, even if they are temporarily illiquid. Bagehot (1873) seems to have thought that if a bank had "good securities" to offer, then it must be solvent and there would be no need to make this distinction (VII: 58). His argument was that most of those in need during a banking panic were "sound people", i.e. not insolvent.

[16]A greater probability of moral hazard exists when the central bank intervenes to help individual banks rather than the system as a whole (Capie et al. 1994).

and was informed about everything pertaining to all other organs of governance. It had eighteen members and its president was the governor.

The crisis in Portugal was part of a widespread phenomenon felt throughout Europe and the USA and was precipitated by the slump which followed the post-war boom of 1919–1920 (Feinstein et al. 1995a, b). It began very gradually in the first half of 1920, became painfully apparent in July, went on in a crescendo until early 1921, and then gradually worked itself out in the following months (Banco de Portugal, various years). Its causes were both international and domestic. Portuguese and colonial firms were hit twice by the world contraction, which was reflected in a sharp drop in foreign orders for exports (−20% by volume from 1920 to 1921), and in a strong increase in competition from imports (+100% by volume in the same period). Some negative influence from abroad, through financial channels, may have been present too, but was probably less important, given that the international links of this sector were weak (Reis et al. 1995). Meanwhile, internally a considerable amount of speculation in merchandise stocks, in company formation and on the stock exchange took place. Its effects were aggravated by a fall in domestic demand caused by expectations of falling prices as a result of the return to peace and normality, and this held back spending (Branco 1950).

3.1 Bagehot's Rules: The LLR Must Lend Freely and Vigorously[17]

During this critical time, Portuguese banks (including unincorporated banking houses) displayed all the expected symptoms. As they experienced rapid deposit withdrawal and a rise in the currency ratio (cash in the hands of the public as a percentage of sight deposits), they took measures to raise their reserve ratios (reserves as a percentage of sight deposits). As liquidity problems became increasingly felt, they turned to the BP for help by rediscounting commercial paper in their portfolios, getting loans on collateral and seeking to raise the limits on their credit allowances at the BP.

Already during the 1st semester of 1920, a rise in the demand for credit by bankers became discernible at the BP. Several bank managers were received by the GC to argue personally their respective cases, usually for a rise in their normal credit allowances. The requests of all the major houses were accepted, though in the case of some smaller or weaker ones, only under certain conditions. In June, it was noted that total rediscounts were getting larger than direct trade discounts, an unusual situation for the BP. Eyebrows were also raised at the GC when the *Banco Nacional Ultramarino* (BNU), one of the biggest banks and the monopoly issuer of notes for

[17]Quotes of Bagehot's rules are from his Lombard Street. In this case, see Bagehot (1873/2006, p. 198): "in time of panic it [the Bank of England] must advance freely and vigorously to the public out of the reserve".

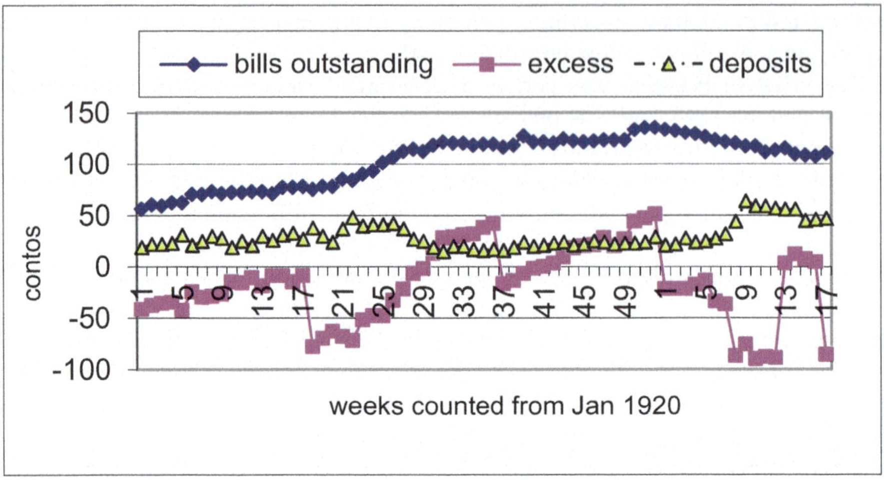

Fig. 1 Bank of Portugal, key variables, 1920–1921. *Notes* a positive "excess" occurs when the private note issue exceeds the legal limit (*Source* Situações semanais, AHBP)

the colonies, asked for a large discount on a guarantee comprising only shares, a sign that it lacked sufficient good paper to rediscount.[18]

By the first week in July, it was obvious that there was reason to worry seriously, as bankers began to stream in, seeking ever more support. By early August, the BNU was asking for credits worth 17,500 contos,[19] when in June it had only needed 2,000, and the private bankers Totta, with a mere 750 contos of capital, had piled up 9,000 of debts to the Bank.

During the next six or seven months, the BP responded to the pressure with vigor and swiftness. Meetings of the CA became daily rather than twice-weekly, in order to attend promptly to all the pressing demands. The weekly outstanding value of discounts at the Bank at the end of each week rose by almost 240% between January 1920 and the peak of this account twelve months later (see Fig. 1). Though we lack precise information on the identity of the recipients of this assistance, the signs are that they were principally in the financial sector. Directors noted the pronounced shift from trade discounting to rediscounting of bills presented by bankers, and the annual report for 1920 echoed this.[20] "[In 1920] The beneficial and decisive intervention of the BP made itself felt principally in the form of rediscounts as a result of the difficulties experienced by several financial establishments" (Relatório 1921, p. 8). The doubling of the average value of bills discounted corroborates the notion that very large customers (i.e. banks) were becoming increasingly frequent. At the same time, the sharp reduction in their mean duration is a sign that they were being used more and more for emergencies.

[18] GC meeting, 04/06/1920.

[19] The conto was the unofficial thousand-fold multiple of the escudo ($): 1 conto equaled 1,000$00.

[20] Director Mota Gomes at GC meeting, 25/06/1920.

Did the BP provide all the support that was needed by banks in trouble which "deserved" nevertheless to be saved? The evidence is contradictory and difficult to assess. The GC itself was uncertain about the magnitude of the remedy required, and for the historian this is even harder to grasp. Interestingly, opinions within the Bank differed widely concerning the robustness of the different institutions which came for help.[21] Information was gathered continually by different methods and through different channels, but was always limited and imperfect, not least because if the BP was seen to be enquiring too deeply into a given bank, this might precipitate a run on the latter.[22]

The BP's posture, both outwardly and inwardly, was that it was the one and only support of the system and had to be prepared therefore to provide the assistance that any bank needed. Consequently, its reply to such requests tended to be quite "Bagehotian". It was ready to lend "without stint, in a timely fashion and as far as necessary and possible, and that it was better to err by excess than on the side of insufficiency".[23] In practice, however, it was not always so. Many requests were accepted but as a fraction of what had been asked for, or under much harsher conditions, and some were refused. Usually, the reason was that the situation did not justify the support. The *Banco Popular Português* (BPP), for instance, was turned down as not really being in trouble but with the proviso that, if it later became desperate and *could offer reasonable paper for rediscount* [my emphasis], its call would be attended. The *Banco Português e Brasileiro* (BPB) received the same treatment on the grounds that not only its problems were already over, but that it ought to liquidate some of its share portfolio first before coming to the BP for help.[24] Such cases do not contradict the concept of a proper LLR. They clearly fall within the purview of Bagehot's rule that assistance must only be given to banks in true need but solvent, though they might face problems of illiquidity.

Refusals or limitations on requests occurred for other reasons too and, in this perspective, the Bank may have behaved less as a LLR than it should have. The first was a prudential consideration. The preoccupation was that to satisfy the wishes of large banks could entail a dangerous concentration of risk. In August, the credits demanded by the BNU were one third of the total available for lending to all banks and greater than the BP's own capital of 13,500 contos. This led to a reduction in the amount conceded, though on the same occasion, the BP gave the much smaller and possibly less solid *Banco Industrial Português* (BIP) all that it had asked for.[25]

[21] At the GC meeting of 29/11/1920, director Ulrich claimed that the total bill would be something in the region of 60–80,000 contos, but lesser figures circulated too. At the meeting of 15/11/1920, the discussion on the current state of the BNU is illustrative. It pitted those who saw it as "comfortable" (e.g. Silva Viana) or "solid" (Seixas) against those who saw it as "highly delicate" (e.g. Ávila Lima)! On the other hand, Seixas cautioned, probably more sensibly, that "the state of the BNU is hard to determine".

[22] Ávila Lima, GC meeting, 15/11/1920.

[23] Burnay, GC meeting, 03/08/1920.

[24] Both cases were discussed at the meeting of the GC on 09/08/1920.

[25] GC meeting, 03/08/1920.

The most important reason for not lending freely during this crisis, however, was external. It arose from the rigid rules governing the note issue, the consequence of which was that the Bank could easily run out of funds if it intervened on a large scale, as desired by many. In the beginning of 1920, the ceiling on the notes it was allowed by the government to employ "commercially", including for rediscounting bank paper, was 100,000 contos. Forty per cent of this lay unused in the till and was more than sufficient cover against deposit withdrawals. By July, this cushion had shrunk to zero, total discounts were around 100,000 contos and there were no notes left to pay out any of the 25,000 contos of claims being made by depositors, let alone inject further funds into the financial system. The only way out was either to restrict the availability of credit to banks in distress, with grave consequences for the market; or to suspend the limit on the issue of notes.

To expand the note issue openly and legally would have had a political cost that none of the successive governments of the time was prepared to face. The authorities feared the reaction of public opinion to a measure which would probably be inflationary and in times of hardship would certainly hit the profits of the monopoly issuer of notes. They chose instead to allow the Bank, covertly, to issue above the legal limit and sanctioned "any excess in the [note] circulation that might be justified by the circumstances of the markets, to which the Bank must give aid, in the general interest of the country and to defend the economy, which is of such great import for the state and for public order".[26] The effect of this decision is displayed in Fig. 1, where the variable "excess" is the difference between the permitted issue and the Bank's true "commercial issue".[27]

This arrangement was effective in stemming the tide of panic that befell the banking system for a while but depended on political factors and on the gravity of the crisis. The Bank disliked it because the ceiling on the "excess" was never formally specified by any government and the duration allowed for it was also left vague—"for as long as market conditions require".[28] By November 1920, with the crisis getting worse, a new and more hostile government pressed for an end to this policy of monetary secrecy. The consequence was that the volume of daily discounts had to be strictly limited to the amounts received from the repayment of bills. The market became frantic once again and started to pressure the government for additional measures.[29]

The solution was found in a new contract, signed whereby the Bank accepted to make new loans to the state totaling 200,000 contos and was therefore allowed to issue the corresponding amount in notes. In return, the BP was permitted to raise

---

[26]This is the view of the government as expressed by Secretary-General Seixas at the GC meeting of 14/07/1920. This secret authorization was later transcribed into the minute book of the GC meetings. See Livro G2-19, fls.10-10vº.

[27]A negative value of the "excess" represents a situation in which notes were being issued above the limit; a positive figure, the opposite.

[28]Seixas at the GC meeting of 14/07/1920.

[29]On 29/11/1920 the governor informed the GC that heads of banks were mobbing the Bank, demanding amounts which were simply impossible to satisfy. By 11 a.m. that day, their requests totaled 4,500 contos and the Bank only had 3,500 available, an "alarming" situation.

the ceiling on its private issue to 115,000 contos. Since this was not enough for the current needs of the market, the government agreed, in addition, to deposit 41,000 contos with the Bank for one year, which could be used for this purpose too.

The conclusion is thus that the Portuguese central bank could not bail out all the banks in trouble unless it was strongly backed by the government of the day. Without this support the LLR was simply unable to "lend freely". Then, as now, or as in the days of the classical gold standard in England, this rule was utterly dependent on the will of those who govern (Bignon et al. 2012; Buyst and Maes 2008), a situation which is not described by the word "freely".

3.2 Bagehot's Rules: The LLR Must Lend at a Very High Rate[30]

Throughout its history, the BP has always been subject to the will of the governments when it came to setting the official discount rate. The habitual discount rate was 5% and the Bank was free to charge below that, but to go above it required a government decree which was not easily forthcoming.[31] Once again its behavior in this matter can therefore not be separated from the factors which determined the preferences of the country's authorities, with their respective views being frequently misaligned. The government, as the country's largest debtor, preferred low rates, while the BP usually sought to accompany the market, while opting to diverge from it only under critical conditions.

In the particular circumstances of 1920–1921, curiously this topic was never high on the list of subjects discussed by the GC. Throughout the war and after, the Bank rate was kept at 5.5%, until in July 1920 the subject attracted attention just as the crisis was beginning. The Bank sought and obtained, with surprising ease, permission to raise it first to 6 and then to 7%. After this, the matter was rarely mentioned again in the minutes of these meetings.

A plausible interpretation is that in the initial stage of the crisis the latter was not expected to last as long and be as intense as actually happened. The Bank then discovered the overwhelming scale of the panic and realized that a small hike in the discount rate would not be enough to solve the problems of the financial system.[32] Another is that the Bank feared that raising its rate would drive many of its customers to other establishments. This would not only deprive it of earnings, which, as a commercial bank, it cared about, but would also make life more difficult for the

[30]Frequently, it is claimed that Bagehot's statement mentioned "at a penal rate". In fact, his words were that "these loans should only be made at a very high rate of interest" (p. 199).

[31]For numerous examples prior to 1891, see Reis (2007) and Esteves et al. (2009).

[32]If the GC had read Bagehot carefully, they would indeed have expected that "if the central bank responded promptly and vigorously, the panic would be ended in a few days", an occurrence which was actually unlikely in the troubled times after World War I. See Humphrey and Keleher (1983, p. 28).

weaker banks, which would be subject to increased client pressure for discounts. A third construction is that there was a realistic fear of provoking public animosity towards a bank of issue which was a monopolist and might be perceived as taking advantage of the difficulties of others to increase its profits.

The first question raised by this evidence is whether this rate was indeed the "very high rate" that Bagehot had in mind in the event of a panic. Unfortunately, we lack weekly or even monthly data on market rates in Portugal with which to compare the Bank's. The annual averages available, for 1920 and 1921, suggest that the market was a little higher than the BP (Branco 1950, un-numbered table). We cannot be sure, however, that this is a true reflection of the price of credit because the BP discounted only very good paper, in accordance with its statutes, while the average quality of paper in the rest of the market was certainly riskier. We can only say that the two rates were close and that the Bank did not lean heavily on this tool in its handling of the banking crisis.

The second question takes us into one of the main, still unresolved debates regarding the LLR function. Should the support to the financial system be meted out on a discretionary, case-by-case basis; or instead on a "blanket" approach, in which market mechanisms—essentially selection on the basis of price—automatically determined those which were going to be assisted?[33] There are several reasons to explain why the BP espoused the former solution and forsook the discount rate as a central part of its intervention program. One was the country's financial underdevelopment, which excluded the possibility of undertaking "open market operations"; and the inexistence of intermediaries between the banks and the central bank, such as the English discount houses, which could have served in a similar way. A second was the obvious difficulty in allocating funds to the market effectively, by price, given the already noted rigidity imposed by the authorities on the Bank's use of the discount rate. A third was the Bank's tremendous stock of expert knowledge regarding this very small financial market of 30–40 houses, which made it tempting to operate by quantity rationing of credit to entities whose condition and aptitude for survival the GC believed it knew well.

Both the state and the Bank converged regarding the notion that there was a public interest above the many private ones, which justified the extremes to which the LLR might have to go. They also recognized the BP's unique independence and capacity to serve this goal in a disinterested fashion, despite its private nature and the pressures of its shareholders for maximizing dividends.[34] As stated by the Bank's secretary-general, the government "trusts its Central Bank [sic] to make the transactions it considers suitable ...It is not the government who decides which operations are appropriate, solvent or opportune".[35] The issue this raised, however, was: did giving

[33]For a balanced view of the respective merits of these two views, see Fischer (1999). For a defense of the second, more systemic approach, see Capie and Wood (2006), for whom the first one is not a proper LLR function.

[34]Curiously, in 1931, the dictatorial government in which Salazar was finance minister, would still express doubts about the Bank's ability to "resist interesting possibilities from the point of view of profit taking" in its new role as official central bank (Banco de Portugal 1946a, VI: 13).

[35]Stated in the meeting of 11/10/1920.

so much latitude to the BP not threaten its market intervention with the specter of moral and political hazard?

Once again, we come up against difficulties in obtaining adequate data for a satisfactory answer to this. As regards the question of favoritism towards particular members of the financial fraternity, it is clear that the Bank cast its LLR net widely. During the second semester of 1920, altogether 29 institutions, both large and small, were in receipt of advances of varying sizes, both in Porto and Lisbon, presumably all or nearly all of them in connection with the critical moment.[36] Some were corporations, others were banking houses, but more importantly, hardly any of the significant names in the field of finance are missing from this list. This suggests that while the crisis struck broadly, the BP's help was no less dispersed. Unfortunately, we still lack a suitable compilation of the amounts made available in each case and cannot determine whether from this angle there was any discrimination.

On the other hand, undeniably special treatment was given to some banks and this represented a breach of a rigorously defined LLR function. Still, the Bank appears to have been well aware of the dangers of moral hazard that this might involve. Two of these instances clearly belonged in the "too big to fail" category, namely the efforts to rescue the BNU and the Totta banking house. The former was always treated by the BP with unusual generosity, either in terms of the amount of credit or by exempting its collateral from the stringent quality requirements imposed on other banks. On several occasions, members of the GC grumbled about this, but the inescapable fact was that "the BNU is very important in the country's economic and financial organization; a crisis in the BNU, if not halted in time, will become a matter of public order; helping it is not only in its own interest [of the BNU] but also in that of Portugal, the market and of the BP, who would not avoid the consequences, if something negative were to happen to it".[37]

The Totta banking house also found itself in difficulties as a result of massive deposit withdrawals, and, in October and December 1920, it had to ask the BP for very large sums at a moment's notice. One stumbling block was the quality of the collateral provided—industrial shares and dubious bills—but it was also drawing cheques on its account at the Bank without cover. In the end, however, it got most of what it wanted, given the imminence of its suspension and the danger that unsatisfied withdrawals by depositors would precipitate a run on the BP, a flight of capital abroad and knock-on effects for other banks.[38]

Political interference was the second risk connected with the Bank's preference for a casuistic approach to dispensing emergency credits. Not many instances have been detected, but those that were show that the potential for this existed, that it was not welcomed by the GC, and that the latter was aware that, in the current climate

[36]During the crisis, we assume that none of the rescue operations undertaken went unregistered in the minutes of the GC, given the delicate nature of these decisions.

[37]Director Burnay to GC, meeting of 03/08/1920, and various speeches at the meeting of 15/11/1920.

[38]See the general discussion at the GC meetings of 07/12/1920, 08/12/1920 and 11/12/1920. The BP tried to get the government to intervene on its own account without result. It also tried to organize a syndicate of banks to shore up Totta, but none of them accepted.

of political instability, the government's posture could change very suddenly and unexpectedly. On the question of the excess note issue, for example, it was pointed out that the BP might receive an authorization for its increase but this was always bound to be provisional, informal and undocumented. "A new minister [can] come and end it all".[39]

In the episodes described above concerning the BNU and Totta houses, the Bank's conduct was not only shaped by its own concern to ensure the stability of the financial system. Political considerations were present too. In July, when the GC pondered over a response to a massive request for funds from the BNU, the minister of finance let it be known that he was in full agreement with this application and would come to the GC that day and defend his view on the matter. A similar message was relayed by the secretary-general in November, when the BNU threatened to go under again.[40] In both instances, the GC's reaction, in spite of many misgivings, was the one desired by the authorities. Totta's case was similar: an important bank, a threat of suspension, profound doubts in the GC about the wisdom of bailing it out and the secretary-general's final and irresistible advice that it would be better for the BP to accept a guarantee consisting of dubious industrial shares than allow it to crash.[41]

Interestingly, a third, much smaller bank illustrates how the LLR might come into action even when the "too big to fail" doctrine was clearly not applicable. In August, the *Banco Português e Brasileiro* (BPB) asked for help after suffering a loss of three quarters of its deposits. The view of the GC was that its share and bill portfolio was healthy enough should be sold instead off as needed, though possibly at a loss. The minister of finance did not agree. He sent a message to the GC that he wanted this rescue to take place without such a sale because "it would be inconvenient for the market if this bank should be forced to suspend payments". A rediscount was promptly arranged and the BPB went on to survive until 1932.

3.3 *Bagehot's Rules: The LLR Must Make Clear Its Readiness to Lend Freely*[42]

Although long-established and publicly recognized but not legally stipulated as a formal duty, by the early 1920s the market, the state and the BP accepted that "in a crisis, when banks see their deposits contract, it is to the Bank they turn in order to mobilize their assets and transform them into the cash needed to satisfy the demands

[39]Speech by director Motta Gomes to the GC meeting of 15/11/1920.

[40]Speeches by the governor to the GC meeting of 30/07/1920 and of the secretary-general at the meeting of 15/11/1920.

[41]Secretary-General's speech to the GC meeting of 07/12/1920.

[42]There is no statement in these precise terms in *Lombard Street* but Bagehot berated the Bank of England for its lack of clarity. See p. 208.

of their depositors" (Diniz 1925, p. 40).[43] Bankers certainly showed in their behavior that this was their view. Throughout this crisis, they came in person to the Bank for assistance in droves, as one only would only do if one believed that it was prepared to act as LLR. The pattern was uniform. They asked to be received by the GC, stated the nature of their difficulties, described and gave evidence on the condition of their institution and the amount needed to recue it, and presented a list of assets to serve as collateral. At times, they told the BP that this was what everyone expected of it. When the governor of the BNU insisted on the Bank's assistance, he stressed the fact that "the BP has never failed the market, especially this bank, whose problems it has always helped to solve, and particularly now that they are due to transitory factors which will disappear once serenity returns and our current worries melt away".[44]

In early 1921, once the crisis was over, the Bank was pleased to conclude in its annual report: "it [the BP] has been the *traditional* [my emphasis] mainstay of the banks and trading houses' (Relatório 1921, p. 8). At the same time, it should be noted that not all of this was the result of a disinterested assumption by the Bank of its mission as LLR. There was self-interest at play too. One the one hand, there was a fear of being accused by the market and by its political enemies of being guilty of allowing some banks to fail.[45] On the other, the Bank worried that if it were known in the market that it was not helping a major house, e.g. Totta, this might be interpreted as a sign that it was short of funds, a perception which might precipitate a run on the LLR itself.[46]

3.4 Bagehot's Rules: Accommodate Anyone with Good Collateral[47]

The definition of what constitutes "good collateral" has been the subject of some debate.[48] The BP never had much doubt on this score and this is substantiated abundantly by the proceedings of its GC during the 1920–1921 crisis. In its perspective, the only acceptable guarantees were bills of first-class houses, with two or preferably three perfectly solvent signatures. They had to be short, rigorously representative of legitimate commercial transactions and not be renewals of older bills. Anything of lesser quality was rejected and apparently there was a good deal of this circulating

[43]The author was the director of the Banco Português do Continente e Ilhas, and had close family relations with the BP's leadership. For a similar though more official view, see the preamble to the 1925 law on banking in Banco de Portugal (1946b, vol. V: 140).

[44]Spoken at the GC meeting of 30/07/1920.

[45]Speeches by Lobo d'Avila and Silva Viana at the GC meeting of 29/11/1920 and by Burnay on the 08/12/1920.

[46]Speech by director Ulrich to the GC on 08/12/1920.

[47]"…these advances should be made on all good banking securities" (p. 199).

[48]Our approach here is the same as that of Bignon et al. (2012), i.e. we are interested in what contemporaries would have considered "good collateral", not what ought to have been, in retrospect, considered "eligible" by the authorities.

in the market. Throughout these critical months it was not uncommon for banks to present lists of bills for rediscounting at the BP, of which only half or less were deemed acceptable. As a result, the Bank was able to tell the minister of finance, in December 1920, that all of its loans to banks were well secured but in achieving this it had had to reject 50,000 contos worth of commercial paper.[49] Several financial institutions which needed help but could not meet these requirements, tried other solutions instead, such as industrial shares or municipal bonds. The BP systematically opposed this, however, and only gave in under duress from the government, or when faced with a dire emergency.[50]

One might question whether the Bank was not going further than it needed or than Bagehot's canon prescribed. It clearly infringed the rule that the LLR should be prepared to accept as security "what in ordinary times is reckoned a good security", even if the market value were temporarily below face value (Bagehot 1876, 2006, VII, p. 59). In some cases, it considered very reluctantly the possibility of industrial shares at 50% of their face value, but absolutely refused municipal bonds of the city of Oporto. Indeed, in its annual report for 1920, it stated, in clear defiance of Bagehot own words, that "for the Bank a good discount to us is not necessarily one with a very large value, but rather one which faithfully represents legitimate commercial operations".[51] At the same time, it was also more stringent than was stipulated by its by-laws, even though GC members alluded to the importance of adhering to them closely. These contained a long list of assets on which advances might be made and the limits on their value as collateral such as gold and silver (90%), national debt (quoted market value), mortgage bonds on land (85%), shares in corporations (75%), and merchandise in storage (50%) (Banco de Portugal 1946a). Yet rarely were these accepted during the crisis, something which now and then involved it in quite bitter confrontation with its clients and the government.

Several circumstances can be invoked to account for this apparent excess of zeal. One is the fact that it often lacked sufficient resources to satisfy all the bankers' demands, and without the means to discriminate on price alone, it had to use criteria of selection based on the quality of the collateral in order to ration credits. A second motive was the difficulty in valuing shares during a period of crisis. This particular one had strong speculative origins which were present throughout its duration, with many shares becoming illiquid or subject to violent price fluctuations, and therefore being impossible to evaluate.[52] A third reason arose from the Bank's difficulty in

---

[49] Report on this exchange in the GC meeting of 08/12/1920. The BNU was the exception: its collateral was usually taken without examination. Director Mota Gomes, GC meeting of 15/11/1920. This volume of rejections was about 40% of outstanding bills at that time. In the balmy days of the gold standard, the rejection rate was of the order of 1%.

[50] As in the cases of Totta and the BPB.

[51] Bagehot however complained that the Bank of England did the same, to his despair, and that in this matter "there is always great uncertainty as to the conduct of the Bank" (VII: 75).

[52] Silva Carvalho's speech to GC meeting of 07/12/1920. This problem became so important that a scheme was floated to found a "bad bank" with a capital of 50,000 contos to take the vast amount of illiquid stock out of the hands of the banks and discount it at the BP. The latter did not adhere to this plan. See GC meeting of 12/12/1920.

reconciling its public role as a LLR with its duty, as a private corporation, to look after its shareholders' interests. A frequently noted issue in the early history of central banking, it is a theme which came up regularly in the GC's discussions. It was compounded by the fear that, if pushed by extraneous influences into rescuing a bank with only weak assets and the latter failed, the BP might thereby cause its shareholders significant losses. The way to reconcile these two responsibilities would have been to back such riskier operations up with a state guarantee, as happened during the 1891 crisis when unsound institutions were rescued unwillingly by the BP but with the government's cover. In 1920, this was rejected every time the issue was raised. As seen earlier, the secretary-general held that the state did not insure the losses from these operations; it only provided the wherewithal to carry them out.[53]

4 Conclusions

This study of the LLR function of the quasi-central bank of a poor and peripheral country in turmoil allows us to draw three conclusions. They are based on an examination of the banking crisis of 1920–1921 in Portugal.

The first has to do with the far less than perfect fit between the performance of the BP and the paradigm supplied by Bagehot in his classic work. Contrary to the latter's prescription, during a severe crisis the BP advanced funds to banks in trouble less generously than was felt to be required by all parties involved. Moreover, its use of the discount rate was much less vigorous than it might have been. Consequently, its assistance was distributed to the financial sector by means of a rationing process, not allocated on the basis of price. Indeed, advances to banks were distributed primarily according to the Bank's private estimation of each institution's need, although at times the interests of the system as a whole were also taken into account. Finally, it was a lot more demanding regarding the quality of the collateral expected for a rescue than Bagehot judged necessary for overcoming a banking panic. In one respect, however, the Bank's intervention was close to the classical standard which we have been tracking. By tradition and by public and explicit admission, it always made it clear to the market that it was ready to lend to any bank in difficulty providing the collateral was good enough.

A second finding has to do with why there was such a gap between the BP's profile as a LLR and Bagehot's then already well known advice to proto-central bankers when they faced a bank crisis. Was this a carefully considered option or was it unavoidable? Politics and financial policy are in this matter the heart of the story. Throughout these events, the BP was kept continually in a regulatory strait jacket as regards its note issuing function. It was thus prevented from lending more liberally and had no way of avoiding credit rationing. Matters might have been somewhat different had the interests of the Bank's owners not been so influential in influencing the decisions taken by its leaders. Owing to its joint-stock corporate nature, the latter

[53]The question was posed by director Ávila Lima in the GC meeting of 11/10/1920.

had no alternative but to try and maximize the return on shares and protect as much as possible the market value of the capital stock. In good measure, this explains the robust posture of the institution on the subject of collateral. Since so many banks found it difficult to satisfy these requirements, it seems hard to avoid the conclusion that a shorter and more benign crisis would have been possible otherwise.

Our third conclusion pertains to the costs and benefits for the Portuguese economy arising from this LLR activity, in particular its financial dimension. In the short-run, the best yardstick is the number of banks which failed. We lack a precise count of the banks and banking houses which were present in the market at this time, but it was certainly in excess of thirty. Only one closed down as a result of the crisis—the private bankers Nunes and Nunes. While we have no information as to its size, it seems to have been small and the immediate impact of its disappearance can hardly have been significant.[54] In the longer run, the negative impact may have been greater although this is hard to gauge. Two more bank crises, in 1923 and 1925, before the monetary and financial stabilization of the late 1920s, witnessed the demise of nine banks altogether. In the present state of this research, it is hard to tell to what extent this was a legacy of an ill-resolved earlier crisis in 1921 and a part therefore of the fall-out from this event. Only further research can clarify this issue.

Acknowledgements The author thanks the Bank of Portugal for allowing him to consult its historical archives and for financial support for this research. Invaluable assistance at this archive was received from Dr. Stella Pereira.

References

Printed

Bagehot W (1873, 2006) Lombard street: a description of the money market. Cosimo Books, New York

Banco de Portugal (1946a) Diplomas Orgânicos e Regulamentares. Banco de Portugal, Lisboa

Banco de Portugal (1946b) Legislação Própria vols V and VI. Banco de Portugal, Lisboa

Banco de Portugal (various years), Relatório do Conselho de Administração. Balanço, Documentos e Parecer do Conselho Fiscal. Imprensa Nacional, Lisboa

Batista D, Martins C, Pinheiro M et al (1997) New estimates for Portugal's GDP, 1910–1958. Banco de Portugal, Lisbon

Betrán C, Martín-Aceña P, Pons MA (2012) Financial crises in Spain: lessons from the last 150 years. Revista de Historia Económica/J Iber Lat Am Econ Hist 30(3):417–446

Bignon V, Flandreau M, Ugolini S (2012) Bagehot for beginners: The making of lending of last resort operations in the mid-19th century. Econ Hist Rev 65:580–608

Bordo MD (1990) The lender of last resort: alternative views and historical experience. Federal Reserve Bank Richmond Econ Quart 73(1):18–29

[54]See Elementos Históricos, AHBP, which shows that Nunes and Nunes suspended payments during 1920. The BP's evidence places this in 1921, undoubtedly as a consequence of the crisis. It was one of the twenty-nine institutions which received support from the Bank.

Branco CS (1950) Aspectos da Questão Monetária Portuguesa. Banco de Portugal, Lisbon
Buyst E, Maes I (2008) Central banking in 19th century Belgium: was the NBB a lender of last resort? Fin Hist Rev 15:153–173
Capie FH, Goodhart C, Fischer S et al (1994) The future of central banking. In: The tercentenary symposium of the Bank of England. Cambridge University Press, Cambridge
Capie FH, Wood GE (eds) (2006) The lender of last resort. Routledge, London and New York
Diniz AA (1925) O Problema do Banco Emissor. Empresa do Diario de Noticias, Lisboa
Esteves RP, Ferramosca F, Reis J (2009) Market integration in the golden periphery: the Lisbon/London exchange, 1854–1891. Explor Econ Hist 46(3):324–345
Feinstein C, Temin P, Toniolo G (eds) (1995a) Banking, currency and finance in Europe between the wars. Clarendon Press, Oxford
Feinstein C, Temin P, Toniolo G (1995) International economic organization: banking, finance and trade between the wars. In: Feinstein C et al (eds) Banking, currency and finance in Europe between the wars. Clarendon Press, Oxford, pp 9–76
Fink C (1984) The Genoa conference: European diplomacy 1921–1922. University of Carolina Press, Chapel Hills
Fischer S (1999) On the need for an international lender of last resort. J Econ Persp 13(4):85–104
Goodhart CAE (2007) Myths about the lender of last resort. In: Forrest C, Wood G (eds) The lender of last resort. Routledge, London and New York, pp 317–337
Gorton G (1985) Clearinghouses and the origin of central banking in the United States. J Econ Hist 45:277–283
Grossman RS, Rockof H (2015) Fighting the last war: economists on the lender of last resort. National Bureau of Economic Research No. w20832, Cambridge, MA
Guarini G, Toniolo G (eds) (1993) La Banca d'Italia e il Sistema Bancario, 1919–1936. Laterza, Roma-Bari
Humphrey T, Keleher RE (1983) The lender of last resort: an historical perspective. Cato J 3:275–321
Kindelberger CP (2007) The lender of last resort: pushing the doctrine too far? Forrest C, Wood G (eds) (2008) The lender of last resort. Routledge, London and New York, pp 338–351
League of Nations (1920) Currencies after the war: a survey of conditions in various countries, compiled under the auspices of the international secretariat of the league of nations. Harrison and Sons, London
Lumbralles, J da CL (1926) Organização Bancária Portuguesa. Coimbra Editora, Coimbra
Mata ME, Valério N (1982) O Banco de Portugal, único banco emissor, 1891–1931. Revista de História Económica e Social 10
Reis J (1995) Portuguese banking in the inter-war period. In: Feinstein C et al (eds) Banking, currency and finance in Europe between the wars. Clarendon Press, Oxford, pp 472–501
Reis J (1999) The Bank of Portugal's first century: from 1846 to the second world war. In: Holtfrerich CL, Reis J, Toniolo G (eds) The emergence of modern central banking from 1918 to the present. Ashgate, Aldershot
Reis J (2007) "An art, not a science?" Central bank management in Portugal under the gold standard, 1863–1887. Econ Hist Rev 60:712–741
Toniolo G (1990) The economic history of liberal Italy, 1850–1918. Routledge, London
Toniolo G (1995) Italian banking, 1919–1936. In: Feinstein C et al (eds) Banking, currency and finance in Europe between the wars, pp 296–314
Valério N, Nunes AB, Bastien C et al (2006) History of the Portuguese banking system, 1822–1931, vol I. Banco de Portugal, Lisboa
Wood JH (2005) A history of central banking in Great Britain and the United States. Cambridge University Press, Cambridge

Manuscript

Actas do Conselho Geral do Banco de Portugal (1920–1921) in Arquivo Histórico do Banco de Portugal (AHBP), scannerized version, books G2-17 to G2-19

Elementos Históricos Relativos a Instituições de Crédito (anteriores a 1975), Departamento de Supervisão Bancária, Secção de Registos e Averbamentos, in Arquivo Historico do Banco de Portugal, #7004001

Situações Semanais, in Arquivo Histórico do Banco de Portugal

What is in a Bond? The Value of Portugal or the Financial Origins of the Portuguese Civil War

Marc Flandreau

Abstract As bonds left untied make us reflect on the places where we never went, this chapter offers an economic, historical and political meditation on a bond between Portugal and Rothschild that was not tied. By discussing what was not and what might have been, the story offers ways to reflect on what Portugal came to be. On September 27, 1823, the Portuguese Minister of Finance signed a loan contract with B. A. Goldschmidt. I follow this contract and the one with James de Rothschild (which Portugal did not sign) from the date of issue through Goldschmidt's failure (1826) until Portugal's default and the eruption of its Civil War in 1828. I conclude that a Rothschild bond might have escaped default, thus avoiding war.

Keywords Sovereign default · Economic history · Financial reputation · Portuguese Civil War

1 Two Loan Contracts and a Decision

Bonds are an excellent subject for a contribution to a Festschrift. If I had not gone to Berkeley in the early 1990s, I would never have become a student of Barry Eichengreen, and as a result, I would never have met Jorge Braga de Macedo in the same way I did. Bonds bind us but sometimes they divide us. At the time I met with Jorge, the European Exchange Rate (ERM) mechanism tied the currencies of Europe in a manner that preceded both the euro's advent and Brexit.

In a way, bonds take us to strange places. Among the most fascinating effects they have on our lives are those that accrue from the bonds that are not tied. Pondering these non-bonds makes us reflect on the places where we never went.

This paper proposes a rumination under this guise. It offers an economic, historical and political meditation on a bond that was not tied, between Portugal and the House of Rothschild and on the consequences that did not accrue. By enabling us to discuss

M. Flandreau (✉)
Department of History, University of Pennsylvania College, Philadelphia, PA, USA
e-mail: mfl@sas.upenn.edu

L. Brites Pereira et al. (eds.), *Economic Globalization and Governance*,
https://doi.org/10.1007/978-3-030-53265-9_3

a Portugal that was not and a Portugal that might have been, the story offers ways to reflect on the *nature* of the Portugal that came to be.

The film starts in September 1823, with the camera set on the Portuguese Minister of Finance, Henrique Teixeira de Sampaio (1774–1833), the Count of Povoa (*Conde da Póvoa*), a forerunner of Jorge Braga de Macedo. He is a Portuguese merchant and financier and the principal architect of the financial policy of King João VI. At the time when the scene begins, he is signing a document as "Secretary of State and of the Finance Department, and President of the Royal Treasury." What follows is the story of this document and of another document, which he did not sign.

The Minister has been in charge of negotiating a loan. Portugal is in the midst of almost continuous political turmoil. Dom Pedro, who is King João's elder son, and the regent of Brazil, has proclaimed Brazil's independence in September 1822 and João has refused to recognize it. The War of Independence that will ensue will end with the Treaty of Separation, but only in 1825.

Meanwhile, at home, the King is treading a thin line between the rival factions of Liberals and Absolutists who are vying for control of the Iberian Peninsula. He has granted the Liberals a constitution (the Portuguese *Cortes*) in September 1822, only to take it back in June 1823, during the Vilafrancada uprising. The uprising has been led by the King's other son, Miguel, who is at the head of the Absolutist faction and is prepared to depose him. Seeing no other escape than taking the uprising into his own hands, João has put both the Liberal Cortes to rest and obliged Miguel to submit. The unruly Miguel persists and he shall soon be exiled to Vienna, where he stays under the watchful eye of Prince Metternich.[1]

These events are disorganizing the country's finances as they cost money and render revenues harder to raise. But the good news is that money is easy in London. These were the days historian Frank Griffith Dawson has described as the "First Foreign Loan Bubble" (Dawson 1990). One country after another is able to raise capital in the City and, in September 1823, the Count of Povoa has managed to drum up two competing offers.

The first is from the House of Rothschild, a bidder that needs no introduction. The other offer is by the House of Goldschmidt—B. A. Goldschmidt and Co., as it is known—which emerges during the sovereign debt boom of the 1820s as an aggressive provider of sovereign loan originations. When it offers to lend money to Portugal, B. A. Goldschmidt and Co. has just issued with another merchant bank (A. F. Haldimand and Sons) a Danish loan, which has experienced a triumphant rally. Goldschmidt will also later issue a Mexican loan and a Colombian one, too.[2]

The Count of Povoa has had to decide with whom Portugal will tie the knot. Concerned with upholding the interests of his country and king, he has looked for the best price. Accordingly, he has secured an offer from Rothschild, an option to be

[1]On the politics of the period see Paquette (2013).

[2]Danish 5% (1821–1822). Mexican 5% loan (1824) Colombian 6% (1824). According to my calculations with Juan Flores, they floated roughly 20% of the loans and about the same share of the money raised. That put them in the third position in terms of market share (See Flandreau et al. 2009).

precise—which he can take up if he wants.[3] But on September 27, 1823, the contract he is signing is the Goldschmidt contract.[4]

In some previous accounts, it has been mistakenly said that Portugal took the Rothschild offer.[5] My discovery of the Goldschmidt loan contract in the Portuguese National Archive and the availability of the Rothschild contract in the Rothschild Archive in London enables us to explore the contours of the decision. The Count, undoubtedly advised by sophisticate actuaries, has done the maths: Rothschilds are outbid. It did cost around 90 basis points more to borrow with them than with Goldschmidt (6.8% with Goldschmidt versus 7.7% with Rothschild). Or, alternatively, for the same nominal debt, the Government of Portugal was receiving, in round numbers, 20% more cash with Goldschmidt (Table 1).

2 More Money with no Strings Attached?

Whether or not this was a wise choice is another matter. Underwriting by Rothschilds provided significant services to borrowers so, in fact, a loan by Rothschilds and a loan by an ordinary underwriter such as Goldschmidt were two different animals. Rothschilds would cajole the borrower, work on it and coerce it if need be, so as to make ends meet. Given that they retained a clientele of reliable investors whose trust they wished to keep, Rothschilds were interested in preventing country they had underwritten from defaulting. If a country sought to default, they were quick to weigh in on it until it changed its mind. They had tons of capital and a mountain of credit to do this.[6]

As a result, a Rothschild price was not the same thing as a Goldschmidt price, and we would be naive to compare them as mere mathematical alternatives. The

[3]Rothschild Archive London 000/401A/5. The date marked on the Rothschild offer is September 8, 1823.

[4]*Torre do Tombo, Ministério dos Negócios Estrangeiros*, cx. 173. The loan was negotiated in Lisbon by Adolphus Goldschmidt (1798–1876), son of Lion Abraham, the senior partner of the House of Goldschmidt.

[5]The error that I allude to was first committed by Hyde Clarke in 1878 in a list of loans he produces Clarke (1878, p. 313); This is a strange error because Clarke was a specialist in the subject and, as Wilson (2015) has argued, Clarke had firsthand knowledge of the Portuguese Civil War whose origins are related to this early loan. The error reappears in Ayer (1905, pp. 18–19), and more recently in Ferguson (1998, p. 142). Dawson (1990, p. 61) makes an even weirder error, giving the contractor as Thomas and King and referring to "Clarke (1878, p. 313)" as the source. By contrast, accurate indications include Gille (1965, p. 103) and Flandreau and Flores (2009, p. 674). Gille declares having relied on the "Portuguese National Archive" (with no further detail being given), which he claims would hold the general bond and a specimen of the security but he gives no call number. I owe it to Helena Carvalho for having located Gille's probable source in the *Tribunal de Contas* archive (AHTC. *Cartórios Avulso*, 55). This archive holds a copy of the general bond and specimens of the security. So, I suspect that this is what Gille (or his correspondents) got his hands upon.

[6]For an illustration of this argument, see Flandreau and Flores (2009) and Flandreau et al. (2009).

Table 1 Comparing propositions: Rothschild v. Goldschmidt

	Rothschild	Goldschmidt
Nominal amount (m £)	1.5	1.5
Dividend (%)	5	5
Issue price (£)	73	87
Commission (%)	3	2
Amount raised (million £)	1.05	1.275
Maturity (number of years)	96	30
Yield-to-maturity (%)	7.7	6.8

Notes For the sake of simplicity, calculations were made assuming that the Rothschild loan had a 96-year reimbursement profile with a constant amortization of 1.05% per year rather than the somewhat complex profile that was actually chosen. The amortization profile of 30 years is given in the contract, and it translates into a constant annual reimbursement of 50,000 lb sterling (£) as described in the general bond. It is also not possible to model completely the amortization procedure, which rested on market purchases if the loan's price was below par, and so a simplified reimbursement at par was adopted for both (*Source* Author using the sources cited in the text)

price difference purchased something. For once, the Rothschild price was bound to prove more robust. Rothschilds sent the right signal but also traded in such a way so that the signal *became* right. For instance, one year before the Count of Povoa made his judgment call, the Austrian Ambassador in Naples (Ficquelmont) was writing in amazement to his boss (Metternich) about a price rally caused by the news of Rothschild's sponsoring of the Kingdom of Naples: "The credit of a foreigner, which is to say that of the House of Rothschild, not that of the Kingdom of Naples, was responsible for the rise of Neapolitan securities" (Gille 1965, p. 98).

To be clear, it was not Naples' "fundamentals" that mattered but the underwriter's identity. Probably, a better way to put it is to say that the underwriter *was* the "fundamentals." This gave Rothschilds monopoly power and enabled them to price their loans on a different scale. The price they set was not the price that would secure the deal, but the price they felt would protect their reputation.

In economic terms, the principle that was mobilized is known as relationship banking. On the one hand, the bank provides insurance to the borrower by guaranteeing access to credit but this comes with strings attached. The desire for the banker to make ends meet subjects the borrower to monitoring. Against this backdrop, tying the knot with a prestigious underwriter is especially advantageous for "new" countries, because the bankers performed a valuable service that resolved early information asymmetries.

This logic was well-known at the time. In my research, I have come across numerous illustrations. One of these, among many others, has been brought to my attention recently. It is due to no lesser an authority than Camillo Benso, Count of Cavour, Premier of the Kingdom of Sardinia and leader of Italy's unification in the 1850s. In a speech in Parliament discussing the reasons for the high yield loan which the French Rothschilds had designed for the Kingdom of Sardinia in 1849, Cavour claimed that issuing with Rothschild was an "immediate sacrifice" for sure but that the upside was that it purchased the ability to "inspire trust to all the capitalists of Europe" and to bring the price of *Rendita* bonds to a very high value: "*E di portarla ad un corso assai elevato*" is the way he puts it.[7]

Of course, after the initial issue, the game became one of competition inside cooperation: Borrowers tried to fight their banker so as to avoid too much capture. Cavour himself, and other Rothschild borrowers too—the Austrians, French, Russians and Prussians—would all come to a point where they would battle Rothschilds. It was the essence of the game: Once the bankers certified a country on the market thereby resolving early information asymmetries, the field became more competitive though never completely, by definition. The dance of the outside offers would begin. Rothschilds never fully surrendered but conceded territory, usually just enough to fend off the threat.

The Portuguese Count's decision to go with Goldschmidts was maybe not only informed by financial costing, however. Rothschilds were concerned with dampening the politically aggressive tendencies of borrowers, given their concern about future repayment. This was one reason for the conflict that would emerge later with the Italian Count (Cavour), for instance. Italian unity was a geopolitical risk and was initially opposed by Rothschilds. King João VI and his ministers may have likewise worried about the financing becoming a vehicle for external interference in Portuguese politics. A Rothschild loan would have reinforced the grip of Metternich's Holly Alliance, which had a bearing on the conflict between the Liberal and the Absolutist factions in Portugal. By contrast, the Goldschmidt loan seemed like a godsend—more money, with no strings attached.

3 An Aspiring Denmark or a Regular Kingdom of Naples?

Against this backdrop, one can only admire the Count's decision to "jump the gun" and escape the grip of the bankers right away. He had tried and apparently succeeded in outbidding Rothschilds, even *before* his country had a financial reputation. This seems miraculous in that, by definition, if the argument about signaling is valid, it is very difficult for an ordinary banker to offer better terms than a prestigious one. What had Goldschmidt done to secure this feat? Using the price of the Portuguese loan of 1823 when it was launched, Table 2 shows the two competing readings of Portugal: Goldschmidt sold Portugal as an aspiring Denmark, Rothschild would have marketed it as your regular Kingdom of Naples. Which one was it going to be?

There was yet a more prosaic phenomenon behind the Count's success at securing excellent terms. During a boom, the market share of prestige tends to decline because the appetite for risk increases. Many underwriters compete aggressively for marginal

[7] Cavour (1942, p. 45). "*Quest'operazione fu, non esito a dirlo, assai vantaggiosa perché, malgrado che essa ci abbia costato un sacrificio immediate, ebbe per effetto pero d'ispirare molta fiducia a tutti I capitalisti d'Europa nella nostra Rendita, di farla conoscere sulle principali piazza del continente europea, e di portarla ad un corso assai elevato.*"

Table 2 Sovereign Bond prices (converted in comparable 5% bonds) at the time of the Portuguese issue (31 October 1823), sovereign debt market Peak (31 October 1824) and Crash (31 January 1826). (Unit: Pound sterling)

	At the Time of the Portuguese Issue	Peak of the Foreign Debt Bubble	Crash
Rothschild			
Austria	82	92.5	92.5
France	90	98	98
Naples	77	n.a	n.a
Prussia	86.5	94	94
Russia	83	84.5	84.5
Portugal (Rothschild alternative offer)	78 (1)	–	–
Non Rothschild			
Chile	58.5	63.5	46.5
Colombia	52	69	50
Denmark	92	103.5	Paid off
Portugal (Actual)	87	93.5	75

Note(1): We know the issue price (73) but not the price at which it would have traded on the market. Rothschild bonds typically experienced a "run-up" on early trading. Based on the realized performance of other Rothschild loans, a likely counterfactual run-up would have taken the price of Portuguese debt to 78. See Flandreau and Flores (2009, p. 650) (*Source*: Author, using the *Course of Exchange*)

loans on the grounds that the liquid market will absorb them. The underwriters of such loans have a lesser concern for their reputation and they worry less about the downturn. In contrast, prestigious banks remain cautious since they factor in the future. The result is the aggressive entry of marginal banks. According to this reading, all that the Count had done was to take advantage of a credit boom, pure and simple. And the price he had secured for himself, was informed by the looming bubble. This was all good and right, of course—there is nothing wrong with paying less. Except that little by little, Portugal was venturing into a more dangerous corner.

Further evidence supporting the notion that Goldschmidt was simply being entrepreneurial and riding the boom can be garnered by looking at the manner in which it employed an informational technique in the Portuguese contract that had also been used in the Danish loan. One difficulty of lending to Portugal was the paucity of reliable fiscal data. Accordingly, it was difficult to give investors a sense of the debt's sustainability.[8] Because people trusted Rothschilds, the mere mention

[8] As Cohen writes in his *Compendium of Finance*: "The accounts respecting the finances of [Portugal] which we have been able to gather, are very limited and unsatisfactory, but at the time we are writing, a Committee is appointed to investigate the resources of the State, and report upon them, with a view to a loan, which it is in the contemplation of the government to negotiate; Should any satisfactory

that they would be involved was enough—*they* were the information.[9] But this could not work for Goldschmidts. As a result, in their contract, the precise amount yielded by the securities pledged (the revenues from the Soap and Tobacco monopolies) was documented at length. In the prospectus that would later be circulated to investors, the numbers were converted into pound sterling to enable comparison and demonstrate the debt's sustainability.[10] Goldschmidt was not adding value with their own good name and so they were adding data instead. In a euphoric market, this was sufficient to get the ball rolling.

With the contract signed, Goldschmidt launched their loan. But the question is, what was really the value of the "Portugal" they had originated? An indication that Goldschmidt had been overly optimistic arose immediately. On October 11, 1823, the City article of the *Morning Chronicle* mentioned that the Portuguese loan was being shorted.[11] Speculators offered 82, when the issue price was, as we saw, 87. Faced with this skepticism, Goldschmidts did their job: They placed forward orders and worked to keep the prices up, with the result that in the subsequent weeks, as the conversation of the bulls and bears progressed, an alternation of mild premiums and mild discounts to the issue price was reported in James Wetenhall's *Course of the Exchange*. But downward pressures persisted, which suggests that the loan struggled to sell out.[12]

4 The Collapse of the "Goldschmidt Bubble"

Eventually, the tide of optimism of 1824 lifted the prices of *all* foreign loans issued in the London stock exchange and the Portuguese bonds reached £94 twice that year

information reach us previous to publication we shall not fail to notice it in an addenda" (Cohen 1822, p. 127). There was no addenda and the subsequent edition (1828) repeated the same language.

[9]Rothschilds, who must have asked for financial data as they always did, had identified certain rights (the Tobacco and Soap state monopolies) as security. They were marked in the contract, without further elaboration, beyond the description of a mechanism for using the resources as loan collateral.

[10]In the general bond (*Morning Chronicle*, December 10, 1823), the two monopolies are said to have been yielding annually in the past "and sometimes exceeding" £300,000 per year. Investors were led to compute for themselves the annual interest burden, or £75,000 and the amortization, or £50,000 per year (the contract only said that the amortization should take place in 30 years which is consistent with the rate indicated). In other words, the annual burden (£125,000) was more than twice covered by the revenues from the monopolies. However, in the original contract given in the annex, the Tobacco and Soap contracts are said to "yield an annual income of one thousand two hundred and one *contos of Reis*." At the current exchange rate, this was about £250,000 only. The Decima which is also mentioned in the original contract, but only alluded to in the general bond, is said to have yielded about eight hundred and fourteen *contos of Reis* or £180,000. It would be interesting to know more about what happened to the numbers between the initial contract and the prospectus.

[11]It is said to have been offered "82" while "85 was demanded." At that date, the markets did not have the contract details, which they expected to arrive with the "first mail from Lisbon."

[12]On October 31, 1823, Wetenhall quoted -0.325 to -0.25 on the Portuguese bonds.

(in the Spring and Fall) but they were unable to stay at that level (See Fig. 1). In fact, Goldschmidt had never been able to fully offload the position. They had merely pumped up the prices and, since they remained long in their own foreign loans, they became vulnerable to the market downturn which was around the corner.[13] It took on an extreme form—the infamous Panic of 1825 in November and December of that year.[14]

All asset classes were battered and sovereign bonds, in particular, plummeted.[15] The balance sheet of Goldschmidt took a hit. The final blow was the default, in January 1826, of the Colombian loan which Goldschmidt had issued in 1824. The bank suspended payment on February 15, 1826, and market commentary had it that it was fully expected. A couple of days later, Lion Abraham Goldschmidt, senior partner of the bank, "threw himself on the divan" after which he was reported to have "passed from this life without a struggle or a groan."[16]

What had happened to B. A. Goldschmidt and Co. is pretty clear. The bank had intoxicated itself with its own "toxic" assets.[17] According to the *London Courier and Evening Gazette*, for instance, "the principal cause of the stoppage of this house is considered to be the efforts made to support the credit of the different Governments on whose behalf they had entered into contracts for loans, and the depreciation of that description of property has been so great that at this moment Portuguese stock is at a discount of 22 [...] below the contract price."[18] I have not been able to retrieve the *post mortem* that was performed at the time by a committee of bankers (including Rothschild) who assisted with the liquidation but according to the *Times*, the bank had liabilities amounting to £1.2 million while assets did not exceed £0.8 million (against £1.5 million one year earlier).[19]

[13]For instance, it appeared later that a nominal capital of £350,000, or about 8% of the total amount outstanding, was with the bankers (see *Examiner*, November 19, 1826, p. 745). According to the *Globe*, February 15, 1826, one minor partner of B. A. Goldschmidt, Hurtz, would have pulled out at the peak with gains of £100,000.

[14]On the Panic of 1825, see Dawson (1990), Gille (1965) and Neal (1998).

[15]From the market peak of 90 to 91 in early 1825, Colombians had plummeted to 61, Mexicans had gone from 80–81 to 60–62 and Portuguese stock had retreated from 90–91, to below 75.

[16]Accounts had Lion Abraham throwing himself on the sofa out of despair and dying afterwards. Reports ascribed the death to the bursting of a blood vessel in his head but it might also have been a suicide. Suicide being illegal, it created difficulties for succession. To resolve the problem, it was not unusual to seek the assistance of the physician, who would confirm the occurrence of a natural death.

[17]See "Messrs. Goldschmidt and Co." in *London Courier and Evening Gazette*, February 16, 1826, and *Morning Post*, February 16, 1826. *Examiner*: (p. 132). According to the *Public Ledger and Daily Advertiser*, February 16, 1826, "We believe that it is an ascertained fact that the house was worth, in the early part of last year (taking the public sureties at the value of the day) at least one million and a half sterling."

[18]*London Courier and Evening Gazette*, February 16, 1826.

[19]After the bank's liquidation, the formerly personal "princely" fortune of the late Lion Abraham would have been reduced to £140,000. This was still a decent figure (see *Public Ledger and Daily Advertiser*, February 22, 1826, for a discussion of the numbers). The matter ought to receive the devoted attention of a careful student in the future. It is likely that more details are available on

Fig. 1 Price of Portuguese bonds of 1823 (*Source*: Author's calculations using the *Course of Exchange*)

The Duke of Palmella, the Portuguese representative in London, announced that he was making arrangements for the payment of dividends on the debt with another bank. It was repeated in various places, that since B. A. Goldschmidt's function had been merely technical, its failure had no meaning whatsoever for the credit of sovereign borrowers.[20] Some countries underwritten by Goldschmidts, like Colombia, could default but others would not. This was an accurate way, if involuntarily ironical, to couch the matter. Since B. A. Goldschmidt did not add value to Portugal, its collapse could not really deduct anything. And indeed, between late January 1826 and late February 1826, the price of Portuguese bonds reflected market trends rather than the specific failure of Goldschmidt which was soon forgotten.[21]

The consequences of the non-issue with Rothschild may be figured out through a parallel with the experience of the Kingdom of Naples, another geographically, economically and politically peripheral Western European state, where the rival politics of Liberalism and Absolutism were being played out. We know from the account by historian Bertrand Gille that the crisis of 1825 took its toll on Neapolitan bonds, forcing Rothschilds to step in. Those Rothschild clients who wanted to sell out Neapolitan bonds were enabled to do so thanks to the aggressive operations of the underwriter. Evidence suggests that the purchases had been massive. The 1826 balance sheet of the Paris branch (dated June 1826) shows Neapolitan bonds representing 15% of total assets, which amounted to one-fifth of the 1824 London issue underwritten by Rothschilds. James de Rothschild in Paris wrote to Charles in Vienna that if it "had not been for their efforts," Neapolitan funds would be trading much lower and perhaps "the discredit could have been complete" (Gille 1965, pp. 164–165 and Flandreau and Flores 2009, pp. 670–672).

This price-support tactic by Rothschilds was not different from what Goldschmidt had attempted to do. Only, Rothschilds had more capital, more credit and they proved more resilient as a result. This overall resilience is illustrated in Table 2, which shows the price of the various bonds, at the date of the Portuguese issue (October 1823), at the last Portuguese peak (October 1824), and in the midst of the debacle (January 1826). As can be seen, the more serious declines were the non-Rothschild securities. It is also intriguing that after the collapse of the "Goldschmidt bubble," Portuguese bonds fluctuated just above a "barrier" corresponding to the price that Rothschild had offered initially (Fig. 1).

---

the fascinating subject of the failure of B. A. Goldschmidt. An original financial structure (in effect, a trust, operated by key foreign loan contractors) was created to liquidate the assets of B. A. Goldschmidt in a manner that would minimize market disruption. For example, see the *Globe*, February 22, 1826, which explains that the assets were put in a trust (bad bank?) responsible for its liquidation. The five trustees appointed were Rothschild, Samuel, Barclay, Gurney and Richardson, which were all important money market operators and, in particular, involved in sovereign debt (except perhaps Gurney, as far as I can tell), including in denominations similar to those in which Goldschmidt traded. As such, they were directly interested in an orderly resolution.

[20] For example, see *Globe*, February 15, 1826: "The real security of these loans cannot be at all affected by the [failure of Goldschmidt]. If Messrs. Goldschmidt had continued solvent, they could not have paid the dividends unless funds were remitted; and, if the Governments remit these funds, the dividends can just as well be paid through any other house as by that of these merchants."

[21] The *Course of Exchange* gives 75 and 74, respectively.

5 Two Brothers at Arms and a Loan Default

A few weeks into these events, King João VI passed away, leaving a thorny political situation. Before his death, the King had nominated his daughter, Isabel Maria, to serve as regent until the legitimate heir returned to the kingdom. It was unclear however who that heir was going to be. Each faction had its candidate, a son of João in both cases. It could either be Miguel, leader of the Absolutist faction and exiled in Vienna. Or, it could Pedro, the Emperor of Brazil, and leader of the Liberals.

A further complication accrued from the fact that Brazil had ended up pledging to provide Portugal with the money to service the loan of 1823, as a result of the Treaty of Separation between Portugal and Brazil in 1825. Meanwhile, Brazil had joined the countries underwritten by Rothschild. In fact, it may well be that this remote effect—of Rothschilds on Brazil and of Brazil on the Portuguese loan of 1823—explains the tendency for this loan to stay above the Rothschild price of 73, until the eventual default broke the dam in 1828 (Fig. 1).

Even more important to my counterfactual reasoning, however, is the fact that, had Rothschilds been contractors for the loan of 1823, they would have had a leverage on both ends of the ensuing political dispute. On the one hand, they would have had been able to bring pressure to bear on the Liberal faction, because they were lending to Dom Pedro's Brazil. On the other hand, had they managed to issue Portugal's loan of 1823, they would have had leverage over Dom Miguel and the Absolutists, and through the connection with Metternich's Holy Alliance. Chances are that, having a finger in each pie, Rothschilds would have been central to any deal making, as they were in many other geopolitical episodes at the time (Flandreau and Flores 2012). What is more, they would have seen to it that the pledges made were honored. The bond that was not tied in 1823 was returning silently, and with a vengeance.

Instead, as is well-known, the succession crisis led to an arrangement brokered by Pedro whereby he would renounce to his rights to the Crown of Portugal, while Miguel would marry Pedro's infant daughter Dona Maria. Miguel would become consort and recognize the Portuguese *Cortes*. The bond of marriage would prove to be elusive, however. In the Spring of 1828, Miguel arrived in Portugal, prepped by Metternich who asked him to be a good boy for the sake of Europe's peace. In Lisbon, he mumbled his solemn pledge to the constitution but denounced it immediately, after which he dissolved the *Cortes* and went after the Liberals. Now isolated, and counting on his own resources, he cut the financial link to the world. He defaulted on the loan of 1823.

Pedro, unwilling to let his brother have it his own way, dispatched the dividend money (which was supposed to go to Portugal's creditors) to Miguel's Liberal opponents. They had a better use for the funds than servicing a loan. On June 1, 1828, the Goldschmidt loan of 1823 was officially in arrears. Installed in the Azorean Island of Terceira, the exiled Liberal government of Portugal—the Terceira Regency—started to plan the landing of troops and the restoration of Dona Maria against the "Usurper." The Portuguese Civil War had begun.

6 Annex

Note: The following is a transcription of the Goldschmidt contract, which was located in the Portuguese National Archive at *Torre do Tombo*, Ministry of Foreign Affairs Box, cx. 173. This document is an *underwriting* contract, thus distinct from the "general bond" which stated the obligation of the borrower towards the holders of bonds. By contrast, underwriting contracts stated the obligations of the contractor and of the underwriter towards one another. As a result, they typically included (as in the case below) material that ends up in the general bond itself, since the underwriter is contracting for a loan with given characteristics and "on behalf" of the final investors. However, an underwriting contract also includes a description of the contractor's obligations: How the money is raised, transferred to the issuer, and in particular what is the commission. Until the discovery of this document, for instance, we did not know how large Goldschmidt's commission was. A transcription of the general bond may be found in the *Morning Chronicle*, December 10, 1823.

Articles of agreement entered into and concluded in Lisbon this twenty seventh of September one thousand eight hundred and twenty-three, between His Excellency Count da Povoa, Councellor of State and Minister & Secretary of State and of the Finance Department, and President of the Royal Treasury on behalf of His Faithful Majesty, on the one part and Adolphus Goldschmidt of London on the other part.

Whereas His Majesty has by His Decree of the twenty fifth of September of the present year vested in His excellency, the Count of Povoa, full powers and authorities for the purpose of negotiating a Loan of Money for the exigencies of the State. His excellency has entered accordingly into a negotiation with the said Adolphus Goldschmidt, who is vested with full powers and authorities to that purpose by his house B. A. Goldschmidt & Co. of London and contracted and agreed with him for a loan of One million five hundred thousand pounds sterling on behalf and for account of the aforementioned B. A. Goldschmidt & Co under the conditions following that is to say.

1st His truthful majesty will cause to be prepared and delivered into the hands of the said B. A. Goldschmidt & Co a general bond for the sum of one million five hundred thousand pounds sterling. This bond shall be executed and completed in due form according to the existing laws of Portugal, so as to be binding legal and effectual upon His Majesty and successors, for the purposes to be set forth in it. The Bond shall be in the form mutually agreed upon by His Excellency the Count da Povoa and Adolphus Goldschmidt.

2nd Pursuant to this general bond the Portuguese Government will cause to have prepared separate special bonds or obligations which shall contain a copy of the general bond with an attestation and authentication attached thereto in the form to be agreed upon, which special bonds shall entitle the bearer thereof to a proportionate benefit of the general bond, and in the securities to be granted by His Faithful Majesty in pursuance of these presents, and also to interest at the rate of five percent per annum upon the sums which shall be respectively expressed in each special bond. All such special bonds to be countersigned by His Majesty Agent or Agents before they are negotiated. Annexed to each special bond or on the same piece or sheet of paper, there shall be printed sixty dividend warrants for the respective dividends. The number of special bonds to constitute the amount of one million five hundred thousand pounds sterling shall be six thousand three hundred and seventy five, and of the following marks and numbers.

A 1 a 3,750:	3,750	Bonds of	£ 100	375,000
B 1 - 1,500:	1,500	….do….	£ 250	375,000
C 1 - 750:	750	….do….	£ 500	375,000
D 1 - 375:	375	….do...	£ 1,000	375,000

The special bonds with the dividend warrants shall be prepared in London at the expense of the Portuguese Government with the necessary precautions in the preparation of the paper to prevent forgery. And it shall not be required that they be sent back to Lisbon prior to being put into circulation, the above-mentioned signatures being held sufficient by the Portuguese Government to entitle them to all the benefits mentioned in the same, and these presents. A regular register is to be formed of each and the whole of these special bonds regularly numbered, a copy of which is to be transmitted to the Portuguese Royal Treasury there to be entered in conformity.

3rd The contractors are hereby bound to pay 87 pounds sterling value for every hundred pounds stock in the installments as follows.

4th The amount of this loan produces thirteen hundred and five thousand pounds sterling money which will be paid in twelve equal monthly installments, the first to commence one month subsequent to the signatures of the general bond. It being however understood that as the two first instalments are to be paid immediately and for which five percent interest is to be allowed for the period of the contractors advance they are to accept bills to the order of the Treasurer of the Royal Treasury for the ten following instalments at such dates as will bring them due at the period before mentioned.

5th For the remittance and delivery of the proceeds of this loan in London or elsewhere as well as for the purchase of Bullion or its investment in Bills of Exchange or in any other way it may be disposed of as may be determined on by the Government of Portugal, the contractors and His Majesty's Agent or Agents are to receive one half percent commission to be equally divided.

6th His Faithful Majesty agrees to allow to the contractors B. A. Goldschmidt & Co a Commission of 2 Percent on the whole amount of one millions five hundred thousand pounds sterling, the said commission to be placed at their credit and to be deducted from the three first installments of the loan.

7th The general bond of His Faithful Majesty majesty with the securities to be granted by him in pursuance of these presents shall upon their arrival in London be deposited for safe custody and for the security of all parties in the Bank of England under the Seal of the Portuguese Minister resident in London, that of the Contractors, the Portuguese Agent or Agents and also of a Notary Public.

8th In order to secure the payment of the interest and reimbursement of the capital of this loan, in pursuance of these presents, the government pledge specifically and exclusively until its final liquidation the whole revenues arising to His Majesty from the Tobacco and Soap contracts which yields an annual income of one thousand two hundred and one contos of reis. His Faithful Majesty is to decree that the present as well as all the future Tobacco and Soap contractors until the whole of the Loan be discharged be bound to retain out of the sums which they have to pay to Government the half yearly Proportion requisite for the payment of Dividends and the repurchase of the stipulated number of bonds for Redemption. Measures shall further be taken forthwith by his Excellency Count da Povoa that these funds may always be lodged in the Bank of England one month prior to the period of paying the respective Dividends and they are to be placed here in the joint names of B. A. Goldschmidt & Co. and His Faithful Majesty's Agent or Agents. It is hereby understood that the sums which the Tobacco and Soap contractors have to furnish for this purpose are not to enter the Royal Treasury, nor to be directly or indirectly otherwise appropriated but to the end above mentioned. As a collateral security His Faithful Majesty further pledges the revenue of the Decima being an income arising from the Land Tax; this amounts annually to about eight hundred and fourteen contos of Reis. These securities are to be assigned and made over to the contractors of the Loan according to the laws of Portugal and be sent to England as soon as possible. It is however expressly stipulated that although the articles of revenue mentioned in this article are specifically pledged to the payment of the interest and liquidation of the loan contracted for, yet that there are also pledged for the punctual fulfilment of the present contract the whole of the revenues of the state.

9th His majesty agrees and engages that the Interest on the full amount of the bonds shall be understood as commencing from the first of December one thousand eight hundred and twenty three, and shall be paid in London at half yearly periods viz. on the first of June and the first of December of each succeeding year, the first payment to be made on the first of June one thousand eight hundred and twenty four, and the payment of which interest shall be made at the counting house of B. A. Goldschmidt & Co by them and the Portuguese Agent or Agents free from all expense to the holders on presentation and the delivery up of the Dividends Warrants when due.

10th His majesty's government agrees and engages to buy up and wholly discharge the said special bonds and obligations for the total of the said one millions five hundred thousand pounds sterling within the period of thirty years from the first of December one thousand eight hundred and twenty three that is to say special Bonds half yearly to the amount of twenty five thousand bonds these purchases to be made as near as practicable to the period of the Dividends falling due. It is understood however that His Faithful Majesty's Government reserves to itself the right of purchasing the special bonds up in the market to any greater amount and also reserves at all times the right to pay off the loan at its option at par. In case the special bonds should be above par at the periods of repurchasing them for redemption, then lots are to be drawn in London in presence of the resident Minister, the contractors and the Agent or Agents two months previous to the time of payment and the result be immediately made known in the public gazette, stating which of the special bonds are to be redeemed on which the interest ceases to be paid in consequence. The special bonds procured for redemption are on each first of June and first of December, respectively, or as near thereto as practicable to be destroyed in the presence of His Majesty's resident Minister in London in that of the contractors, the Portuguese Agent or Agents and a Notary public, being cut into halves the one of which to be afterwards remitted to the Portuguese Treasury and the other to remain deposited in the Bank of England until the whole loan is repaid. Immediately on the expiration of each period of repurchase the numbers and amounts of the special bonds or obligations canceled are to be advertised in the *London Gazette.*

11th The payment of the dividends and the repurchase of the Bonds for redemption is to be effected by B. A. Goldschmidt & Co. In these proceedings, they are to act jointly with His Faithful Majesty's Agents in consideration of which it is hereby agreed that the Portuguese Government allows them jointly a commission of one half per cent on the interest paid every sixth months as well as on the amount of the special Bonds which they are jointly to purchase for the account of the Portuguese government, and all the minor charges of Postages &ca. &ca.

12th His Majesty's Government engages not to raise any further money out of Portugal for two years from the date of these presents, or sell any Public Securities by commission within that period unless with the consent and through the medium of the contractors.

13th The engagement now entered into on the part of His Faithful Majesty is to be declared inviolable and not to be affected by any political change or circumstance whatsoever and to be held equally sacred in time of peace as well as in War between Portugal and any other country in or out of Europe and lastly the present article are entered into upon the most implicit good faith, His Faithful Majesty pledging himself and his heir and Successors on his part and the contractors themselves, their heirs, executors and administrators on their part to the punctual fulfilment of their respective engagements and id any misunderstanding or doubt should arise regarding such articles or the construction thereof, the contractors are fully assured from the known liberality of His Majesty that he will allow the same to be explained and construed favorably for them.

Thus done and concluded, signed and ratified in Lisbon this twenty seventh day of September one thousand eight hundred and twenty-three, two copies of these presents having been made one whereof is retained by His Majesty's Government and the other by the contractors B. Goldschmidt.

Signed: Conde da Povoa [seal].

Adolphus Goldschmidt (in virtue of power of attorney for B. A. Goldschmidt).

Acknowledgements and Disclaimer I am grateful to Helena Carvalho for her remarkable help in the Portuguese archive. I thank the Rothschild Archive in London and in particular to Justin Cavernelis-Frost for supplying the Rothschild loan. Many thanks to Geoffroy Legentilhomme for assistance with the data. I am also grateful to Stefano Pietrosanti for the Cavour reference. Errors are mine.

References

Ayer J (1905) A century of finance 1804–1904. The London House of Rothschild, Neely, London
Cavour C (1942) Discorsi parlamentari. Giulio Einaudi, Torino
Clarke H (1878) On the debts of sovereign and quasi-sovereign states. Owing by Foreign Countries, Bristol Selected Pamphlets, Bristol
Cohen B (1822) Compendium of finance. containing an account of the origin, progress and present state of the public debts, revenue, expenditures, national banks and currencies, of France, Russia, Prussia, etc. W. Phillips, London
Dawson FG (1990) The first latin American debt crisis. The City of London and the 1822–1825 Loan Bubble. Yale University Press, New Haven
Ferguson N (1998) The world's banker: the history of the house of rothschild. Weidenfeld and Nicolson, London
Flandreau M, Flores JH (2009) Bonds and brands: foundations of sovereign debt markets, 1820–1830s. J Econ History 68(3):646–684
Flandreau M, Flores JH (2012) The peaceful conspiracy: bond markets and international relations during the Pax Britanica. Int Org 66(6):211–241
Flandreau M, Flores JH, Gaillard N et al (2009) The end of gatekeeping: underwriters and the quality of sovereign bond markets, 1815–2007. NBER Int Seminar Macroecon 6(1):53–92
Gille B (1965) Histoire de la Maison Rothschild, Tome I, Des Origines à 1848. Droz, Geneva
Neal L (1998) The financial crisis of 1825 and the restructuring of the British financial system. Federal Reserve Bank of St. Louis Review (May), pp 53–76
Paquette G (2013) Imperial Portugal in the age of Atlantic revolutions: the Luso-Brazilian world, c.1770–1850. CUP, Cambridge
Wilson D (2015) Hyde Clarke (1815–1895). Available online. www.levantineheritage.com. Accessed on 28 Mar 2020

A Thirteenth-Century Fiscal Constitution

António Castro Henriques

Abstract The thirteenth century was an era of bold constitutional experiments in Europe. During this age, for the first time in history, fiscal constitutions, i.e., limits on the fiscal prerogatives of the state, emerged. In Portugal, this manifested itself as a monetary constitution that prevented the use of the kings' minting rights and a hidden tax, namely the 1261 *Instrumentum Super Facto Monete*, which was presented as a contract. It was a genuine monetary constitution insofar as it had the credible commitment of the state and was enforced by the public, via the *Cortes* until 1369, when it likely outlived its utility for the markets. The beneficial effects of this constitution in reining potential monetary mischief can be observed in the comparatively low nominal interest rates prevalent in Portuguese capital markets.

Keywords Economic history · Europe · Fiscal constitution · Middle ages · Portugal

1 Introduction

Jorge Braga de Macedo (2003) argued that Portugal's successful real convergence that allowed the country to qualify for the Eurozone in 1998 was halted by the political incapacity for organizing fiscal reforms. Successive governments failed to rein in the politically strong social coalition who happened to be the main beneficiaries of state expenditure, European structural transfers, and of the low interest rates brought about by the Euro. This was manifest in the loss of competitiveness vis-à-vis the European Union (EU) counterparts (Braga de Macedo 2003). In Braga de Macedo's imagery, twentieth-first-century Portugal is a "good student" whose convergence progress is being thwarted by a "bad fiscal constitution" (Braga de Macedo 2003). The failure to create a virtuous fiscal constitution, in which investment and risk-taking are rewarded, is thus a factor that explains the two (and counting) "lost decades" of the Portuguese economy.

A. Castro Henriques (✉)
Faculdade de Economia, Universidade do Porto, Porto, Portugal
e-mail: ahenriques@fep.up.pt

L. Brites Pereira et al. (eds.), *Economic Globalization and Governance*,
https://doi.org/10.1007/978-3-030-53265-9_4

In this paper, I take on the issue of the "fiscal constitution" and its effects on economic performance, albeit in an earlier historical period: the thirteenth and fourteenth centuries (roughly from 1200 to 1370). This comparison is especially important because the thirteenth century amounted to what James D. Buchanan called a "constitutional moment" for most European states. From Rome, whence bold legal theorist Innocent III pontificated, to Runnymede, where King John signed the *Magna Carta*, the limits of monarchical power became more concrete and acquired formality. From the Low Countries to León, parliaments also acquired the capacity to enforce proper constitutional rules that constituted deliberate restrictions on the, hitherto formally unhinged, executive power.

This period serves as the first testing ground for the observation of constitutionalism's economics effects. The Portuguese experience, in particular, provides an interesting case. In fact, in 1261, Portugal developed a unique set of restrictions regarding the role of the state as the issuer of money of the state, in the middle decades of the thirteenth century, which clearly qualify as a monetary constitution.

The structure of this chapter is as follows: in Sect. 2, we argue for the applicability of the concept of "fiscal constitution" to the thirteenth century's "constitutional moment." Section 3 discusses the different monetary constitutions that emerged in Portugal, in comparison with those of other Christian Iberian kingdoms. Section 4 shows that these monetary constitutions led to contrasting nominal interest rates and capital markets in the respective states while Sect. 5 concludes.

2 The Constitutional Moment

Circa 1200, a specter was haunting Europe—the specter of constitutionalism. The monarchies of old Europe could not exorcise this specter, as their prerogatives in taxation, justice, and coinage were challenged by representatives of the general public, whose practical demands were often grounded in new legal theories and abstract principles. As a consequence, sovereigns across the continent had to acknowledge that their rights were limited by principles.

This constitutional moment captured the attention of legal historians but not of their economic counterpart. New legal ideas, like the new political theology or the rebirth of the Roman Law, were important in this constitutional moment. Nevertheless, such ideas emphasized the submission of the monarch to law and public interest, but they also underlined the monarch's independence from the remaining political bodies in the realm. This aspect is visible in the Portuguese *Leis Gerais* issued by Afonso II in the 1211 *Cortes* of Coimbra and, more so, in the monumental *Constitutions of Melfi* issued by the Holy Roman Emperor Frederick II. The contention over resources between the colliding forces of the markets and the state was even more important than the new ideas.[1] As long remarked by Wim Blockmans, there was

[1] Not all constitutional struggles revolved around property rights and fiscal issues, as the procedures and scope of the king's judicial officers were another bone of contention.

no need for high-minded constitutional texts in Flanders, where the industrial and mercantile towns acquired a direct say on the decisions of their sovereign (Blockmans and Uyten 1969). What challenged the prerogatives of European monarchies was not the Roman Law or the new political theological theses, both of which argued for the centralization of power, but rather the broad coalitions uniting towns, merchants, and landlords (including church institutions) that sought to defend their rights and resources. The emergence of the *Magna Carta* would have been unconceivable without the challenge posed to the landowners by the sophisticated tax machinery of revenue-maximizing English Plantagenet Kings.

In the political economic literature, the term "fiscal constitution" is most often used as a heuristic concept. It refers to the articulation of principles, practices, and attitudes of both the rulers and the ruled with respect to taxes and transfers from the state budget (Bonney and Ormrod 1999, pp. 1–3). In this sense, every state has its own fiscal constitution, however despotic it could be. Nevertheless, the same term can also be used, as it will be here, with a precise meaning: fiscal constitution describes a situation in which the limits of the state's taxing and spending powers are defined by rational taxpayers without consideration for their present individual interests. This concept was developed by Brennan and Buchanan in the 1970s, who assumed that the state, for all its protests of benevolent intentions, is by definition revenue-maximizing and that pleas for self-regulation on behalf of the state are intrinsically impossible (Brennan and Buchanan 1980, p. 163). While this might appear a tall order for the thirteenth century, it has been argued that Portugal had one such a fiscal constitution (Henriques 2009b). More specifically, thirteenth-century Portugal had what can be called a "monetary constitution" that defined the rules under which the monarchy could exert its most important prerogative—issuing money.

3 The Emergence of the Portuguese Monetary Constitution (1261)

In the states born out of the *Reconquista*, where plunder and rights over border trade offered the kings alternatives to direct taxes, the constitutional fight over coinage was more important than the disputes over taxation that led to the *Magna Carta*. In fact, Iberian monarchs claimed the minting of money as their prerogative. In the twelfth century, under the pretext of keeping the quality of the coinage, they were entitled to collecting all the coins circulating in the realm every seven years and replace them with a new, typically lighter, type of coins. This prerogative was detrimental to the interests of the public.

For the monarchs, such re-coinage (*fractio monete*) typically followed by debasement provided two advantages. On the revenue side, it allowed for the extraction of a fee for each coin produced. This payment, known as *seigniorage*, was justified by the need to cover money's production costs but, in practice, it far exceeded these. This amounted to a tax on the owners of money. On the expenditure side, debasing a currency allowed for the devaluation of nominal sums, with the values determined by custom (like military wages), as well as debts owed by the monarchs. Socially, however, this practice had devastating effects, especially in the context of a metallic currency, where nominal prices adjust to changes in the metallic content of coins. The owners of capital saw their interests' value plummet while landowners saw the value of nominal rents decrease accordingly. The re-coinage also disrupted the price structure and, via seigniorage, was essentially a hidden tax, i.e., a forcible transfer from the public to the state. Also, it should be noted that the fiscal effects of debasement were minor, if not neutral, whenever the state was also a landowner that purchased relatively few tradable goods (Henriques 2014).

This issue was first dealt with in León whose *Cortes* secured a pact, around 1202, whereby the monarch would not exert his right to renew the coinage in exchange for a tax payment every seven years, named *moneda forera*. This tax was agreed as a compensation for the monarch not exercising his re-coinage prerogative. The same solution was adopted in Castile, at least after 1215 (O'Callaghan 1969, pp. 1517–1523). However, the unified monarchy of Castile–León continued to mint new coinages and debase older ones without foregoing the *moneda forera* (Crusafont et al. 2013, pp. 297–305). In fact, constant negotiation with the *Cortes*, especially under kings Sancho IV (1284–1295), Fernando IV (1295–1312), Juan II (1406–1454), Enrique III (1454–1475), allowed these monarchs to adopt successive different monetary systems. Monetary discipline was a forlorn aspiration of Castilian towns for centuries until the Catholic Kings finally built a stable monetary system.

The same tension was found in the Crown of Aragon, where a *monedatge* ad valorem tax was likely first collected under King Peter I in 1208 (Crusafont et al. 2013, pp. 121–122). Nevertheless, it appears that the military difficulties of Peter I forced him to mint coinages with decreasing fineness, irrespective of this constitutional limitation. The composite nature of the Crown of Aragon meant that each polity (the kingdoms of Valencia, Aragon, and Mallorca and the territories of Barcelona or Montpellier) had its own monetary units. The currency flows among these realms exerted a powerful pressure on the revenue-maximizing monetary policy of the Aragonese kings. Markets could backfire and circulate coins by weight rather than by tale (Crusafont et al. 2013, pp. 121–122).

In February 1222, the need to alleviate the real weight of his debts led James I to mint the *doblenc*, a billon coin with a fineness of 16.6% (Crusafont et al. 2013, pp. 124, 563). This decision meant an abrupt debasement, as the circulating coin was a *diner ternal* (i.e., 33.3% fine). This was disruptive for the whole economy, as lenders saw the worth of their loans halved and contracts denominated in the old coinage became difficult to enforce. We may deduce that the opposition to this change was intense because James I did not enforce the circulation of his new coinage by tale and accepted that it could be valued by weight in the markets (Crusafont et al. 2013, p. 124). This move aroused such opposition that, in December, James I issued a *constitucio* stating the he accepted the exchange rate between his new *dinero doblenc* and the *dinero ternal* created by the market (Tréton and Bénézet 2009). At some point, James I also swore that he would keep the *dinero doblenc*.[2] Yet, his commitment to this promise would not stand: In 1254, James I was released by the pope from honouring his oath of 1222 and yet again change the coinage. Instead of a credible commitment, the monarch managed to bootstrap the constitutional oath.

The custom of holding a lucrative re-coinage every seven years was also followed by Portugal's earlier kings, who come across as entirely self-serving in their monetary policy: Sancho I (1185–1211) and his grandson Sancho II (1223–48) debased their gold and silver currencies multiple times (Henriques 2009). While the poor quality of the coinage might have contributed to the civil war that toppled Sancho II, there is no evidence of any opposition to the king's prerogative. Nevertheless, in the winter of 1253, Afonso III (1248–79) envisaged a re-coinage of the country's silver *dinheiros* (or pence) for the seventh year of his rule. Anticipating the rise in prices that the new, debased coinage would cause, Afonso enlarged the royal council to obtain the assent of the municipalities in order to issue a comprehensive price setting. However, this did not allay the tensions and the municipal representatives continued to contest the new coinage. The two sides later met at the *Cortes* of 1254 in Leiria, during which Afonso III agreed to withhold his plans for a *fractio monete* in exchange for a kingdom-wide subsidy (*monetagium*) to be paid by all the realm's households, which was then the solution found in the other peninsular kingdoms.

However, Portugal followed a different route from its peninsular counterparts, however. The public likely knew that trading re-coinage for a tax had not definitively eliminated the royal monetary prerogatives in Castile and Aragon and the tension continued. One year later, in response to the municipalities' "humble and insistent supplications," Afonso III formally swore that he, and the kings after him, would not demand another *monetagium,* would not debase the coinage and would only collect seigniorage. This compromise clearly matched the ambitions of the municipal representatives. Formal letters testifying to the oath (*kartae Iuramenti*) were issued and sent to the head of the major clerical institutions and to the pope.

However, when a new septennial period was about to expire, Afonso III announced the minting of a new (silver-richer) species of *dinheiro*. This was a cunning move as the *Karta Iuramenti* forbade the crown to debase and to order a new wide re-coinage, but it did not forbide to issue a new coinage. This new coinage entailed the devaluing by tale the old (silver-poorer) coinage. This disruptive change was within the terms dictated by the oath of 1255, but it flew in the face of the aspirations of the municipal representatives. Facing yet again the opposition of "prelates, barons, friars, and the people of the realm," Afonso summoned the *Cortes* to be held in Guimarães in 1261. There, he agreed to halt the facial value change of the existing coin in exchange for a new and final *monetagium*. This was eventually agreed with by the barons, prelates, and municipal representatives but only in exchange for the king's firm commitment to never again change the currency nor demand another tax.

[2]Later, in 1236, the Estates of Aragon obtained from James I the promise that he would keep the currency's characteristics, however, they had to pay a *monedatge* with three times the usual rate (Crusafont, Balaguer & Grierson 2013, p.124).

The document importantly, it was dubbed an *instrumentum* not a *carta*, that is to say that it was regarded as a binding contract between two parties not as a charter issued out of the royal will. The *instrumentum* contained declarations and concessions in the name of both parties of the agreement. Thus, the term *instrumentum* (written version of a contract) was more adequate. Like the *Karta Iuramenti* of 1255, the it contained a king's oath, but this worked only as a supplementary warranty. The force of the decision rested on its negotiation between parts. Was the *Instrumentum Super Facto Monete* the basis for a monetary constitution?

What defines a fiscal constitution is the commitment of the executive to abide by the restrictions pertaining to its fiscal and monetary powers. The substance of the *Instrumentum* was challenged at least twice. The first attempt is not very well known. There is evidence that, around 1293, King Dinis (1279–1325) summoned the *Cortes* to discuss the possibility of changing the intrinsic content of the *dinheiros*.[3] Given that Dinis' *dinheiros* were "practically the same as those of his father" (Crusafont et al. 2013, p. 441), the likely outcome of this meeting was the rejection of the king's proposal and, hence, the maintenance of the monetary standard of 1261.

The evidence is somewhat more substantial for Afonso IV (1325–57), who in his first regnal year summoned *Cortes* "for paying me homage and for the matter of the coins." It is likely that Afonso IV wanted to negotiate the minting of a new coinage and, hence, circumvent the terms of the 1261 *Instrumentum*. Once again, numismatic evidence (Crusafont et al. 2013, pp. 442, 443) precludes the possibility that the king attained his goal. The refusal of the realm's estates is consistent with a statement by Afonso IV, which was recorded by the chronicler Fernão Lopes: "if my people had consented to change currency again, I would rank among the world's richest kings."[4]

The *Instrumentum* was still in force by 1369, when King Fernando I launched his over-ambitious bid for the Castilian throne. Fernando I ordered a general re-coinage which was well-received by the public, possibly because the money supply was too restrictive. The constitutional principle was still invoked in the *Cortes* against this measure (Henriques 2009a, p. 71). However, the permanent condition of the life-or-death war against Castile that followed the reign of Fernando I called for large-scale debasements and, consequently, the end of the monetary constitution.

---

[3] As Ferro (1972) noted, there is a short entry in Dinis' chancery record mentioning a "*carta de concillis super immutationem de moneta*."

[4] "Se lhe o seu poboo conssetira outra vez mudar a moeda, que elle fora huum dos ricos Reis do mundo."

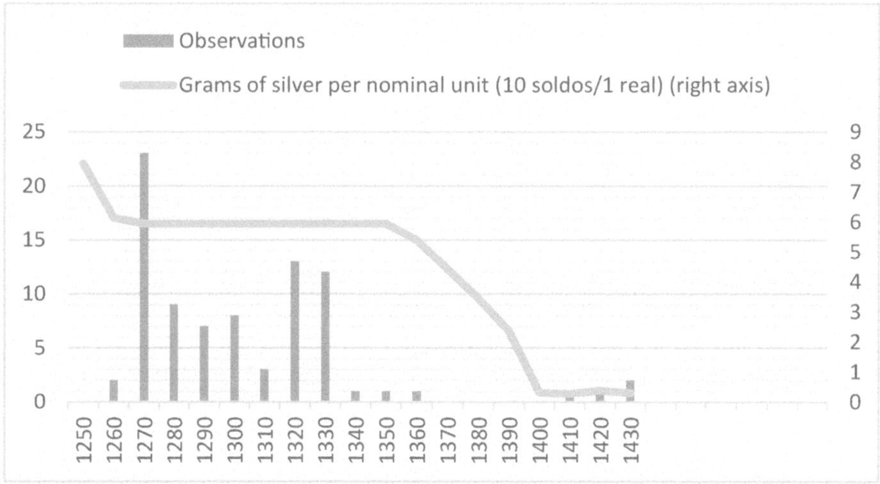

Fig. 1 Number of annuities contracted in Portugal (1250–1430) and metallic content of nominal monetary unit. (Source: Henriques 2019, Fig. 3)

4 Assessing the Economic Effects of Constitutionalism

The Portuguese monetary constitution worked for about one century, whereas its Iberian counterparts proved less consistent. Its effects on economic performance can be measured by looking at interest rates.

The credibility of the coinage's stability (in both quantity and quality) is likely to have an important positive effect on capital markets. In the context of metallic money, the commitment on behalf of the state to a coinage with a stable fineness meant that money kept its value.[5] This can be seen in the interest rates observed in the three cases mentioned here for the same type of contract: the perpetuity. A perpetuity, also known as an annuity or a rent charge, was essentially the selling of a fixed nominal sum (normally assigned to a rent or other stable monetary flow). As such, it was akin to a credit contract, in which the perpetual sum was equivalent to the interest and the price paid to the principal.

In Portugal, no perpetuities were sold before 1261, the year of the *Instrumentum Super Factio Monete*, as shown in Fig. 1. In contrast, in Castile, where the monarchy kept its minting rights and commitment was not credible, there are simply no perpetuities until the time of the Catholic Kings (Henriques 2019). Figure 2 shows that the constitutional limitation of 1261, after which the Portuguese credit market emerged,

[5]Although we do not have estimations (solid or otherwise) of Portuguese money supply in the period, there is little doubt that the restrictions set out in the *Instrumentum Super Factio Monete* had a stabilizing effect on the quantity of coinage in circulation. The minting capacity set out in the *Instrumentum* was a paltry 309 *libras* (Crusafont, Balaguer & Grierson 2013, p.458), at a time when royal revenues (let alone total output/money supply) were only a few hundred thousand *libras*. Foreign and gold coinages complemented the money supply.

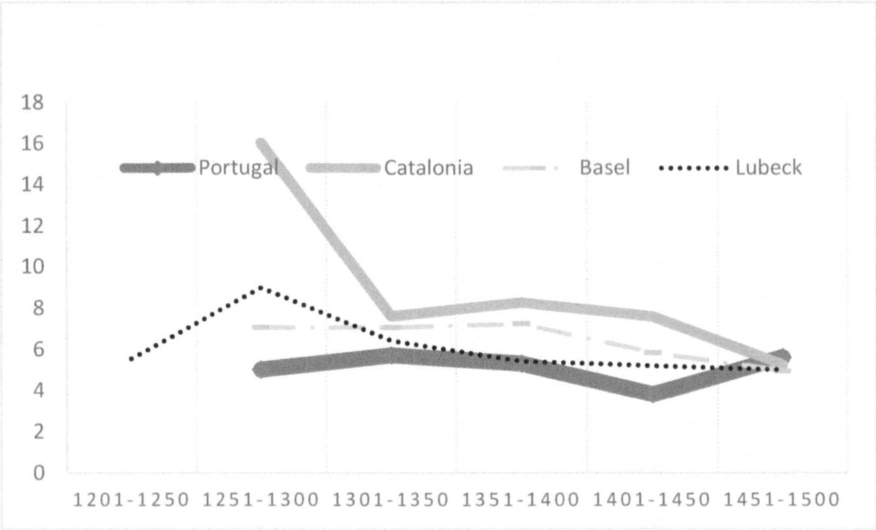

Fig. 2 Interest rates on perpetuities (Iberia and German-speaking city-states)

led the country's interest rates to the low levels prevailing in the self-governing towns, which typically had strong incentives to keep their currencies stable (Crusafont et al. 2013, p. 124). By contrast, in Catalonia, whose Aragonese kings did not credibly commit to a stable coinage, interest rates in the thirteenth century appear excessive. The positive economic effects of the Fiscal Constitution can be seen in the surprisingly low interest rates enjoyed by Portugal, a territorial monarchy. The interest rate levels are comparable to those prevalent in city-states, i.e., polities whose rulers were typically more responsive to the interests of the public.

5 Conclusion

In Europe, the thirteenth century not only redefined the right to tax but also created proper fiscal constitutions for the first time in history. In Portugal, the constitutional limits took the form of a monetary constitution which prevented the use of the kings' minting rights and the hidden tax of seigniorage. The 1261 *Instrumentum Super Facto Monete*, which was presented as a contract between the state and the public, was a genuine monetary constitution insofar as it gained the credible commitment of the state and was enforced by the public, via *Cortes* until 1369. The beneficial effects of this constitutional limitations can be seen in the comparatively low nominal interest rates prevalent in Portuguese capital markets, which were on pair with those practiced in the European city-states.

References

Braga de Macedo J (2003) Portugal's European integration: the good student with a bad fiscal constitution. South Eur Soc Polit 8(1–2):169–194

Blockmans W, Van Uytven R (1969) Constitutions and their application in the Netherlands during the middle ages. Revue Belge de Philologie et d'Histoire 47:399–424

Bonney R, Ormrod WM (eds) (1999) Crisis, revolutions and self-sustained growth: towards a conceptual model of change in fiscal history. Stamford, Shaun Tyas

Brennan G, Buchanan JM (1980) The power to tax. Cambridge University Press, Cambridge, Analytical Foundations of a Fiscal Constitution

Buchanan JM, Lee DR (1994) On a fiscal constitution for the European Union. Journal des Economistes et des Etudes Humaines 5(2–3):219–232

Crusafont M, Balaguer AM, Grierson P (2013) Medieval European coinage, vol 6. Cambridge University Press, Cambridge, The Iberian Peninsula

Ferro MJP (1972) Para o Estudo da Numária de D. Dinis. Do Tempo e da História 5:201–228

Henriques AC (2009) State finance, war and redistribution in Portugal, 1249–1527. PhD Thesis. University of York

Henriques AC (2014) The rise of a tax state: Portugal, 1371–1401. E-J Portuguese Hist 12(1):49–66

Henriques AC (2019) Capital in a frontier economy: Portugal, 1230–1500. Revista de Historia Económica. J Iberian Latin Am Econ Hist 1–34

Henriques AC (2009b) Primeira Constituição Fiscal Portuguesa (1254–1369). In: Amaral L, Henriques A, Braga de Macedo J, Ferreira da Silva A (eds) Nove Ensaios na Tradição de Jorge Borges de Macedo. Tribuna *da História*, Lisbon, pp 97–216

O'Callaghan JF (1969) The beginnings of the Cortes of León-Castile. Am Hist Rev 74:1517–1523

Tréton R, Bénézet J (2009) El Llibre de les monedes de Barcelona i dels florins d'or d'Aragó. Compilació redactada per Jaume Garcia, arxiver reial de Barcelona, per aus de la seca de Perpinyà. Fundació Nogue, Barcelona

Russell JC (1962) The medieval monedatge of Aragon and Valencia. Proc Am Philos Soc 106(6):483–504

Economic History and History of Economics: Complementary Approaches to Portuguese Economic Development

José Luís Cardoso

Abstract This chapter focuses on how the problems of economic development were addressed by the Portuguese historiography of the late nineteenth and twentieth centuries. The ensuing discussion benefits from the simultaneous consideration of two historiographical domains that complement each other: economic history and the history of economics. On the one hand, there are the authors and texts of economic history that seek to describe the facts and circumstances related to the functioning and dynamics of economic reality, for a given period or succession of periods, in order to establish evolutionary trends. On the other hand, there are the authors and texts of the history of economics that seek to adopt analytical forms (principles and laws) and doctrinal and programmatic frameworks (visions and ideologies) aimed at providing explanatory meaning to the observed economic changes, phenomena and regularities. A true understanding of the important issues pertaining to Portuguese economic development is to be found, however, in the intersection of these distinct but complementary historiographical perspectives.

Keywords Economic development · Economic history · History of economics · Methodology · Portugal

1 Introduction

The title of this contribution refers to an important methodological issue when studying the problems of Portuguese economic development: the simultaneous application of two complementary historiographical domains, namely economic history and history of economics.[1] These approaches are sometimes erroneously presented

[1] The present contribution is largely based on the duly authorized translation of a chapter written in Portuguese, namely (Cardoso 2017), which is included in a book of limited circulation within academic circles.

J. L. Cardoso (✉)
Instituto de Ciências Sociais, Universidade de Lisboa, Lisbon, Portugal
e-mail: jcardoso@ics.ulisboa.pt

L. Brites Pereira et al. (eds.), *Economic Globalization and Governance*,
https://doi.org/10.1007/978-3-030-53265-9_5

as one and the same, and sometimes also wrongly claimed to be autonomous from one another.

Indeed, the historical memory brings different and seemingly appropriate words to the discussion of the developmental problems of the Portuguese economy and society throughout the period being considered here (the early 1870s to the early 1970s). In the lexicon of concepts, words such as modernization, improvements, advances, regeneration, promotion and progress are often used to express the dynamic movement of structures that support, and project into the future, a sense of collective purpose, i.e., words that convey the notion that things change even when everything seems to remain as before.

Other form of expressions referring to the constraints that hinder the processes of change and modernization is also frequently used. The discussion on this matter essentially leads to the naming of physical and moral causes of economic backwardness (i.e., the circumstances and factors of a natural or political nature) or simply the explanatory reasons for economic decline.

To be sure, we observe a certain degree of continuity and persistence in the use of these concepts and expressions throughout the period under consideration. The reason is that these are recognized to be useful as diagnostic tools, as well as a blueprint of the strategic orientations to be pursued in the future. This is evident, for example, in the writings of the Royal Academy of Sciences of Lisbon during the late eighteenth century regarding improvements to be implemented in different sectors of economic life and also in the 1960s writings on developmental issues which called for a break with the *Estado Novo* growth model.[2] The recurrent use of these expressions reveals the potentialities and virtues of inquiring into the conditions and factors that contribute toward Portuguese economic and social development.

Now, the discussion employing expressions such as expansion and decay, progress and backwardness and improvements and obstacles has always been present in the Portuguese economic literature since the dawn of the mercantilist era. In methodological terms, this discussion relied on two distinct disciplinary approaches even though neither claimed complete autonomy. On the one hand, some authors and studies sought to describe the facts and circumstances of relevance to the functioning and dynamics of economic phenomena (such as consumption, production, population growth, currency, credit, taxes) for a given period or a succession of periods. These studies thus sought to distil evolutionary trends from observable facts. On the other hand, other authors and studies focused on the analytical forms (principles and laws) and doctrinal and programmatic frameworks (visions and ideologies) that gave explanatory meaning to both the observed regularities and the changes in economic facts or phenomena.

These two distinct approaches, respectively, bring us to the historiographical fields of economic history and the history of economic science and ideas (or more succinctly, the history of economics), which nowadays have well-identified lineages and historiographical sequences.

---

[2]The *Estado Novo* (New State) refers to the authoritarian, corporatist and statist period of rule in Portugal during 1933–1974.

Given that these two disciplinary fields initially appeared as only one (as it was difficult to separate the history of economic facts from the history of interpreting these facts), there is no point in strictly separating them, however. This is especially true because the authors who most advanced knowledge in the two domains, which we now consider to be autonomous, were often one and the same. Examples of this disciplinary ambivalence are evident in the works of authors such as José Frederico Laranjo, António Sérgio, Moses Amzalak, Armando Castro, Virgínia Rau, Vitorino Magalhães Godinho and Jorge Borges de Macedo. In other words, these authors had the double facet of being both historians of economic facts and historians of economic ideas. In Sect. 5 below, the discussion's focus will be on the contributions of Magalhães Godinho and Borges de Macedo, given their proximity to contemporary historiography.

2 The First Steps Toward Economic History Scholarship

In any historiographical review focused on Portugal, it is easy to understand what leads us to recall the pioneering contribution of Alexandre Herculano. When it comes to economic historiography, the inevitable recollection of his name is not due to his heuristic ambition of systematically tackling the intellectual territory where economic and financial facts and themes are displayed and discussed. Above all else, the relevance of Herculano's contribution stems from the way in which he used and adapted the influences of German historicism in search of a narrative about the "nature of societies," as opposed to one built upon the deeds and shadows of heroes. The readers of his works were able to analyze and evaluate the importance and weight of institutions, economic structures and problems, especially in some of his *Opúsculos,* which included economic considerations on the feudal and seigneurial regime, the land property regime of the church, crown and nobility and also savings banks and mutual aid insurance systems in Portugal (Herculano 1873).

Oliveira Martins is another noteworthy figure of nineteenth-century Portuguese historiography. His historical incursions were mostly focused on specific economic and financial problems, which were addressed using an analytical framework and a short-term pragmatic perspective, for the study of economic reality (Martins 1872, 1883). Regarding the latter, he sought to propose solutions for concrete problems that he felt should not be overlooked, given both his interventionist and publicist vein and his eagerness to take on a reformist political responsibility (Martins 1885). In fact, Oliveira Martins' attributes of being a public intellectual and politician led him to focus especially on economic and financial matters.

At the theoretical level, Oliveira Martins was influenced by, and particularly receptive to, the contributions of the then current school of thought known as "socialism of the chair (*catedra*)" and also by the German historical school from which he inherited a critical sense regarding the supposed universality of abstract laws in political economy. In his view, such universality was either unattainable or would lead to the adoption of economic developmental concepts that did not properly value the effort needed to create conditions for the full allocation of national resources. At the political level, these same influences highlighted the need for national development strategies that were adapted to the historical and geographical specificities of the economic reality under study, which could then be marshaled into a project of change.

According to Oliveira Martins, the reliance on history to study economic reality was a source of learning aimed at affecting the present time, enabling the construction of explanatory interpretations as to the country's economic backwardness in relation to the observed pace of progress in most developed nations. It could also help with the design of proposals that would improve, regenerate and promote various sectors of economic activity, especially agriculture. Historical reflection on economic issues (or even only historical exemplification) was understood to be a form of political and civic intervention needed to create an opportunity for the country to overcome its long cycle of economic decline. This view, which was not always supported by irrefutable proof or historical evidence, would later have repercussions in the historiographical work of authors such as Cortesão (1930) and Sérgio (1924), who were greatly influenced by Oliveira Martins. In general terms, this view also served to consolidate a pessimistic tradition regarding the country's real economic potential, which has since been accepted and echoed in the public imagination.

The names of João Manuel Esteves Pereira and Basílio Teles also deserve to be singled out among the politicians and historians that were contemporaries of Oliveira Martins. They too contributed to the creation of a historiographical canon dealing with economic issues in the late nineteenth and early twentieth centuries. The former historian is best known due to his two studies on the Portuguese industry's history, which were published in the *Ocidente* journal in 1897 and 1900 (collected in Pereira 1979), and the latter due to his historical essays on work organization, agriculture, credit and taxation systems (Teles 1901).

The political economy textbooks used at the University of Coimbra should also be mentioned, namely those of José Frederico Laranjo and, especially, Marnoco e Sousa. Both authors made slight incursions into economic history and always through the influence of political economy–historical schools that sought to contextualize the application of laws and principles, which were supposedly valid for any given country and time (Laranjo 1891; Sousa 1910). The works of these authors also include side reflections on the evolutionary process of economic ideas, leading to the emergence of autonomous studies in the field of the history of economic thought (Laranjo 1881–1884).

A very special mention is also due to Alberto Sampaio for his concise interpretation of historical exercises entailing a high level of abstraction. His monographic studies on the economic habits and customs of the populations in northern Portugal reveal quite well the methodological accuracy of his thinking:

> It is superfluous to stress the importance of the issues being broached in this work; the author believes, however, that few readers who will enjoy a story without characters, and lacking the appeal that arises from the drama of passions and the play of interests; however, the reader will be satisfied should the experts deem the story to bring any value, however small, to knowledge about the origins; should an outline also result from the elements that the author

> collects regarding the establishment of property and agricultural systems in the north of the country, even if only it be a rough one; and finally, if in this manner, should one be able to slightly extend one's historical horizon. (Sampaio 1923 [1899], pp 5–6)

While succinct, this reflection undoubtedly accords Alberto Sampaio a role as a forerunner when it comes to identifying the benchmarks to which economic history should measure itself.

3 In Search of the Systematization of a New Disciplinary Field

During the first three decades of the twentieth century, the Portuguese editorial scene witnessed the publication of the first works that identified, in their very titles, a new discipline with historical scope, namely economic history.

Adriano Antero's voluminous compendium is such a case in point. This work comprises long tracts on the history of economic life in ancient Greece and Rome, which also reveal his ultra-descriptive, ultra-factual and semi-geographical view of the emerging discipline:

> Economic history studies the influence that economic factors have or have had on society, in general, or on any given country or region. And these main economic factors are—the situation, area, appearance, climate, population, products, industries and communications. (Antero 1905, I, v)

In contrast, Carneiro de Moura considered that the practice of economic history entailed other requirements, namely the knowledge provided by relevant statistical documentation, which was not sufficiently advanced in our country, in his opinion. As a result, he argued for a methodological renewal that was influenced by the German historical school's tenets:

> History, based on social causality explained by environmental and social factors, illuminates the modern world in the light of the data studied and purified by science. (…) Portugal's economic history is the living and noteworthy testament of the laws that govern all human societies in the pursuit of wealth, and if our plan does not encompass the detailed theoretical exposition of these laws, we will nonetheless explain and verify the facts described (…)
>
> The historical economic school despises a priori conceptions and observes economic phenomena by careful historical analysis. Unfortunately, in our case, we lack the statistical data and other analytical elements needed to accurately formulate economic laws. (Moura 1913, pp 8–19)

Carneiro de Moura presents economic history as a history based on the knowledge of how the factors of production evolved over time. His approach undoubtedly denotes modernity and an alignment with contemporary international contributions:

> And other laws may be induced from our economic history. Through them, as we shall see, one observes the evolution of the three factors of production land, capital and man, or nature, capital and labor - first, beginning with the predominance of nature, followed by that of labor, and finally capital, towards a solidarity solution for the world economy, which re-establishes communal structures. (Moura 1913, p 19)

A few years later, João Lúcio de Azevedo produced one of the most remarkable works of Portuguese economic historiography, giving rise to an interpretative model based on economic cycles associated with the temporary predominance of certain products (pepper, sugar, gold and diamonds). Notwithstanding the poor coherence or validity of the epochs (*épocas*) he considered, the clarity and pertinence of his approach remain unchallenged. Economic history proceeds to balance the costs and benefits that the country faces cyclically, as it moves between economic prosperity and decline:

> The studies that comprise this volume adopt the materialist approach which, while not unique, is certainly indispensable in understanding history. Nations do not live on heroism alone, their beloved subject. For each nation there is a debt and credit account, as is there for individuals, which gives us insight into the nature of their prosperity, and the way in which the signs of decline manifest themselves early on, even for the greatest of empires.
>
> With respect to Portugal, it will be interesting to inquire what price it paid for its past glory, and what effect it had on the country's general conditions. These pages are intended to provide those answers by attempting to outline the economic currents that shape our history. (Azevedo 1928, p 7)

Finally, the work of Francisco António Correia should be highlighted as we exhaust the set of authors who innovated methodologically in search of a discipline capable of providing consistent answers and explanations for the problems of modernization and blockages, improvement and backwardness. Indeed, it is in his book that we find a fuller systematization of an "Economic History of Portugal" based on successive cyclical movements, where the notion of continuity and path dependence on earlier states of evolution is maintained.

In order to understand well the national economy of our times, it is indispensable to study its evolution, all the forward and backward movements, and the causes that influenced the allocation and use of natural resources.

The economic organization of our country, as well as that of the rest of our social organization, may reflect the spirit of the reforms undertaken to improve it, but its structure, in fact, corresponds to a slow transition from previous modalities, which are linked to older ones, and where all are intimately interrelated (Correia 1929, v).

In conclusion, it is important to see a clear approach in these authors' work regarding the methodological orientations that economic history encompass in order to assert itself as an autonomous historiographical domain, notwithstanding their lack of originality in managing historical sources and processing relevant data. Moreover, it is an approach where economic history harbors the central concern of understanding the reasons that explain the country's backwardness, and the factors that drive its progress. This effort should be seen an academic complement to a greater civic purpose grounded in the wider public sphere, as seen in the reflections of academic and journalistic circles like, for example, the so-called *Seara Nova* generation.[3]

---

[3]Given the wider political and cultural scope of the *Seara Nova* journal, the discussion of its contents is beyond the scope of the present contribution. To be sure, this journal is an example of the modernity of Portuguese intellectual circles in the early 1920s, prior to the rise of the *Estado Novo* authoritarian regime. For more details on this topic, see Magalhães (2009).

4 Contributions from the History of Ideas

As stated above, it is not always easy or even possible to distinguish the contributions that belong exclusively to the history of economic thought. In addition to the already mentioned contributions of J. Frederico Laranjo and Marnoco e Sousa, who sought to create a distinct field of inquiry, it is worth noting the multiple contributions that comprise the immense written heritage of Moses B. Amzalak. This heritage includes a very significant number of reading notes, bio-bibliographical sketches, excerpts from transcripts, new editions of out-of-print works and unpublished works. Amzalak is worthy of our attention due to his exhaustive survey of printed sources of great relevance for the study of the history of Portuguese economic thought. His contribution does not stand out either due to importance of his analytic commentary or due to the brilliance of his critical analysis. Instead, Amzalak surpassed his readers' expectations by drawing their attention to the way that the various generations of Portuguese economists contributed to an original reflection on economic problems, at the theoretical, doctrinal and political levels, or otherwise adapted the reflections of foreign authors to a domestic audience.

His style moves between the apology or glorification of Portuguese authors' originality, as well as those of Portuguese ascendency (Amzalak 1934 among many other titles), and also the organization of concise bio-bibliographical information on the authors that he read, transcribed and edited (Amzalak 1928 to cite only the most significant collection of his writings). In both instances, Amzalak was not concerned with distancing himself from the published authors and texts and was perhaps only enthused by the news that he brought to his readers. Notwithstanding his hermeneutic limitations, he nonetheless contributed to normalizing and stabilizing the manner in which the evolution of economic thought was recorded, in order to then become available as a tool for the most demanding craft of the historians who were to subsequently follow in his pioneering steps.

Another important contribution was that of António Sérgio who relied on the writings of the seventeenth century's most representative authors, such as Luís Mendes de Vasconcelos, Manuel Severim de Faria and Duarte Ribeiro de Macedo. In his approach, António Sérgio sought to construct an argumentative strategy around the great national designs, the great options imposed on the country on a permanent basis as opposed to a given moment in time (Sérgio 1924). In his eyes, Portugal faced the challenge of constantly choosing between "fixation or transport policies," the threats of decline and desire for a "*Risorgimento*," and the inevitability of the "crisis of intelligence" and the need for "corrective mind-sets." This was another way of looking at the factors of progress and the reasons for economic backwardness, in a framework shaped by the pessimistic tradition that was very much inspired by Oliveira Martins's intellectual legacy.

On a very different register, José Calvet de Magalhães would later provide an interpretative sequence for many of the authors briefly discussed by Amzalak and António Sérgio. This was undertaken with reference to a period that encompassed the economic literature from the medieval and mercantilist eras. Specifically, he enriched these two Portuguese authors' discussions by broadening the scope of their writings to include international comparative approaches (Magalhães 1967).

5 The Consolidation of a Disciplinary Field

Among the authors who sought to pay systematic attention to the history of economic doctrines and theories in Portugal, Armando Castro occupies an undisputed place, especially considering the final phase of his career. He was responsible for establishing a coherent interpretative model, inspired by Marxist methodology, that considered the legitimizing function of conceptual constructions and doctrinal elaborations associated with the development of the capitalist economy's material basis, at the social and political levels.[4]

The same Marxist programmatic orientation is to be found in his approach to the interpretation of Portuguese economic history, as is clear in the following excerpt:

> We think it is preferable to approach our economic history in such a way to easily understand the fundamental aspects of economic laws, and evolution of social relations related to production. Historical-economic studies of this kind are of real scientific and cultural interest, as the mere compilation of retrospective data, which interests those who study these questions, is unable to provide a causal explanation for the facts; in order to attain this scope of analysis, it is necessary to identify the social classes in action, the type of relations existing between them, and to examine the repercussions of the material productive forces' development on production's social relations. (Castro 1947, pp 9–10)

Vitorino Magalhães Godinho also cultivated a faithful commitment to a coherent model of interpretation that yielded many and fruitful empirical research results. Undoubtedly, he was one of the authors who best and most contributed to the development of an interpretative canon of Portuguese economic and social history.[5]

Without ever losing his passion for archives, respect for sources and concern for taking great care of documents, the history that Vitorino Magalhães Godinho pursued, in keeping with the practices of the *Annales* French school, is particularly demanding in terms of the theoretical construction process and the necessary conceptual elaboration, which allows for a better understanding of the succession of events. He also never yielded to the acritical positivism that characterized the work of many historians of his generation, given that he did not see economic and social history simply as narrative of sequential facts that had been positively assessed and linked together without any causal explanation (Godinho 1947). The events that have been painstakingly reported and reproduced from secure and trustworthy sources must be seen within a long-term perspective. They require, above all else, an interpretative effort that makes use of rational understanding based either on the construction

[4]Given the chronological scope being considered here, the texts published by Armando Castro after 1974 are not discussed. For the discussion of these and other later contributions covering the most recent historiography of Portuguese economic thought, see Cardoso (1991).

[5]A more detailed approach to Magalhães Godinho's innovative contributions in this field is provided in Cardoso (2011), which is also the source for the paragraphs that follow.

of ideal types (in the best Weberian tradition) or on problem formulations that then require the historian to provide both explanations and solutions. Two examples taken from his work help us to understand his positioning and proximity to the spirit of the *Annales* school on this matter.

The first example relates to the concept of a "historical–geographical complex" which he himself invented, and through which he sought to discern the linkages between spatial or territorial structures located in space but whose time possessed both rhythms and cadences, thus capturing both short and long dynamics, i.e., spaces that change with the rhythm of history itself. In this complex, actors and institutions come to interact (with their own directions but joint dynamics), economic, social and political relationships are established along different spatial scales (local, regional, national, worldwide), and cultural and ritual practices are defined, thus affording specificity to the historical realities being analyzed (Godinho 1966).

His study of trading networks and commercial fleets in the Indian and South Atlantic Oceans, within the broader perspective of the study of global markets, allowed Magalhães Godinho to develop the heuristic validity of this concept. In doing so, he intertwined the following elements: the dialectic relations and tensions between space and time, conjuncture and structure, short and long term, micro- and macro-analysis, and facts and ideas. More importantly, this concept allowed him to explore the paths that lead to a better historical understanding of complex social phenomena.

In this sense, and to take one of his more preferred themes as an example, merchant fleets are, above all else, the collection of vessels that comprise them. In another sense, however, they are also the cargoes that the vessels transport, the men that build, equip and sail in these vessels, the institutions and powers that determine and finance the voyages and trade they undertake, the science that allows for maritime navigation, the risks and insurance schemes that make the sailing feasible, the markets that allow for the free movement of goods transported and the currencies used to transact them, the trading bills of exchange that circulate, the myths facing the vessels' crews as well as the purpose and vision motivating them.

The second example is related to the concept of Portugal as a "blocked society," which Magalhães Godinho developed in one of his more remarkable (and more controversial) essays. He used this notion to coherently explore the vicissitudes of blockages at different moments in Portuguese history, which illustrate or provide a pretext for studying the problems of backwardness, dependence and decadence, waste and misuse of resources, mind-sets and cultural aspects that are not much given to innovation and the advancement of knowledge (Godinho 1971). This approach represents a new encounter with the works of historians Oliveira Martins and António Sérgio, as discussed above, and thus provides clear evidence of the weight of this tradition in Portuguese economic historiography.

For a perspective that is less attached to the need for paradigm changes, the studies and essays written by Virginia Rau during the 1940s, 1950s and 1960s are worth mentioning. Her contributions cover themes pertaining to the a*ncient* regime's economic and social history (collected in Rau 1984). The works on Portuguese and foreign merchants, trading places, bankers, shipbuilding, foreign trade relations, as well as on the economic thought of mercantilist era writers (sixteenth to eighteenth centuries), reveal an extreme caution when it comes to analyzing sources and explaining their relevance to the study of historical problems. They also reveal a fundamental concern with the framing of facts and people, and a keen perception regarding the flow of goods, capital and currencies, as well as the analysis of technical conditions, contractual regimes, and labor and power relations.

One last author deserving our attention in this brief assessment of Portuguese economic historiography prior to 1974 is Jorge Borges de Macedo.[6] His works are mainly motivated by the need to contradict the subaltern interpretations of economic ideas and practices, as espoused by numerous Portuguese authors regarded as being representative of a certain national elite. Seeking to chart new paths to better understand the modernization and blockage processes of the Portuguese economy, Borges de Macedo focused instead on diplomatic and political conjunctures and external competitive factors that could affect the development of economic sectors, especially industry. In doing so, he produced groundbreaking studies in which he demonstrated a skillful handling and problematization of hitherto untapped archival sources. His studies have contributed decisively to renewing the interpretative legacies of the economic reality during the Marquis of Pombal's rule, the history of industry in the eighteenth century, the Methuen Treaty (1703) and the economic consequences of the Continental Blockade in the early nineteenth century.

However, his most solid contribution to the understanding of Portuguese development problems was his interpretation of the history of industrial equipment, banking and port activities, as well as the economic and political strategies defined by sovereign decision makers in the eighteenth century in the face of a contingent framework of complex international relations (Borges de Macedo 1963). In this regard, his historical inquiry offers a variety of readings about Portuguese economic and political thought in the eighteenth century, which is always seen from the perspective of innovative application of principles that may be used to interpret economic and social reality, while simultaneously helping to define strategies and policies with a view to their reform and/or development.

Without exhausting or foreshadowing the development of other categorizations that might help us to understand the essential features of the economic doctrines and policies that prevailed in Portugal throughout the eighteenth century, I believe it is pertinent to suggest three central ways of organizing economic discourse during this period, which deliberately takes the reflections provided by Jorge Borges de Macedo in his essays as our starting point.

---

[6]For an overview of Borges de Macedo's role in the renewal of economic history and the history of economic thought, see Cardoso (2013), from which the following paragraphs on are adapted. By including this analysis, I wish to pay tribute both to Jorge Borges de Macedo and to his son, Jorge Braga de Macedo, to whom I dedicate the present contribution. In addition, by attempting to replicate a style that is so typical and so unique in Jorge (the son)—for whom the nature of academic texts does not rule out the inclusion of personal remembrances and emotions—when evoking the work of Jorge (the father), I am also following the steps of the father's tradition "*Saber Continuar*" (knowing how to go on), as explained in Braga de Macedo et al. (2009).

The first of these ways relates to the definition of the direction that economic policies should follow. Such a view applies specifically to the study of mercantilism which, for Borges de Macedo, "is not a systematic theory, but rather a series of useful items of knowledge that do not form a chain leading to a systematic interpretative coordination of the whole economic reality" (Borges de Macedo 1966a). He therefore sought to identify and highlight a variety of influences, and a range of strategic options converging in such a way so as to achieve an objective or a central purpose that, in effect, strengthened the state's economic performance.

The second path that faithfully portrays another dimension of Portuguese economic discourse in the last quarter of the eighteenth century may be expressed as follows: getting to know the kingdom better in order to change it. Once again, we rediscover the insightful attention that Borges de Macedo paid to a remarkable group of authors who acted either independently or under the institutional auspices of the Academy of Sciences of Lisbon and other learned institutions during the governments of Dona Maria I and the Prince Regent Dom João. The following citation summarizes clearly this situation:

> The end of the eighteenth century was overcome by a genuine anxiety for analysis and creativity that led to the formation of the richest, most varied and most fertile Portuguese technological bibliography, with the appearance of books ranging from the debate about metropolitan and overseas agrarian problems to studies of accountancy, mechanics, ballistics and medicine. The problems were studied from a practical point of view and were clearly adapted to the national realities. (Borges de Macedo 1966b, pp 131–32)

Such "anxiety for analysis and creativity" resulted in the definition of a strategy making the fullest possible use of available natural and human resources, which in turn presupposed the undertaking of a stringent diagnosis of both the favorable conditions and the limits that were imposed on economic activity. Science and technology, together with the knowledge of the natural and social world, were instruments placed at the service of economic development. However, it was also important to understand that agents had to be free to act as they wished if human activity were to be effective in the economic field, and that principles and measures favoring the extension and enhancement of mercantile relations should also be pursued.

Finally, and in a similar vein, the third path may be summarized as: managing the economic conjuncture in order to develop the country. Jorge Borges de Macedo's works also elucidate us about the need for pragmatism in the face of an external political alignment that imposed negotiated trajectories, as well as a cautious and prudent mind-set needed to deal with domestic financial difficulties. In this regard, the testimony provided by Dom Rodrigo de Sousa Coutinho's activity between 1796 and 1803, in the exercise of his governmental responsibilities, as well as in the programmatic texts that he bequeathed to us, merits a special mention. In fact, this explanatory context enables us to understand the extent of economic and financial reforms designed to guarantee an indispensable political and institutional stability. The correction of past mistakes due to the uncontrolled issue of fiat money, plans for the creation of a banking institution, financial restructuring programs and colonial administration reforms were some of the matters warranting Dom Rodrigo de Sousa Coutinho's full attention as part of his public mission. Moreover, he showed to himself to possess a sense of proportion and priority in facing the international conjuncture where Portugal's fate was at stake. This is the hallmark of great statesmen, where it was important to manage affairs but without jeopardizing the future of the country.

6 Epilogue

Magalhães Godinho and Borges de Macedo provide relevant inputs into the advancement of innovative approaches on economic history and history of economic ideas, especially regarding the study of historical factors and conditions needed for Portugal's economic growth and development. In both cases, their point of departure, and motivation, is grounded in their concern with history. As such, they were able to extend and challenge a historiographical tradition going back to the nineteenth-century works of Alexandre Herculano and Oliveira Martins, which was prolonged into the early twentieth century by João Lúcio de Azevedo and Francisco António Correia.

However, a different stream of thought associated with a reflection on development issues emerged toward the end of the period being considered here. It was led by economists and sociologists with strong ties to the Latin American structuralist school, which encompassed the work produced for the United Nations Special Commission for Latin America (CEPAL—*Comisión Económica para América Latina*). The CEPAL writings and action programs had their followers in Portugal, both in the renewed environment of teaching economics at the Institute of Economic and Financial Sciences (ISCEF—*Instituto Superior de Ciências Económicas e Financeiras*) and in the most modest circle of social scientists collaborating at the Social Research Office (GIS—*Gabinete de Investigações Sociais*) together with its *Análise Social* academic journal. It was, after all, a current of economic and social thought that took into account the importance of history in understanding the conditions conducive to modernization and development, which demanded from politicians the initiative to favor the indispensable conditions needed to break the ties of dependency and intra-country asymmetrical relations (cf. Nunes 1968).

This interpretative trend would remain active well beyond this contribution's temporal scope, notwithstanding the cliometric orientations of a new economic history committed more to providing hypotheses and quantitative-driven essays of relevance to the functioning of the Portuguese economy than to reactivating the specter of economic backwardness and decline. While these times are interesting given their critical conjunctures associated with processes of historiographical renewal, they clearly warrant a future contribution that goes beyond the present one.

References

Amzalak MB (1928) Do estudo e da evolução das doutrinas económicas em Portugal. Oficinas do Museu Comercial, Lisboa

Amzalak MB (1934) Trois précurseurs portugais. Sirey, Paris
Antero A (1905) História económica (6 vols). Tipografia A. J, Silva Teixeira, Porto
Azevedo JL (1928) Épocas de Portugal económico. Livraria Clássica Editora, Lisboa
Borges de Macedo J (1963) Problemas de história da indústria portuguesa no século XVIII. Associação Industrial Portuguesa, Lisboa
Borges de Macedo J (1966) Vias de expressão da cultura e da sociedade portuguesas nos séculos XVII e XVIII. Boletim da Academia Internacional da Cultura Portuguesa 1:121–133
Borges de Macedo J (1966a). Mercantilismo. In: Serrão J (ed) Dicionário de história de Portugal. Iniciativas Editoriais, Lisboa
Braga de Macedo J et al (eds) (2009) Nove ensaios na tradição de Jorge Borges de Macedo. Tribuna, Lisboa
Cardoso JL (1991) A recente historiografia do pensamento económico. Ler História 21:146–153
Cardoso JL (2011) Vitorino Magalhães Godinho and the Annales school: history as a way of thinking. E-J Portuguese History 9(2)
Cardoso JL (2013) Jorge Borges de Macedo: problems of the history of Portuguese economic and political Thought in the eighteenth-century. E-J Portuguese History 11(2)
Cardoso JL (2017) Modernização e bloqueios. Problemas do desenvolvimento económico na memória histórica. In: Matos SC, João MI (eds) Historiografia e res publica nos dois últimos séculos. Centro de História da Universidade de Lisboa, Lisboa, pp 163–182
Castro A (1947) Introdução ao estudo da economia portuguesa (fim do século XVIII a princípios do século XIX). Edições Cosmos, Lisboa
Correia FA (1929) História económica de Portugal. Empresa Nacional de Publicidade, Lisboa
Cortesão J (1930) Os factores democráticos na formação de Portugal. New edition s.n. (1964). Portugália, Lisboa
Godinho VM (1947) História económica e social da expansão portuguesa. Terra Editora, Lisboa
Godinho VM (1966) Complexo histórico-geográfico. In: Serrão J (ed) Dicionário de história de Portugal. Iniciativas Editoriais, Lisboa
Godinho VM (1971) A estrutura da antiga sociedade portuguesa. Arcádia, Lisboa
Herculano A (1873) Opúsculos. Viúva Bertrand, Lisboa
Laranjo JF (1891) Princípios de economia política. Imprensa da Universidade, Coimbra
Laranjo JF (1881–1884) Economistas portugueses. New edition s.n. (1976). Guimarães editores, Lisboa
Magalhães JC (1967) História do pensamento económico português. Da Idade Média ao mercantilismo. Imprensa da Universidade, Coimbra
Magalhães JR (2009) Oração de sapiência proferida na abertura solene do ano lectivo. Notas Económicas 30:41–62
Martins JPO (1872) Teoria do socialismo. Evolução política e económica das sociedades da Europa, Guimarães Editores, Lisboa
Martins JPO (1883) O regime das riquezas (elementos de crematística). Livraria Bertrand, Lisboa
Martins JPO (1885) Política e Economia Nacional. Guimarães Editores, Lisboa
Moura C (1913) História económica de Portugal. Tipografia do Anuário Comercial, Lisboa
Nunes AS (1968) Sociologia e ideologia do desenvolvimento. Estudos e ensaios, Moraes Editores, Lisboa
Pereira JME (1979) A indústria portuguesa: subsídios para a sua história, 1897 e 1900. Guimarães Editores, Lisboa
Rau V (1984) Estudos sobre história económica e social do antigo regime. Editorial Presença, Lisboa
Sampaio A (1923) Estudos históricos e económicos, vol I. Livraria Chardron, Porto
Sérgio A (1924) Antologia de economistas portugueses: Séc XVII. Biblioteca Nacional, Lisboa
Sousa JFM (1910) Ciência económica. Imprensa da Universidade, Coimbra
Teles B (1901) Estudos históricos e económicos. Livraria Chardron, Porto

US Inflation and the Imbalances of the Bretton Woods System, 1965–1973

Michael D. Bordo

Abstract This chapter argues that the key deep underlying fundamental for the growing international imbalances leading to the collapse of the Bretton Woods System between 1971 and 1973 was rising US inflation since 1965. It was driven in turn by expansionary fiscal and monetary policies—the elephant in the room. What was kept in the background at the Camp David meeting on August 15, 1971 (when President Richard Nixon closed the US gold window, as well as imposing a ten per cent surcharge on all imports and a ninety-day wage–price freeze), was that US inflation, driven by macro-policies, was the main problem facing the Bretton Woods System, and that for political and doctrinal reasons was not directly addressed. Instead, President Nixon blamed the rest of the world rather than correcting mistaken US policies. In addition, at the urging of Federal Reserve Chairman Arthur F. Burns, Nixon adopted wage and price controls to mask the inflation, hence punting the problem into the future. I argue the case that the pursuit of sound monetary and fiscal policies could have avoided much of the turmoil in the waning years of Bretton Woods. Moreover, I point out some of the similarities between the imbalances of the 1960s and 1970s—especially fiscal and the use of tariff protection as a strategic tool, as well as some differences—relatively stable monetary policy and floating exchange rates.

Keywords Bretton Woods System · Fiscal policy · Global imbalances · Monetary policy · The Great Inflation

1 Introduction

The Nixon shock of August 15, 1971, was a critical event in the twentieth-century history of the international monetary system. It was on a par with the ending of the classical gold standard at the outbreak of World War I in August 1914 and the UK's departure from the gold exchange standard in September 1931.

M. D. Bordo (✉)
Department of Economics, Rutgers University, New Brunswick, NJ, USA
e-mail: bordo@economics.rutgers.edu

L. Brites Pereira et al. (eds.), *Economic Globalization and Governance*,
https://doi.org/10.1007/978-3-030-53265-9_6

President Richard Nixon's speech to the nation on that Sunday ended the history of gold convertibility that underlay the Bretton Woods System and that was a major underpinning of the global monetary system for two centuries. The rest of the Bretton Woods System (the adjustable peg) collapsed with the advent of generalized (managed) floating exchange rates in March 1973.

One of the driving motivations for President Nixon's actions was the perception that growing imbalances between the USA, with an exploding balance of payment deficit, and Germany and other countries of Western Europe and Japan, with burgeoning surpluses, was harmful to the competitive position of US manufacturing and the country's overall prosperity. President Nixon's New Economic Policy had three principal prongs: closing the gold window to protect the remaining US gold reserves; a ten per cent surcharge on imports of all countries to force the surplus countries to revalue their currencies; and a ninety-day wage–price freeze to control US inflation.

This paper argues that the key deep underlying fundamental for the growing international imbalances was rising US inflation since 1965, in turn driven by expansionary monetary and fiscal policies—the elephant in the room. What was kept in the background in August 15, 1971, was that US inflation, driven by US macro-policies, was the main problem facing the Bretton Woods System, and that for political and doctrinal reasons was not directly addressed. Instead, President Nixon blamed the rest of the world instead of correcting mistaken US policies. In addition, at the urging of Federal Reserve Chairman Arthur F. Burns, Nixon adopted wage and price controls to mask the inflation, hence punting the problem into the future.

This paper revisits the story of the collapse of the Bretton Woods System and the origins of the Great Inflation. Based on narratives as well as conversations with the Honorable George P. Shultz, a crucial player in the events of the period 1969–1973, I argue the case that the pursuit of sound monetary and fiscal policies could have avoided most of the turmoil in the waning years of Bretton Woods. Moreover, I point out some similarities between the imbalances of the 1960s and 1970s—especially fiscal and the use of tariff protection as a strategic tool, as well as some differences—relatively stable monetary policy and floating exchange rates.

Section 2 provides the background of the Bretton Woods System (BWS), established in 1944 but its operational form only ran from 1959 to 1973, after the Western European countries declared current account convertibility. The monetary and fiscal policies of the USA as center country of the BWS were crucial to its successful operation and survival. In Sect. 3 we document the connection between US domestic policies and the eventual collapse of the BWS between 1968 and 1973.

Section 4 tells the story of the genesis of the Great Inflation which began in 1965 and ended in 1983. The early years of the Great Inflation are closely tied to the dynamic forces that eventually destroyed Bretton Woods.

Section 5 focuses on the international policy coordination between the USA and the other major players in the Bretton Woods System to try to preserve the system, namely the Group of Ten (G10), International Monetary Fund (IMF) and Bank of International Settlements (BIS). Section 6, in conclusion, considers some parallels between the events of the crisis of the early 1970s and the current US situation. Unlike the 1960s and 1970s, monetary policy and inflation are not a serious force pointing to a crisis. But there is some similarity to the 1960s and 1970s in the burgeoning fiscal deficits and a run-up in the ratio of debt to GDP consequent upon the resolution of the great financial crisis and the recent tax cuts. This may lead to a fiscal crisis and eventually a dollar crisis which has some echoes to the events of 1968 to 1973.

2 Bretton Woods

The BWS came out of the Bretton Woods Conference in 1944. The adjustable peg system was conceived as a compromise between the fixed exchange rate gold standard and the floating exchange rates of the 1920s (Bordo 1993; 2017). Its purpose was to optimize the global trading system and yet allow domestic demand management to preserve full employment. It required capital controls, and the IMF was established to help alleviate short-term current account imbalances.

The BWS only became fully operational in December 1958 after the Western European countries declared current account convertibility. The system quickly evolved into a gold dollar standard. The USA as center country pegged the dollar ($) into gold at $35 per ounce, and the rest of the world pegged their currencies to the dollar. The US dollar emerged as a key reserve currency for the rest of the world as a substitute for scarce gold.[1] The demand for international reserves grew with the growth of real output and trade and was satisfied by the USA running ever-larger balance of payment deficits. As center country, the USA did not have to adjust to its balance of payment deficits by pursuing tight financial policies.[2] The dollar was held as international reserves because of its unique properties as an international unit of account, medium of exchange and store of value. The crucial requirement for the system to work was that the USA maintains stable monetary and fiscal policies, i.e., maintains price stability.

In 1960, Robert Triffin pointed out the problem of having one country's currency, the dollar, as the reserve currency for the world (Bordo and McCauley 2018). He posited that as the rest of the world grew the demand for dollars as international reserves would eventually exceed the US monetary gold stock leading to the possibility of a run on Fort Knox. Were the Fed to tighten, world depression would follow, like in the 1930s. The only solution according to Triffin was to create a substitute for dollars as international reserve. He preferred Keynes's (1943) bancor, eventually the international community produced Special Drawing Rights (SDR) as a form of paper gold. Despres et al. (1966) and McKinnon (1969) argued counter to Triffin that the USA was the banker to the rest of the world and a dollar standard could persist as long as the USA followed stable macro-policies.

---

[1]The British pound was also a reserve currency in the BWS, but its role declined steadily throughout the period. See Schenk (2010).

[2]It was the (*n-1*)th currency in a system of *n* currencies. See Mundell (1969).

Friedman (1953) predicted that the adjustable peg would eventually break down because it depended on capital controls and because the adjustment mechanism both between countries and the rest of the world and the USA would not work in the face of downward nominal rigidities and the full employment mandate that came out of the Employment Act of 1945. As it unfolded, Friedman's predictions came true. He favored: freely floating exchange rates, rule-based monetary and fiscal policy and no controls on current account and capital account transactions. All of these were adopted in the 1970s and 1980s.

US and international officials were convinced by the Triffin story, especially after the London price of gold spiked at $40 per ounce on the news that John F Kennedy would win the 1960 election and follow an inflationary set of policies. They became obsessed over growing US balance of payment deficits and declining gold reserves as European real incomes recovered from the devastation of World War II increasing the demand for dollars. See Fig. 1 which shows that by 1959 the US monetary gold stock equaled total external dollar liabilities and the rest of the world's gold stock exceeded that of the USA.

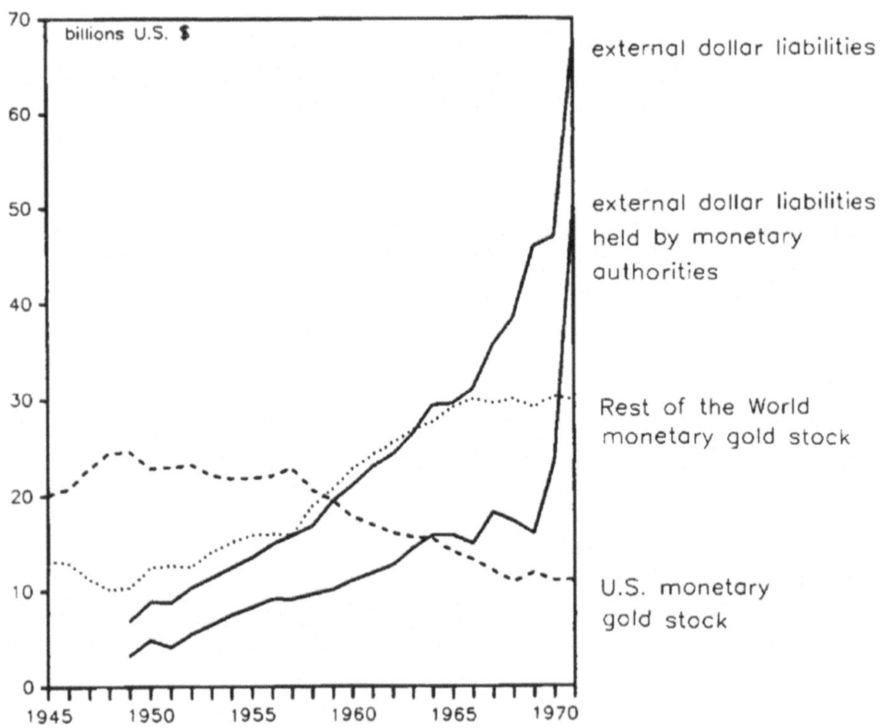

Fig. 1 Monetary gold and dollar holdings, the USA and the rest of the world, 1945–1971 (Source: Bordo 1993)

By 1966, official dollar liabilities held by foreign monetary authorities exceeded the US monetary gold stock, dollar holdings. This led to the creation of many official facilities to staunch the gold drain (Bordo 1993; Coombs 1976; Solomon 1982). These included: US capital controls (The Interest Equalization Tax 1963); Operation Twist 1962 (combining tight monetary policy with expansionary fiscal policy to both encourage capital inflows and stimulate domestic investment); the Gold Pool in 1961 (in which eight key countries pooled their gold resources to intervene in the London gold market and protect the $35 peg (Bordo 2017)); moral suasion (threatening Germany that it would remove US troops if it converted its outstanding dollars into gold); the GAB (General Arrangements to Borrow 1961, which increased the IMF's line of credit to the USA in the face of a speculative attack); and, the swap lines (IOUs between central banks as substitutes for gold conversions (Bordo et al. 2015).

In general, these stopgap measures worked, at least until 1965. More important as we expand on below, the Federal Reserve Chairman William McChesney Martin followed a policy of low inflation before 1965 and the Federal Open Market Committee (FOMC) did pay attention to the US balance of payments and gold reserves in its deliberations (Bordo and Eichengreen 2013). Europeans complained about US inflation, but they were wrong—US inflation adjusted for output growth was below theirs before 1965 (Meltzer 2010). The French also resented the exorbitant privilege of the dollar and its "adjustment without tears" (Bordo 2017).

3 Crisis and Collapse: 1965–1971

The key driving force for the growing imbalances beginning in 1965 was money financed fiscal policy in the USA to pay for the Vietnam War and the Great Society of Lyndon Baines Johnson (LBJ). The increases in fiscal deficits and money growth (relative to real output growth) led to the beginning of the Great Inflation (see Figs. 2 and 3).

The increase in US money growth led to larger US balance of payment deficits (Fig. 4) and increases in the international reserves of Germany, Japan and other surplus countries (Fig. 5), in turn putting pressure on them to expand their money supplies and push up prices (Bordo 1993). This led to increased resentment against the USA.

In this period, the dollar was increasingly under threat seen in a series of currency crises and unsuccessful policy responses. The first serious threat to the dollar was the sterling crisis of November 1967 which led to great pressure on the price of gold in the London gold market and stressed the Gold Pool. Much of the resources used to shore up sterling (the second reserve currency of the BWS believed by the US monetary authorities as the first line of defense for the dollar (Bordo 2017) came from the US Treasury gold window which reduced the monetary gold stock.

Once sterling was devalued and the pound ceased to be a major reserve asset, speculation turned against the dollar. The Gold Pool kept raising the quotas required of the members until first France dropped out in June 1967 and then the others

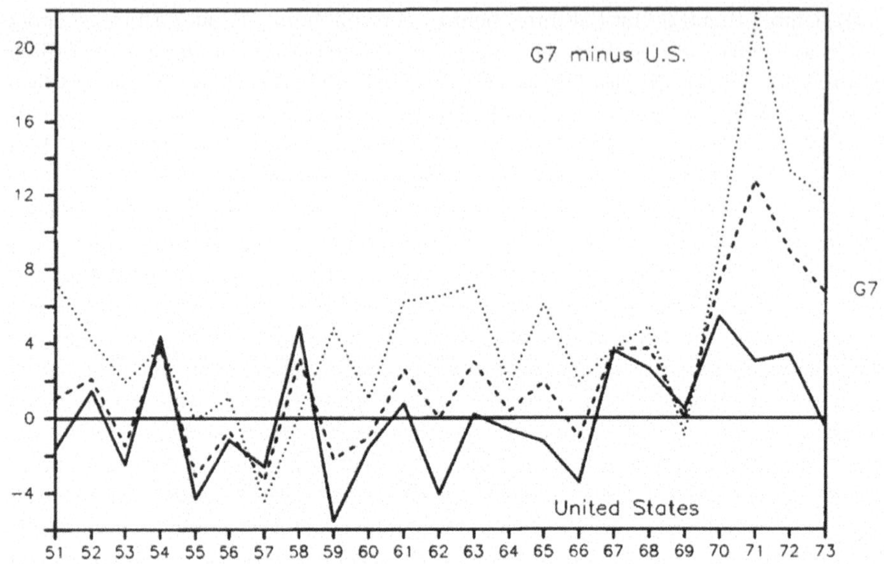

Fig. 2 Money (M1) growth less real output growth in the USA, the G7 countries and the G7 excluding the USA, 1951–1973 (Source: Bordo 1993)

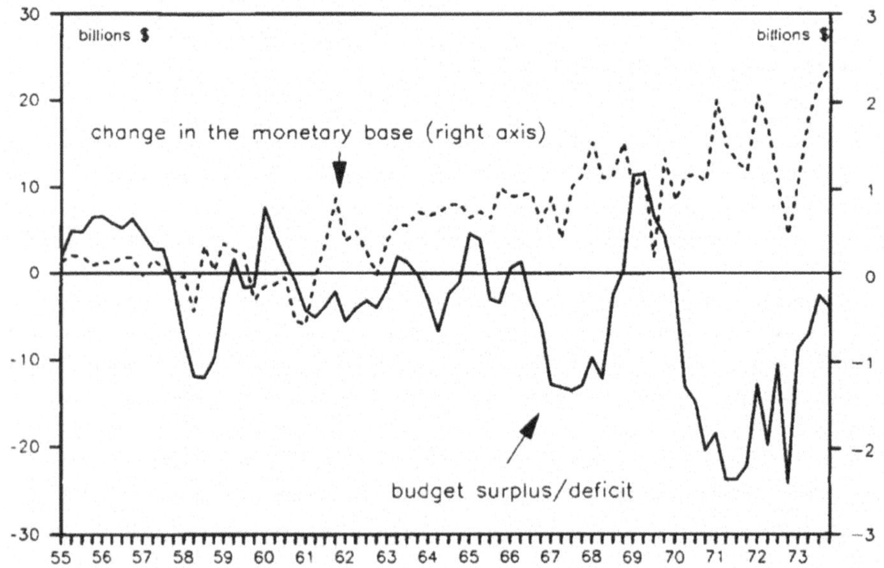

Fig. 3 US budget deficit and the changes in the monetary base, 1955–1973, y-o-y change of quarterly data (Source: Bordo 1993)

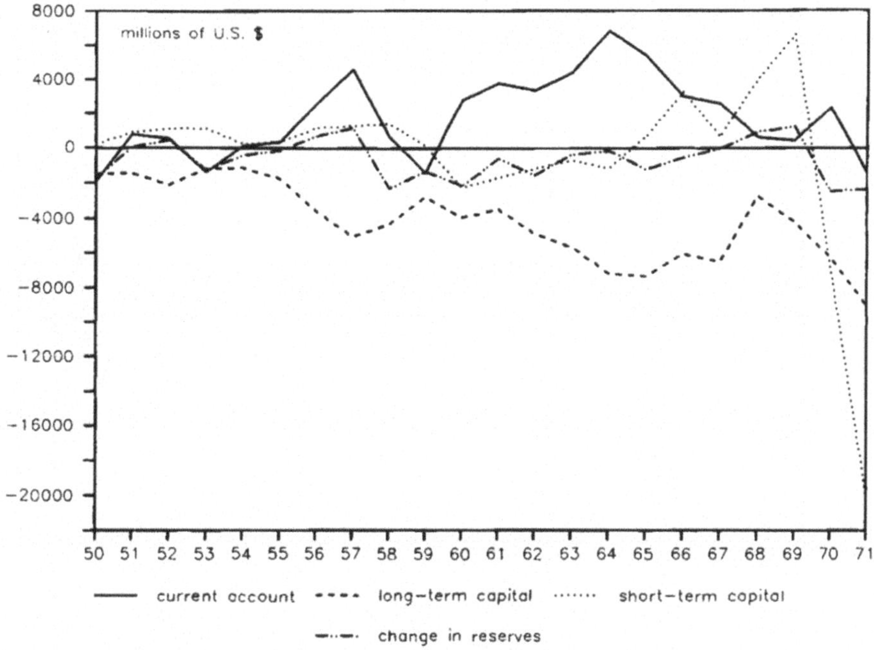

Fig. 4 Balance of Payments, USA, 1950–1971 (Source: Bordo 1993)

objected. By March 1968, the USA and the other partners in the Pool agreed to close it and create a two-tier gold market—the private market in London and an official arrangement open only to monetary authorities. Meltzer (2010) declared this event as the beginning of the end of the Bretton Woods System.

Two other US actions greatly weakened the US defenses—eliminating the gold reserve ratio behind member bank reserves in 1965 and then eliminating the gold reserve ratio behind Federal Reserve notes in 1968. Both of these measures designed to release more gold resources to defend the dollar ultimately made things worse by reducing the USA's credibility.

The crisis abated somewhat in 1969 following a tightening in both fiscal (the 1968 tax surcharge) and monetary policies. These policies temporarily led to capital flows into the USA and less pressure on US gold reserves. However, the tight policy was quickly reversed because the Nixon administration feared that the continuation of the 1970 recession into 1971 would threaten the following year's election and it put pressure on Burns and the FOMC to loosen its monetary policy (Meltzer 2010; Stein 1994; Wells 1994). This prompted the attack on the dollar to resume leading to a capital outflow of $4 billion in May 1971 (Meltzer 2010, p 749).

The reaction to the growing balance of payment crisis by the Nixon administration was to increasingly blame the surplus countries for running large surpluses and deliberately undervaluing their currencies to gain a competitive advantage over the USA. There was deep reluctance to recognize that the key source of the problem

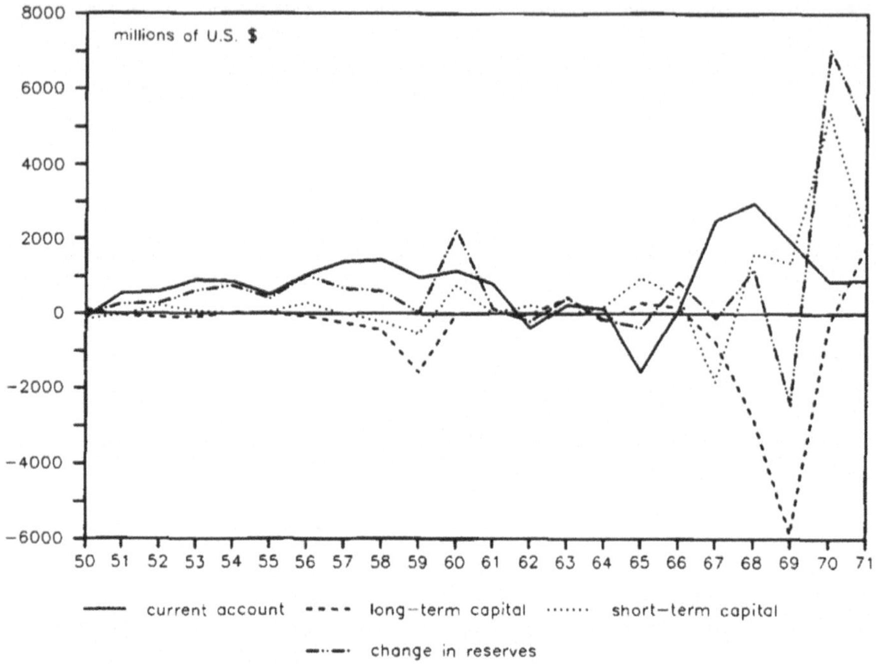

Fig. 5 Balance of Payments, Germany, 1950–1971. (Source: Bordo 1993)

was US inflation.[3] To do so would require the following monetary contraction and, hence, producing a severe recession. Nixon feared such an outcome would harm his reelection chances in 1972. As we discuss below, Fed Chairman Arthur Burns accommodated the President's demands.

The crisis peaked in August 1971 when fears that the British would convert their dollar holdings into gold led President Nixon to announce his New Economic Policy on 15 August. The policy had three principle components: closing the gold window; a 10% surcharge on imports; and a 90-day wage–price freeze. The objective of the first two actions was to preserve US gold reserves and to pressure the surplus countries to revalue their currencies. The wage–price freeze (which later turned into controls) reflected the belief by Burns and others that inflation was primarily driven by non-monetary cost-push forces and, more fundamentally, that the domestic political costs of the correct monetary policy required to really kill inflation were just too high.

[3]This is not to argue that the only cause of the global imbalances of the 1960s and 1970s was US inflation. The surplus countries did follow export-led growth policies and were reluctant to revalue their currencies. However, rising US inflation became increasingly the major problem leading to the collapse of Bretton Woods (Bordo 1993).

4 The Beginning of the Great Inflation in the USA

During World War II, the USA financed only a small part of wartime expenditures with the inflation tax compared to World War I and much of it was suppressed by price controls (Friedman and Schwartz 1963). During the war, the Federal Reserve was subservient to the Treasury and was constrained in its actions by enforcing pegs on both short-term and long-term government securities. After the war, inflation jumped when the controls were lifted, reaching a peak in 1948. The Fed began pressing for a return to its operational independence which was finally achieved in the Federal Reserve Treasury Accord of February 1951. In the following decade, under the direction of Chairman William McChesney Martin, the Fed followed a policy geared to price stability. This was consistent with the conservative fiscal policies of the Eisenhower Administration (Meltzer 2010; Stein 1994). Martin also paid considerable attention to the gold constraint of the Bretton Woods System and the balance of payments and monetary gold reserves.

The succeeding Kennedy and Johnson administrations attached high priority to increasing US growth and reducing unemployment using Keynesian aggregate demand management policies. The 1964 Kennedy tax cut increased the fiscal deficit, and in this period, the Martin Fed began accommodating fiscal policy by its even keel operations (Meltzer 2010).[4]

Martin attached considerable importance to cooperating with the administration, and his concept of central bank independence was "independent within the government." As a consequence, money growth began increasing along with fiscal deficits (see Figs. 6 and 7).

The underlying ideology of macroeconomic policy changed in this period from classical orthodoxy to Keynesianism. The Council of Economic Advisors Chairman Walter Heller and then Arthur Okun adopted the Phillips Curve as their policy guide. Following the mandate of the Employment Act of 1945, their main emphasis was on maximizing employment. Reducing unemployment below 4% was the goal at the expense of higher inflation. The welfare costs of inflation were perceived as lower than the costs of unemployment. The Keynesians also believed that fiscal policy was a more potent tool of demand management than monetary policy and that both monetary and fiscal policies should be used to fine-tune the business cycle (Stein 1994).

Inflation increased slowly after 1962 and then more rapidly in 1965 with the build-up in government expenditures for the Vietnam War and LBJ's Great Society programs (Fig. 8). Meltzer (2010, p 485) posited that the Fed's expansionary monetary policy accommodated one half of the increase in the fiscal deficit. As inflation increased, the Martin Fed began following a tighter monetary policy in late 1965. President Johnson greatly opposed this for fear that his domestic agenda would be

[4]See Humpage (2015) who attaches less weight to Fed accommodation via even keel operations.

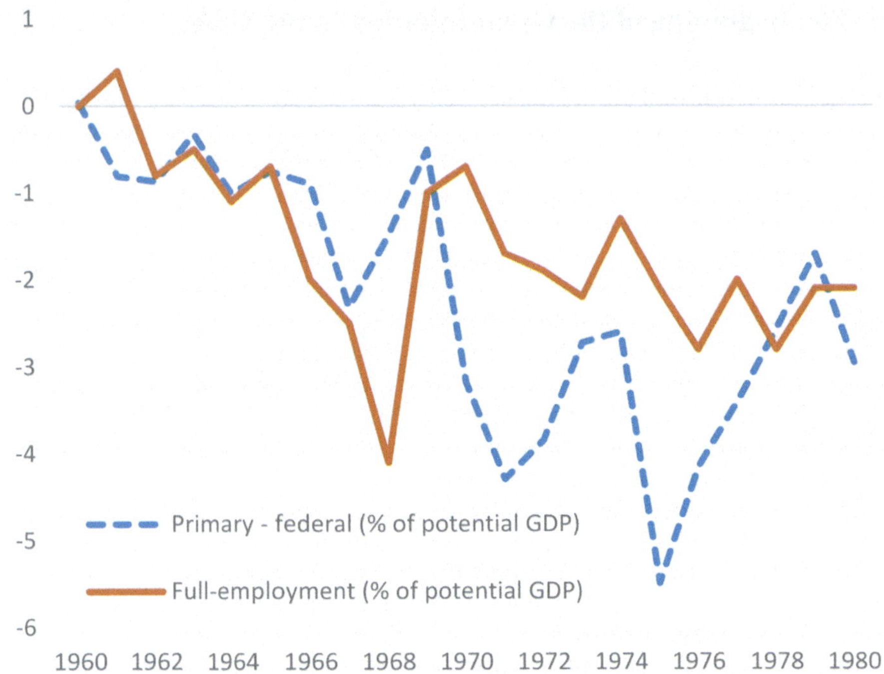

Fig. 6 US budget balance. Notes: Primary budget balance is defined as the difference between current expenditures and current receipts (Sources: BEA, CBO and FRED)

sabotaged and he put considerable pressure on Martin to avoid tight money.[5] The Congress also favored low interest rates in this period.

In 1966–67, Fed tightening (in part due to concerns over the balance of payments) led to the Credit Crunch of 1966 when rising rates surpassed the regulation Q ceiling on time deposits and led to a decline in mortgage finance. This led to considerable pressure from Congress and the administration to shift to a more expansionary policy (which it did). In the years 1965 to 1969 (with a few exceptions), the FOMC reduced its attention to the rest of the world, to the US balance of payments and to the monetary gold stock in favor of its domestic objectives (Bordo and Eichengreen 2013).

Meltzer (2010, Chap. 4) summarized Fed policy in the early years of the Great Inflation as increasingly attaching more weight to unemployment than inflation. This reflected both ideology—the adoption of Keynesian doctrine and politics—and increased pressure from the administration to avoid rising unemployment. As a consequence, expansionary monetary (and fiscal policy) would lead to a reduction in unemployment then followed by an increase in inflation. The Fed would then tighten to reduce inflation but once unemployment started increasing political pressure would

[5]The urban legend is that LBJ invited Martin down to his ranch and took him for a rough drive in a jeep when he made the point that Martin should not raise the discount rate in December, which he did anyway (Bordo and Eichengreen 2013; Meltzer 2010).

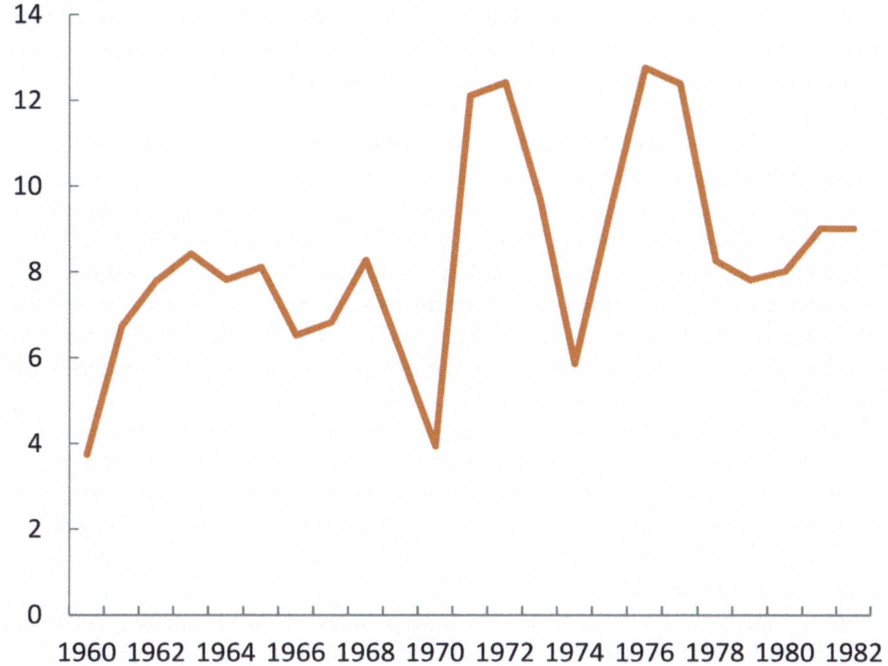

Fig. 7 M2 growth in the USA, 1960–1982, % change (Source: FRED)

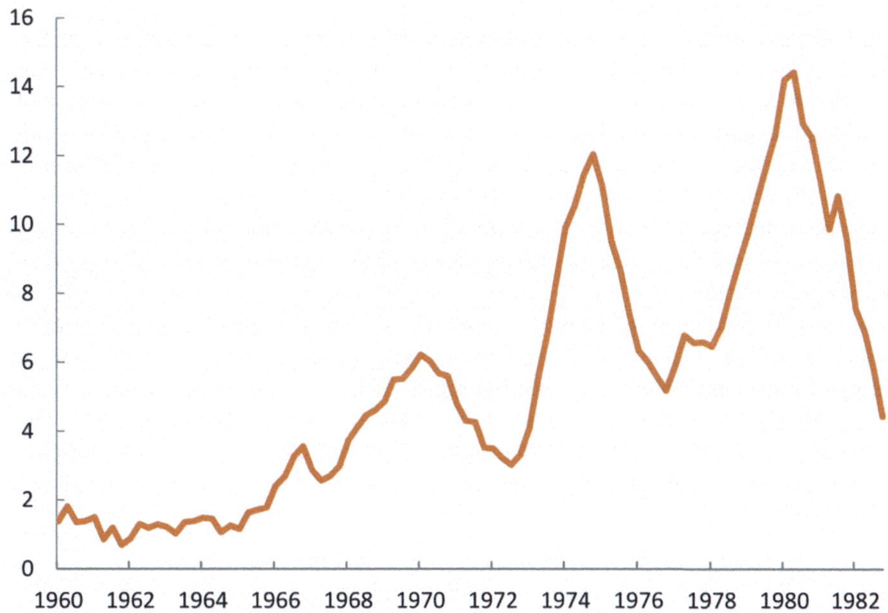

Fig. 8 CPI inflation in the USA, 1960–1982, y-o-y% change (Source: FRED)

encourage the Fed to abandon its tightening. According to Meltzer, these actions convinced the public that the Fed did not attach high priority to inflation which became more and more persistent as inflationary expectations became embedded in the public conscience.[6]

Richard Nixon became President in November 1968, and he campaigned on a platform to roll back the expansionary aggregate demand policies and the liberal agenda of the preceding democratic administrations. He was influenced by the views of Milton Friedman. He posited a greater role for free markets, the pursuit of a policy of monetary gradualism to reduce inflation and full employment balanced budgets. In October 1969, he appointed Arthur Burns as Chairman of the Fed. Burns was close to Milton Friedman (his teacher at Rutgers University in the 1930s). Burns was viewed as an advocate of sound money but not of monetary rules (Meltzer 2010; Wells 1994). He also had been a close advisor to Nixon since 1960.

Before leaving, Martin began pursuing a tight monetary policy. This was also coincident with the 1968 tax surcharge (passed in early 1969). This led to the beginning of a recession in late 1969 which did reduce inflation close to 3% from a peak of 6%. Burns followed through with the inherited policy, and the Nixon administration did not roll back the Johnson tax surcharge. This contributed to a recession in 1970 and rising unemployment.

Burns, under pressure from Nixon, reversed policies and began expanding money growth in early 1971. Burns both remembered that he had correctly warned Nixon in 1960 that a recession was coming, which would threaten his election chances, and had acceded to Nixon's promise on the day he was installed as Chairman "You see to it: no recession" (Wells 1994, p 42).[7]

Monetary expansion rekindled inflation in 1971. Burns was increasingly reluctant to tighten monetary policy. In 1970, he began to publicly state that the key determinant of inflation was now cost-push pressure by big labor unions and large firms with considerable market power. During that year, in varying venues, he began advocating income policies—wage and price controls.[8] As mentioned above, the big upsurge in US inflation spilled over into the balance of payment deficit, the international reserves of the surplus countries and inflationary pressure abroad. This precipitated the balance of payment crisis in the summer of 1971 and led to Nixon's Camp David speech on 15 August.

A key component of the New Economic Policy was a 90-day wage–price freeze. Arthur Burns was successful in overcoming the opposition of Milton Friedman and George Shultz and convincing first Secretary of the Treasury John Connally and then President Nixon that income policy would deal with the inflation problem. This decision, in turn, reflected both Burns and the Nixon administration's unwillingness to recognize the elephant in the room and use monetary policy to reduce inflation

---

[6]For other explanations of the Great Inflation, see Bordo and Orphanides (2013).

[7]Nixon also said about Burns, "I respect his independence. However, I hope that independently he will conclude that my views are the ones that should be followed" (Wells 1994, p 42).

[8]See Shultz (2018) who unearthed a letter from Burns to Nixon dated June 22, 1971, when he explicitly advocated wage–price controls.

directly. This reflected Nixon's fear of a recession weakening his reelection chances in the forthcoming 1972 presidential election and Burns' surrendering the Federal Reserve's independence to political pressure.

5 International Policy Considerations

The Bretton Woods System was designed as a cooperative exercise, and the IMF was established to coordinate international and domestic macro-policies of all the members. As described in Bordo and Schenk (2017), increasing policy coordination was required to manage the ongoing currency crises facing many countries (e.g., France 1958, Italy 1961, Canada 1962), as the BWS evolved. Of greater importance to the BWS was the chronic sterling crisis, which played out intermittently from 1947 to 1968 (Bordo et al. 2009). The final episode was the crisis of the dollar from 1968 to 1973.

In addition to the IMF, which was an organization of finance ministers, the G10 advanced countries plus Switzerland and the BIS, an organization of central bankers emerged as the key players in the major rescues of the 1960s (Bordo and Schenk 2017).

As mentioned above, in response to the Triffin dilemma, the US authorities and the other international agencies set up many facilities to preserve US gold reserves.

All of these mechanisms came under great strain once the USA began inflating and its balance of payment deficits expanded.

Richard Nixon changed the international perspective of the USA away from providing a favorable institutional and political environment for the development of the international economy embodied in the New Deal Bretton Woods institutions. He turned inward and made domestic US concerns "national renewal" his prime focus (Sargent 2015, p 102). He attributed the global imbalances threatening US gold reserves and the position of the dollar on the surplus countries of Western Europe and Japan, who he believed intentionally undervalued their currencies to gain a competitive advantage over the USA. They also pursued an export-driven growth model. This perception dominated the deliberations leading to the Camp David announcement.

Nixon, Connally and his other advisors viewed cutting the link with gold as a measure to force the others to adjust by revaluing their currencies. The temporary import surcharge was also viewed as a strategic measure to force the others to come to the bargaining table. It was believed that once the rest of the world revalued their currencies US investment and manufacturing industry would regain the position lost to foreign competition (Irwin 2013).[9]

After the Camp David announcement, Nixon sent Connally and Paul Volcker, Under Secretary of the Treasury, to the capitals of the world to convince them to adjust the values of their currencies. The chief holdout was President Pompidou

[9] Irwin (2013, p 32) also argued that the Nixon administration took a mercantilist position on trade issues for political reasons—to get domestic political support.

of France who believed that the USA should devalue the dollar (raise the dollar price of gold). A meeting between Nixon and Pompidou in November 1971 led to a compromise at a meeting of the major countries at the Smithsonian Institution in Washington D.C. on December 11, 1971.

At the Smithsonian, the USA agreed to devalue the dollar by 8.5%, the Europeans revalued their currencies by a similar amount and Japan agreed to revalue the Yen by 16.9%. In addition, the revamped par value system would have wider exchange rate bands of 2.25% instead of the original 1% (Volcker and Gyothen 1992).

Through this period, US inflation was still going strong and the pressure on imbalances continued. George P. Shultz, newly appointed Secretary of the Treasury, proposed a plan at the IMF Annual Meetings in September 1972 (dubbed Plan X) to correct the imbalances (Shultz 1973). This plan, earlier formed with the aid of Milton Friedman and Paul Volcker, was an attempt to create a quasi-flexible exchange rate system and ultimately move to free floating. Under the plan, countries would convert their reserves into SDR. Each member would adjust their currencies to imbalances measured by a series of indicators based on the size of their reserves relative to some normal measure, which in turn were based on their IMF quotas (Schenk 2017). Countries with reserves below normal would have to devalue their currencies by 3–4% per year. Countries with reserves larger than normal would have to revalue their currencies by 3% per year, countries whose reserves exceeded 175% of normal would be penalized and lose access to convertibility. In a sense, this was an actualization of Keynes's (1943) scarce currency clause which was blocked by the USA at the Bretton Woods Conference in 1944. Both the IMF and France were opposed to the plan, and it never was adopted.

Throughout 1972, one country after another left the par value system and floated: Canada (May 1970), Germany (May 1971) followed by Austria, Belgium, the Netherlands and Switzerland, the UK (June 1972). The USA devalued a second time by 10% in February 1973. By March 1973, the par value system had disappeared. It was replaced by generalized managed floating.

6 Conclusion: Some Lessons for Today

In the 1960s and 1970s, the major problem in the USA, and the rest of the world, was inflation. That is not the case today although it could be if the Fed is too slow to tighten. Rather, the key problem today is fiscal. Like the 1960s and 1970s, the source of the problem was a run-up in fiscal deficits beginning in 1965 and continuing through the 1970s. In recent years, major fiscal expansion to stem the Great Recession and a significant run-up in the debt-to-GDP ratio has not been rolled back. The recent tax cuts have increased the fiscal imbalance and are raising the debt-to-GDP ratio into historically high levels. As the Fed tightens to normalize monetary policy and was inflation to pick up much beyond the 2% level, debt service costs will rise which will add to the fiscal imbalances. Aggravating the problem are entitlements that cannot be cut. This means that the room for a fiscal consolidation without an increase in fiscal space could move the USA in the direction of a debt crisis (Slok 2018). This is a different imbalance than in the 1960s and 1970s but is still a serious one. Indeed, a sovereign debt crisis would threaten the credibility of the dollar as an international currency (Eichengreen 2010).

A second source of resonance from the earlier crisis is the use of tariff protection. At Camp David, the 10% temporary import surcharge was imposed as a strategic bargaining tool to force the surplus countries to adjust. It was successful in leading to the Smithsonian Agreement but, in the end, the only solution to the problem of the imbalances of the BWS was floating exchange rates. Today, the use of tariffs as a threat to force trading partners (especially China) to change their industrial policies risks the same kind of reaction that ultimately made the Camp David strategy fail, in the sense that the Smithsonian Agreement only lasted several months as the underlying deep fiscal and monetary imbalances became even worse. It also raises the specter of a trade war, such as occurred in the 1930s, which greatly exacerbated the Great Depression.

References

Bordo MD, Humpage O, Schwartz AJ (2015) Strained relations: US monetary policy and foreign exchange market operations in the twentieth century. University of Chicago Press, Chicago

Bordo MD, Orphanides A (2013) The great inflation. University of Chicago Press, Chicago

Bordo M (1993) The bretton woods international monetary system: a historical overview. In: Bordo MD, Eichengreen B (eds) A retrospective on the bretton woods system: lessons for international monetary reform. University of Chicago Press, Chicago, Ch 1

Bordo MD, Schenk C (2017) Monetary policy cooperation and coordination: an historical perspective on the importance of rules. In: Bordo MD, Taylor J (eds) Rules for international monetary stability: past, present and future. Hoover Institution Press, Standford, CA, Ch 5

Bordo M, Erceg C, Levin A, Michaels R (2007) Three Great American Disinflations. NBER Working Paper 12982, March

Bordo M, Oliver M, MacDonald R (2009) Sterling in Crisis 1964–67. European Review of Economic History, October

Bordo MD (2017) The operation and demise of the bretton woods system: 1958–1971. NBER Working Paper 23189

Bordo MD, McCauley RN (2018) "Triffin: Dilemma or myth". NBER Working paper 24195

Bordo MD, Eichengreen B (2013) Bretton woods and the great inflation. In: Bordo M, Orphanides A (eds) The great inflation. University of Chicago Press, Chicago, ch 9

Bordo MD, Monnet E, Naef A (2017) The gold pool (1961–1968) and the fall of the bretton woods system: 1958–1971. NBER Working Paper 24016

Coombs C (1976) The arena of international finance. John Wiley and Sons, New York

Despres EC, Kindleberger C, Salant W (1966) The dollar and world liquidity: a minority view. Economist 5 (February) 526–529

Eichengreen B (2010) Exorbitant privilege: the rise and fall of the dollar and the future of the international monetary system. Oxford University Press, New York

Friedman M, Schwartz AJ (1963) A monetary history of the United States 1867–1960. Princeton University Press, Princeton

Friedman M (1953) The case for flexible exchange rates in Friedman M, essays in positive economics. University of Chicago Press, Chicago

Humpage O (2015) Even keel and the great inflation. Federal Reserve Bank of Cleveland Working Paper 15:32. December

Irwin D (2013) The Nixon shock after forty years: the import surcharge revisited. World Trade Review 12(1):29–56

Keynes JM (1943) Proposals for an international clearing union in the international monetary fund, 1945–1965: twenty years of International Monetary Cooperation. By Horsefield JK (1969) Documents vol 3. International Monetary Fund, Washington D.C., pp 19–36

McKinnon R (1969) Private and official international money: the case for the dollar. Princeton Essays in International Economics. Princeton University, International finance Section, Princeton

Meltzer A (2010) A history of the Federal Reserve, vol 2. University of Chicago Press, Chicago

Mundell R (1969) Problems of the International Monetary System. In: Mundell R, Swoboda A (eds) Monetary Problems of the International Economy. University of Chicago Press, Chicago, pp 21–38

Sargent D (2015) A superpower transformed: the remaking of American Foreign Relations in the 1970s. Oxford University Press, New York

Schenk C (2010) The decline of sterling: managing the retreat of an International Currency 1945–1992. Cambridge University Press, Cambridge

Schenk C (2017) Coordination failures during bretton woods. In: Ghosh A, Quereshi M (eds) From great depression to great recession: the elusive quest for international policy cooperation. International Monetary Fund, Washington DC, Ch 4, 2017

Slok T (2018) Deutsche bank blog April. Available online. https://www.db.com/newsroom_news. Accessed on Mar 29 2020

Solomon R (1982) The International Monetary System, 1945–1981. Harper and Row, New York

Stein H (1994) Presidential Economics, 3rd edn. American Enterprise Institute, Washington DC

Volcker PA, Gyothen T (1992) Changing Fortunes: The World's Money and the Decline of American Supremacy. Times Books, New York

The Gold Standard and the Euro: Conjoined Twins or Distant Relations?

Barry Eichengreen

Abstract I provide a structured comparison of the nineteenth-century classical gold standard and the Euro, basing my analysis heavily on recent research. Both similarities and differences are evident in the historical record. Both regimes were vaunted as engines of convergence, but in both cases convergence was incomplete. Both were seen as delivering fiscal discipline, but in both cases such discipline was erratic. But whereas the gold standard was always a contingent monetary regime, there is nothing contingent about Euro-area membership. Finally, the gold standard operated in a simpler political setting, one in which mass participation in electoral politics was the exception to the rule.

Keywords Economic convergence · Economic history · Euro · Gold standard · Monetary regimes

1 Introduction

Jorge Braga de Macedo has long been interested in the classical gold standard for the light it sheds on contemporary monetary problems. In 1996, he explored the parallels between currencies convertible into gold before 1913 and the European currencies rendered convertible by the removal of capital controls in the 1990s.[1] That analysis was informed by recent experience, the 1990s being the first time in six decades when European currencies were fully convertible on both capital and current account. It was informed by Europe's turbulent experience with the European Monetary System, the 1992–1993 EMS crisis having driven countries out of that system, temporarily in some cases, permanently in others, and forcing the remaining members to move from narrow 2¼% fluctuation bands to 15% bands.[2] These events pointed up the contrasts between the gold standard and the EMS. In contrast to the EMS, the gold

[1] See Braga de Macedo (1996) and also Braga de Macedo et al. (1996) in this same volume.

[2] As finance minister, Braga de Macedo had brought Portugal into the EMS in the spring of 1992.

B. Eichengreen (✉)
University of California, Berkeley, CA, USA
e-mail: eichengr@econ.berkeley.edu

L. Brites Pereira et al. (eds.), *Economic Globalization and Governance*,
https://doi.org/10.1007/978-3-030-53265-9_7

standard gained members over time, rather than losing them; countries adopting gold convertibility were never forced to adopt gold import and export points as wide as 15%.[3] This perspective suggested that the EMS was less robust than its gold-standard predecessor. At the same time, Braga de Macedo cautioned against reading too much into the events of 1992–1993. While that experience "might be thought of as throwing cold water on the prospects for [a single European currency] in the 1990s and beyond..." Braga de Macedo instead concluded that "a perspective grounded in the history of the international monetary system suggests that the prospects for EMU may not be so dim."[4] This prediction proved accurate when the Euro came into being at the end of the 1990s. At the time of writing, the single currency has remained firmly in place for more than two decades. The Euro area has gained members over time rather than losing them. This perspective suggests that the Euro area is now as robust as its gold-standard predecessor.

In this chapter, I revisit these comparisons in light of subsequent research, the intervening quarter century having provided an opportunity for additional analysis of both historical and contemporary international monetary arrangements.[5] These two strands are not unrelated. Twenty years of the Euro, not all of which have proceeded smoothly, encouraged scholars, in Europe and elsewhere, to reconsider gold-standard experience. And recent work on the gold standard has directed attention to previously neglected aspects of Euro-area experience.

2 Convergence

A theme of Braga de Macedo (1996) was convergence: nominal convergence, real convergence, and political convergence.[6] His discussion of nominal convergence focused on inflation rates and long-term interest rates, these being two of the Maastricht Treaty's "convergence criteria."[7] The nominal convergence underway in the first half of the 1990s continued up to the advent of the Euro and, especially, thereafter—until the 2008–2010 crisis erupted, after which it abruptly did not. Inflation rates converged across member states as a result of the decline of inflation in Southern European economies such as Portugal, Greece, and Italy.[8] The standard deviation

[3]The gold import and export points, determined by transactions costs of shipping gold between national markets, were on the order of ± 1 percent. Some central banks were able to maintain wider bands by imposing additional costs (paying out only clipped or worn coin) or redeeming currency notes only at remote offices. See Bloomfield (1959) and Officer (2007).

[4]Braga de Macedo (1996), p 242.

[5]The Braga de Macedo piece cited above was in fact prepared for a conference held in Arrábida in 1994.

[6]This discussion of nominal and real, but not also political, convergence draws on Eichengreen (2019).

[7]Along with budget deficits and debt ratios.

[8]My focus here is on Western Europe, the transition economies of Eastern Europe being a somewhat special case.

of annual inflation rates, expressed in percentage terms, fell from 6% in the early 1990s to less than 1% in 1999, where it has remained since (statistics cited in this paragraph are for the 12 original Euro-area members).

Interest rate convergence was even more dramatic. Nominal rates on 10-year Greek government bonds fell from 18% (a full 10 percentage points above German levels) in the mid-1990s to just 5% (mere basis points above German levels) in 2001, when Greece adopted the Euro, and to even lower levels and narrower spreads in the mid-2000s. Spreads then widened explosively following the bankruptcy of Lehman Brothers in 2008, with the development of banking problems in Ireland and elsewhere in the Eurozone, and following revelations in late 2009 of budgetary deception by a previous Greek government. Experience was similar, if less dramatic, in Portugal: ten-year yields fell from 12% in 1995 to 3.9% in January 1999 when the country adopted the Euro. Yields then fell further, to a low of 3.4% in 2005, before reversing in 2009–2010 and reaching 10.5% in 2012, after which they fell back to 2–3%.

Nominal convergence occurred for reasons both good and bad. It was good in the sense that such convergence is a normal feature of an integrated monetary zone. A single monetary policy should make for similar risk-free interest rates across an integrated economic zone. But nominal convergence was bad in that it reflected an unfortunate tendency to confuse the elimination of exchange risk with the elimination of default risk. Ten-year government bonds are not always and everywhere risk free. Yet this was evidently the belief after the turn of the century. This misperception may have reflected confusion between exchange risk and default risk, where only the former was eliminated by monetary union. It may have reflected the existence of zero risk weights and zero capital charges on banks holding sovereign bonds. It may have been confounded by the fact that the European Central Bank (ECB), though applying different haircuts to different maturities of government bonds, reflecting their different degrees of liquidity risk, did not distinguish them by degree of default risk.

Have these problems now been solved? Any confusion between exchange risk and default risk was dissolved by post-2008 events; this has been at least one beneficial effect of the crisis. In 2011, the ECB introduced a schedule of graduated valuation haircuts on assets rated BBB+ to BBB-, replacing the uniform haircut applied previously. The new haircuts were at least as high as the old haircut and in some cases higher. But regulatory capital charges for risky sovereign debt are still absent. Basel III foresees changing this, but governments, worried about burdening weak banks, have hesitated to implement the recommended reforms.

There was interest rate convergence in the gold-standard era as well. The period saw improvements in information and communications with the rollout of a global submarine telegraph network (see, e.g., Foster 1994; Hoag 2006). It saw the development of institutions mediating international capital and information flows: investment banks, rating agencies, and bondholders' representative committees (Esteves 2013; Flandreau and Zumer 2004). It is argued that the gold standard itself sent an important signal about creditworthiness—about the stability and reliability of policy and institutions—much in the manner of the Euro. Insofar as adherence to the gold standard presupposed the maintenance of balanced budgets and limited debt, going onto that standard could be taken as a signal that a government was committed to precisely those policies, reassuring investors. Bordo and Rockoff (1996) famously argued that the gold standard functioned as a "good housekeeping seal of approval." This view has not gone undisputed, just as the idea that the Euro provided automatic protection against budget deficits and debt restructuring has not gone undisputed. For example, Ferguson and Schularick (2006) criticized Bordo and Rockoff's evidence and suggested that British colonial status was at least as important as gold-standard adherence and the sustainability of fiscal policies for the cost of borrowing in London.[9]

Braga de Macedo (1996) showed that the record of real convergence was mixed in Stage I of the transition to the Euro. True to form, there was then continued lack of real convergence, as measured by the dispersion of per capita incomes, following the advent of the Euro. For the 12 original members of the Euro area, the coefficient of variation of per capita GDP in purchasing-power-parity terms was flat from the mid-1990s up until the crisis; between 2008 and 2015 that coefficient of variation then nearly doubled.[10]

Several factors contributed to post-2008 real divergence. First, there was the asymmetric impact of the China shock. China's accession to the World Trade Organization and integration into the global trading system were good for Germany, which specialized in the production and export of machinery and transport equipment, for which China had voracious appetites. But these same events were bad for countries such as Italy and Portugal, which had considerable product-specialization overlap with China.

Second, Germany benefited from the integration of Eastern European countries into the Single European Market. German firms outsourced labor-intensive activities to Eastern Europe and specialized in skilled-labor-intensive stages of production. Companies in other member states, in Southern Europe in particular, failed to do likewise, whether because their products were less conducive to this kind of supply-chain management, because they lacked the same historical links to the region, or simply because management was stuck in its ways.

Third, because of inefficient banking and financial systems, countries like Portugal that might have been expected to experience catch-up did not see productivity rise with capital inflows. Instead of flowing into manufacturing, capital flowed into relatively inefficient, technologically antiquated service sectors (Blanchard 2007; Reis 2013).

Finally, countries such as Portugal, Spain, and Greece experiencing capital inflows suffered from overvalued exchange rates. This phenomenon of capital flows from Northern to Southern Europe can be thought of as a corollary of the nominal convergence discussed above. But the resulting Dutch-disease problem made investment in

---

[9]"Colonial" status is used here as shorthand for membership in the British Commonwealth and Empire.

[10]If one considers instead all 19 members of the present-day Euro area, there was strong convergence up to 2008, reflecting catch-up growth in the Central European and Baltic members and also strong if unsustainable growth in Southern Europe, fueled by capital inflows, which then halted in 2008.

manufacturing unattractive. More precisely, investment in both manufacturing and high-tech services was unattractive. The result was a failure to invest more in the new generation of information technologies (IT) and to reorganize production to capitalize more fully on their productivity-enhancing potential.

Again, one can ask: which of these problems has been solved? The China shock has diminished in the sense that China is no longer growing its economy and exports at double-digit rates. The production and export of manufactures have picked up in Spain and Portugal. Overvalued currencies are less overvalued, what with the weakness of the Euro relative to the Dollar, internal devaluation, and the end of indiscriminate capital flows between Northern and Southern Europe. Banking systems have been strengthened and reformed in most European countries.

The result has been the recovery of productivity growth across the Euro area, and specifically in the crisis countries where such recovery was needed most acutely. Between 2014 and 2016, Ireland and Spain had two of the three fastest rates of total factor productivity (TFP) growth among the major Eurozone countries, according to AMECO. Portuguese and Greek TFP growth rates were respectable, at 0.6 and 0.5% per annum, respectively.

Finally, the Euro area and the European Union (EU) have not displayed the political convergence anticipated by their architects. The EU's accumulated body of law (the *Acquis Communautaire*) obliges its members to preserve the stability of democratic institutions and to respect rule of law and the fundamental rights of citizens. For Portugal in particular, membership in the EU was associated with, and followed immediately on, the transition to democracy. The expectation was that democratic values and practices would not just deepen within incumbent EU and Euro-area members but also spread to the new member states.

It has not turned out this way. According to the most recent report of the World Justice Project for 2017–2018, rule of law has been falling in Poland, Hungary, Bulgaria, and Austria.[11] Hungary has seen a sharp decline in fundamental rights: Viktor Orban's government has taken control of the media, criminalized efforts to help migrants and refugees, taxed NGOs that support immigration, and restricted the work of civil society more generally; Poland has seen a decline in constraints on government powers, a decline in open government, a decline in fundamental rights, and a decline in criminal justice: specifically, the government of Jaroslaw Kaczynski has undermined judicial independence and sought to cultivate domestic political support by picking fights with the European Commission; and, in early 2019, Austria far-right Interior Minister Herbert Kickl was accused of threatening the rule of law by calling into question the country's commitment to international rights conventions.

This rise of right-wing nationalism in what were formerly known as the accession economies of Eastern Europe is partly a reaction against disappointing living

[11] Also, in Belgium whose inclusion on this list may surprise the reader (it certainly surprised this author). Belgium's decline reflects a falling score on "order and security" due mainly, it would appear, to a low rating for the prevalence of civil conflict. In contrast, the rule of law rating has been improving in Portugal.

standards, EU membership not having automatically delivered the promised real convergence. In seeking to understand these political trends, Berglof (2018) points not just to disappointing growth but also to low absolute real incomes (by European standards), the impact of the post-2008 financial crisis, and weak official safety nets. In addition, there was a post-2015 reaction against immigration, both in Eastern Europe, where there had been little actual experience with immigration, and in many Western European countries, where traditionally dominant groups were perturbed by the increasingly multi-cultural nature of society.

At the same time, there has been growing political support across Western Europe for political parties with a nationalist orientation, most often of the Right but sometimes of the Left. These nationalist parties criticize the EU as infringing on national policy autonomy and the Euro as limiting their economic policy autonomy. They push back against the EU's fiscal rules, although such parties tend to be more critical of those rules when campaigning than when actually gaining office (viz. the cases of Greece in 2015 and Italy in 2018).

Nationalists, by definition, oppose deeper European integration as inimical to their core values. The participation of such parties in government, and even the political constraints they impose on other parties participating in a governing coalition, can make it more difficult for member states to agree on reforms, such as those proposed by European Commission (2017) for deepening Europe's monetary union. Facing Eurosceptical parties at home, it then becomes correspondingly more difficult for the French and German governments, traditionally the dual locomotives of further integration, to agree on deepening measures.

3 Fiscal Discipline

Fiscal discipline has long been at the center of debates over the viability and robustness of monetary arrangements. Thus, the debate over the reasons for the collapse of the Bretton Woods System long focused on whether lax fiscal policy or lax monetary policy was the precipitating factor. Even authors focusing on Federal Reserve policy point to chronic budget deficits as a reason why the central bank was pressured and felt compelled to keep interest rates artificially low (Bordo 2018).

This same fear of fiscal dominance haunted the framers of the Maastricht Treaty. Braga de Macedo (1996) highlights their concern over deficits in countries that aspired to membership in the Euro area, for example, Portugal, which had a budget deficit in excess of 7% of GDP in 1994. Officials displayed limited faith in the power of market discipline to rein in excessive deficits, notwithstanding evidence that market had some restraining impact on municipal debts and deficits in the United States (Goldstein and Woglom 1992). Their skepticism gave rise to the convergence criteria for deficits and debts governing entry into the monetary union and to the excessive deficit procedure applied subsequently.

Post-1999 experience has reinforced this early skepticism of the disciplining effects of financial markets. As described above, interest rates on sovereign bonds converged quickly to German levels following the advent of the Euro. This was true equally of countries with high debts and low ones. It was true equally of countries with large and small budget deficits. Starting, then, around 2009, market discipline kicked in with a vengeance.

This erratic record would not have come as a surprise to students of the gold standard. Le Cacheux and Zumer (1998) considered the response of interest rates to debts and deficits in gold-standard countries between 1880 and 1913. They found only a weak response of interest rates over a considerable range of debts and deficits, beyond which interest rates rose abruptly. To put it ironically: history suggests that investors pay close attention to debt and deficit ratios when pricing securities, except when they do not.

Flandreau, Le Cacheux and Zumer also found that the sustainability of debts was influenced by the monetary regime—that debt problems were less once price levels began trending upward in the 1890s. To be clear, this was not fiscal dominance: price levels rose starting in the 1890s because of global gold discoveries, not because of changes in central bank policies due to fiscal policies and other factors. This finding for the gold standard suggested that fiscal sustainability would be shaped by ECB policy even if the ECB adhered to its mandate to maintain low and stable inflation. The accuracy of the conclusion became clear with the contrast between the Trichet ECB, which raised interest rates in 2008 and 2011, and the Draghi ECB, which refrained from equally restrictive policies and in 2015 turned to quantitative easing to prevent the European economy from slipping into deflation. The two policy regimes had visibly different implications for public debt sustainability.

Braga de Macedo (1996) did not question the viability of the fiscal rules adopted in Europe as an alternative, or supplement, to market discipline. But he observed that such rules will be enforceable only if there is support for their objectives in the countries to which they are applied, and not when the rules are imposed from outside absent that support. Subsequent experience is consonant with this conclusion. Europe's fiscal rules have been adhered to consistently to only in countries where fears of fiscal dominance (known locally as "stability culture") are deeply ingrained.[12] Elsewhere, violations have been repeated, and there has been a reluctance by the European Commission to apply the associated fines and sanctions for fear of feeding nationalistic sentiment in the subject countries.

In the case of US states, the budget rules in place since the nineteenth century have had a significant impact on debts and deficits because they are self-imposed. However, they lead not just to lower levels of debt and smaller deficits but also to more procyclical budget outcomes (Lutz and Follette 2012). Europe's fiscal rules have also had the unintended consequence of accentuating fiscal procyclicality (European Commission 2018). This problem has prompted successive revisions to diminish procyclicality but at the cost of increased complexity.

Market discipline is imperfect, but so, inevitably, are fiscal rules. It follows that there is no easy alternative to building stability culture at home. But such stability culture has deep historical roots. History suggests that it is not easily transplanted.

---

[12]Even there, there have been occasional violations, as in Germany in 2003.

4 Capital Flows

It was not just domestic investors who purchased government bonds indiscriminately before 2009 and somewhat more discerningly thereafter. This brings us to the role of foreign investors, international capital flows, and their relationship to the monetary regime.

There is an extensive literature on capital flows under the pre-1914 gold standard. Synthesizing what was known, Kindleberger (1973) argued that the stability of the gold-standard system hinged on British overseas lending, and that stability benefited in particular from the fact that British lending tended to fluctuate countercyclically. When economic activity in Britain turned down, leading to a decline in the country's import demands, overseas lending turned up, reflecting the existence of a relatively stable domestic savings rate. Thus, the negative impact on other countries of the decline in export demand was offset by a capital-inflow induced fall in interest rates and increase in domestic investment. This was in contrast to the 1920s, when capital outflows, now mainly from the USA, fluctuated procyclically rather than countercyclically.

Europe after 1999 more closely resembled the 1920s. The explanation lies in the structure of domestic financial systems. Under the classical gold standard, credit aggregates were relatively stable. Given that stability, domestic and foreign investment fluctuated inversely.[13] In the 1920s and even more in the early twenty-first century, credit was more elastic. During the upswing, more lending for financial as well as real investment pushed up asset prices, which in turn increased collateral values and underpinned additional lending, in the operation of what economists refer to as the leverage cycle (Geanakoplos 2010). Bank capital ratios were lower than in the nineteenth century, making for more leverage and greater elasticity. The adoption of mark-to-market regulatory rules further accentuated procyclicality.[14] Nor were asset valuations and collateral values restrained by perceptions of rising exchange and default risk in the capital-importing countries, the Euro having providing assurance that exchange risk had been eliminated and encouraging the misapprehension that default risk was removed along with it. Reflecting this combination of factors, capital flows from Northern Europe to Southern Europe surged in 2001–2007, when the source countries, notably Germany, were expanding robustly, but reversed in the crisis, when German, European and global growth all fell.

Moreover, unlike in the nineteenth century, when overseas lending was mediated by the bond market and when securities were sold to retail investors, a substantial fraction of Southern European sovereign issues now were held by banks, including foreign banks. Thus, when questions arose about debt sustainability in Southern Europe, only did Northern European banks grow more reluctant to lend overseas, but they also grew more reluctant to lend at home due to the resulting balance sheet problems. Again, the implication was that domestic and foreign lending fluctuated together, not inversely.

---

[13]This being the central point of Cairncross (1953).

[14]See also Sect. 2 above.

In the nineteenth century, foreign capital was heavily invested in projects related to the production of traded goods (ports, railways, and other projects supporting export capacity).[15] In the opening years of the twenty-first century, in contrast, it was invested in non-traded goods and services production, in residential construction in particular. Home construction in countries like Ireland and Spain expanded enormously with impetus from capital inflows.[16] Schularick and Taylor (2015) suggest that this association between credit booms and capital flows, on the one hand, and housing booms, on the other, is distinctively modern; their evidence suggests that it is more pronounced than earlier historical periods.

Eventually, European policy-makers sought to address these issues by applying countercyclical buffers and capping loan-to-value ratios. Closing the barn door after the horse has bolted may be better than not closing the barn door at all. But what is stunning, in hindsight, is that the dangers of procyclical lending and capital-flow-induced housing booms were not on the radar of the Euro's architects prior to the crisis.

5 Labor Flows

Labor mobility has been acknowledged as an optimum currency area criterion ever since Mundell (1961). Interestingly, however, while the late nineteenth century is referred to as the age of mass migration, the connections between labor mobility and the gold standard were not made until recently.[17] Khoudour-Casteras (2006) showed that variations in the rate of emigration fostered balance of payments adjustment in countries experiencing adverse shocks. This mechanism operated more powerfully in countries with convertible rather than inconvertible currencies, insofar as the latter also had the option of adjusting the exchange rate. Hatton and Williamson (1998) referred to this phenomenon as "capital chasing labor" (meaning that where emigration led, financial investment followed), but Khoudour-Casteras showed that there was also a tendency for labor to chase after capital when the latter was the source of the shock. When capital again reversed direction and flows resumed to the countries of the European periphery, migration similarly reversed direction. One in three immigrant arrivals in the USA between 1850 and 1913 returned to Europe subsequently. More than half of temporary moves to the USA lasted less than five years (Boustan and Eriksson 2017). Some European migrants moved to the new world—from Italy to Argentina for example—for a period as short as the spring planting and fall harvest seasons, matching the seasonality of interest rates, which spiked at those same times of year, attracting capital to complement the labor.[18]

---

[15]This was more prominently the case of British overseas lending as compared to lending by French and German investors (see Feis et al. 1931 and Fishlow 1985).

[16]The corresponding expansion was less in Greece and Portugal.

[17]See however Panic (1992) and Eichengreen (1996).

[18]The reference here is to the planting and harvest seasons in the New World.

Relatedly, Khoudour-Casteras and Esteves (2009) documented how emigrants' remittances played a stabilizing role in periods of financial stress. In periods when commercial capital flows to a country of the European periphery dried up, remittances remained relatively stable. Where remittances dominated the capital account, the incidence of crises, as measured by sudden stops and current account reversals, was less. The explanation for financial stability in the countries at the center of the gold standard is no mystery: these countries had powerful central banks with influential discount rates that could "draw gold from the moon."[19] For countries at the periphery, many of which lacked central banks, Khoudour-Casteras and Esteves suggested that the solution to that mystery had a lot to do with emigration and remittances. Interestingly, Correia and Martins (2016) find a similar pattern for Greece in the Euro crisis: when Greek government bond yields spiked, indicating that investors were retreating from the country, remittances increased, buffering the impact on the balance of payments.

Late twentieth-century comparisons with the USA warned that labor mobility in response to asymmetric regional shocks was disturbingly low in Europe.[20] Subsequent analyses (e.g., Beyer and Smets 2015; Dao et al. 2014) found some evidence of a tendency for the gap to close. They found evidence of declining interstate mobility in the USA because of high housing costs and for other reasons. At the same time, they found that mobility between regions was rising in Europe. However, the latter increase in labor mobility has been mainly between the accession economies of Central and Eastern Europe on the one hand and Western Europe on the other: westward prior to the crisis and back toward the countries of origin thereafter.[21] The causes of this increase in labor mobility—whether it reflects the development of information networks among migrants, Ryanair, or something else—remain to be determined.

In addition, the continued decline in air travel and related costs made for increased emigration from the Euro-area crisis countries to non-European destinations, from Portugal to Brazil for example.[22] As it had under the gold standard, this last mechanism provided another margin for responding to asymmetric shocks in Europe.

6 Lender of Last Resort

Both the gold standard and the Euro are portrayed as automatic, non-discretionary systems. Under the gold standard, the textbooks suggest, there was a mechanical link between the stock of gold and the monetary circulation. The Maastricht Treaty and

[19]The phrase is from the Committee on Currency and Foreign Exchanges after the War (1919), which was looking back nostalgically at the prewar situation of the Bank of England in particular.

[20]See Blanchard and Katz (1992), Eichengreen (1993), and Decressin and Fatas (1995).

[21]On this see Dao et al. (2014) and Jauer et al. (2018).

[22]See Phillips (2011) and, for a longer-term perspective, Marques and Gois (2016).

Treaty of European Union made no provision for parity adjustments within the monetary union, for the issuance of parallel currencies, or for exit and the reintroduction of a national currency.[23] The ECB in its early years officially followed a two-pillar strategy, where inflation and the money stock were both intermediate targets, but in practice it closely targeted 2% inflation.

Careful observers of the gold standard always understood that the historical reality was more complex, suggesting that the same might be true of the Euro area. The maintenance of convertibility was contingent; it could be suspended, in England, for example, at the discretion of the Bank of England and with approval from Parliament, in the event of war or economic and financial crisis (Bordo and Kydland 1995). As a consequence of the French Wars, convertibility was suspended in 1797, and the Bank of England expanded its balance sheet in support of wartime fiscal policies. The government, for its part, committed to converting the Bank's short-term bills into long-term bonds and backing the latter with future tax revenues, allowing convertibility to be restored in 1821 (Antipa and Chamley 2017). In 1847, in response to a harvest failure that induced a banking crisis, the bank suspended Peel's Act and issued unbacked fiat money in support of the financial system, following the failure of earlier efforts to provide that support while also maintaining convertibility (Dornbusch and Frenkel 1984). In 1866, the Bank of England's efforts to reconcile convertibility with support for the banking and financial system were more successful; it refused to bail out Overend Gurney, but lent freely against collateral to other financial institutions while raising bank rate to high levels to limit the drain of gold (Flandreau and Ugolini 2014). Historians disagree on when the Bank of England and by implication other central banks explicitly acknowledged their responsibility as a lender of last resort. But they agree that even under the gold standard the monetary authority had to be attentive to the state of the government's finances and the condition and stability of the banks. And that when moving from attention to action, it had to exercise judgment.

Early critics of the ECB worried that its statute defined its mandate too narrowly, given its emphasis on the pursuit of price stability and all but total neglect of the need to maintain a stable financial and payments system. This official framing reflected German preoccupation with price stability and recognition that, without German support, monetary union would not go forward.

Critics warned that a rigid mandate might force regulators to suppress the development of securitized financial markets where the danger of liquidity crises is most severe. In turn, this would favor preservation of the historically prevalent bank-intermediated financial system where the need for central bank intervention was less (see Folkerts-Landau and Garber 1993).

They were partly right. The development of securitized markets posed the risk of runs and liquidity crises, just as advertised. Rather than suppressing them, however, regulators in their wisdom allowed those markets to develop and flourish. Rather than being competed out of business, the banks turned to wholesale funding and more leverage as ways of countering narrowing spreads between their lending and deposit

[23] All three of which were recommended by critical observers during the Euro crisis.

rates. The result was not one but two risks to financial stability: the risk of liquidity crises in securitized markets and the risk of runs on highly leveraged banks by their wholesale funders.

When two BNP Paribas-linked hedge funds seized up in the summer of 2007, the ECB was quick to inject liquidity into the financial system. But it was also too quick to conclude that its work was done and to raise interest rates in 2008 and 2011, two occasions when modest increases in headline inflation trumped officials' residual concerns with financial stability. Together with a sharp turn to fiscal consolidation, this delayed Europe's recovery from the crisis. An extended recession meant more non-performing loans for banks and disappointing revenues for their governments, on both counts feeding doubts about debt sustainability. Only with the transition from Trichet to Draghi and the decision of the ECB board to back Draghi's "do whatever it takes" pledge with Outright Monetary Transactions (purchases of bonds of governments that had negotiated rescue programs) was it finally clear that the ECB was prepared to act on its lender-of-last-resort responsibilities. Had its board taken a closer look back at gold-standard history, it might have gotten there earlier.

7 Conclusion

So, are the Euro and the gold standard best understood as conjoined twins or distant cousins? The obvious answer is also the accurate answer: both characterizations contain an element of truth. Both regimes were vaunted as engines of convergence, but in both cases convergence was incomplete. Both were seen as delivering fiscal discipline, but in both cases fiscal discipline was erratic. Both were predicated on the existence of high international capital mobility, but the effects of that capital mobility were not always as promised by its champions. Both relied for their operation on the mobility of labor, but labor mobility was endogenous to the monetary regime, not an exogenous precondition for optimum-currency-area status.[24] Both required central banks to operate as lenders of last resort rather than to follow mechanical monetary rules.

From other perspectives, however, the resemblance is harder to see. The gold standard was always a contingent monetary regime. In contrast, there is nothing contingent about Euro-area membership; German finance minister Wolfgang Schauble's suggestion in 2015 that Greece might take a temporary holiday from the Euro was not something, given economic and political realities, that Greek and other European leaders could reasonably pursue.

Finally, the gold standard operated in a simpler political setting, one in which mass participation in electoral politics was the exception to the rule. The Euro, in contrast, operates in a setting where the pressure on monetary policy from populist politicians and parties is intense. The response has been to buttress the independence of the European Central Bank, to the point where it is the most independent central

[24] A distinction made in a related connection by Frankel and Romer (1998).

bank in the world. But this creates complaints, understandably, about its political accountability. The institution has responded by enhancing the transparency of its decision making and operations in order that it can be better held accountable in the court of public opinion. Whether this will be enough, time will tell.

References

Abramitzky R, Boustan L, Eriksson K (2017) To the new world and back again: return migrants in the age of mass migration. ILR Review 72(2):300–322. https://doi.org/10.1177/0019793917726981

Antipa P, Chamley C (2017) Monetary and fiscal policy in England during the French Wars, 1793–1821. Bank of France Working Paper #627

Berglof E (2018) A tale of two crises—populism in former Soviet Space. Unpublished manuscript, Institute of Global Affairs, London School of Economics

Beyer RCM, Smets F (2015) Labour market adjustments and migration in Europe and the United States: how different? Economic Policy 30:643–682. https://doi.org/10.1093/epolic/eiv011

Blanchard O (2007) Adjustment within the Euro: the difficult case of Portugal. Portuguese Econ J 6:1–21. https://doi.org/10.1007/s10258-006-0015-4

Blanchard O, Katz LF (1992) Regional evolutions. Brook Papers Econ Activity 1:1–75

Bloomfield AI (1959) Monetary Policy under the International Gold Standard, 1880–1914. Federal Reserve Bank of New York, New York

Bordo MD (2018) The imbalances of the bretton woods system 1965 to 1973: US Inflation, the Elephant in the Room. NBER Working Paper No. 25409. https://doi.org/10.3386/w25409

Bordo MD, Kydland F (1995) The gold standard as a rule. Explor Econ Hist 32:423–464. https://doi.org/10.1006/exeh.1995.1019

Bordo M, Rockoff H (1996) The gold standard as a 'good housekeeping seal of approval.' J Econ History 56:389–428. https://doi.org/10.1017/S0022050700016491

Braga de Macedo J (1996) Converging towards a European Currency Standard: Convertibility and Stability in the 1990s and Beyond. In: Braga de Macedo J, Eichengreen B and Reis J (eds) Currency convertibility: the gold standard and beyond. Routledge, London, p 3–10

Braga de Macedo J, Eichengreen B, Reis J (1996) Introduction: Currency Convertibility in Historical Perspective—the Gold Standard and Beyond. In: Braga de Macedo J, Eichengreen B, Reis J (eds) Currency convertibility: the gold standard and beyond. Routledge, London, p 241–265

Cairncross AK (1953) Home and Foreign Investment, 1870–1913. Cambridge University Press, Cambridge

Committee on Currency and Foreign Exchanges the War (1919) HMSO Report. 6 Nov 1919, London

Correia L, Martins P (2016) Are remittances an instrument of stabilization and funding in the Euro area? Appl Econ Lett 23:1177–1181. https://doi.org/10.1080/13504851.2016.1142647

Dao M, Furceri D, Loungani P (2014) Regional Labor Market Adjustments in the US and Europe. IMF Working Paper 14/26 (February)

Decressin J, Fatas A (1995) Regional Labor Market Dynamics in Europe. Euro Econ Rev 39:1627–1655. https://doi.org/10.1016/0014-2921(94)00102-2

Dornbusch R, Frenkel JA (1984) The Gold Standard Crisis of 1847. J Int Econ 16:233–271. https://doi.org/10.3386/w1039

Eichengreen B (1993) European Monetary Unification and Regional Unemployment. In: Lloyd Ulman L, Eichengreen B, Dickens W (eds) Labor and an Integrated Europe. Brookings Institution, Washington D.C., pp 188–223

Eichengreen B (1996) Déjà vu All over again: lessons from the gold standard for European Monetary Unification? In: Bayoumi T, Eichengreen B, Taylor M (eds) Modern Perspectives on the Gold Standard. Cambridge University Press, Cambridge, pp 365–387

Eichengreen B (2019) Convergence and Divergence in the EU: Lessons from Italy. Intereconomics 31:14–19

Esteves RP (2013) The Bondholder, the Sovereign, and the Banker: Sovereign Debt and Bondholders' Protection before 1914. Euro Rev Econ History 17:389–407. https://doi.org/10.1093/ereh/het016

Esteves RP, Khoudour-Casteras D (2009) A Fantastic Rain of Gold: European Migrants' Remittances and Balance of Payments Adjustment during the Gold Standard Period. J Econ History 69:951–985

European Commission (2017) A Roadmap for deepening Europe's economic and monetary union. In: Further steps towards completing Europe's economic and monetary union: a roadmap. European Commission, Brussels, 6 December. Available online. https://ec.europa.eu/commission/publications/completing-europes-economic-and-monetary-union-factsheets_en. Accessed 29 Mar 2020

European Commission (2018) Review of Flexibility under the Stability and Growth Pact. In: Commission Staff Working Document SWD (2018) 270 final, Brussels, 23 May.

Feis H (1931) Europe, the World's Banker. Yale University Press, New Haven

Ferguson N, Schularick M (2006) The Empire Effect: The Determinants of Country Risk in the First Age of Globalization, 1880–1913. J Econ History 66:283–312. https://doi.org/10.1017/S002205070600012X

Fishlow A (1985) Lessons from the past: capital markets during the 19th century and the interwar period. International Organization 39(3):383–439. https://doi.org/10.1017/S0020818300019135

Flandreau M, Le Cacheux J, Zumer F (1998) Stability without a Pact? Lessons from the European Gold Standard, 1880–1914. Economic Policy 13:115–162

Flandreau M, Ugolini S (2014) The Crisis of 1866. Graduate Institute of International and Development Studies Graduate Institute, Geneva Working Paper No. 10/2014

Flandreau M, Zumer F (2004) The Making of Global Finance 1880–1913. OECD, Paris

Folkerts-Landau D, Garber P (1993) The ECB: A Bank or a Monetary Policy Rule. In: Canzoneri M, Grilli V, Masson P (eds) Establishing a Central Bank: Issues in Europe and Lessons from the US. Cambridge University Press, Cambridge, pp 87–110

Foster E (1994) Movements of Exchange Rates and Interest rates under the Pre-World War I Gold Standard. Routledge, London

Frankel JA, Romer D (1998) The Endogeneity of the Optimum Currency Area Criteria. Economic Journal 108:1009–1025

Geanakoplos J (2010) The Leverage Cycle. NBER Macroeconomics Annual 25:1–65

Goldstein M, Woglom G (1992) Market-Based Fiscal Discipline in Monetary Unions: Evidence from the US Municipal Bond Market. In: Canzoneri M, Grilli V, Masson P (eds) Establishing a Central Bank: Issues in Europe and Lessons from the US. Cambridge University Press, Cambridge, pp 228–270

Hatton T, Williamson J (1998) The Age of Mass Migration: Causes and Economic Impact. Oxford University Press, Oxford

Hoag C (2006) The Atlantic Telegraph Cable and Capital Market Information Flows. J Econ History 66:342–353. https://doi.org/10.1017/S0022050706000143

Jauer J, Liebig T, Martin JP, Puhani PA (2018) Migration as an Adjustment Mechanism in the Crisis? A Comparison of Europe and the United States 2006–2016. IZA Discussion Paper No.11328, February

Jorda O, Schularick M, Taylor AM (2015) Betting the House. J Int Econ 96:S2–S18. https://doi.org/10.1016/j.jinteco.2014.12.011

Kindleberger C (1973) The World in Depression 1929–1939. University of California Press, Berkeley

Khoudour-Casteras D (2006) Exchange Rate Regimes and Labor Mobility: The Key Role of International Migration in the Adjustment Process under the Classical Gold Standard. Unpublished manuscript, Universidad Externado de Colombia

Lutz B, Follette G (2012) Fiscal Rules: What Does the American Experience Tell US? Finance and Economic Discussion Paper 2012–38, May 2012
Marques JC, Gois P (2016) Structural Emigration: The Revival of Portuguese Outflows. In: Lafleur JM, Stanek M (eds) South-North Migration of EU Citizens in Times of Crisis. Springer, Berlin, pp 65–82
Mundell R (1961) A Theory of Optimum Currency Areas. Am Econ Rev 51:657–665
Officer LH (2007) Between the Dollar-Sterling Gold Points: Exchange Rates. Cambridge University Press, Cambridge, Parity and Market Behavior
Panic M (1992) European Monetary Union: Lessons from the Classical Gold Standard. St. Martin's Press, New York
Phillips T (2011) Portuguese Migrants Seek a Slice of Brazil's Economic Boom. The Guardian, 22 December. Available online. www.theguardian.com/world/2011/dec/22/portuguese-migrants-brazil-economic-boom. Accessed on 29 Mar 2020
Reis R (2013) The Portuguese Slump and Crash and the Euro Crisis. Brookings Papers Economic Activity 1:143–193

European Macroeconomics

Part II is devoted to European issues but it also provides a narrative for the economic consequences of the 1974 revolution in Portugal, already evoked in Part I. Moreover, it bears explaining that Portugal in Europe was always seen by the honoree as being complementary to the country's leading role in the first wave of globalization. However, Portugal feared the second wave for reasons evoked in Part I, which draw on the work of his father, the historian Jorge Borges de Macedo (1921–1996). After the Second World War, performance was also mixed, as documented in many of the honoree's contributions, due to Portugal's inability to durably combine economic interdependence and mutual political responsiveness, notwithstanding NATO and OECD membership.

More recently, Portugal joined the Eurozone following the macroeconomic regime change of the early 1990s but delayed the implementation of required budgetary procedures and other structural reforms until the 2011–2014 bailout. While the jury is still out as to how successfully Portugal adapted to the third wave of globalization, the honoree has consistently affirmed his vision of Europe and Portugal, with the latter open to the world economy and firmly committed to the Community of Portuguese-speaking countries, which was established in 1996. This is particularly true for the academic and policy debates with each one of the contributors to this part, as well as a large part of the research that is detailed in the Appendix.

Part II begins with the contribution by Aníbal Cavaco Silva, who discusses the absence of a macro stabilization function for the Eurozone. The author is well placed to broach this topic since he was Prime minister at the time of the Maastricht treaty and President of the Republic during the Eurozone sovereign debt crisis. It was under his premiership that Jorge Braga de Macedo, then the Minister of Finance, signed the Maastricht Treaty on behalf of Portugal, as the contributor points out. Before that time, they had been colleagues at the Catholic and Nova Universities in the early 1970s. The contribution's argument is that EMU remains highly vulnerable to shocks without some fiscal risk sharing. While EU technical debates recognize this desideratum, the same cannot be said about politics across member states. Since history reveals that EU leaders act decisively when confronted with a crisis, the next recession may well see them establish such function in the Eurozone.

Along the same lines, the second contribution by Paul De Grauwe advocates the creation of a Eurozone budget. During crises, the inherent instability of the sovereign bond markets in a monetary union becomes systemic and no amount of financial engineering can stabilize an otherwise unstable system. The willingness of the European Central Bank to provide liquidity in the Eurozone sovereign bond markets during times of crisis (through the Outright Monetary Transactions program, say) will be counterproductive because this program is loaded with austerity conditions. Hence the need for a Eurozone budget.

Jürgen von Hagen, who visited Portugal's parliament in 1994 and subsequently served on the board of the Fiscal Council, takes the opposing view in the third contribution. After reviewing the development of the EMU fiscal framework, he argues that transfers dealing with asymmetric shocks are less important than commonly argued because fiscal discipline is the critical issue. Since a debt union with decentralized authority is not sustainable, choosing between fiscal union and fiscal freedom is a decision between collective coercion combined with individual safety, on the one hand, and the ability to choose one's own best policies combined with individual responsibility, on the other.

The contribution by Annette Bongardt and Francisco Torres deals with the topic of variable geometry. This topic had been pursued previously by the honoree in academic and political collaboration with the second co-author, as well as at the Ministry of Finance and the European Affairs Committee in the Portuguese Parliament. This contribution argues that (treaty-based) variable geometry or differentiated integration in the core EU institutions is not sustainable after the Eurozone crisis and Brexit. The rationale is that EMU has in the meantime become the (economic and political) core of the Union and of the integration process. Accommodating member states' preferences that are too divergent from the Union's by means of more institutional flexibility, at the expense of the objective of an evercloser union, would entail keeping the EU as an intergovernmental organization without political ambition. Therefore, all EU countries should be in EMU and Schengen, or leave the Union and opt instead for membership in the European Economic Area or a Free Trade Agreement.

The fifth contribution, by António Pinto Barbosa and Luís Catela Nunes, has the intriguing title of "The Peculiar First Semester of 2012" and was recently presented at the Lisbon Academy of Sciences by the first co-author. It is also worth recalling that Luís Catela Nunes co-authored several papers with the honoree about the transition from Portuguese escudo to euro, one of which drawing on foreign exchange data provided by Luís Campos e Cunha, then vice governor of the Bank of Portugal, who wrote a personal tribute for this volume. Using the case of Portugal, this contribution provides evidence on an often-neglected positive effect of the austerity packages implemented during the Eurozone crisis. While the Keynesian view stressing the contractionary effect on the economy is well documented in the deterioration of basic macroeconomic indicators, the austerity package also provided an important and less often acknowledged ingredient to the economy's recovery, namely an increase in investors' confidence, as expressed by a sustained decline of the yields in financial markets.

In the sixth contribution, Miguel Lebre de Freitas and Miguel Faria e Castro revisit a small open economy approach to the Portuguese economy, which the first co-author attempted to apply in Belarus in the 1990s in collaboration with the honoree. The authors estimate sequences of real exchange rates that are consistent with internal and external balance and use these estimates to study the evolution of the Portuguese economy during the 1971–2017 period. They find that after a period of prolonged appreciation, the real exchange rate fell below its equilibrium level during the recent 2011–2015 adjustment phase, driven both by declining nominal wages and improvements in the terms of trade.

Last but not least, Paul Krugman states in the seventh contribution, and with his usual elegance, that "Portugal can claim much of the credit for the gratifying resilience of its late commitment to democracy, avoiding economic catastrophe." With "generally responsible policies," the disappointments stem from the euro's structural flaws and, since the 1980s, the underlying forces causing trouble for peripheral regions in all advanced economies. To be sure, Portugal achieved only limited convergence on wealthier European nations and is still vulnerable to macroeconomic crisis. Nonetheless, Nobel Krugman argues that it has to be considered a major success story relative to the grim prospects in 1975, in the wake of the revolution mentioned in the first sentence of this Foreword.

Miguel Rocha de Sousa

A Macro-stabilization Function for the Euro Area

Aníbal Cavaco Silva

Abstract This chapter explores an institutional challenge still facing the European Monetary Union (EMU) after the Eurozone sovereign debt crisis. One of these is the absence of a centralized macroeconomic stabilization function to deal with possible asymmetrical shocks, in addition to the common monetary policy. Indeed, the EMU remains highly vulnerable to shocks without some fiscal risk sharing. To be sure, a centralized fiscal stabilization implies a common budget and, hence, some risk sharing. However, it also makes future economic crises less likely and relieves the pressure on the common monetary policy, among other advantages. While the European Union (EU) technical debate recognizes this desideratum, the same cannot be said for the political debate across EU Member States. However, history has taught us that EU leaders act decisively when confronted with a crisis. Thus, the next recession may see them accept and establish a macro-stabilization function for the Euro area.

Keywords Eurozone · Macroeconomic stabilization function · Policy coordination · Political feasibility · Portugal

1 The European Reaction to the Sovereign Debt Crisis

The international financial crisis that began in the USA in 2007–2008 led the EU into a severe recession—the deepest since World War II. The ensuing sovereign debt crisis raised questions about the EU's stability and the Euro's irreversibility. Indeed, the two crises made it clear that the economic and monetary union (EMU), established in Maastricht by the Treaty of the EU in 1992, was an unfinished endeavor.[1]

In order to stabilize the financial situation and preserve the integrity of the Euro area, the European political leaders adopted an important set of measures aimed at reinforcing the EMU's financial, budgetary, and economic pillars.

[1] The Minister of Finance, Jorge Braga de Macedo, signed the Treaty on behalf of Portugal.

A. Cavaco Silva (✉)
Gabinete do Sacramento, Convento do Sacramento, Lisbon, Portugal
e-mail: geral@gabinetesacramento.pt

L. Brites Pereira et al. (eds.), *Economic Globalization and Governance*,
https://doi.org/10.1007/978-3-030-53265-9_8

The European Stability Mechanism was created to support countries facing a situation of financial emergency and lacking access to the foreign-debt market. It was based on the concession of loans coupled with the imposition of economic policy conditionality.

The fiscal discipline rules, and mechanisms of supervision and coordination of Member States' economic policies, were improved and strengthened, both in their preventive and corrective functions. For this purpose, the so-called *six-pack* and *two-pack* were approved, as well as the Treaty on Stability, Coordination and Governance in the EMU, which came into force in January 2013.

Regarding the procedural framework of the European economic and budgetary policy, known as the "European Semester," Member States were required to detail their fiscal stability and economic reform plans for the next three years, and submit them to the European Commission and the Economic and Financial Affairs Council (ECOFIN) in April. Governments were also obliged to submit their budget proposals each October, before the approval by national parliaments.

In the second half of 2012, after a series of banking crises in several countries such as Ireland and Spain, the decision was taken to create the Banking Union with three pillars, not yet totally implemented, namely: a Single Supervisory Mechanism, a Single Resolution Mechanism, and a European Deposit Insurance Scheme.

In addition, the European Central Bank (ECB) followed the lead of the central banks of the USA, Japan, and England and adopted a more active stance. In particular, it pursued a series of non-conventional monetary policy measures and also acted like a lender of last resort.

These were, undoubtedly, correct political decisions that significantly increased the degree of risk sharing across Member States. The EMU project showed itself to be strong and the analysts that predicted the Euro area's disintegration were proved wrong.

However, some shortcomings in the EMU's initial architecture remain. One of the most important of these is the absence of a centralized macroeconomic stabilization function beyond the single monetary policy, as I underlined in a recently published essay (Silva 2018). The correction of this shortcoming, though essential for reinforcing the resilience of the Euro area, has been facing great difficulties in the political debate to date.[2]

The inexistence of a central fiscal capacity in the EU is particularly relevant for two reasons: one, the fact that countries in the Euro area have lost control of their monetary and exchange rate instruments, having transferred those to the ECB; second, the fact that budgetary policy of these countries is subject to strong restrictions by the Treaty of the EU, the Stability and Growth Pact and the Treaty on Stability, Coordination and Governance in the EMU.

These constraints place a large burden on monetary policy to mitigate economic recessions and on national fiscal policies to stabilize external shocks affecting a country. In face of a decline in aggregate demand, a country may lack sufficient

[2]Eyraud et al. (2018) provide evidence that political factors created policy distortions and have negatively affected fiscal outcomes in the Euro area between 1999 and 2015.

economic policy space to achieve the adequate anticyclical adjustments without violating the European rules of fiscal discipline, which may have negative spillovers on other EMU members. Such situations need not only arise from inappropriate policies of Member States.

It is true that supranational rules for fiscal discipline are a beneficial means of pressuring Member States to pursue appropriate policies. However, one has to recognize that there is a cost resulting from countries losing flexibility when seeking to stabilize their economies through fiscal adjustments in case of exogenous shocks. To be sure, this cost justifies an offsetting European intervention.

This is particularly true in the case of negative production and employment shocks that afflict one member state specifically—the so-called asymmetrical shocks. It is also true in the case of significant economic recessions like the ones that occurred during 2009 and 2012 in the Euro area.

In the context of the EMU, Portugal—a medium size country with a productive structure showing some vulnerability and very dependent on oil, natural gas and food imports—has always defended the creation of a EU transfer mechanism to offset the loss of national monetary and exchange rate policies, thus helping countries to smooth out asymmetric shocks, a problem that the single monetary policy obviously cannot solve. Moreover, it is a solution in line with Robert Mundell's theory of optimum currency areas (Mundell 1961).

The economic recession in Spain during 2012–2013 was a true asymmetrical shock for Portugal, which coincided with the Financial Assistance Program negotiated with the EU, the ECB, and the International Monetary Fund (IMF). Portuguese exports to Spain represent 25% of total exports, something that has no comparison with any other country in the EU. In 2012, Portuguese GDP fell by 4% while the export of goods and services to Spain fell by 4.5% in nominal terms.

2 The Insufficient Coordination of National Economic Policies

It is through the coordination of national fiscal policies that European authorities have tried to compensate the absence of a macro-stabilization function over the business cycle, and as a response to possible asymmetrical shocks.

The relevance of this coordination was recognized by the Delors Report (1989) on EMU in the European Community:

> In particular, uncoordinated and divergent national budgetary policies would undermine monetary stability and generate imbalances in the real and financial sectors of the Community. Moreover, the fact that the centrally managed Community budget is likely to remain a very small part of total public sector spending and that much of this budget will not be available for cyclical adjustments will mean that the task of setting a Community-wide fiscal policy stance will have to be performed through the coordination of national budgetary policies. Without such coordination it would be impossible for the Community as a whole to establish a fiscal/monetary policy mix appropriate for the preservation of internal balance, or for the

> Community to play its part in the international adjustment process. Monetary policy alone cannot be expected to perform these functions. Delors Report (1989, pp 19–20)

In this sense, the Maastricht Treaty established that Member States should consider their economic policies as a matter of common interest, and that the necessary coordination should take place within the Council based on the approval of general guidelines for Member States' economic policies.

Despite measures taken to reinforce the supervision of economic and budget plans as a result of the sovereign debt crisis, and also the coordination of national economic policies, these continue to be "clearly insufficient to ensure coherent and consistent national policies and an aggregate budgetary stance of the Eurozone that could be placed in parallel with the single monetary policy defined by the ECB in order to favor macroeconomic stability in the area as a whole" (Silva 2018).

While on the monetary side there is a single policy centralized at the ECB, on the fiscal side there are nineteen separate policies mostly reflecting each Member States' different circumstances and priorities. Negotiations envisaging an agreement on a coordinated Euro area fiscal initiative with a stabilization purpose will not be easy. On the one hand, differences will persist as to how to read the global and European economic situation, as well as differences on the best way to deal with crises. On the other, the adjustments in national budgets will also be difficult and slow because budgetary institutions and procedures are very different across countries.

An example of coordination insufficiency is evident in the systematic refusal of Germany—a country with recurrent trade surpluses—to undertake expansionary economic measures as means to compensate contractionary policies in countries with an excessive deficit situation.

The same can be said about the Commission and Council's attempt to fight the strong economic recession that hit the UE at the end of 2008 by encouraging expansionary fiscal policies in the Member States. This European incentive did not take into account the different wiggle room that countries had to raise their public spending. As a result, it contributed to aggravate the unsustainability of public finances in Greece, Ireland, and Portugal, thus making their financial assistance programs inevitable.

The coordination of Member States' economic policies also failed during the double dip in the Euro area economic growth in 2012–2013. While Ireland, Greece, Spain, and Portugal were forced to implement contractionary fiscal policies to correct their economic imbalances, Germany, The Netherlands, and Austria also pursued the same path even though these countries had a margin to adopt expansionary policies. The result was a sharp procyclical fiscal contraction that exacerbated the downturn in the Eurozone.

The sovereign debt crisis clearly highlighted the need to endow the EMU with a central stabilization function over the economic cycle and in the event of asymmetrical shocks. This would allow authorities to determine the appropriate combination between fiscal and monetary policies that is compatible with non-inflationary economic growth and a high level of employment. Within the context of the EMU, the question of the appropriate policy mix does not arise at the level of each individual country but rather at the level of the nineteen Member States as a whole.

Indeed, several authors have emphasized that the EMU will remain highly vulnerable to shocks without adding some degree of fiscal risk sharing (see Berger et al. 2018).

3 A Euro Area Macroeconomic Stabilization Budget

A strong and sustainable EMU requires a macroeconomic stabilization budget, as recognized at a technical level by the European institutions.

A fiscal stabilization policy in the Euro area, alongside a more effective institutional coordination mechanism of national economic policies, will help to define a better mix between fiscal and monetary policies capable of dealing with Euro area-wide shocks. It is a solution that reduces the probability of future economic crises, and that better guarantees a balance between the interests of individual Member States and the Euro area as a whole.

In addition, it would prevent the pressure to rely solely on the common monetary policy in order to ensure the EU's macroeconomic stabilization. As is the case today, monetary policy may have little room to give an adequate response because it has been used so intensely as a result of the sovereign debt crisis, and so is effectively constrained at its lower bound.

The EMU's intrinsic problem of having a single monetary policy on one side, and nineteen fiscal policies on the other, would be thus mitigated. Moreover, the macroeconomic needs of the Euro area as a whole would thereby be taken into due account.

A European fiscal stabilization capacity, and the risk sharing that it implies, is also essential to make the EU a stronger and more influential player in the international scene. This would also help the EU to compete with the USA and China in many strategic areas pertaining to our future while also reinforcing the Euro as a global currency. This desideratum is particularly important in an environment of widespread uncertainty and geopolitical tension, as highlighted by President Emmanuel Macron in his speech at the Sorbonne in September 2017.[3]

The existence of a central stabilization function is essential to prevent economic and political fragmentation among Member States and to mitigate contagion risks, especially as the severity of economic downturns may differ across Euro area countries characterized by different economic structures and dissimilar fiscal policy space.

A genuine EMU macro-stabilization capacity naturally requires a common budget for the Euro area to mitigate economic shocks, as espoused by the former President of

---

[3]President Macron stated in his speech: "Only the Eurozone with a strong and international currency can provide Europe with the framework of a major economic power" (Macron 2017).

the ECB, Mario Draghi,[4] or a specific budget line within the EU budget, as defended by the former President of the EU Commission, Jean-Claude Juncker.[5]

Such a budget would support Euro area countries when pursuing public investments and would offset costs arising from Member States' provision of unemployment benefits.

The creation of a stabilization fund, financed by Euro area Member States in times of economic growth, seems to be the most economically adequate and possibly the more politically acceptable way to finance such a budget. This fund would make transfers to countries in need during bad times, thereby operating as countercyclical fiscal policy. Only in extraordinary situations would the fund be allowed to borrow from the market.[6]

To help countries to smooth out the effects of idiosyncratic shocks or of a global recession, transfers would take place almost automatically. Ideally, this should depend on an easily observable threshold cyclical indicator, like a negative unemployment rate deviation from the trend, in order to reduce the scope for disagreements and discretion. Country transfers would complement the functioning of national automatic stabilizers.

To avoid delays, the question of the degree of flexibility left open to countries when choosing how to spend incoming transfers from the stabilization fund should be resolved beforehand. However, large multiplier expenditures should be prioritized to increase the degree of stabilization provided.

A recent IMF analysis refers that the buildup of assets during typical good times, amounting to an annual contribution of 0.35% of GDP, would have been sufficient to finance a large part of the automatic stabilizers' operation in past Euro area recessions (Arnold et al. 2018).

To avoid the moral hazard problems, the creation of a centralized European fiscal capacity must be accompanied by reinforced supervisory mechanisms and European intervention in national economic and budget policy decisions. This reinforcement will prevent deviations from fiscal discipline rules and persistent delays of reforms aimed at improving competitiveness, as well as ensuring sound fiscal policy making at the national level. It is vital that countries are dissuaded from running less sustainable fiscal rules as a result of knowing that they will receive support from the Euro budget when faced with external shocks.

A centralized macroeconomic stabilization function should provide an *ex-ante* incentive for fiscal discipline by conditioning support in bad times on past compliance with the fiscal rules. Only then will it be possible to avoid suspicion by some Member

[4] In an interview with the Financial Times, Mario Draghi declared that: "To have a stronger EMU, we need a common Eurozone budget" (Draghi 2019).

[5] A Eurozone budget has recently been linked to the proposal of a so-called Minister of Finance and Economy for the Euro area (European Commission 2018).

[6] Other alternatives that have been suggested are less convincing: national contributions based on a percentage of gross national product (GDP) or value-added tax; revenues from specific taxes on consumption, fees, or taxes on companies; a common unemployment insurance fund that would make transfers to unemployed persons; and, a borrowing-lending scheme in which a central entity would borrow from the market at low costs and would lend on to Member States.

States that they will be paying for the costs of wrong political decisions made by other states. Only then will it be possible to avoid the feeling that it is a risk sharing system that creates permanent transfers from more to less developed countries. Fiscal discipline rules in the Growth and Stability Pact should be simplified to ensure transparency and make their enforcement more automatic (Arnold et al. 2018).

Politically it will not be easy to effectively discourage moral hazard while providing fiscal risk sharing as it requires rules that bind national policy-makers.[7] Steps in this direction will raise the question of more democratic accountability of European institutions.

4 The Problem of Political Feasibility

The technical debate that has been made at the European institutions has recognized the importance of endowing the EMU with a fiscal capacity that ensures macroeconomic stabilization, and this has also been favored by European central banks. However, the same cannot be said for the political debate across the different Member States.

At the EU level, the so-called Five Presidents' report on "Completing Europe's Economic and Monetary Union" includes a proposal to reinforce the EMU's foundations through the creation of a Euro area-wide fiscal stabilization function by 2025 at the latest. The report's authors emphasize that all mature monetary unions have put a common macroeconomic stabilization function in place to better deal with shocks that cannot be managed alone at the national level (European Commission 2015).

The report's proposals were later developed and expanded in a reflection paper that was signed by the European Commission Vice-President responsible for the Euro, as well as the Commissioner responsible for Economic and Financial Affairs (European Commission 2017). In this paper, some of the guiding principles of a Euro area macro-stabilization function, possible objectives, and financing aspects are laid out in more detail, thereby contributing toward the debate on how this new fiscal capacity is to be conceived.

At a political level, meanwhile, the debate regarding the EMU's completion, particularly the creation of a macro-stabilization function, has been overshadowed by the attention that European leaders were forced to direct to other questions, such as migration, Brexit, and Italy's budgetary crisis.

The Eurogroup meeting of December 2018 discussed the Commission's proposal to establish a new budgetary instrument for convergence, competitiveness, and stabilization in the EMU, which aimed to further strengthen the Euro area's resilience. Regarding the Budgetary Instrument for Convergence and Competitiveness (BICC), the ministers reached a common view but they did not agree on the need and design

[7]The more fiscal risk sharing is put in place and the greater the concern for moral hazard, the more relevant rules enforced by the center will become (Berger et al. 2018).

of a stabilization function. The same position was adopted some days later at the Euro Summit meeting.

Since then, the Eurogroup's discussions have been confined to the main features of the BICC within the Euro area, which would support both structural reforms and public investment. An agreement was reached on the design of this instrument in the Euro Summit of June 2019, but not on the appropriate source of financing.

Such an instrument differs from the creation of a fiscal stabilization capacity for the Euro area. It is not a European response either to asymmetric or to Euro area-wide shocks. The BICC will be part of the EU budget, and will be delivered in the form of grants to enable Member States' key reforms and public investment projects that reflect the strategic guidance for Euro area convergence, as defined by the Euro Summit and Eurogroup (Council of the EU 2019).

Will the creation of the BICC make it more likely to approve a true European macro-stabilization capacity in future? It is not possible to answer this question at present because the political debate at the Council of Heads of State and Government is very much influenced by the Member States' internal politics.

Nonetheless, and from a stabilization perspective, the creation of a convergence instrument between Member States is undoubtedly a positive step provided it has an adequate dimension. It cannot, however, replace the creation of a specific macro-stabilization capacity in the Euro area.

In addition to politically strengthening of the Union, convergence makes the economic structures of lesser developed Member States stronger, thus reducing their vulnerability to asymmetric economic shocks.

On the other hand, convergence reduces cyclical divergence between Member States in times of recession, while also favoring the leveling of productive structures. This will allow a single monetary policy to be more efficient as a stabilization instrument for the Euro area as a whole. Convergence will therefore reduce the size of a Euro macroeconomic stabilization budget.

In any case, convergence will always be a long-term trend even with the creation of a European budgetary instrument. It is not implausible that a Euro area country or region will be affected by negative external shocks in a different manner from other countries or regions. A common stabilization function should not be viewed by the European leaders just as the culmination of a convergence process. Politically, it should be preceded by the completion of the banking union.

It is very unlikely that the instrument for convergence and competitiveness will be operating before 2021. The Eurogroup meeting of October 2019 reached an agreement on some elements of governance and allocation of the funds for the new Euro area budgetary instrument. However, the appropriate financing solutions and instrument's size remain undefined, awaiting the negotiations of the Heads of State and Government in the context of the EU budget.

The political debate on the creation of an instrument that provides meaningful macroeconomic stabilization during a downturn will certainly be more difficult than that on the instrument for convergence, given the legal, technical, and operational problems that it entails. The enlargement of shared competencies and decisions over national budgetary matters to prevent moral hazard will certainly lead to a very complicated discussion. Therefore, it is only with some optimism that we can anticipate such an instrument being created and operational before 2025, the date set out in the Five Presidents' report.

History has taught us that EU leaders act decisively when they are confronted with a crisis, however. Thus, it is entirely possible that we shall have to wait for the next recession to convince them that the creation of a macro-stabilization function is critical to making the EMU much more resilient to adverse shocks.

References

Arnold N, Barkbu B, Ture E, Wang H, Yao J (2018) A Central Fiscal Stabilization Capacity for the Euro Area. IMF Staff Discussion Notes 18/03

Berger H, Dell'Ariccia G, Obstfeld M (2018) Revisiting the Economic Case for Fiscal Union in the Euro Area. IMF Departmental Paper 18/03

Council of the European Union (2019) Term Sheet on the Budgetary Instrument for Convergence and Competitiveness. Press Release. Available online. www.consilium.europa.eu/en/press/press-releases/2019/06/14/term-sheet-on-the-budgetary-instrument-for-convergence-and-competitiveness/. Accessed 17 Nov 2019

Delors Report (1989) Report on Economic and Monetary Union in the European Community. Committee for the Study of Economic and Monetary Union. Available online. www.ecb.europa.eu/ecb/access_to_documents/archives/delors/html/index.en.html. Accessed 17 Nov 2019

Draghi M (2019) Mario Draghi declares victory in battle over the euro. Interview with L. Barber and C. Jones, Financial Times, Frankfurt, 30 September. Available online. www.ft.com/content/b59a4a04-9b26-11e9-9c06-a4640c9feebb. Accessed 17 Nov 2019

European Commission (2015) Completing Europe's Economic and Monetary Union. Report by Jean-Claude Juncker in close cooperation with Donald Tusk, Jeroen Dijsselbloem, Mario Draghi and Martin Schulz. Available online. https://ec.europa.eu/commission/five-presidents-report_en. Accessed 17 Nov 2019

European Commission (2017) The Deepening of the Economic and Monetary Union. Reflection Paper. Available online. https://ec.europa.eu/commission/publications/reflection-paper-deepening-economic-and-monetary-union_en. Accessed 17 Nov 2019

European Commission (2018) A European Minister of Economy and Finance. Directorate-General for Economic and Financial Affairs. Available online. https://op.europa.eu/en/publication-detail/-/publication/f9afe657-ff3a-11e7-b8f5%E2%80%9301aa75ed71a1. Accessed 17 Nov 2019

Eyraud L, Gaspar V, Poghosyan T (2017) Fiscal Politics in the Euro Area. IMF Working Paper 17/18

Macron E (2017) Initiative pour l'Europe—Discours d'Emmanuel Macron pour une Europe souveraine, unie, démocratique. Sorbonne University, Paris, 26 September. Available online. www.elysee.fr/emmanuel-macron/2017/09/26/initiative-pour-l-europe-discours-d-emmanuel-macron-pour-une-europe-souveraine-unie-democratique. Accessed 17 Nov 2019

Mundell RA (1961) A theory of optimum currency areas. Am Econ Rev 51(4):657–665

Silva AC (2018) Portugal and the Future of the European Union. Brown J World Affairs XXIV(II):7–22

Aníbal Cavaco Silva served as President of Portugal from 2006–2016. Previously, he was Prime Minister of Portugal from 1985–1995. He also served as Professor of Public Economics at the Nova University of Lisbon and at the Portuguese Catholic University.

Toward a Sustainable Eurozone

Paul De Grauwe and Yuemei Ji

Abstract We argue that the various proposals aimed at stabilizing the Eurozone using financial engineering do not eliminate the inherent instability of the sovereign bond markets in a monetary union. During crises, this instability becomes systemic and no amount of financial engineering can stabilize an otherwise unstable system. The real stabilization of the Eurozone entails two mechanisms. The first is the willingness of the European Central Bank (ECB) to provide liquidity in the Eurozone sovereign bond markets during times of crisis. The ECB has set up its Outright Monetary Transactions (OMT) program to do this. However, OMT is loaded with austerity conditions, which will be counterproductive when used during recessions, which is when crises generally occur. That is why a second mechanism is necessary, which consists in creating a Eurozone budget.

Keywords Eurozone · Fiscal union · Economic and monetary union · Lender of last resort · Optimum currency areas

1 Introduction: Booms and Busts in the Eurozone

It is well-known that monetary unions cannot easily deal with asymmetric shocks (Mundell 1961). The surprising thing is that the nature of the asymmetric shocks that hit the Eurozone has been quite different from the traditional asymmetric shocks analyzed in the optimum currency area (OCA) literature. In fact, business cycles in the Eurozone have been relatively well synchronized, as shown in Fig. 1.

We observe that most Eurozone countries were booming during 2000–2007 and experienced a downturn since then. If there was asymmetry, it was in the amplitudes of the same cycle. Some countries (Ireland, Spain, Greece) experienced a very strong

P. De Grauwe (✉)
London School of Economics and Political Science, London, UK
e-mail: p.c.de-grauwe@lse.ac.uk

Y. Ji
School of Slavonic & East European Studies, University College London, London, UK
e-mail: yuemei.ji@ucl.ac.uk

L. Brites Pereira et al. (eds.), *Economic Globalization and Governance*,
https://doi.org/10.1007/978-3-030-53265-9_9

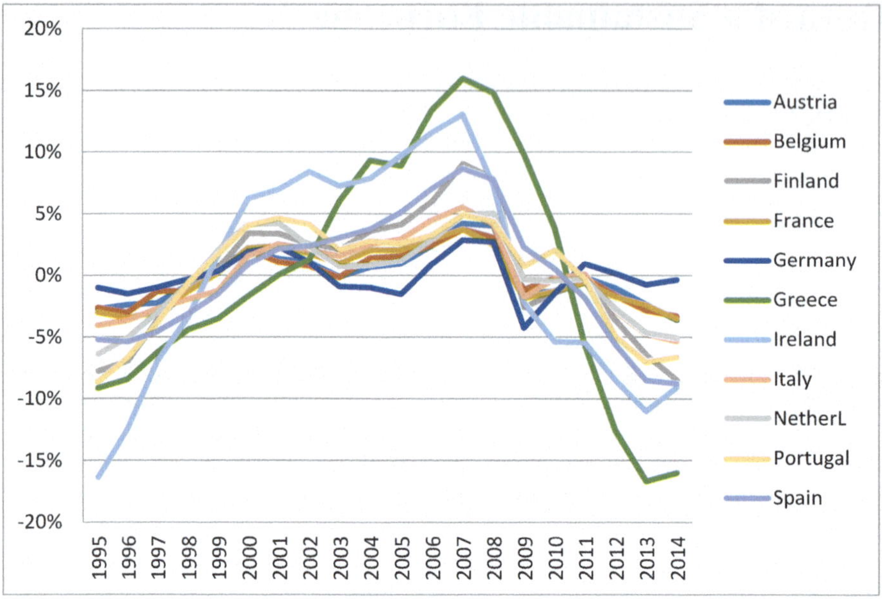

Fig. 1 Business cycle component of GDP. Note: the business component is obtained by applying a HP-filter to observed GDP (*Source* Eurostat)

boom and a deep and protracted recession afterwards. Other countries (Belgium, Germany, France, Italy, Netherlands) experienced a much more modest period of booming conditions followed by less intense recessions. Germany stands out as having experienced booms and busts with the lowest amplitude.

If there is asymmetry in the Eurozone business cycle movements, it is in the amplitude of these cycles. In the group experiencing the highest amplitudes, this asymmetry led to a situation in which countries first experienced an unsustainable boom, often accompanied by asset price bubbles, and were hit very hard with deep recessions when the crash came, leading to an explosion of government debt.

The problem with the monetary union lies in the fact that it had great difficulties in dealing with the asymmetric occurrence of such boom-bust scenarios, for two reasons. First, the European monetary union lacks a mechanism that can deal with boom-bust scenarios characterized by different amplitudes. These lead to divergent developments with large external imbalances, where some countries built up current account deficits and other countries surpluses.

When these imbalances had to be redressed, it appeared that the mechanisms to redress these in the Eurozone ("internal devaluations") are very costly in terms of growth and employment, leading to social and political upheavals. Countries that have their own currency and that are faced with such imbalances can devalue or revalue their currencies. In a monetary union, countries facing external deficits are forced into intense expenditure-reducing policies (austerity) that inevitably lead to rising unemployment and much hardship to millions of people. This problem has been recognized by the economists that pioneered the theory of optimal currency areas (Kenen 1969; McKinnon 1963; Mundell 1961).

In Figs. 2, and 3, we show one dimension of these imbalances. Figure 2 shows the evolution of relative unit labor costs in periphery countries. It shows how these countries experienced a massive reduction in competitiveness (increase in relative unit labor costs) produced by unsustainable booms that tended to raise prices and wages relative to other member countries. After the crash, they were forced to adjust with large internal devaluations. These introduced strong deflationary forces leading to deep recessions and large increases in unemployment. From Fig. 3, we observe that the core countries did not lose competitiveness during the boom years. After the crash, they also did not reflate their economies which would have led to internal revaluations. As a result, the whole of adjustment costs was borne by periphery (deficit) countries and a net deflationary dynamic was imposed on the system as a whole.

That is when the Eurozone's second problem arose. As stressed by De Grauwe (2011), the Eurozone's fragility arises from the fact that member countries of the monetary union issue debt in a currency that they have no control over. As a result, these countries' governments can no longer guarantee that the cash will always be available to roll over government debt. In turn, this lack of guarantee provided by Eurozone governments can trigger self-fulfilling liquidity crises (a

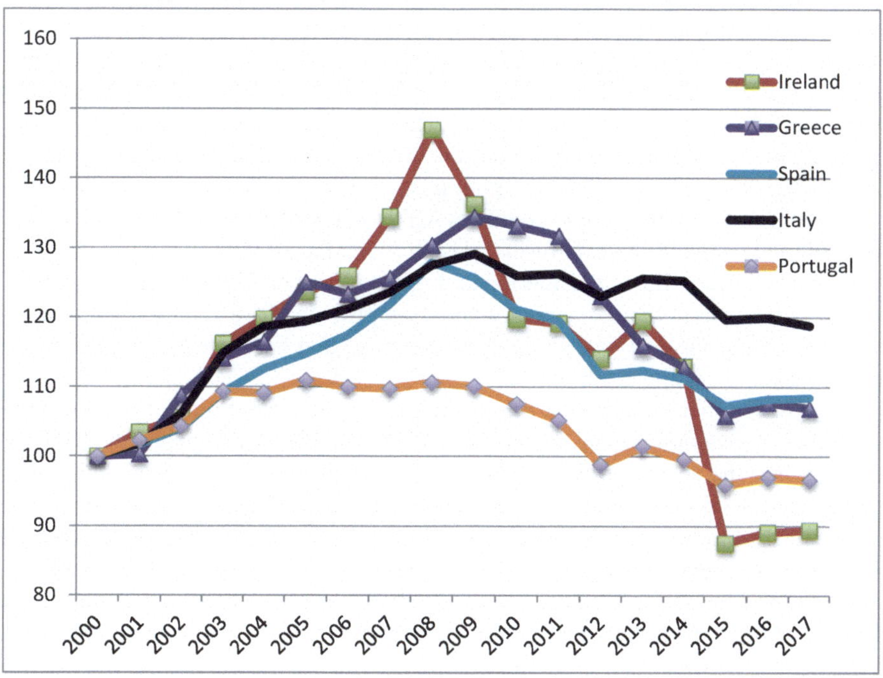

Fig. 2 Relative unit labor costs in periphery Eurozone (2000 = 100) (*Source* Eurostat)

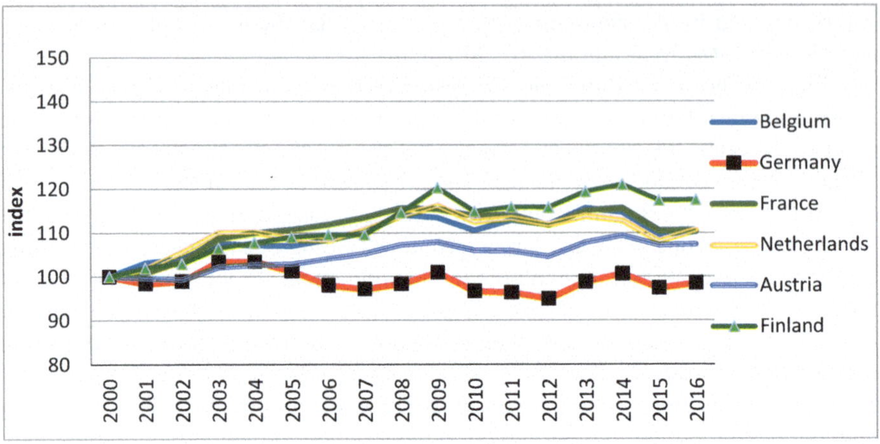

Fig. 3 Relative unit labor costs in core Eurozone (2000 = 100) (*Source* European Commission, AMECO)

sudden stop) that can degenerate into solvency problems. When this occurs, it leads to a massive outflow of liquidity from problem countries, making it impossible for their governments to fund the rollover of their debt at reasonable interest rates.

This dynamic can force countries into a bad equilibrium characterized by increasing interest rates that trigger excessive austerity measures, which in turn lead to a deflationary spiral that aggravates the fiscal crisis (De Grauwe 2011 and De Grauwe and Ji 2013). This is exactly what happened during the 2010–2012 sovereign debt crisis. Markets singled out these countries, leading to massive capital outflows from the first group of countries and into the second one. The whole of the Eurozone was destabilized. This problem risks popping up each time the Eurozone is pushed into a recession, and each time some countries will be hit harder than others. As a result, large internal capital flows risk further destabilizing the system.

This episode also illustrated how unstable government bond markets in a monetary union can become in the absence of a backstop provided by a central bank. This is illustrated in the surge of spreads in those countries that had been hit more severely by the crash.

The absence of a backstop for the sovereign in a monetary union also creates the possibility of generating a "deadly embrace" between the sovereign and the banking sector. When the sovereign is pushed into a bad equilibrium, it is very likely that the domestic banks will experience solvency problems because they are the major holders of sovereign bonds. A hellish doom loop is set in motion where the sovereign debt crisis engenders a banking crisis. The reverse causality is equally possible, as the Irish crisis has demonstrated: a domestic banking crisis forces the sovereign to step in to save the banking system. This typically requires the government to take on more debt thereby creating a risk of insolvency.

2 Redesigning the Eurozone

We identified two problems of the Eurozone. The first one arises from the fact that it has poor instruments to deal with asymmetric shocks. We call this the OCA-problem. The second problem arises from the instability of government bond markets in the Eurozone. We discuss next the way in which we can deal with the two problems.

2.1 How to Deal with the OCA Problem?

The standard response derived from the OCA theory is that member countries of a monetary union should undertake structural reforms so as to make their labor and product markets more flexible. By increasing flexibility through structural reforms, the costs of adjustments to asymmetric shocks can be reduced and the Eurozone can become an optimal currency area. This has been a very influential idea and has led Eurozone countries into programs of structural reforms.

It is often forgotten that although the theoretical arguments in favor of flexibility are strong, the fine print of flexibility is often harsh. It implies wage cuts, less unemployment benefits, lower minimum wages, easier firing. Many people hit by structural reforms, resist and turn to parties that promise another way to deal with the problem, including an exit from the Eurozone. From an economic point of view, flexibility is the solution. From a social and political point of view, flexibility can become a problem. Stressing flexibility too often as the way out of the conundrum risks creating enemies of the monetary union which, as time moves on, leads to an increasing political momentum in favor of exiting the union.

The traditional OCA-analysis assumes that asymmetric shocks are typically permanent and structural in nature (a change in preferences, a supply-side shock). We have found, however, that most of the shocks hitting the Eurozone have been temporary and the result of a boom-bust scenario. They are also typically demand-side shocks. In De Grauwe and Ji (2017), we provided a further discussion that business cycle shocks, albeit with different amplitudes, have been the dominant forces.

The implications of this finding for Eurozone governance, namely the overwhelming importance of the cyclical and temporary component of output growth, is that efforts at stabilizing the business cycle should be strengthened relative to those made to impose structural reforms. We are not implying that structural reforms are unnecessary but rather that efforts at creating mechanisms aimed at stabilizing the Eurozone business cycles should be strengthened.

Inter-country versus inter-temporal smoothing There have been many proposals made to create a fiscal space at the Eurozone level in the form of a common unemployment insurance system (e.g., Alcidi and Thirion 2015; Beblavy et al. 2015; Benassy-Quéré et al. 2018; Enderlein et al. 2012).[1]

Such an insurance system has both an inter-country and inter-temporal insurance dimension. It is easier to deal with the inter-country dimension, which has also received more attention in the past. When one country experiences a recession, and thus increasing unemployment, the other country experiences a boom, and declining unemployment. This facilitates the workings of the common unemployment insurance system. The booming country transfers resources to the country in a recession and thereby smoothens the business cycles in both countries. Such a system encounters relatively few technical and political problems.

However, problems arise when business cycles in the different member countries are relatively well synchronized but with very different amplitudes. In this case, most countries will tend to experience a recession at about the same time but the recession will be mild in some countries while very intense in others. This creates both an economic and a political problem. First, countries with a mild recession are asked to transfer resources to countries experiencing a stronger recession. This tends to reduce the recession's intensity in the latter country at the expense of making it more intense in the former. It is not clear that this is welfare improving. Second, it is likely to create important political problems in the country which is asked to transfer resources when its economy is not doing well.

The previous analysis suggests that common unemployment insurance schemes should put sufficient emphasis on smoothing over time. This can be achieved by allowing the common unemployment insurance scheme to accumulate deficits and surpluses over time. The fiscal rule that could be imposed is that the insurance scheme balances over the business cycle.

In principle, inter-temporal smoothing could be done at the national level, by allowing the national budgets to do the job. However, the large differences in amplitude of business cycle movements make a purely national approach problematic, as it leads to large differences in budget deficits and debt accumulation between countries. These differences quickly spillover into financial markets when countries that are hit very hard by a decline in output are subject to sudden stops and liquidity crises. This is likely to force them to switch off the automatic stabilizers in their national budgets (De Grauwe and Ji 2017). In addition, these liquidity outflows are inflows in other countries in the monetary union, typically those that are hit least by the recession.[2] The latter's economic conditions improve at the expense of the former. The stabilization of common business shocks with different amplitudes at the national level makes the system unstable.

[1]There is an older literature making similar proposals, namely Hammond and von Hagen (1993), Italianer and Vanheukelen (1993), and Mélitz and Vori(1993).

[2]This is confirmed by the empirical work of Furceri and Zdzienicka (2013) and Hoffmann and Nitschka (2012) who find that risk sharing through financial markets declines dramatically during recessions.

National stabilization does not work and actually introduces an element of instability in a monetary union, mainly because it leaves the countries that are most affected by business cycle shocks unable to stabilize. Thus, when business cycle shocks dominate, a common approach to stabilization must be followed. A budgetary union can provide this stabilization. By centralizing part of national budgets in a common budget managed by a common political authority, the different increases in budget deficits following from a (common) recession lead to a budget deficit at the union level. As a result, the destabilizing liquidity flows between countries disappear, and the common budgetary authority can allow automatic stabilizers in the union budget to do their role in smoothing the business cycle. In fact, the countries with the deepest recession will profit most from the automatic stabilizing features of the common budget because such a budget also generates implicit inter-country transfers. As a result, a common budget provides the most effective way to stabilize the business cycle.

A small step in the direction of creating a Eurozone budget was taken at the end of 2018 when the European Council decided to set up a "Budgetary Instrument for Convergence and Competitiveness" (BICC). No decision has as yet been taken about the size of this budget. The European Commission, however, had proposed an amount of 17 billion euros, spread over the 2021–2027 European Union (EU) "multiannual financial framework," be set aside for the Eurozone budget. This is 2.4 billion euros a year or 0.01% of Eurozone GDP (which in 2018 stood at 13.7 trillion euros). The aim of BICC is to make public investments that will "strengthen convergence" and improve competitiveness in the Eurozone (see Consilium 2019 for more details).

There are two ways one can judge this micro-step forward. First, it is so small that it will be negligible from a macroeconomic perspective, and as a result will do nothing to stabilize the Eurozone. The second interpretation is that it is a step, albeit a minuscule one, in the right direction. Let us hope this interpretation was the driving force behind this Eurozone budget.

2.2 How to Deal with the Instability of Government Bond Markets?

Let us now turn to the question of how to deal with the Eurozone's second problem, namely the instability of government bond markets.

The ECB has a central role to play here. By promising to provide unlimited support to government bond markets in times of crisis, it can stop liquidity crises that are likely to emerge each time the Eurozone experiences a recession; liquidity crises that destabilize the system, leading to large capital outflows from some countries to others within the same monetary union.

The ECB recognized this problem when it started its OMT-program in 2012. This certainly helped to pacify financial markets at that time and avoided the Eurozone's collapse. When the OMT-program was announced, the yields in government bond markets of periphery countries started to decline steeply. The beauty of that announcement was that the ECB did not have to buy one euro in government bond markets.

The issue arises regarding the credibility of the OMT-program when used in future. This credibility problem arises from the fact that the ECB will have to decide whether it is facing a liquidity crisis or a solvency problem when using the OMT-program. If it determines it is a liquidity problem, it should step in. If it decides it is a solvency problem, it should not. In the latter case, the decision of whether or not to support the troubled government should be taken by the other governments.

This creates political problems that the ECB cannot tackle. It is generally very difficult to determine in real time whether the problem is due to lack of liquidity or due to insolvency. The uncertainty surrounding liquidity versus solvency problems makes it difficult for the ECB to step in without creating political controversy. In the 2015 Greek crisis, the ECB decided that the Greek problem was one of insolvency and therefore refused to support the Greek government bond market, precipitating the crisis and leading to intense political conflicts in the Eurozone.

All this raises doubts about the ECB's willingness to provide liquidity to governments in times of future crises. As a result, the OMT's credibility is limited, which means that it is not a foolproof insurance mechanism to stabilize markets in future crises.

This problem does not exist in standalone countries. The central bank's commitment to support a standalone sovereign in times of crises is unconditional mainly because the sovereign prevails over bureaucrats at the central bank. This comes at a price for it also implies that the credibility of the central banks' commitment to price stability is less than 100%. Paradoxically, one may argue that the ECB's commitment to price stability is stronger than in standalone countries precisely because its commitment to supporting 19 different national governments is weak.

The only way to solve the ECB's lack of credibility as lender of last resort in government bond market is to create a budgetary union that includes the consolidation of a significant part of national debts into a single Eurozone debt. This could be achieved by the issuance of Eurobonds that are backed by a joint liability of issuing governments (see De Grauwe and Moesen 2009 and Delpla and von Weizsäcker 2010). Such a consolidation mimics the relation between the central bank and the government that exists in standalone countries. It makes the credibility of liquidity support for the sovereign watertight and eliminates the danger of destabilizing capital flows within the union. Clearly such a consolidation can only occur if it is embedded in a political union, characterized by a central government that has the democratic power to tax and to spend. These are very intrusive, if not revolutionary transformations of the Eurozone, for which today there is little appetite in official circles. These have now taken for granted that a further significant budgetary union, together with a political union in which the budgetary union must be embedded, is out of reach for the foreseeable future (which undoubtedly is true). As a result, they tend to embrace technical solutions that can solve the problem while avoiding the need to create a budgetary and political union.

3 The Search for Technical Solutions Aimed at Enforcing Market Discipline by Financial Engineering

Official Eurozone institutions have embraced the intellectual idea that financial markets can be used to impose budgetary discipline and that suitably constructed financial assets can promote financial stability in the Eurozone. This idea has become popular among Eurozone policy-makers because of an understanding that achieving discipline and stability by political means, such as political integration, has hit a wall which prevents any further progress.

During 2018, a group of French and German economists proposed various schemes such as sovereign bankruptcy procedures and triggers that would force governments to issue different debt tranches in the hope of garnering the market's disciplining powers (Benassy-Quéré et al. 2018; Lane and Langfield 2018).[3] The European Systemic Risk Board (2018) published a report containing a proposal to create a "safe asset" for the Eurozone that is based on the repackaging of sovereign bonds risks. The European Commission followed up on this and came forward to support the idea of creating a safe asset (European Commission 2018). The hope is that this financial engineering will stabilize an otherwise unstable system of Eurozone sovereign bond markets. During 2018, official policy has thus become very much based on using market forces to discipline and stabilize the Eurozone.

In a way, all this is quite surprising. One thing we have learned from the financial crisis is that financial markets cannot be trusted as a disciplining device. During the boom years prior to the crisis, euphoria dominated in financial markets leading consumers, banks, firms, and investors to be blind to risk. As a result, they took on massive amounts of debt, encouraged by equally euphoric rating agencies and disregarded risks to their balance sheets. During this time, financial markets considered Greek sovereign bonds to have the same risk as German sovereign bonds.

When the crash came, financial markets panicked. Suddenly, they detected risks everywhere, forcing consumers, firms, and governments into excessive austerity, thereby deepening the recession (De Grauwe and Ji 2013). Financial markets became engines of excessive discipline.

All this is not new. Economic historians have taught us for some time that financial markets almost never apply the right amount of discipline (Kindleberger 1978 and Minsky 1986). During booms, markets apply too little discipline, thereby amplifying the boom, and during recessions, they impose too much discipline, thereby making the downturn worse.

In this section, we concentrate on several proposals aimed at enforcing market discipline through financial engineering. The first proposes to replace the existing structural budget balance rule by an expenditure rule that, if exceeded, would force governments to issue junior debt. The second proposal wants to enforce sovereign debt default procedures on governments that have become insolvent. The third one

---

[3]For a more general criticism of the French-German reform proposals, see Messori and Micossi (2018).

focuses on introducing a safe asset for the Eurozone. Let us discuss each of these proposals in order.

3.1 Tranching Government Debt

The idea behind the proposal to force governments to issue junior debt if their expenditures exceed some threshold value is that this will subject governments to more market discipline. The reasoning is the following: When governments spend too much, they are forced to finance the extra spending by issuing junior bonds. As a result, buyers of these bonds will face more risk and demand a risk premium. Thus, the issuing governments will pay a higher interest rate, which will enforce more discipline. The market will do its job of reigning in the tendency of excessive government spending.

All this sounds plausible. The evidence of past boom-bust financial cycles, however, is that this disciplining mechanism typically fails. During booms, euphoria prevails and few investors perceive risks. As mentioned earlier, during the Eurozone boom years, investor saw no difference in risks between Greek and German sovereign bonds. It is likely that they will see no significant difference in risks between the different tranches of outstanding government bonds when euphoria prevails.

During the downturn, exactly the opposite will happen. In fact, the existence of junior bonds will work as wake-up call and set in motion panic reactions of flight. As a result, the governments that issued junior bonds are more likely to be hit by a self-fulfilling liquidity crisis, forcing them into excessive discipline and austerity.

The reality is that financial markets are not well equipped to enforce discipline on sovereigns. The introduction of some new financial instrument will not change that reality.

3.2 Sovereign Default Procedures

The second proposal aimed at using market forces to discipline governments relies on a formal sovereign debt restructuring procedure. Governments that are insolvent should be forced to restructure their debt. In other words, the holders of these governments' bonds should be forced to accept losses. As a result, investors would realize that their investments would be risky in the absence of a possible bailout of the sovereign. This would lead them to ask for a risk premium, thereby disciplining the sovereign's behavior.

Again, this sounds reasonable at first sight. The same criticism, however, applies here to the one we leveled against the forced issue of junior bonds. There is very little evidence that investors ask for risk premia during boom phases, when euphoria blinds them to seeing risks properly. And during the bust phase, the opposite occurs and that is when the knowledge about the existence of debt restructuring procedures will trigger fear and panic. Indeed, such a sovereign restructuring procedure may actually trigger crises more easily than before.

There is an additional problem with this proposal, which has to do with identifying when governments are insolvent. It is easy to say that an insolvent sovereign should be forced to restructure its debt. It is much more difficult, during crisis moments, to distinguish between sovereigns' solvency and liquidity problems. This difficulty arose during the 2010–2012 sovereign debt crisis. For the case of Greece, it was relatively easy to conclude that its government was insolvent. What about the cases of Ireland, Spain, and Portugal? These countries were gripped by massive sales of their sovereign bonds leading to a liquidity crunch that made it impossible to rollover their debt at normal market conditions. Quite a lot of economists concluded that these countries were insolvent and should restructure their debt. It turned out that this advice was wrong and that these countries were solvent but had become illiquid. Economic recovery would have been much more difficult for these countries had they been forced to restructure their debt.

3.3 The Safe Asset Proposal

The proposal to create a safe asset in the Eurozone, which was made by the European Systemic Risk Board (ESRB), explicitly aims to eliminate destabilizing capital flows across the monetary union's national borders and to stabilize the system. Will it be able to achieve this? This is the question that we now address.

In contrast with earlier proposals to create Eurobonds, which assume that participating governments are jointly liable for the service of national debts (De Grauwe and Moesen 2009 and Delpla and von Weizsäcker 2010), the "safe asset" proposal makes no assumption of joint liability. Instead, national governments are individually liable for their own debt, so there is no pooling of risks.

The "safe asset" is created when financial institutions (private or public) buy a portfolio of national government bonds (in the primary or secondary markets) and use this portfolio as a backing for their own bonds issue, called "sovereign bond backed securities" (SBBS). The latter have the following characteristics. One tranche, the junior tranche, is risky. This tranche takes the hit when losses are posted on the underlying portfolio of government bonds.[4] The second tranche, the senior tranche, is safe. The proponents of SBBS take the view that a 30% junior tranche is a large enough buffer to take potential losses on the underlying sovereign bonds, so as to make the senior tranche (70%) risk free. Based on simulations of underlying risk patterns, the authors claim that their proposal will more than double the size of safe assets in the Eurozone. In addition, they claim that SBBS will replace the destabilizing capital flows across national borders in the Eurozone by a movement from the risky

[4]In the ESRB (2018) proposal, this tranche is split further into two tranches, a junior tranche proper with the highest risk (10%) and a mezzanine tranche (20%) which takes the losses after the junior tranche has been depleted.

asset (the junior tranche) into the safe asset (the senior tranche), thereby eliminating Eurozone instability.

How likely is it that these SBBS will stabilize the Eurozone? Note that in the way we formulate the question, we do not dispute that the creation of a safe asset may not increase the financial system's efficiency during normal times in the Eurozone. It probably will do so by supplying a new asset type that provides a better diversification of normal risks. The issue is whether the safe asset will be an instrument for dealing with systemic risks in times of crisis. Our answer is no for the following reasons:

First, the creation of a safe asset does not eliminate the national government bond markets. This is recognized by the safe asset's proponents (Brunnermeier et al. 2016 and ESRB 2018). In fact, they have made the continuing existence of national sovereign bond markets a key component of their proposal. According to the ESRB "the SBBS issuance requires price formation in sovereign bond markets to continue to be efficient" (p 33). The markets for sovereign bonds must remain large enough to maintain their liquidity. That is also why the ESRB proposes to limit total SBBS issuance to at most 33% of the total outstanding stock of sovereign bonds.

This constraint on SSBS issuance implies that national sovereign bond markets will still be "alive and kicking." As a result, the major problem that we identified earlier remains present, i.e., the potential for destabilizing capital flows across the borders of the monetary union's constituent countries.

Second, we observe that during crises, the yields' correlation pattern changes dramatically. During normal times, all yields are highly positively correlated (see Tables 1 and 3). During crises, the safe assets' yields tend to decline sharply and become negatively correlated with high risk yields, as investors look for safe havens. This pattern was very pronounced during the 2010–2012 sovereign debt crisis. In their simulations of SBBS risks, Brunnermeier et al. (2016) do consider the fact that risks can be correlated. However, their correlation pattern is fixed while correlation patterns change dramatically during crisis periods, as we show in Table 2. We find that during the 2010–12 sovereign debt crisis, the government bond yields of periphery countries under stress were highly positively correlated. At the same time, these yields were negatively correlated with the yields of core (safe) countries like Germany, Finland, France, and the Netherlands.

The implication is that it is very unlikely that the SBBS senior tranche can maintain its safe-asset status during crises, as it will consist of bonds that investors dump and "safe-haven" bonds. The senior tranche will continue to depend on the cash flow generated by bonds that panicking investors deem to be extremely risky. The perception that this senior tranche is equally safe as the safe-haven sovereign bonds (e.g., German bonds) is very unlikely when markets are in panic mode. As a result, it is also likely that investors will flee the SBBS' senior tranches to invest in the "real thing," i.e., super safe sovereign national bonds.

A third problem is related to the previous one. During normal times, the safe asset will have been used in the pricing of derivatives and other financial instruments, and it will be an important part of the repo market providing liquidity in that market. As a result, a large part of Eurozone financial markets will depend on the perceived safety and liquidity of the SBBS construction. When during crisis periods, the safety

Table 1 Correlation of yields before crisis, 2000M1-2009M12

	Germany	Finland	Netherlands	Austria	France	Belgium	Italy	Spain	Ireland	Portugal	Greece
Germany	1.00										
Finland	0.97	1.00									
Netherlands	0.97	1.00	1.00								
Austria	0.94	0.99	0.99	1.00							
France	0.98	1.00	1.00	0.99	1.00						
Belgium	0.95	1.00	0.99	1.00	0.99	1.00					
Italy	0.89	0.97	0.96	0.99	0.96	0.98	1.00				
Spain	0.94	0.99	0.99	1.00	0.98	1.00	0.99	1.00			
Ireland	0.61	0.78	0.76	0.83	0.74	0.81	0.88	0.83	1.00		
Portugal	0.90	0.98	0.97	0.99	0.96	0.99	0.99	0.99	0.87	1.00	
Greece	0.68	0.83	0.82	0.87	0.80	0.86	0.92	0.88	0.96	0.91	1.00

Source European Central Bank and authors' own calculation
Note The yields are yields on ten-year government bonds

Table 2 Correlation of yields during crisis, 2010M1-2012M09

	Germany	Finland	Netherlands	Austria	France	Belgium	Italy	Spain	Ireland	Portugal	Greece
Germany	1.00										
Finland	0.98	1.00									
Netherlands	0.99	0.99	1.00								
Austria	0.89	0.93	0.91	1.00							
France	0.83	0.89	0.87	0.98	1.00						
Belgium	0.45	0.58	0.54	0.74	0.80	1.00					
Italy	-0.66	-0.57	-0.58	-0.34	-0.21	0.28	1,00				
Spain	-0.62	-0.60	-0.55	-0.48	0.34	0.02	0.81	1.00			
Ireland	0.16	0.24	0.24	0.28	0.38	0.68	0.38	0.44	1.00		
Portugal	-0.62	-0.52	-0.54	-0.32	-0.19	0.29	0.88	0.73	0.54	1.00	
Greece	-0.82	-0.79	-0.78	-0.62	-0.50	-0.13	0.81	0.81	0.23	0.85	1.00

Source European Central Bank and authors' own calculation
Note The yields are yields on 10-year government bonds

Table 3 Correlation of yields after crisis, 2012M10-2017M12

	Germany	Finland	Netherlands	Austria	France	Belgium	Italy	Spain	Ireland	Portugal	Greece
Germany	1.00										
Finland	1.00	1.00									
Netherlands	1.00	1.00	1.00								
Austria	1.00	0.99	1.00	1.00							
France	0.99	0.99	0.99	0.99	1.00						
Belgium	0.99	0.99	0.99	0.99	0.99	1.00					
Italy	0.92	0.91	0.92	0.93	0.95	0.95	1.00				
Spain	0.90	0.90	0.90	0.92	0.92	0.94	0.97	1.00			
Ireland	0.93	0.93	0.93	0.95	0.95	0.96	0.97	0.99	1.00		
Portugal	0.78	0.78	0.79	0.82	0.83	0.85	0.93	0.93	0.92	1.00	
Greece	0.31	0.31	0.31	0.35	0.34	0.38	0.45	0.58	0.55	0.57	1.00

Source European Central Bank and authors' own calculation
Note The yields are yields on ten-year government bonds

of that construction is put into doubt (as we argued in the previous section), liquidity will tend to disappear and the whole Eurozone financial sector will be at risk. In the end, we may have less, rather than more, financial stability in the Eurozone.

There is an historical analogy here. During the boom years, Collateralized Debt Obligations (CDO) were created which were backed by different types of securities, e.g., mortgages. At the time, many people were enthusiastic about this and believed that CDO would make the financial markets more efficient by spreading risks better. It was believed that this would ultimately lead to more financial stability. The SBBS proposed by the ESRB has the same CDO structure as the previous ones. It would be surprising that financial engineering, which in the past failed dismally in stabilizing financial markets, would manage to stabilize them in future.

4 Conclusion: The Inevitability of Political Union

We have argued that the various proposals aimed at stabilizing the Eurozone by financial engineering will not eliminate the inherent instability of sovereign bond markets within a monetary union. During crises, this instability becomes systemic and no amount of financial engineering can stabilize an otherwise unstable system.

Stabilization using financial engineering will not work. The real stabilization of the Eurozone entails two mechanisms. The first is the willingness of the ECB to provide liquidity in Eurozone sovereign bond markets during times of crisis. While the ECB has set up its OMT-program to do this, it is loaded with austerity conditions which will be counterproductive during recessions (which is when crises generally occur). That is why a second mechanism is necessary, which implies the creation of a Eurozone budget.

With the election of Emmanuel Macron as French president in 2017, there was some hope that such a gradualist strategy could be set in motion. Macron's proposal to create an embryonic Eurozone budget seemed to open the door for such an approach and led to the European Council's decision to create a Eurozone budget in 2018. It was called BICC in order to avoid using standard English to give the baby a proper name, namely Eurozone budget. Although it is a step in the right direction, the size of this budget is so small (0.01% of Eurozone GDP) that it will make no significant contribution to stabilize the Eurozone in the foreseeable future. This is due to the unwillingness to create a political union in which a budgetary union is embedded.

Although this willingness does not exist today, it is important to keep the momentum for a political union alive because it remains a necessary condition for the Eurozone's long-term survival. Such a momentum can be created by a strategy of small steps (Enderlein et al. 2012), such as the creation of a limited fiscal space at the Eurozone level. In this sense, notwithstanding the extremely small size of the BICC, its creation in 2018 can be seen as a positive development. Other proposals come to mind as part of this gradualist strategy, such as a common unemployment insurance mechanism (Alcidi and Thirion 2015; Van Rompuy et al. 2012). Only time will tell if these small steps allow for a bigger leap toward the desired destination.

References

Alcidi C, Thirion G (2015) Feasibility and added value of a european unemployment benefit scheme. Interim Report, CEPS, Brussels

Beblavy M, Marconi G, Maselli I (2015) European unemployment benefits scheme: the rationale and the challenges ahead. Centre for European Policy Studies Special Report, Brussels

Benassy-Quéré A et al (2018) Reconciling risk sharing with market discipline: a constructive approach to euro area reform. CEPR Policy Insight, no. 91. Available online https://cepr.org/sites/default/files/policy_insights/PolicyInsight91.pdf. Accessed 28 Mar 2020

Brunnermeier M, Langfield S, Pagano M, Reis R., Van Nieuwerburgh S, Vayanos D (2016) ESBies: safety in the tranches. In: ESRB working paper series, No. 21

Consilium (2019) Explainer on the euro area budgetary instrument. Available online www.consilium.europa.eu/en/policies/emu-deepening/bicc-faq/. Accessed 28 Mar 2020

De Grauwe P (2011) The Governance of a Fragile Eurozone. CEPS Working Documents, Economic Policy, May. Available online www.ceps.eu/book/governance-fragile-eurozone. Accessed 28 Mar 2020

De Grauwe P, Moesen W (2009) Gains for all: a proposal for a common eurobond. Intereconomics 44(3):132–141

De Grauwe P, Ji Y (2013) Self-fulfilling crises in the eurozone: an empirical test. J Int Money Finance 34:15–36

De Grauwe P, Ji Y (2017) Booms, busts and the governance of the Eurozone. In: Vandenbroucke F, Barnard C, De Baere G (eds) A European social union after the crisis. Cambridge University Press, Cambridge, pp 160–191

Delpla J, von Weizsäcker J (2010) The blue bond proposal. Bruegel Policy Brief, May, Brussels. Available online https://www.bruegel.org/2010/05/the-blue-bond-proposal/. Accessed on 29 Mar 2020

Enderlein H et al (2012) Completing the Euro. a road map towards fiscal union in Europe, Report of the "Tomaso Padoa-Schioppa Group". Notre Europe, June. Available online https://heurope-solidarity.eu/documents/ES_CompletingTheEuro_Report_June2012_01.pdf. Accessed on 29 Mar 2020

European Commission (2018) Press release memo-18-3726. Available online https://europa.eu/rapid/press-release_MEMO-18-3726_en.htm. Accessed 28 Mar 2020

European Systemic Risk Board (ESRB) (2018) Sovereign bond-backed securities: a feasibility study, January. Available online www.esrb.europa.eu/pub/task_force_safe_assets/shared/pdf/esrb.report290118_sbbs_volume_I_mainfindings.en.pdf. Accessed 29 Mar 2020

Furceri D, Zdzienicka MA (2013) The Euro area crisis: need for a supranational fiscal risk sharing mechanism? IMF Staff Discussion Note No. 13-198, Washington, DC: International Monetary Fund, September

Hammond G, von Hagen J (1993) Regional insurance against asymmetric shocks: an empirical study for the European Community. University of Mannheim, Mimeo

Hoffmann M, Nitschka T (2012) Securitization of mortgage debt, domestic lending, and international risk sharing. Can J Econ 45(2):493–508

Italianer A, Vanheukelen M (1993) Proposals for community stabilization mechanisms. Econ Commun Publ Finances Euro Econ 5(93):493–510

Kenen P (1969) The theory of optimum currency areas: an eclectic view. In: Mundell R, Swoboda A (eds) Monetary problems of the international economy. University of Chicago Press, Chicago, IL, pp 41–60

Kindleberger CP (1978) Manias, panics and crashes: a history of financial crises. Wiley, New York

Lane PH, Langfeld S (2018) The feasibility of sovereign bond backed securities in the euro area. Available online https://voxeu.org/article/feasibility-sovereign-bond-backed-securities-euro-area. Accessed 28 Mar 2020

McKinnon R (1963) Optimum currency areas. Am Econ Rev 53(4):717–725

Mélitz J, Vori S (1993) National insurance against unevenly distributed shocks in a european monetary union. Recherches Économiques de Louvain 59(1–2):81–104

Messori M and Micossi S (2018) Counterproductive proposals on euro area reforms by French and German economists. Centre for European Policy Studies. Available online www.ceps.eu/system/files/PI2018_04_MMandSM_PI91.pdf. Accessed 28 Mar 2020

Minsky H (1986) Stabilizing an unstable economy. Yale University Press, New Haven, Connecticut

Mundell R (1961) A theory of optimal currency areas. Am Econ Rev 51(4):657–665

Van Rompuy H, Barroso JM, Juncker JC, Draghi M (2012) Towards a genuine economic and monetary Union. European Council. Final Report, 5 Dec. Available online www.consilium.europa.eu/uedocs/cms_Data/docs/pressdata/en/ec/134069.pdf. Accessed 28 Mar 2020

Fiscal Governance in the Euro Area: What Kind of Union?

Jürgen von Hagen

Abstract Political debates over the fiscal framework of the European Monetary Union have focused on two issues, dealing with asymmetric shocks and maintaining a high degree of fiscal discipline. After reviewing the development of the EMU fiscal framework, we argue that transfers dealing with asymmetric shocks are less important than commonly argued. Fiscal discipline is the critical issue. Three stark alternatives exist, a fiscal union, a debt union with decentralized authority, and a monetary union with fiscal freedom and a sovereign default framework. The debt union is not sustainable. Choosing between fiscal union and fiscal freedom is a decision between collective coercion combined with individual safety, on the one hand, and the ability to choose one's own best policies combined with individual responsibility, on the other.

Keywords Eurozone · Debt and fiscal union · Economic and monetary union · Fiscal discipline · Optimum currency areas

1 Introduction

European Monetary Union (EMU) has always been about fiscal as much as about monetary policy. Indeed, the implications of a common currency for the member states' fiscal policies have been the subject of intense political debates. Some governments hoped that the euro would enable them to borrow more and at more favorable rates. Others feared that they would become liable for the debts of profligate partners and face less favorable borrowing terms than before (Fratianni and von Hagen 1992). In the end, the governments could not agree on a common fiscal policy. The perceived loss of national sovereignty was obviously too large. This has often been regarded as a source of instability of the euro area. Instead, the relevant treaties contain many rules and procedures for the coordination of national fiscal policies, which have been revised and extended many times since the start of the euro. Today, there still seems to

J. von Hagen (✉)
Department of Economics, University of Bonn, Bonn, Germany
e-mail: vonhagen@uni-bonn.de

L. Brites Pereira et al. (eds.), *Economic Globalization and Governance*,
https://doi.org/10.1007/978-3-030-53265-9_10

be a need for further reform (European Fiscal Council 2019). The fiscal dimension of the EMU thus remains underdeveloped and in flux. Some claim that the EMU needs a fiscal union to be more resilient (e.g., Berger et al. 2018). Others hold that a fiscal union requires a political union which is currently not in sight. As in other areas of European integration, many policy-makers seem to think that one can leave the issue open and wait until some, and perhaps the right, kind of fiscal union emerges spontaneously.

In this chapter, we discuss the implications of EMU for the fiscal policies of the member states with a focus on fiscal governance. Two issues have commonly been discussed in the EMU context: insurance against asymmetric shocks and the sustainability of public finances. We argue that the latter is the more critical question in the EMU context and that the current approach will not lead to stable results.

2 The EMU Fiscal Framework

Recognizing that the stability of the common currency could be undermined by the fiscal profligacy of individual member states, the Maastricht Treaty devised the "Excessive Deficit Procedure" (EDP), later extended by the "Stability and Growth Pact" (SGP). It is an elaborate system of rules and procedures based on a host of statistical indicators, all aiming to ensure a high degree of fiscal discipline and the sustainability of public finances in each member state. Governments must comply with conditional and unconditional fiscal targets, and publish annually their fiscal strategies, intentions, policies, and outcomes. They must keep public debt below 60% of GDP, budget deficits below three percent of GDP and should maintain budget balances "close to zero or in surplus." Conditional on being above 60%, they have to reduce the debt ratio by five percent annually until the gap to 60% is closed. Governments submit to the European Commission annual Stability Reports explaining their fiscal strategies over the next three years. Because of its strong reliance on numerical targets, this approach has been dubbed "government by statistics" (Pisani-Ferry 2010, p 2). It assumes that the commitment to common numerical rules can compensate for the lack of a strong fiscal authority coordinating the fiscal policies of the member states.

Since the European fiscal crisis that started in Greece in 2010, the scope and depth of "government by statistics" have been expanded. In 2011, the "Six Pack" was introduced to strengthen the enforcement of the EDP and the SGP by giving more weight to the 60% limit for the debt-GDP ratio, adding government spending rules, and introducing a "Macroeconomic Imbalance Procedure," similarly based on a range of statistical indicators. The "Two Pack" was introduced in 2013 and further develops the monitoring procedures for the member states' public finances and their efforts to correct deviations from the EDP and SGP targets. Governments must now seek approval for their budget plans from the EU Commission.

Yet, "government by statistics" has neither prevented the building up of large fiscal imbalances nor contributed much to identifying the risks in public finances that emerged with the European fiscal crisis. A first reason is that, while the fiscal indicators measure the outcomes of past policies, they provide only a very limited information about the future. Second, they fail to take into account the riskiness of government assets and liabilities (von Hagen and Chen 2018), and largely ignore the implications of budgetary operations on the net wealth of government (Milesi-Ferretti and Moriyama 2004). In Germany, for example, successive governments have boasted about their achievement of a balanced budget several years in a row, while letting important infrastructure assets rot and thus accumulating large hidden debts. Such behavior clearly works against the goal of sustainability.

Third, there is no coherent and consistent conceptual framework within which the information gleaned from the indicators is organized, and compliance with or deviations from the rules are analyzed. How abiding by the rules would ensure the sustainability of public finances, and how deviating therefrom would endanger it, still remains unclear. If anything, "government by statistics" has created a culture of problem denial, allowing policy-makers to argue that everything is fine as long as the numbers comply with what the rules require.

Although the EU Treaty clearly rules out that an EMU member state or the EMU as a whole make itself, or be made, liable for another member state's public debt, the EMU member state governments in 2010 (by an agreement outside EU law) set up the European Financial Stability Facility (EFSF) as a bailout fund for member states in fiscal distress. It later morphed into the European Stability Mechanism (ESM) as a permanent bailout fund. With a capital of 80 billion euros, one of the largest international financial institutions, it stands ready to rescue states with unsustainable public debts combining loans with painful, IMF-style adjustment programs.

3 Fiscal Insurance Against Asymmetric Shocks

In a monetary union, the common monetary policy cannot react to temporary shocks affecting individual member countries in different ways. In the presence of such shocks, the monetary policy stance will often not be optimal for the individual countries. Optimum currency area theory in the tradition of Mundell argues that a monetary union should be complemented by a fiscal union that facilitates risk sharing among the members and provides more macroeconomic stability at the country level. Its main purpose would be to implement transfers from countries in boom to countries in slump.

There are several problems with this proposal. Conceptually, such a mechanism would dampen the fluctuations of individual economies around the average cyclical position of the union. Whether or not this leads to more stability of output and employment at the country level is an open question, since the average may be more volatile over time than (some of) its components. One would need a lot of information about the stochastic nature of relevant shocks (Kletzer and von Hagen 2001). Such a transfer scheme may well imply transfers from relatively poor to relatively rich countries and, therefore, be perceived as unfair. This is the main reason why East European countries currently reject the idea (Heinemann 2019).

A host of empirical studies of fiscal insurance in federations has shown that the response of fiscal transfers to temporary, asymmetric shocks is weak at best. Estimates commonly suggest that ten percent or less of asymmetric shocks are offset. One would have to believe in very large multipliers to think that such transfers provide significant macroeconomic stabilization. Capital and factor markets are much more effective absorbers of asymmetric shocks (Hepp and von Hagen 2012, 2013). Instead fiscal transfers serve primarily to reduce permanent income differentials. They are an outflow of solidarity among citizens of the same nation. Clearly, this is an issue unrelated to monetary union and it is bound to create conflicts among the members of the EMU whose citizens do not share similar feelings of mutual solidarity. Finally, asymmetric shocks can be the result of different national economic policies. Therefore, fiscal insurance will create moral hazard problems. As the member states will not want to pay for the bad policies of other members, fiscal insurance will lead to calls for even tighter monitoring and controls of economic policies at the national level. It is far from obvious that this is feasible and, if so, that it is more desirable than self-insurance through capital markets.

4 Fiscal Governance of the European Monetary Union

With a national currency, controlling the rate of inflation is key to solving sovereign debt crises. Facing an unsustainable level of public debt, a government can reduce the real value of its debt through surprise inflation or by defaulting on (part of) its debt. Inflation spreads the implied losses over all holders of the currency and nominal debt. Default, in contrast, concentrates the losses on bondholders and often causes instabilities in the national banking system. Historically, governments have preferred inflation to default, because the consequences of default are viewed as more painful than the consequences of inflation. Default leads to a decline in aggregate demand and tax revenues, while inflation comes with an expansion of both.

By renouncing control over the rate of inflation, member states of the euro area have given up the preferred way to keep their debts sustainable. This implies that, for any level of debt, the probability of partial default has increased. Realizing this, bondholders demand interest premiums compensating them for the greater default risk. One should, therefore, expect sovereign bond yields in the euro area to depend positively on the levels of debt of the individual governments. Empirical research using data from before the crisis indeed shows that interest rate spreads in the euro area were correlated with differences in government debt and deficits, although these correlations were quite small (Schuknecht et al. 2009). Once the European fiscal crisis hit, the link between bond yields and government debt grew much stronger (Schuknecht et al. 2011). Large sovereign bond yield spreads are not a sign of dysfunctional markets. Before the introduction of the euro, yield spreads reflected different inflation expectations. Today, they reflect different degrees of sovereign risk.

Once inflation control has been removed from the governments as a tool to maintain public debt sustainability in a monetary union, the question arises of who is responsible for debt sustainability in the new regime. There are three stark alternatives: fiscal union, debt union, and fiscal freedom.

4.1 Fiscal Union

A fiscal union is defined by the centralization of fiscal resources and competences and the allocation of the responsibility for the sustainability of public finances at the central government, the "Center" for short. All public debt is merged into a common debt issued and guaranteed by the Center. Individual member state governments are not allowed to borrow in their own right; only the Center issues debt. Therefore, a fiscal union has no need for emergency lending mechanisms such as the ESM. The Center apportions the funds it borrows to the governments of the member states in an arrangement similar to the Australian Loan Council (von Hagen et al. 2000). The member states benefit from the Center's superior status in the financial markets and the assurance that they can never fall into a debt crisis.

The fiscal union needs a mechanism through which the member states and the Center agree on the annual amount of borrowing and its partitioning among the members. The Australian experience teaches that such agreements are not easy to reach and maintain, when states have different growth perspectives and different financing needs. Annual borrowing could be allocated to the member states according to a fixed rule, allowing them to accumulate and draw from reserve funds according to their individual borrowing needs. Such an arrangement, however, could lead to macroeconomic disturbances if the states use it in uncoordinated ways. Alternatively, member states could exchange rights to fiscal union debt among themselves, allowing states with larger financing needs to borrow from states with smaller financing needs under the common deficit ceiling (e.g., Casella 1999).

The Center needs sufficient fiscal resources to assure the sustainability of the union's public debt. In terms of the intertemporal budget constraint, this requires that the Center can credibly commit to a future stream of sufficiently large primary surpluses. The larger the union's debt, the larger would have to be the Center's resources to generate such surpluses. In addition, the Center needs sufficient resources to remain liquid and able to refinance its debt in times of economic and financial distress. The more volatile the union economy and its parts, the larger the Center's resources have to be to achieve that objective.

Germany's experience in the early twentieth century teaches us that a fiscal union in which the Center depends entirely on transfers from the member states would be very fragile. States might withhold transfers in times of fiscal distress leaving the Center unable to meet its financial obligations. Therefore, the Center must have its own tax resources large enough to guarantee the union's debt, a fiscal administration collecting its own taxes throughout the union, and the ability to adjust these resources to a growing debt stock. Finally, since the possibility of fiscal distress cannot be excluded at the level of the union, the Center needs some degree of authority over the union's inflation rate in order to be able to fend off a fiscal crisis without having to resort to partial default. For example, the rules of the union could allow the Center to temporarily suspend the central bank's independence and oblige the central bank to buy union debt during a fiscal crisis (Lohmann 1992).

The Center needs strong authority over the member states to assure a debt path consistent with sustainability of the union. Since the member states will often be tempted to circumvent the ban on borrowing, the Center needs strong coercive powers over the member states to enforce it. It must be able to oversee the members' entire financial operations at all levels of government and have police powers to enforce union rules. Beyond that, the fiscal union has no need to control the fiscal policies of its member states in any detail. States are completely free to do as they wish within their budget constraints.

The existence of a large budget at the Center might create the adverse dynamics dubbed the Law of the Attraction of the Central Budget, or *Popitz' Law*. Thinking that they can benefit from the resources of other members of the union to finance their own public policies, member state governments will be inclined to transfer ever more policy competences to the Center, which will be happy to assume these competences in order to increase its own power and resources. Germany is a prime example of this process. In the early years of the Federal Republic, most fiscal and policy competences were allocated with the state governments. Over time, the states transferred more and more of them to the federal government in exchange for federal funding. Obviously, such a powerful Center would need strong democratic controls, hence fiscal union and political union are closely linked.

4.2 Debt Union

In a debt union, member states borrow in their own right, but their debt is guaranteed by the union. In contrast to a fiscal union, the Center is weak in terms of financial, political, and legal resources. A debt union can consist of the mutual commitment of the member states to guarantee their public debts through a rescue fund like the ESM. Alternatively, the member states could merge all or large parts of their existing public debts and issue jointly guaranteed "Eurobonds." Various kinds of "Eurobonds" have been proposed in recent years. The idea is that governments could issue safe Eurobonds up to a certain limit and risky national bonds beyond that. But clearly, the distinction between Eurobonds and national bonds would be irrelevant from the markets' perspective. A true distinction between the two would exist only if member states can default on national bonds but not on Eurobonds. But a default on national bonds would cause the very economic and financial turmoil for the euro area that the member states wish to avoid by setting up the debt union in the first place. Therefore, the threat of letting member states default on national bonds is not credible. In a fiscal crisis, the debt union would always stand ready to convert national bonds into Eurobonds. Anticipating this, markets would price both equally, creating the illusion that each member state's quality as a borrower is as good as the quality of the union as a whole. For the same reason, all EMU members will always want to increase the resources of the common bailout fund. Limiting the fund's financial power is therefore not a credible promise. The ESM is open ended.

The debt union creates a classical fiscal common pool problem, giving governments access to the tax revenues of other member states without facing the political costs of taxation. As a result, all governments have an incentive to borrow more than they would otherwise. This incentive is particularly strong for small member states, which feel the common pool externality less than large states and anticipate that large states will always want to protect the credibility of the common debt from being damaged by the default of a small state. In a debt union, therefore, small members are "too small to fail."

In view of this adverse incentive problem, the debt union has a vital interest in controlling the fiscal policies of its member states tightly to assure that each state maintains sustainable public finances. Debt unions try to achieve that through a system of budgetary rules much tighter than those of a fiscal union and a machinery of fiscal plans and programs, ambitious fiscal targets and detailed norms all monitored by the Center. The debt union puts its members into fiscal straightjackets constraining their short-term flexibility much more than what is required for maintaining sustainable public finances. Member states will seek ways to circumvent the rules by creative accounting and finding new debt instruments.

The tragedy of the debt union is that the Center lacks the information and coercive powers to keep its members from borrowing excessively. It must rely on the information provided by the members and on their administrations to enforce its rules. It is able to constrain fiscal plans, but not fiscal outcomes. In the end, the idea that the debt union controls the fiscal policies of the member states remains an illusion.

This illusion is the mark of the framework for fiscal governance in the euro area. Experience has shown that peer pressure and public exhortation are not enough to keep member state governments from embarking on unsustainable policies. The EU Commission is not the kind of neutral and competent judge over fiscal policies that an ideal debt union requires. Instead, it tends to focus on headline numbers such as the budget balance instead of looking at the structural issues that cause unsustainable policies. It is interesting in this regard to notice that the Commission's 2012 Fiscal Sustainability Report (p. 43) singled out Italy as the one EMU member state with sustainable public finances. This was justified by the assumption that all reforms intended by the Italian government in power at the time would be carried out fully and effectively. They were not.

The more closely the debt union monitors the budgetary policies of its members, the more it implicitly assumes responsibility for their outcomes. If a member state finds itself in fiscal distress, its government will turn to the debt union and ask for help, arguing that it did what it was told to do by the Center. The union will find it difficult to reject such requests, and rescue operations will become more frequent as a result. In the end, the opposite of what was intended comes about: more debt and more bailouts. In sum, the debt union is itself an unsustainable arrangement.

Historical experience shows that debt unions sooner or later end up being drowned in debt or in high inflation.

4.3 Fiscal Freedom

A monetary union with fiscal freedom operates under the firm principle that each member state is solely responsible for its own public finances. It leaves the member states complete freedom over their finances and has no need to subject them to any strictures and controls. Member states are free to adopt the policies they consider best for themselves. They pay interest rates on their public debt reflecting the quality of their policies and they bear the consequences of their own actions. The EMU experience so far has shown that fiscal freedom needs some important institutional features to be credible. In particular it needs a framework for an orderly sovereign default (Gianviti et al. 2010). Four things need to be addressed.

First, a member state's debt crisis must not lead to its expulsion from the monetary union, because even the threat of that happening would aggravate its financial problems. Second, a set of rules must be in place by which a state in fiscal crisis and its creditors are brought together to negotiate a restructuring of the unsustainable debt. A sovereign default court could be set up for this purpose. Third, the link between sovereign debt and the banking sector must be addressed. Openly acknowledging the possibility of sovereign default will already make banks more cautious in investing in public debt. In addition, banks should be required to hold capital against public debt similar to other risky assets. Central bankers might object that monetary policy operations rely on the existence of risk-free public debt, but this only implies that the ECB would have to change its operating procedures appropriately. Finally, the liquidity shortage a state undergoing default will find itself in must be addressed. The common fund like the ESM could be used to make bridge loans to governments in default, but only on the condition that an agreement for restructuring has been reached with its creditors and approved by the court of default. Such loans do not have to come with painful adjustment programs as ESM loans currently do. They will, therefore, not create the same divisiveness among the member states EMU has witnessed in recent years.

With fiscal freedom, the member states have a vital interest in sound fiscal institutions. For some, this may mean fiscal rules and constitutional debt brakes, for others it may mean having a finance minister with strong control over public finances or creating a powerful national fiscal council. There is no need to have a one-size-fits-all approach to fiscal institutions.

The open flank of the monetary union with fiscal freedom is that it rules out the use of monetary financing to resolve an excessive debt problem. It leaves the common money stock untouched as a base for the inflation tax. Note that the inflation tax required to solve an excessive debt problem would be much smaller in a monetary union than with national currencies, as it is spread over more countries and holders of money. Realizing this, highly indebted governments will wish to find ways to tap into that fiscal resource, e.g., by inducing the central bank to buy disproportionately large amounts of their debt. Preventing such strategic behavior might be a justification for some light monitoring the member states' fiscal policies even in a monetary union with fiscal freedom. But there are more natural ways to do that, such as holding the central bank accountable for its policies.

Conclusions

EMU has already gone a long way toward a debt union. But a debt union is not a sustainable arrangement. It does not create the incentives to reduce public debt, it will keep the fiscal crisis lingering, and, ultimately, result in high inflation or a collective debt crisis. Both can destroy the euro. Sooner or later, the members of the euro area must choose between a fiscal union and a monetary union with fiscal freedom. This is not the choice between a federal Europe and a union of sovereign states. Federations can be fiscal unions such as Australia, debt unions such as Argentina and Germany, or monetary unions with fiscal freedom such as the USA.

In the fiscal union, sustainability will be achieved by a powerful Center forcing the member states to pursue the policies it desires. In the monetary union with fiscal freedom, each member state will seek its own preferred way to achieve and maintain sustainability. As always, the price of freedom is individual risk and responsibility.

References

Berger H, Dell'Ariccia G, Obstfeld M (2018) The Euro Area Needs a Fiscal Union. IMF Blog February 21. Available online https://blogs.imf.org/2018/02/21/the-euro-area-needs-a-fiscal-union/. 29 Mar 2020

Casella A (1999) Tradable deficit permits: an efficient implementation of the stability pact in the European Monetary Union. Econ Policy 14:321–362

European Commission (2012) Fiscal sustainability report. European Economy 8. European Commission, Brussels. Available online https://ec.europa.eu/economy_finance/publications/european_economy/2012/index_en.htm. Accessed 29 Mar 2020

European Fiscal Board (2019) Annual Report. European Commission, Brussels. Available online https://ec.europa.eu/info/publications/2018-annual-report-european-fiscal-board_en. Accessed 29 Mar 2020

Fratianni M, von Hagen J (1992) The European Monetary system and European Monetary Union. Westview Press, Boulder, Colorado

Gianviti F, Krueger AO, Pisani-Ferry J et al (2010) A European mechanism for sovereign debt crisis resolution. Bruegel, Brussels

Heinemann F (2019) Osteuropäer lehnen EU-Transferunion ab. ZEW News 1–2 July–Aug 2019. Available online www.zew.de/presse/pressearchiv/osteuropaeer-lehnen-eine-euro-transferunion-ab/. Accessed 29 Mar 2020

Hepp R, von Hagen J (2012) Fiscal federalism in Germany: stabilization and redistribution before and after unification. Publius J Federal 42(2):243–259

Hepp R, von Hagen J (2013) Regional risk sharing in Germany: 1970–2006. Oxford Econ Pap 65(1):1–24

Kletzer K, von Hagen J (2001) Monetary Union and Fiscal Federalism. In: Wyplosz C (ed) The Impact of EMU on Europe and the developing world. Oxford University Press, Oxford

Lohmann S (1992) Optimal commitment in monetary policy: credibility versus flexibility. Am Econ Rev 82(1):273–286
Milesi-Ferretti GM, Moriyama K (2004) Fiscal adjustment in EU Countries: a balance sheet approach. Working Paper 04/143, IMF, Washington DC
Pisani-Ferry J (2010) Euro-area governance: what went wrong? How to repair it? Policy contribution 2010/05. Bruegel, Brussels
Schuknecht L, von Hagen J, Wolswijk G (2009) Government risk premiums in the bond market: EMU and Canada. Eur J Polit Econ 25(3):371–384
Schuknecht L, Wolswijk G, von Hagen J (2011) Government risk premiums in the EU revisited. Eur J Polit Econ 27(1):36–43
von Hagen J, Chen Y (2018) Fiscal risk and public sector balance sheets. Working Paper, University of Bonn
von Hagen J, Bordignon M, Dahlberg, M et al (2000) Subnational government bailouts in OECD countries: four case studies. IADB research network WP R-399. Washington. Available online https://idbdocs.iadb.org/wsdocs/getdocument.aspx?docnum=788028 Accessed 28 Mar 2020

On the Limits of EU Differentiated Integration: Lessons from the Eurozone Crisis and from Brexit

Annette Bongardt and Francisco Torres

Abstract Variable geometry ought to imply "variably geometry Europe" as variable geometry or differentiated integration in the European Union has reached its limits. Drawing on the lessons of the Eurozone crisis and of Brexit, this chapter argues that (treaty-based) variable geometry or differentiated integration in the core European Union (EU) institutions—especially economic and monetary union (EMU)—is not sustainable. EMU has in the meantime become the (economic and political) core of the Union and of the integration process. It is therefore the Euro area, and no longer the internal market, on which one would have to anchor EU integration. From an EU point of view, it does not make sense to accommodate member states' preferences that are too divergent from the Union's by means of more institutional flexibility at the Euro areas' expense and the objective of ever-closer union. This would mean transforming the EU into a mere intergovernmental organization without a common currency (and for that matter without political ambitions). Therefore, all EU countries should be in all main EU (treaty-based) institutions, most notably EMU and Schengen, or leave the Union and opt for membership of the European Economic Area only or for a lesser preferential trade agreement like a free trade agreement.

Keywords Brexit · Differentiated integration · Economic and monetary union · Sovereign debt crisis · Variable geometry

1 Introduction

Jorge Braga de Macedo's research agenda, intellectual curiosity, and policy and political engagements have spanned many diverse areas, some of which are discussed in the chapters of this Festschrift. In our chapter, we concentrate on one specific

A. Bongardt (✉)
CICP – Research Center in Political Science, Universidade de Évora, Évora, Portugal
e-mail: bongardt@ufp.edu.pt

F. Torres
Católica Lisbon School of Business & Economics, Universidade Católica Portuguesa, Lisbon, Portugal
e-mail: ftorres@ucp.pt

L. Brites Pereira et al. (eds.), *Economic Globalization and Governance*,
https://doi.org/10.1007/978-3-030-53265-9_11

topic of his very prolific contributions to the broader area of European integration, as an academic, policy advisor/maker and politician. This chapter's object is variable geometry, which we defend ought to imply "variably geometry Europe" as variable geometry or differentiated integration in the EU has reached its limits and is no longer politically sustainable.

Although Jorge Braga de Macedo is possibly mostly known as an international and development economist in his academic career, over the years he has contributed various essays and books to the political economy of European integration. Moreover, in late 1988, three years before chairing the ECOFIN Council as minister of finance and taking the escudo into the Exchange Rate Mechanism (ERM) of the European Monetary System (EMS), he moved on from academia to the European Commission, as Director of National Economies at DG EcFin (at the time known as DGII). Although one of us had taken his graduate course in International Monetary Economics at Nova University and written a thesis under his supervision, it was in Brussels during the exceptional year of 1989 that we first engaged in discussions on the process of European integration and its implications for economic policy in Portugal, which were never to cease thereafter. Such continuous discussion moved from the purely academic domains to policy-making and politics and back again. It covered many topics, most notably Portugal's monetary integration strategy and its various adjustment/convergence phases in the then European Economic Community (EEC) and later the EU as well as the broad European process of ever-closer Union. We will focus here on the intersection of the two and examine the question of variable geometry after the Maastricht Treaty, which Jorge Braga de Macedo signed on behalf of Portugal.

In choosing this topic, we would like not only to pay tribute to Jorge Braga de Macedo's earlier work on variable geometry but also to highlight its present-day relevance. It is an issue that regained political and academic prominence due to the sovereign debt crisis, the various scenarios for the EU's future put forward by the previous Commission and, more recently, Brexit.

In a way, variable geometry or differentiated integration has always remained on the EU's agenda. It is even already considered a permanent feature of the EU,[1] with a center open to participation of all member states, very much along the lines of the concept of "positive variable geometry," adopted in a resolution of the Portuguese Parliament when Jorge Braga de Macedo was President of the European Affairs Committee.[2] In fact, the European Commission in its White Paper on the future of Europe (European Commission 2017b) presented five scenarios that depart from the current situation but allow the EU to evolve in line with the wishes of the member states ("carrying on," which lacks ambition; "nothing but the single market," which in our view would lead to disintegration; "those who want more do more," which introduces differentiation with a potential negative impact on the Union's sustainability; "doing less more efficiently"; and "doing much more together"). In our view,

[1] See Leruth and Lord (2017).

[2] Resolution 21/95, Official Journal, April 8. See Braga de Macedo (1995, 1996), the latter published in a volume with several other contributors to this volume and Torres (1995, 1996).

these scenarios suggest a lack of political determination to pursue the project of European integration as established in the treaties. This is possibly due to the fact that heterogeneity of preferences has increased with successive enlargements and with differentiated integration, resulting in insufficient convergence of preferences.

The predominant vision in the 1990s was that the EU's single market with the four freedoms (made politically viable by the coordination of economic policies) would be the common base, while other forms of open cooperation would allow for the necessary flexibility in light of the club's larger heterogeneity (Dewatripont et al. 1995; Demertzis et al. 2018, have a similar approach). The Maastricht Treaty raised the level of economic integration from common market to EMU and therefore the need for coordination. EMU has in the meantime become the economic and political core of the Union and of the integration process. Therefore, one would have to anchor EU integration in the Euro area instead of the internal market.

Nevertheless, there are EU members (notably Sweden and Poland) that committed to join EMU at the time of accession but apparently no longer wish to do so. Instead, they only want to be part of the internal market, a lower integration level. For those countries, it would possibly make more sense—it certainly does for the EU—that they exit the Union to only be part of the European Economic Area (EEA).[3] Of course, this option might ultimately not be attractive when EU funds and geo-strategic considerations go the other way. Nevertheless, now that Brexit took place, the EU should pursue deepened economic integration in order to sustain the currency of the Union, the Euro, and further its integration project.

Drawing on the lessons of the Eurozone crisis and of Brexit, we argue that (treaty-based) differentiated integration or variable geometry in the core EU institutions—especially EMU—is not sustainable[4]: it may only work in what are today secondary matters or new "open partnerships." Not only EMU but other early exercises of variable geometry, such as the Schengen agreement, have in the meantime moved into the EU core. For example, the Permanent Structured Cooperation (PESCO) in the area of defense may evolve to become central institutions at the core of the European integration process. Therefore, countries with divergent preferences may well consider invoking Article 50 of the Treaty on European Union, the exit provisions to leave the EU. This has been the option of the UK, which finally left the EU on January 31, 2020, after having dithered over Brexiting between 2016 and the end of 2019. Some former European Free Trade Association (EFTA) countries have opted not to join the EU but stay closely within in its orbit (Norway, Iceland, Liechtenstein, all in the EEA, and Switzerland with a series of complicated bilateral agreements that shadow EEA membership).

[3]Although we focus on EMU, a similar reasoning applies with respect to other major policies of the Union. Member states that refuse to participate in common asylum policies and to accept a fair quota of refugees should probably opt for a lower level of integration in the EEA or at least not claim solidarity from the rest of the Union in other domains.

[4]Holzinger and Schimmelfennig (2012) distinguish between treaty-based differentiation, which they deem politically more relevant, and differentiation in ordinary Community legislation and EU secondary law.

Our thesis is that only a "variable geometry Europe" but not a "variable geometry EU" allows the Union to deliver on its objectives and ensure the politically sustainability of the European integration process (Begg et al. 2015). That implies that all EU countries should be in all main EU (treaty-based) institutions, notably EMU and Schengen. Alternatively, they should leave the Union and opt for membership of the EEA only or opt for a lesser preferential trade agreement (like a free trade agreement). A free trade agreement with the EU seems to be the preferred option of the UK, apart from being the only viable one for the EU, given UK red lines.

The remainder of the chapter is organized as follows: the next section discusses the UK's experience with European integration from 1973 until its exit from the EU in 2020. Section 3 puts forward the argument that the EU's deepening integration toward EMU implied an important qualitative change, which made the UK position in the EU untenable. Section 4 explains why differentiated integration in the Union reached its limits and discusses the EU club's optimum size. Section 5 concludes with a possible outlook.

2 Increasing Differentiation Until Separation: The Case of the UK and European Integration

The UK had been opposed to the model of European integration since the beginning of the process in the 1950s. Although part of the preparatory Spaak Committee of what would become the EEC created by the 1957 Rome Treaty, in 1955 it left in disagreement with the proposed supranational model of integration. Having decided not to become a member of the EEC, the UK was the principal promoter and architect of the EFTA set up in 1960 as a rival club of European economic integration. EFTA settled for a lower level of economic integration, based on intergovernmental rather than supranational coordination. Yet, the UK decided to abandon its new EFTA partners already shortly after 1961, applying for EEC membership. The move was motivated by not wanting to lose out on the economic benefits associated with access to such an important market and customs union, overriding sovereignty concerns that had thus far been dominant. In the event, the UK was only allowed to join the EEC/European Community (EC) in 1973 (together with Denmark and the Irish Republic, as Norway decided to stay out after a negative referendum outcome) in what was the first EC enlargement.

Once a club member, the UK kept ever more to the margins of European integration, with the Maastricht Treaty as a watershed moment.[5] The UK's position in the EU became characterized by substantial cherry picking on EU policies and its non-participation in what has de facto become the EU's core, the Euro area. It never joined the border-free Schengen area and did not adhere to multiple aspects

[5] As early as 1975, the UK held an in–out referendum on its EC membership, which resulted in a majority for remaining. For a more detailed discussion of the UK's experience in the EU, see Bongardt and Torres (2017) and Bongardt and Torres (2020).

of judicial and police cooperation. As for the latter, it got a block opt-out, meaning that the UK chose to reject the whole policy area, while still selectively opting in into those aspects of cooperation of its liking. Also, and despite having opted out of the Schengen agreement, it benefited from access to European databases in security matters, most notably the Schengen Information System.[6] It also obtained a special protocol (like Poland) with regard to the application of the European Charter of Fundamental Rights. In addition, it negotiated a derogation (along with Denmark) with respect to the adoption of the common currency of the Union, the Euro, which was to become the political and economic core of the EU club. Subsequently, it did not participate in almost any of the economic governance institutions that were created in the wake of the sovereign debt crisis so as to make the common currency sustainable. It furthermore refused any (financial) solidarity toward the rest of the Union and, in particular, the countries that endured adjustment programs. The UK's distancing within the Union meant that the UK had become the member state with the least participation in European institutions and policies before it left the Union on January 31, 2020 (Bongardt and Torres 2017).

For the UK, the benefits from membership in the EU club had thus become very much confined to the economic benefits associated with the internal market (Bongardt and Torres 2016, 2017). And yet, even in that domain, which was then at the core of UK participation, the European regulatory model based on decision making by qualified majority was resisted in the name of (a perceived loss of) national sovereignty and arguably different socio-economic model (Bongardt 2020). Indeed, the preferences revealed by the UK (and also Ireland) with regard to market regulation of goods and services, labor markets and financial markets, tend to be closer to North American preferences (OECD 2015) while most other EU member states tend to follow the continental values of a welfare state and environmental sustainability.

The UK focused on obtaining economic advantages from the club while at the same time demanding compensations for policies deemed less favorable. It avoided participating in common objectives throughout its membership in the European integration project. For the EU, every time there were revisions to the European treaties, the outcome would lead to inferior solutions in light of red lines (veto threats) imposed mostly by the UK, i.e., leading to insufficient integration and treating the European objectives and model as secondary. That in turn stoked popular discontentment in many countries of the EEC/EU, including the UK itself. With some countries having a preference for less integration (more national sovereignty, albeit illusionary in a globalized world) and others for more sovereignty sharing as to effectively tackle common challenges, the blame for unsolved problems is put on the EU club, albeit for different motives.

For the Union, the costs associated with this blocking mindset became greater and greater, either in relation to the deepening of defense cooperation, the strengthening

[6]The UK was granted access to the Schengen Information System even after having invoked Article 50 to leave the EU and even during the transition period when it no longer was member. Its alleged abuse and lack of reciprocity were strongly criticized by MEPs (see euobserver.com/justice/147,084).

of economic union or a vast range of policies in the internal market sphere. For an EU that needs to continuously reform its institutions and further integrate in order to keep up with, and respond to, the manifold challenges that it faces, the situation became untenable. Brexit put an end to an unsustainable situation of differentiated integration.

3 EMU: From an Open Partnership to the Core of European Integration

The UK's preferences became incompatible with EMU's economic agenda and the EU's political sustainability, ever since the move from a single market to an EMU.[7] The reason is that with EMU, the economic union part, which includes the internal market, can no longer be treated as stand-alone and independent of the monetary union. Rather, EMU's good functioning requires that economic union go hand in hand with monetary union, together with the necessary coordination to sustain the latter. The UK preference for a stand-alone economic union ultimately put it on a collision course with EU integration objectives and, in particular, Eurozone policies (Bongardt and Torres 2017).[8]

That clash of preferences is rooted in the fact that the internal market can no longer be treated as static. For the Eurozone to work well, it is in the legitimate interest of current and future members that the economic union be deepened with regard to Eurozone requirements—these include, after Brexit, all EU member states except Denmark, which benefited from an opt-out (although Denmark follows all the Eurozone' decisions in terms of monetary policy, its self-exclusion implying that it only does not participate in the decision making). The increased interdependencies between monetary union's members and enhanced coordination needs implied a qualitative change in European integration.

While obviously important for the sustainability of the monetary union, the issue goes much beyond and to the core of the integration process. The EU needs to complete EMU, notably through more coordinated economic, fiscal, and budgetary policies and a banking and capital markets union (Jones and Torres 2016), in order to deliver positive (economic, environmental, and social) results to the entire Union, and therefore sustain the political integration project.

The UK preferences and interest in the economic union part (highlighted by the specificity of, and dependency on, its financial sector concentrated in the City of

---

[7]In the monetary domain, the UK was the only member state not to take part in the ERM at its inception in 1979. It was also the only one to later leave it without coming back to participate in EMU, after the country had been forced (by speculation against the pound sterling) to abandon the ERM after a short spell lasting from 1990 to 1992.

[8]As stated by Jorge Braga de Macedo (2017, p 10–11), "The UK, before the exit referendum, did not see better Eurozone governance as complementary to a broader and deeper single market, and this slowed the progress of the financial union as much as Germany's insistence on the need to retain national fiscal backstops."

London) became incompatible with EMU sustainability, the good functioning of European institutions and their response to the challenges facing the EU. The UK had not only opted out of the monetary union altogether but it also refused to take part in the economic union's deepening, thus hindering the necessary strengthening of its institutions and governance. The UK did not participate in the Euro Plus Pact and even vetoed the Treaty on Stability, Coordination and Governance in Economic and Monetary Union, which in turn required other member states to settle for an intergovernmental pact beyond the Union framework, at a time of great Eurozone fragility and perils for its survival.

In the sovereign debt crisis, the UK did not participate in the newly created institutions of the European Financial Stability Fund (EFSF) and the European Stability Mechanism (EMS), while also not providing solidarity to the Eurozone member states most affected by the crisis. It only accepted the ESM in exchange for the European Financial Stability Mechanism (EFSM), which involves a guarantee of the EU budget for granting loans, no longer being used to support Eurozone countries. It only made an exception to support Ireland when its national interest, linked to the British financial system, was at stake. At the same time, the UK nevertheless continued to benefit substantially from the Euro area. British banks continued to have privileged access to the European Central Bank (ECB)'s liquidity operations throughout the global economic and financial crisis. Above all else, a large proportion of Euro-denominated financial activities (the so-called Euro clearing and the negotiation of sovereign debt by investment banks) takes place on the London financial market, which is outside the Euro area.

It obviously does not make much sense that the Eurozone's financial stability, in general, and that of countries more affected by market turbulence, in particular, should be put at risk by Euro-denominated financial activities taking place in London, beyond the reach of the ECB's jurisdiction. Yet, this is precisely what happened during the sovereign debt crisis. The UK maintained an almost continuous non-constructive attitude with respect to Eurozone's problems, putting EMU architecture and viability at risk. It also criticized the so-called austerity and adjustment programs but refused to contribute constructively (and financially) to fellow EU member states in need, as it deemed their problems to be within the purview of the Euro area. It also opted not to participate in the creation of the European Banking Union (EBU) in spite of the European Banking Authority (EBA) being headquartered in London.

Brexit triggered the EBA's move from London to Paris, and so into the Eurozone. More importantly, Brexit opened up the opportunity for the EU to finally direct internal market financial regulation toward the common good of financial stability across the Eurozone, and thereby reinforce the economic union in the crucial area of the monetary union. It should also make it easier to bring intergovernmental economic agreements that were made at the margins of the EU due to the UK's veto into the Community framework, and to complete the institutional architecture with a full banking union, a European monetary fund, a Eurozone budget and greater integration/budgetary coordination. For that to happen, it is essential that the Euro area be the EU political core that all member states join or, at least, which they do not obstruct. The Eurozone countries could then strengthen both the efficiency and political responsiveness of monetary and financial institutions by completing EMU and advancing the integration process (European Commission 2017a; Jones and Torres 2016).

EMU calls for more homogeneous preferences across member states in order to function and deliver, namely, to complete institutional reform and ensure that its economic union side fulfills the prerequisite of a sustainable monetary union. For that, it is necessary to have an EU core (the Euro area) that is more cohesive, homogeneous, and more integrated.

Until now the completion of EMU had been rendered more difficult due to the fact that the Euro area remained smaller than the EU club, not only because of the derogations granted to the UK and Denmark at Maastricht, but above all else due to the UK's insistence on institutionalizing this difference in a permanent way, with the support of other member states like Sweden and Poland. As a result, prior to Brexit, the division between the Euro area members and other EU countries had made the crisis response and attempts to strengthen EMU, more difficult, thereby putting at risk the sustainability of EMU and EU.[9]

The economic and political weight of the UK enabled it to block EU reforms in a systematic way. All other member states that do not wish to be part of the Eurozone, despite having committed to do so upon joining the EU, are likely to conclude sooner or later that they are at the periphery of the European integration process, and thus less able to influence it, as they lack the power of the UK or are unable to draw on it post-Brexit.

Brexit came to solve a pending issue regarding the extent to which the artificial divide between Eurozone insiders and outsiders will tend to disappear. This opens up, for instance, the possibility of the Eurogroup functioning as a formation of the Council (see European Commission 2017a). After all, Denmark already follows the Euro area's monetary policy whereas all other member states (including Sweden and Poland) are committed in their accession treaties to adopt the Euro as their currency. It follows therefore that it is not the EU that has to de-characterized itself in order to adapt to a change of preferences by countries that seek to renege on the objectives that they committed to at the time of their accession to the Union.[10] Those countries will probably have to decide at one point whether they want to comply with their

---

[9]Ireland and the Netherlands have also recently (2019) sided with non-Euro member states on the Eurozone budget question in the "new Hanseatic league." In spite of having received unconditional solidarity from the other EU member states throughout the entire financial and sovereign debt crises and, especially, during the Brexit negotiations, Ireland maintains a less than fully committed relation with the EU. This is also exemplified by its stance on taxation, data protection, EU symbols, and self-exclusion from Schengen.

[10]The result of the UK December 2019 elections confirmed that the democratic mandate for Brexit had to be respected, namely the 2016 referendum and the overwhelming parliamentary majority in favor of triggering Article 50 to leave the EU by March 2019. Fortunately for the EU integration project, the various attempts (from the UK and also from within the EU) to stop Brexit through such a de-characterization of the Union, as negotiated with the UK government in February 2016, failed.

accession treaties and Union objectives or whether they intend to invoke Article 50 TEU to exit the EU.[11]

The UK's exit from the Union can contribute to more homogeneous preferences and allow EMU to function better by some accounts. To start with, it opens up the possibility to better gear financial regulation in the single market toward the Euro area's public good of financial stability. Without internal opposition by the UK, it could also prove easier to bring what are today intergovernmental European economic agreements into the Community framework at some stage. Last but not least, Brexit established a precedent, which opened the door for any discontented EU member state to exit the club (whether current or potential EMU members or EU members with an opt-out of monetary union), which should reduce any member state's capacity to hold up decisions that are in the common interest and, in turn, should facilitate decision making and problem solving.

4 The Eurozone as the EU Club's Optimum Size

The EU faces a major challenge due the fact that the club became not only larger but also more (and possibly too) heterogeneous over the years. Its problem-solving capacity is at stake when permanently divergent preferences block the decision-making process. This issue leads us to the question of an optimum (or sustainable) size of the club.[12]

In its successive enlargements, the initial EEC (later EC/EU) largely increased the number of its members (from 6 to 28 member states, 27 after Brexit), whereby it came to include also countries that had stayed out initially, not least because of harboring different views on supranational governance and European economic integration as a political project. On a variety of accounts (not merely on living standards), the Union integrated countries as diverse as EFTA members (among whom the UK, the free trade area's chief promoter), former Council for Mutual Economic Assistance (COMECON) members and former non-aligned countries. The UK was possibly the main promoter of the successive EU enlargements, notably the ones in this millennium, as an alternative (national) strategy to the club's deepening. In 2004, it was also the UK (under the Blair government) that accelerated the free movement of workers (to be phased in) from the new EU member states. This had a negative impact on European public opinion and possibly contributed to the rejection of the ill-fated Constitutional Treaty in 2005 in the French and Dutch referendums (Sternberg 2015), as well as on UK public opinion (freedom of movement was one

[11]This is also in the spirit of the concept of "positive variable geometry." As Braga de Macedo (1995) puts it: "Nevertheless, member States cannot block the need for Union deepening expressed by a majority of member States (…) this has been called positive variable geometry."

[12]Framed in the terminology of the economic theory of clubs, whether the benefits from integration at the margin, be it for the Union as such or for each member state, are larger or at least equal to the costs from increased club heterogeneity. See Alesina and Spolaore (1997, pp 1027–1056) and Torres (2009). For the notion of sustainable integration, see Begg et al. (2015).

of the main arguments presented for Brexit). The UK would later come to complain (under the Cameron government) about the free movement of persons on its soil and try to undo the EU principle, rather than making use of the available instruments at its disposal to control EU immigration used by the other EU members.[13]

The problem of the EU club's sustainability is that too much heterogeneity—of preferences regarding the model of society—may undermine trust between member states, which is fundamental in a common market whose functioning rests on the principle of mutual recognition, and for political integration that is based on trust and shared values. On the upside, participation in common institutions and sovereignty sharing tends to create and strengthen a European identity beyond the various national identities, thus overcoming the problem of heterogeneous preferences and cultural diversity between the member states (Alesina et al. 2017, p 4; Bongardt and Torres 2017).

The UK was a particularly problematic case in this regard. It expressed its differences by maintaining itself ever more at the margin of European integration, having limited its cooperation in policies and common institutions with its partners, vetoed institutional reforms, and demanded new exceptions until it became the EU member state that least participated in common institutions.[14] Not surprisingly in this light, the country ended up invoking Article 50 and finally, after prolonged dithering, exited the Union in 2020.

The case of Brexit suggests that openness to European integration is crucial to allow for a convergence of preferences. It is not by chance that those member states that form part of the Euro area tend to support it ever more (76% in favor, on average, with a variation between 65 and 88%), even despite the crisis effects, whereas the countries that stayed out of the Euro area tend not to support it (25% in the UK).[15] Put differently, there is a certain endogeneity in the convergence of preferences. Preferences tend to converge when countries have the opportunity to cooperate through institutions and common policies (as are the cases of Belgium, Germany, Portugal, Spain, Slovakia, and Slovenia, for example) and to diverge when they do not (the cases of Denmark, Poland, Sweden and UK, among others).[16]

---

[13]In 2017, French President Macron complained about the lasting negative effects of the British choice with respect to the European social model in the context of the posted worker directive.

[14]The New Framework for the UK in the EU (February 2016) would have created an ever more institutionalized differentiated integration. It did not come about only thanks to Brexit.

[15]Source: Standard Eurobarometer 91, European Commission, Spring 2019. All Eurozone countries support EMU and the Euro and are above the EU average. Most of non-Eurozone countries' public opinions are against both. The exceptions are Bulgaria and Romania, although with levels of support below the EU average.

[16]An exit index defining three cores of Europe computed by Gastinger (2019) along three dimensions (social, economic, and political) also ranks these four countries high (in the third core). Italy, Greece, and France also rank high in their propensity to leave the EU although other considerations put forward by the author, such as Greece's dependency on EU funds, Italy's membership of EMU, and France's high share of citizens feeling European, reduce that risk. Vollaard (2014), Leruth and Lord (2015), Leruth et al. (2017), and Jones (2018) theorize the notions of EU integration and disintegration.

At present, only eight countries, namely Austria, Belgium, France, Germany, Greece, Italy, Portugal, and Slovenia, participate in all of the EU's main institutions and enhanced cooperation mechanisms (König 2015, updated in Wolfstädter and Kreilinger 2017). Those institutions include EMU, Schengen, PESCO, the European Charter of Fundamental Rights, multiple aspects of judicial and police cooperation, the Euro Plus Pact, the Treaty on Stability, Coordination and Governance in Economic and Monetary Union, the EBU, the EFSF, the ESM but also include enhanced cooperation in such fields as divorce law, European unitary patent, (matrimonial) property regime rules, the European public prosecutor's office, and the financial transaction tax. The UK stood out as the least integrated of all member states, followed by the Czech Republic, Sweden, Denmark, Poland and Hungary.

Any solution that builds more flexible European institutions, better able to accommodate different preferences, may well contribute to a smoother functioning of the EU (Braga de Macedo 2001; Spolaore 2013). However, this is only true in the short run. In the long run, it leads to preference divergence and the erosion of the European integration project as an "ever closer Union." If differentiation offers a way out of a stalemate, it only does so in the short term and/or for secondary institutions, for which there are already many examples of sub-clubs (exemplified by the European unitary patent or the divorce law).[17] In the long term, it risks cementing or promoting the divergence of preferences and puts the cohesiveness and sustainability of the EU project at risk. In other words, it is the very differentiation that tends to explain the separation.[18] To function, the Union needs a political core and a shared identity and destiny.[19] It is the Eurozone that has, in the meantime, established itself as the core of European integration.

It makes no sense that the EU should adapt to the very divergent preferences of given countries (even less so since some of them joined the Union subject to the condition of joining all of its institutions, including EMU, but seem to have changed their intentions afterward). Rather, it is those countries that need to decide whether they want to stay in the Union and its political integration project or leave.[20] For

---

[17] According to Jorge Braga de Macedo (2002), not all combinations of flexibility and integration are possible, let alone desirable. Among others, furthering integration constrains purely contractual arrangements.

[18] See Dustmann et al. (2017).

[19] In the words of former Prime Minister of Luxembourg, Joseph Bech, quoted by Pope Francis on the occasion of the 60th anniversary of the Treaty of Rome in 24 March 2017, "the European economic community will prove lasting and successful only if it remains constantly faithful to the spirit of European solidarity that created it, and if the common will of the Europe now being born proves more powerful than the will of individual nations." Pope Francis concludes: "That spirit remains as necessary as ever today, in the face of centrifugal impulses and the temptation to reduce the founding ideals of the Union to productive, economic and financial needs."

[20] The main attempts at revoking Brexit defended a loose and flexible EU in lieu of the Eurozone as its political core and of an ever-closer Union. According to Soros (2017), the EU should transform itself into an organization that countries like the UK would want to join, which would have implied granting a special treatment to the UK that should have revoked Brexit. This had been David Cameron's (and the UK government's) stance before the 2016 referendum and of other prominent anti-Brexiteers like Tony Blair after the referendum, until the December 2019 elections made it

this reason, it is important to have explicit provisions for entry as well as for exit (Bongardt and Torres 2016; Spolaore 2015). In this context, Brexit was arguably a necessary, although not sufficient, condition for further EU integration (Bongardt and Torres 2020).

Pursuing the option of binding third countries into existing intergovernmental agreements, as suggested for instance in Pisani-Ferry et al. (2016), at the very least carries the risk of a backlash on EU dynamics because it makes the evolution of governance toward the Community sphere more difficult, even if preferences converged among EU member states. In our view, therefore, differentiated integration is only sustainable if anchored to a solid core, the Eurozone.

If the EU needs to heed a lesson from Brexit, it is that there are limits to what differentiated integration can achieve and that the Union will need to focus and deliver on EU common goods in order to be economically and politically sustainable. EMU—the EU's treaty-based integration objective since the Maastricht Treaty—is the case that best illustrates this point. With divergent interests across member states, too much differentiation through opt-outs and reinforced cooperation can erode the cohesiveness of the EU project. In our view, a shared identity is crucial, but difficult to achieve in the absence of a core project.

5 Conclusion

The fundamental lesson from both the Eurozone crisis and Brexit is that the EU needs to focus and deliver on EU common goods in order to be sustainable. From this perspective, it is not necessary to have more EU (treaty-based) differentiation or flexible integration. On the contrary, what the EU's complicated relation with the UK and its subsequent exit from the club illustrate is that are the very limits of variable geometry or differentiated integration within the Union.

In the case of the EU, countries that share a currency and common external borders and that identify more with the Union and the spirit of integration (the case of the six founding members, Portugal, Slovakia, Slovenia, Spain, among others) seem less prone to abandon the EU. Until the elections in the Netherlands and in France, in 2017, there was a certain expectation (and *Schadenfreude*) in (not only) the UK that Brexit contagion could reach Euro area members, contributing to a weakening or end of the EU. As anticipated by Bongardt and Torres (2016), there was no domino effect. Indeed, the effect was precisely the opposite, namely the apparent strengthening of the resolve to accelerate the European integration process (see also Eurobarometer 87 and Hilmer 2017).

---

clear that the democratic mandate and Parliament's decision to leave had to be respected. So far, only Greece and Ireland have either ignored the result or repeated referenda on Europe (with side agreements to get the "necessary result"). Anti-Brexit forces have tried to go the Greek or Irish way but, in the end, a new parliament unblocked Brexit.

However, countries that are less or little integrated in the main institutions of the EU, and above all out of its political core, the Euro area and Schengen, and benefiting from other exceptions, tend to depict a more permanent divergence with respect to the Union's objectives and policies—the cases of Sweden, Denmark, Poland, the Czech Republic and Hungary. Interestingly, some regions/nations within member states, while manifesting a strong preference for EU integration, debate and/or give serious consideration to exiting the states which they are now part of, Scotland and Northern Ireland, in the case of the UK, or Catalonia in the case of Spain (Bongardt and Torres 2018).

On the other hand, from a EU point of view, it does not make sense to accommodate excessively divergent preferences of countries like the UK, Sweden or Poland by means of more institutional flexibility at the expense of the Euro area and the objective of ever-closer union. This would mean transforming the EU into a mere intergovernmental organization without a common currency and political ambitions, which only accommodated the interests of the UK, impeding the deepening of the integration process.

After the upgrading of the European integration objective to EMU at Maastricht, it is now the Euro area, and no longer the internal market, that anchors EU integration. The Euro zone has become de facto the EU's common base, even more so since the Euro crisis. If the countries that committed to join EMU at the time of their accession to the club do not wish to do so any longer (the cases of Sweden and Poland) and only want to be part of the internal market, it could make sense for them—it certainly does so for the EU—to exit the Union and to join the EEA. Those countries cannot make a claim to heterogeneity when it suits them (EMU and/or different preferences in the redistribution of refugees in the Union) and decline it under treaty-based obligations.

It does not seem compatible for countries to want to simultaneously have a Union without differentiation (in which a group of countries is not able to progress faster than laggards on integration) and different objectives and trajectories. It follows that countries with excessively different preferences should leave the EU and participate in a second tier of integration (with much less shared sovereignty and solidarity), notably EEA membership. Somewhat lesser integration in the EU orbit is afforded by participation in the customs union or free trade agreements (apparently the UK preferred option). This amounts to "variable geometry Europe" and not "variable geometry EU."

It is obvious that upon exiting the Union, those countries exclude themselves from other common policies in the domains of cohesion, agriculture, defense, etc. However, they convey the wish to follow another path by not wanting to be part of the political core of the Union and not providing solidarity with it. Those countries may always cooperate with the EU in various domains, as is the case of Norway and Switzerland and even other non-European countries. For that reason, it is important that there are explicit provisions not only for joining the Union (Article 49 TEU)—there are various candidates in waiting—but also for exiting the EU, as established in Article 50. Brexit, the first member state to leave the Union was undoubtedly a watershed moment, making clear that the door is now open for any permanently discontented member to exit and to seek to redefine its trade (and wider) relationship with the EU in line with its different preferences on integration.

References

Alesina A, Spolaore E (1997) On the number and size of nations. Q J Econ 112(4):1026–1056

Alesina A, Tabellini G, Trebbi F (2017) Is Europe an optimal political area? Brookings papers on economic activity conference draft, March

Begg I, Bongardt A, Nicolaïdis K, Torres F (2015) EMU and sustainable integration. J Euro Integr 37(7):803–816

Bongardt A (2020) UK Dithering over Brexit: On the European single market and its regulatory model. In: Bongardt A, Talani S, Torres F (eds) The politics and economics of Brexit. Edward Elgar, Cheltenham

Bongardt A, Torres F (2016) The political economy of Brexit: why making it easier to leave the club can allow for a better functioning EU. Intereconomics 51(4):214–219

Bongardt A, Torres F (2017) Brexit: Uma questão de racionalidade política. Universidade Católica Editora, Lisbon

Bongardt A, Torres F (2018) Sobre as Fronteiras Externas e Internas da União Europeia. Brotéria 186:21–32

Bongardt A, Torres F (2020) Brexit as a question of political rationality: hard choices for the UK, lessons for EU sustainability. In: Bongardt A, Talani S, Torres F (eds), The politics and economics of Brexit, Edward Elgar, Cheltenham

Braga de Macedo J (1995) Multiple allegiances as fate: the Portuguese Idea of Europe. Draft, November. Available online www.jbmacedo.com/courses/euroec.html. Accessed 29 March 2020

Braga de Macedo J (1996) Selling stability at home, earning credibility abroad. In: Torres F (ed) Monetary reform in Europe: an analysis of the issues and proposals for the intergovernmental conference. Universidade Católica Editora, Lisbon, pp 23–58

Braga de Macedo J (2001) Globalization and institutional change: a development perspective. In: Malinvaud E, Sabourin L (eds) Globalization, ethical and institutional concerns. Vatican City, Pontifical Academy of Social Science, pp 223–267

Braga de Macedo J (2002) A 'Eurocentric' perspective on global governance. In: Paper presented at the conference democracy and governance in the EU. Institute for European Studies, Universidade Católica Portuguesa, Lisbon, 18 Oct

Braga de Macedo J (2017) Reform complementarity and policy coordination in Europe: a view from Portugal. CIGI Papers No. 132, June

Demertzis M, Pisany-Ferry J, Sapir A et al (2018) One size does not fit all: European integration by differentiation. Policy Brief 3, Bruegel, Brussels

Dewatripont M, Giavazzi F, Harden I et al (1995) Flexible integration: towards a more effective and democratic Europe, monitoring European integration 6. Centre for Economic Policy Research, London

Dustmann C, Eichengreen B, Otten S et al (2017) Europe's trust deficit: causes and remedies, monitoring international integration 1. CEPR Press, London

European Commission (2017a), Reflection paper on the deepening of EMU. European Commission, Brussels, 31 May. Available online https://ec.europa.eu/commission/publications/reflection-paper-deepening-economic-and-monetary-union_en. Accessed 29 Mar 2020

European Commission (2017b) White paper on the future of Europe. Reflections and Scenarios for the EU27 by 2025, COM(2017) 1 Mar 2025, European Commission, Brussels. Available online https://ec.europa.eu/commission/future-europe/white-paper-future-europe_en. Accessed on 29 Mar 2020

Gastinger M (2019) Brexit! Grexit? Frexit? Considerations on how to explain and measure the propensities of member states to leave the European Union. In: EUI Working Paper RSCAS 2019/85
Hilmer R (2017) What holds Europe together? The EU in the wake of Brexit, Friedrich-Ebert Stiftung, Bonn
Holzinger K, Schimmelfennig F (2012) Differentiated integration in the European Union: many concepts, sparse theory, few data. J Euro Publ Policy 19(2):292–305
Jones E (2018) Towards a theory of disintegration. J Euro Publ Policy 25(3):440–451
Jones E, Torres F (eds) (2016) Governance of the European Monetary Union. Routledge, London, New York
König N (2015) A differentiated view of differentiated integration. Policy paper 140, Jacques Delors Institut, Berlin
Leruth B, Lord C (2015) Differentiated integration in the European Union: a concept, a process, a system or a theory? J Euro Publ Policy 22(6):754–763
Leruth B, Gaenzle S, Trondal J (2017) Differentiated integration and disintegration in the European Union: state-of-the-art and ways for future research. University of Agder, ISL WP1
OECD (2015) Economic Policy Reforms. Going for Growth, Paris: OECD
Pisani-Ferry J, Röttgen N, Sapir A, Tucker P, Wolff G (2016) Europe after Brexit: a proposal for a continental partnership, Bruegel, Brussels, 29 Aug
Pope Francis (2017) Address to the heads of state and government of the European Union in Italy for the celebration of the 60th anniversary of the Treaty of Rome. Vatican, 24 Mar
Soros G (2017) Standing up for Europe. Project Syndicate, 1 June
Spolaore E (2013) What is European integration really about? A political guide for economists. J Econ Perspect 27(3):125–144
Spolaore E (2015) Monnet's chain reaction and the future of Europe. https://VoxEU.org, 25 Jul. Available online https://voxeu.org/article/monnet-s-chain-reaction-and-future-europe. Accessed on 29 Mar 2020
Sternberg C (2015) What were the French telling US by voting down the 'EU constitution'? A case for interpretive research on referendum debates. Comparative Euro Polit 16(2):145–170
Torres F (1995) A Geometria Variável da União Monetária. In: Vasconcelos A (ed) Portugal no Centro da Europa. Edições Quetzal, 1st, 2nd edn, Lisbon, pp 129–148
Torres F (1996) The political economy of monetary reform in Europe. In: Torres F (ed) Monetary reform in Europe. an analysis of the issues and proposals for the intergovernmental conference. Universidade Católica Editora, Lisbon, pp 59–83
Torres F (2009) The role of preferences and the sustainability of EMU. In: Talani SL (ed) The future of EMU. Palgrave Macmillan, Basingstoke, pp 54–74
Vollaard H (2014) Explaining European integration. J Common Market Stud 52(5):1142–1159
Wolfstädter L, Kreilinger V (2017) European Integration via flexibility tools: the cases of EPPO and PESCO. Policy Paper 209, Jacques Delors Institut, Berlin

The Peculiar First Semester of 2012

António S. Pinto Barbosa and Luís Catela Nunes

Abstract In 2011, Portugal was subjected to one of the most stringent austerity packages implemented during the Eurozone crisis, a package known as the troika program. The interpretation of the effects of this program led to a vivid confrontation between two opposing views. A Keynesian view stressed the contractionary effect on the economy, well documented in the deterioration of basic macroindicators. We believe, however, that the austerity package might have simultaneously provided an important and less often acknowledged ingredient to the economy's recovery, namely an increase in investors' confidence as expressed by a sustained decline of the yields in financial markets. To some extent, this opposing German view also accounts for the Portuguese macroeconomic adjustment.

Keywords Eurozone crisis · Keynesian view · Macroeconomic adjustment · Portugal · Troika

1 Introduction

The international financial crisis that hit the world economy in 2007, and the reaction that followed through the implementation of austerity programs in several economies, provides a unique opportunity to evaluate the relative merits of two competing arguments. On the one hand, the argument that such austerity essentially produced a contraction in the economies in which it was applied, causing a reduction in output and an increase in unemployment. This corresponds to the Keynesian view of austerity, with the implicit suggestion that its detrimental effects would tend to aggravate rather than attenuate the impact of the initial shock (see Krugman 2013).

A. S. Pinto Barbosa · L. Catela Nunes (✉)
Nova School of Business and Economics, Universidade Nova de Lisboa, Carcavelos, Portugal
e-mail: lcnunes@novasbe.pt

A. S. Pinto Barbosa
e-mail: abarbosa@novasbe.pt

L. Brites Pereira et al. (eds.), *Economic Globalization and Governance*,
https://doi.org/10.1007/978-3-030-53265-9_12

In contrast, there is the argument stressing the potential improvement in the level of confidence of economic agents, in particular investors, which might result from the application of smart austerity packages. This corresponds to the German view of austerity.[1] From this standpoint, an appropriately designed austerity program may induce economic agents to believe that the economy will soon resume a healthy path via the control of its main macroeconomic disequilibria. This positive impact on economic agents' expectations will tend to stimulate aggregate spending and produce a beneficial expansionary effect in the economy.

Portugal could not easily escape this controversy, as it was subjected in 2011 to one of the most stringent austerity packages implemented during the crisis, a package known as the *troika* program. As one would perhaps expect, the interpretation of the effects of this program led to a vivid confrontation between these two opposing views.

Our purpose here is to bring some brief thoughts on this subject. We start by acknowledging that the Keynesian view is well documented in the data that show a significant contractionary effect in the Portuguese economy and a deterioration in basic macroeconomic indicators. Indeed, it seems that there is no need to question this fact's importance. As to the second view, which points to a positive effect on expectations of the austerity package and which might possibly coexist with the first, the available information is scant and debatable.

We thus thought it would be of interest to concentrate on this more controversial topic by asking the following two questions: First, was the *troika* program's implementation able to raise to some extent the confidence of economic agents, namely investors? Second, if so, did this expectations effect translate into some positive impact on aggregate spending, however limited and partial, so that, in its absence, an even sharper fall in demand would have occurred? We acknowledge, however, that an answer to this important second question is clearly beyond the scope of this paper. As such, we concentrate on the first one, assuming that the answer is still of interest to academics and policymakers.

2 The Portuguese Government Bond Yield During the Crisis

Has the implementation of the austerity program in Portugal been able to lift expectations and raise the confidence level of economic agents? An answer to this question requires a preliminary identification of an indicator that may, to some extent, signal modifications in the confidence levels of economic agents. The yield of Portuguese ten-year government bonds would seem appropriate for this purpose, as it is an indicator normally used for similar analyses. To be sure, this indicator reflects the

[1] Several authors discussed this argument, e.g., Giavazzi and Pagano (1990) and Alesina and Ardagna (2012).

influence of many other factors, namely the observed and expected evolution of reference rates set by the European Central Bank (ECB). But it also reflects the country risk premium, which largely represents the assessment of the country's financial and economic health by investors in the international capital market.

How did the ten-year Portuguese sovereign debt yield react to the implementation of the *troika* program? Figure 1 depicts its evolution between January 2010 and January 2013. The formal start of the *troika* program in May 2011 is also identified in the figure by the first vertical line (it was approved by European Finance Ministers on 16 May 2011).

During this entire period, we note a clear increasing trend in the yield until January 30, 2012, when it reaches a maximum of 17.4%. From that date onward, the rate trends downward with oscillations. Since this downward path occurs when the austerity program had been running for about eight months, the question emerges whether this might be a consequence of its implementation? In other words, a plausible conjecture may be that the successful way in which the program was being implemented might have boosted investor perceptions that things were starting to get under control, and that the main macroeconomic disequilibria were being adequately addressed.

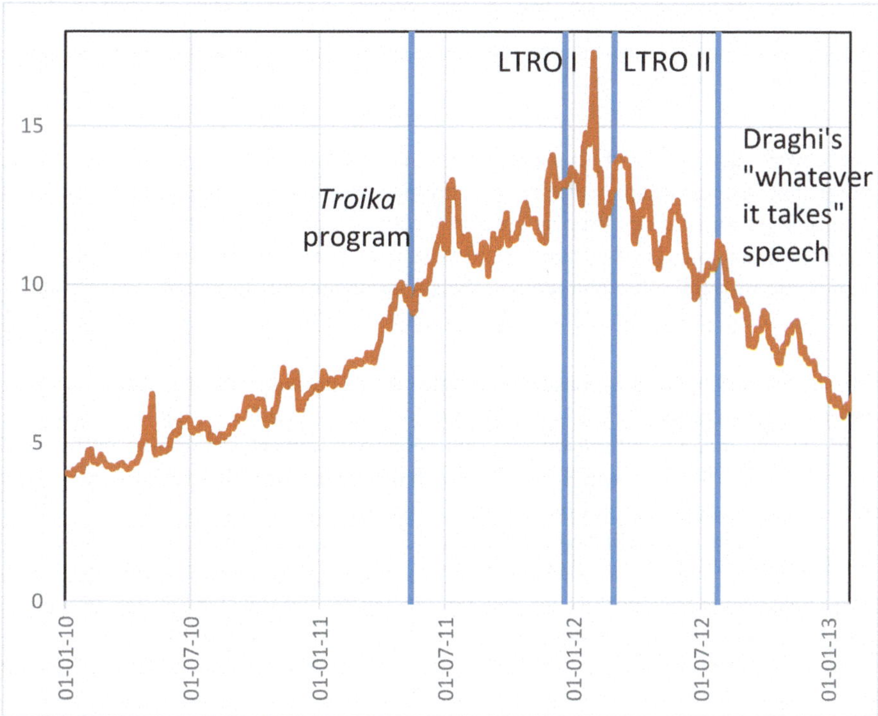

Fig. 1 The ten-year Portuguese government bond yield (*Source* Bloomberg, Thomson Reuters Datastream, and authors' calculations)

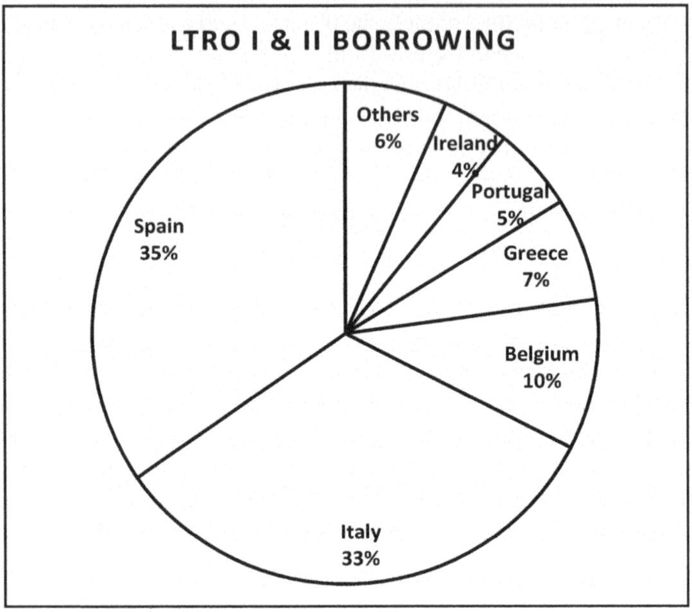

Fig. 2 Distribution of the total amount of the two LTROs between countries (*Source* Daetz et al. (2018), and authors' calculations)

One basic difficulty with this interpretation stems from the fact mentioned above, namely that sovereign yields often reflect multiple influences, some of them unrelated to national circumstances. In particular, the role of the ECB in setting the reference rate in the Eurozone is of paramount importance. The central bank's influence can also operate through other channels such as announcements that may signal more or less willingness to provide financial assistance to Eurozone-crisis countries facing acute liquidity shortages.

In the latter context, it is possible to single out the three most important ECB interventions. On December 8, 2011 (prior to the Portuguese yield reaching its maximum), the ECB announced two long-term refinancing operations (LTRO), both with three-year maturities, through which the central bank made liquidity available to banks under more favorable conditions. The first LTRO was allotted on December 21, 2011. The second LTRO was allotted on February 29, 2012, with an even larger liquidity injection. Finally, the famous Mario Draghi's phrase pronounced on July 26, 2012, should be mentioned: "Within our mandate, the ECB is ready to do whatever it takes to preserve the euro. And believe me, it will be enough" (Draghi 2012).

The first LTRO liquidity injection amounted to 489 billion euros while the second one increased to 529 billion euros.[2] Figure 2 shows the distribution of the total amount

[2]Banks were allowed to roll existing ECB loans into the two LTROs. Net new borrowing was 210 billion euros in the first LTRO and 310 billion euros in the second.

Table 1 Ten-year government bond yields when LTROs were announced (December 8, 2011) and at the peak period in Portugal (January 30, 2012)

Date	Germany (%)	Portugal (%)	Spain (%)	Ireland (%)	Italy (%)	Greece (%)
December 8, 2011	2.1	12.9	5.8	8.6	6.8	33.5
January 30, 2012	1.8	17.4	5.1	7.4	6.1	34.3

Source Bloomberg and Thomson Reuters Datastream

banks in the respective Eurozone countries borrowed through the two LRTOs.[3] From this total, Portugal received about 5%, corresponding to 49 billion euros, a share considered to be relatively small.[4]

Note that this type of intervention tends to favor a decline in the corresponding sovereign yields through a reduction in the risk premium. In the Portuguese case, however, and in contrast to what happened with Spain and Greece, the ten-year yield continued to rise after this first intervention until it reached its maximum by the end of January (see Table 1). This reinforces the belief that the ECB interventions might not be the sole factor behind the sovereign yields' evolution. Other country-specific factors would have also presumably contributed to this evolution.

The third important ECB intervention during this period is the famous "whatever it takes" statement by Draghi, made on July 26, 2012, and the accompanying declaration of the willingness of the ECB to conduct whatever liquidity injections (Outright Monetary Transactions—OMT) might be necessary to give support to that statement. This important intervention was interpreted by the market as the willingness to provide unlimited support, if necessary, to countries facing acute liquidity crises that could endanger the monetary union itself. This would broadly correspond to the role of the ECB as a lender of last resort. The legal basis for such a bold move, and its conformity with the statutes of the central bank, was vigorously questioned in some quarters but the European Court of Justice refrained from considering it out of the bank's remit.

What effects on Portuguese yields, if any, followed from these interventions? In Fig. 1, the dates of the two LTRO interventions and the Draghi statement are identified by vertical lines. One can see that the Portuguese yields started to fall from the January maximum but only sometime after the first LTRO. The central bank interventions had certainly contributed to this decline.

On the other hand, the Draghi speech and the accompanying announcement of OMT, which many consider to be the decisive factor in restoring Eurozone market confidence, do not seem to have had a significant impact on the declining path of the

[3]The LTRO amounts are obtained from Daetz et al. (2018).

[4]Alphaville (2012) mentioned Portugal's limited participation in the first liquidity injection: "Portugal is also the only peripheral Eurozone bond market that has failed to rally since the European Central Bank announced plans to offer three-year loans to the Eurozone's banks on December 8, a move that averted a credit crunch."

Portuguese yield that had begun about six months earlier. This issue is raised in a study on the implementation of the Portuguese *troika* program:

The evidence regarding the impact of the Draghi speech and the announcement of the outright monetary transactions program is more ambiguous. The decline in yields on Portuguese bonds began well before the Draghi speech and seems to have stalled by June 2012, but it resumed after the Draghi speech in July (Eichenbaum et al. 2016, p. 44).

It is possible, of course, to speculate that the evolution of Eurozone instability might have somehow contributed to a gradual build-up of the anticipation of some forthcoming drastic intervention on the ECB's part to assure the ultimate survival of the monetary union. To use an expression common during that period of instability, the market might be expecting the central bank to use a "bazooka" or even an "atomic bomb." But if this "expectational" phenomenon did occur, its anticipation would have spread its beneficial stabilization effects across the whole Eurozone, especially on the periphery, where instability was more acute. Does this correspond to what we observed in that special semester that preceded the Draghi speech?

Figure 3 additionally incorporates the behavior of the ten-year government bond yields of Spain and Italy, two peripheral countries also afflicted by financial markets'

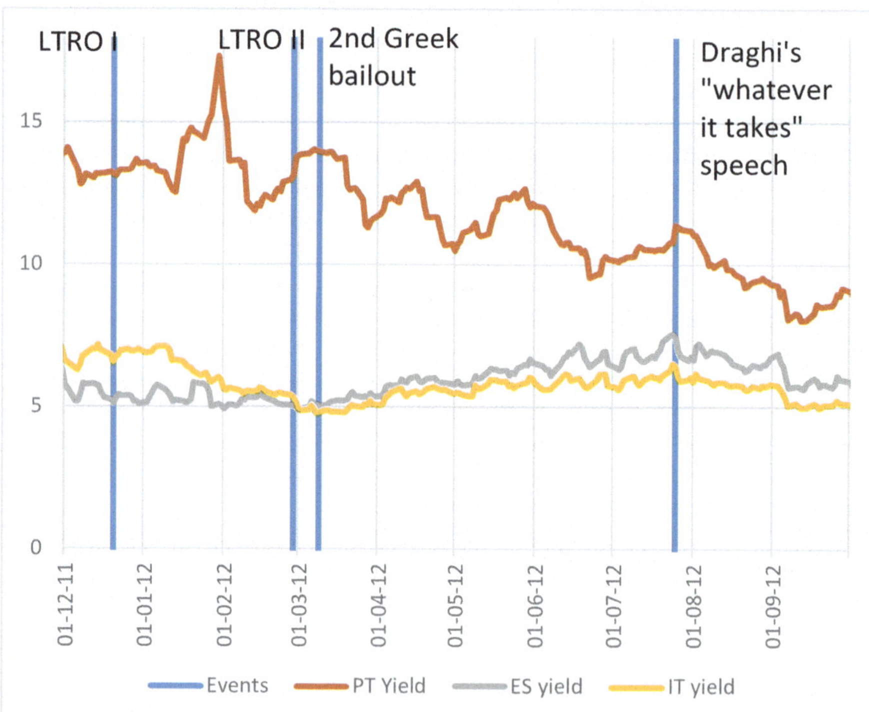

Fig. 3 Ten-year government bond yields for Portugal, Spain, and Italy (*Source* Bloomberg and Thomson Reuters Datastream)

instability. The comparison with the Portuguese yield shows a sharp contrast. While the Portuguese rate shows a downward trend during this period, the Spanish and Italian yields show an increasing trend instead (especially after March, when a restructuring of the Greek debt, also indicated in the figure, took place) and they start to decline much later, only after the Draghi speech.[5]

3 Dating the Sovereign Debt Crises

A more comprehensive analysis of the behavior of Portuguese sovereign debt yields, vis-à-vis other peripheral countries, also suggests that the first semester of 2012 stands out as a peculiar period. In particular, we identify stress regimes in the yields of each country. These regimes are defined as periods of an increasing trend in the time series of the ten-year government bond yields for each of the peripheral countries most under pressure during the crisis (sometimes referred to as the PIIGS countries): Portugal, Italy, Ireland, Greece, and Spain.

Since there is a large volatility in the yields' behavior over time, and even more so during crisis periods, we first extract the corresponding trend components from each country's observed yields. One of the most popular trend-extraction approaches is the Hodrick–Prescott filter, which has received strong criticism in recent years (Hamilton 2018). As such, we adopt the recently proposed boosted HP filter that is described in Phillips and Shi (2019).[6]

In order to identify the stress regimes in each country's yields, we adopt a two-step approach. First, the boosted HP filter is used to extract the trend component for each country. For this task, we consider a longer period that extends from January 1, 2007, until September 21, 2018. In a second step, the following approach is used to identify regimes of stress in each country's yields: Stress regimes correspond to periods of sustained increases in the trend component. These periods begin when the trend component starts increasing (when there is a trough in the trend component) and end when the trend component starts decreasing (when a peak is reached). To avoid identifying periods where the trend yield is increasing but only marginally, we disregard regimes with an average increase in the trend yield that is below 0.5 percentage points per day.

Figure 4 depicts the resulting stress regimes for each country and clearly shows that the stress regimes tend to occur simultaneously in all peripheral countries. In the case of Portugal, there was at least some other country (during all identified stress periods)

[5]It is sometimes speculated that had the instability not contaminated larger economies like Spain and Italy, there might not have been a Draghi speech in the first place.

[6]This study shows that the boosted HP filter is able to recover the trend mechanisms present in a wide variety of situations, with various degrees of volatility, persistence, and trend behaviors, such as time series with unit root processes, deterministic polynomial drifts, and polynomial drifts with multiple structural breaks even without knowledge of the number of such breaks. Given the typical behavior of yield time series, characterized by large volatility swings and multiple structural changes over time, the boosted HP filter is a natural choice to estimate the trend component.

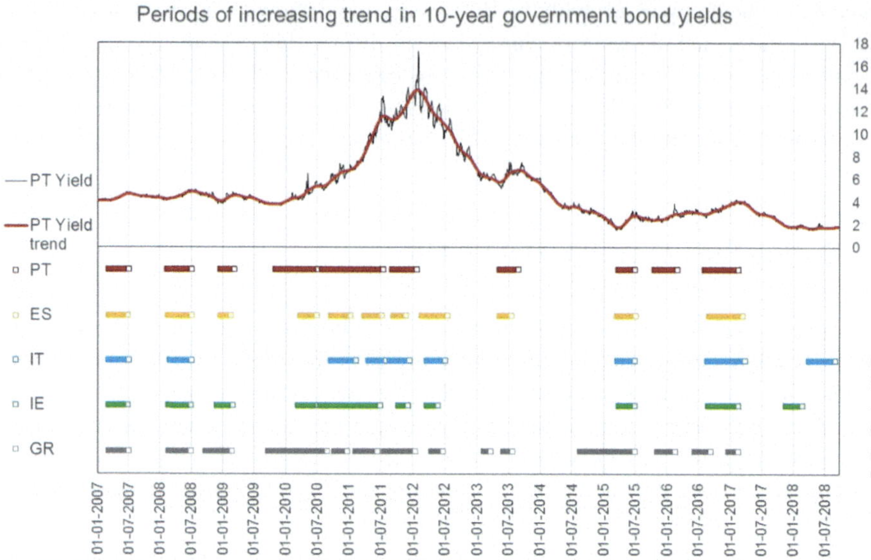

Fig. 4 Portuguese ten-year yield and trend component, and stress regimes in the yields of peripheral countries (*Source* Bloomberg, Thomson Reuters Datastream, and authors' calculations)

where a stress occurred during part of that period. Moreover, the first semester of 2012 stands out. During this period, other countries exhibited stress regimes with rising yields while Portugal's yields were decreasing. And this peculiarity—Portugal displaying declining yields in contrast with the other peripheral countries—only took place during that time period.

4 Discussion

Could the observed decline in Portuguese yields during the first semester of 2012 reflect the effect of the country's rating being regularly published by the main agencies? Did any rating upgrade occur during that period? If so, the improvement in market confidence, as expressed by the reduction in yields, may reflect the information thus conveyed to some extent.

The only known rating modification in this period was that of Standard and Poors (S&P) on January 13, 2012, which was a downgrading to BB from BBB—(set previously on December 5, 2011). If any effect was to be expected from this announcement, it would have been an increase in the yield, and this indeed happened. The already rising yield experienced a further sharp increase, until it reached its maximum at the end of January, as noted above. Therefore, the increase in market confidence, which we believe expressed itself after 31 January, occurred notwithstanding this

Table 2 Sovereign bond holdings by OMFIs, million euros

	Portugal	Italy	Spain
Dec 2011	22,651	265,408	186,427
June 2012	30,305	354,286	225,796

Source Bruegel Data Set

earlier negative S&P news. At the same time, we should mention that the other two ratings agencies (Fitch and Moody's) kept their previous ratings unchanged during this period (both below investment grade).

Another influence that is often suggested as an important explanation for the sovereign yields' behavior is the role of banks, particularly domestic ones. In the case of Portugal, banks increased their exposure to sovereign debt during the first semester of 2012. To what extent could this increase explain the downward trend in the ten-year yields observed during that period when compared with the Spanish and Italian ones? Note that the possible relevant role of this explanation is not incompatible, in principle, with our previous interpretation. In fact, it could similarly express a move by banks toward a more optimistic view about the evolution of the Portuguese economy. Given that we cannot exclude the possible role of other relevant factors, it is useful to also consider the evolution of peripheral banks' (other monetary financial institutions) exposure to sovereign debt (Table 2).

In the first semester of 2012, we note a significant increase of around 7.6 billion euros of Portuguese banks' exposure to domestic sovereign debt, which represents a 33.8% increase relative to the holdings in December 2011. At the same time, however, there is a concomitant rise in Italian and Spanish debt (respectively 88.9 and 39.4 billion euros, representing increases of 33.5% and 21%). It is thus difficult to explain the yields' contrasting behavior based solely on the banking factor.

Only other factors, over and above the common influences (like the ECB interventions), could explain the yields' different behavior in periphery countries. Those factors should express the impact of country-specific circumstances. In the Portuguese case, we conjecture that the financial markets started, at a certain point in time, to entertain the possibility that the Portugal's economic and financial difficulties were somehow beginning to be controlled. Note that Portugal was under a specific stabilization program, which was not the case of Spain and Italy. Under this interpretation, the nature and quality of the policies implemented under that adjustment may have been a relevant factor in explaining the yields' idiosyncratic behavior. In this regard, the first semester of 2012 provided us with a rare opportunity to observe the discriminating behavior of an indicator—the ten-year sovereign bond yield—that was subject to strong common influences at the same time.

5 Conclusion

In addition to the well-documented negative Keynesian effects, we conclude that the austerity package implemented in Portugal may have simultaneously provided an important, and often less acknowledged, ingredient regarding the economy's recovery, namely an increase in investors' confidence as expressed by a sustained decline in financial-market yields. In this light, it might be said that the *troika* program also included an expansionary component in the sense that a sharper contraction of the economy would have most likely occurred in its absence. The possible coexistence of the two competing arguments about austerity's macroeconomic effects should therefore not be excluded a priori. Indeed, during Portugal's crisis period, the first semester of 2012 seems to provide singular evidence that reinforces this interpretation.

References

Alesina A, Ardagna S (2012) The design of fiscal adjustments. NBER Working Paper 18423

Daetz SL, Tang DY, Subrahmanyam MG et al (2018) Can central banks boost corporate investment: evidence from the ECB liquidity injections. Danmarks Nationalbank Working Papers, No. 126

Draghi M (2012) Speech by the president of the European Central Bank, 26 July. Global investment conference, London. Available online www.ecb.europa.eu/press/key/date/2012/html/sp120726.en.html. Accessed 4 Mar 2020

Eichenbaum M, Rebelo S, de Resende C (2016) The Portuguese crisis and the IMF. IEO background paper BP/16-02/05. International Monetary Fund, Washington

FT Alphaville (2012) Portugal, back in the frame, financial times, London, 26 January. Available online https://ftalphaville.ft.com/2012/01/26/853131/portugal-back-in-the-frame/. Accessed 29 Mar 2020

Giavazzi F, Pagano M (1990) Can severe fiscal contractions be expansionary? Tales of two small European Countries. NBER macroeconomics annual 1990, vol 5, National Bureau of Economic Research Inc., Chicago, pp 75–122

Hamilton JD (2018) Why you should never use the Hodrick-Prescott filter. Rev Econ Stat 100(5):831–843

Krugman P (2013) Europe's Keynesian Problem. The Conscience of a Liberal blog, 25 May. Available online https://krugman.blogs.nytimes.com/author/paul-krugman/. Accessed 4 Mar 2020

Phillips PC, Shi Z (2019) Boosting the Hodrick-Prescott filter. https://arXiv.com/1905.00175

The Krugman–Macedo Diagram Revisited

Miguel Lebre de Freitas and Miguel Faria-e-Castro

Abstract We revisit the diagram developed by Krugman and Macedo (The economic consequences of the April 25th revolution, Krugman and Braga de Macedo, Economia III:435–483, 1979) to study the adjustment path of output and real wage gaps in a small open economy. Using time series data, we estimate sequences of real exchange rates that are consistent with internal and external balance for the Portuguese economy and use these estimates to plot its evolution during 1971–2017. Following a period of prolonged appreciation, we find that the real exchange rate fell below its equilibrium level during the 2011–2015 adjustment phase, which was driven by both declining nominal wages and improvements in terms of trade.

Keywords Economic regimes · External and internal balance · Macroeconomic adjustment · Portugal · Small open economy

1 Introduction

Forty years have passed since Jorge Braga de Macedo and Paul Krugman published "The Economic Consequences of the April 25 Revolution" (Krugman and Macedo 1979). In that article, the authors analyzed Portuguese macroeconomic developments, starting in the years that preceded the 1974 Revolution until the completion of the first standby arrangement that was negotiated with the International Monetary Fund (IMF) in 1977. At that time, Portugal was adjusting to an adverse combination of domestic and external shocks that moved the economy away from full employment and external balance. This situation included a global recession, high oil prices, a massive return migration from the former Portuguese colonies in Africa, and political and social instability following the military coup. On the policy front, the economy underwent a wave of government interventions, which the authors identified as a movement

M. Lebre de Freitas (✉)
Universidade de Aveiro and NIPE, Aveiro, Portugal
e-mail: afreitas@ua.pt

M. Faria-e-Castro
Federal Reserve Bank of St. Louis, St. Louis, MO, USA

L. Brites Pereira et al. (eds.), *Economic Globalization and Governance*,
https://doi.org/10.1007/978-3-030-53265-9_13

toward a "politicized market economy," i.e., "one in which the distributional role of prices becomes a justification for their manipulation" (p. 456).

The article's main contribution was that of a visual tool used to map the trajectory of a small open economy, which focused on two policy goals, "internal balance" and "external balance," and on two strategic variables—the "real output gap" (defined as the actual relative to potential output) and the "real wage gap" (defined as the real wage relative to the "warranted level," i.e., the level that would be consistent with internal and external balance). Using this tool, the authors analyzed the Portuguese economy's macroeconomic adjustment during 1974–1978. The Krugman–Macedo (KM) diagram was revisited by Braga de Macedo (1984, 1990) in the analysis of economic and political dilemmas associated with Portugal's process of European integration, as well as resulting policy responses. As the author points out, excessive wage growth was no longer the main issue in the subsequent macroeconomic episodes. Instead, the rivalry between the two main trade unions (which eroded their bargaining power) together with the emergence of short-term renewable labor contracts allowed employers to overcome rigid labor laws and adjust to changing economic circumstances.

Portugal has changed much in the last four decades. Democracy has been consolidated, economic institutions were developed in the context of the European Union (EU), and its productive structure has been modernized. Nevertheless, the recent crises revealed a macroeconomic environment that was highly vulnerable to changes in international borrowing conditions. By 2011, Portuguese authorities requested international financial assistance for the third time since the 1974 Revolution. The previous decade had witnessed the accumulation of large external imbalances fueled by capital inflows. During that period, real wages had increased faster than the corresponding EU average, fiscal conditions remained fragile, and oil prices had risen. In an influential paper, Blanchard (2007) argued that external competitiveness had been eroded because unit labor costs had increased faster at home than abroad. Thus, in the absence of an exchange rate tool, the required adjustment in relative prices would doom the country to a long period of disinflation until downward wage and price pressures brought the economy back to external balance. The view that rapid wage growth was the cause of external imbalance (rather than its consequence) is controversial (Campos e Cunha 2008). Still, Blanchard and Portugal (2017) contended that much of the current account's recovery during 2011–2013 was the result of a negative and large output gap ("import compression"). Reis (2015), on the other hand, emphasized the considerable expansion of exports, "in spite of small changes in relative prices" (p. 443).

This paper's purpose is to revisit the main phases of Portuguese macroeconomic adjustment using the lens of the KM diagram.[1] We depart from the original work in that our assessment of the real wage gap is based on an index of relative unit labor

[1]Blanchard and Portugal (2017) also summarize the recent macroeconomic adjustment of the Portuguese economy in terms of a diagram showing the deviations from "internal balance" and "external balance" but do not disentangle the contribution of relative prices.

costs vis-à-vis the EU. Instead of calibrating a production function, we use regression analysis. We find that oil prices continue to play an important role, even though this influence has been declining. Our analysis suggests that the emergence of large current account deficits during the 2000s was indeed associated with a departure of the real exchange rate from its warranted level, and also that much of the external adjustment during 2011–2013 was achieved through expenditure reduction, as argued by Blanchard and Portugal (2017). However, the real exchange rate also adjusted downward—in line with the contraction in demand—pulled by declining nominal wages. Moreover, an improvement in terms of trade at the outset of the adjustment program implied an increase in the "warranted real wage," driving the real exchange rate gap below zero. The downward adjustment in wages, together with benign external conditions, has thus allowed the Portuguese economy to return to external balance under full employment but without a long process of "competitiveness through disinflation."

The remainder of this chapter is organized as follows: In Sect. 2, we present the KM diagram. In Sect. 3, we propose an approach, based on the real exchange rate, to measure the gap between the actual real wage and the one that would be consistent with internal and external balance. In Sect. 4, we describe our empirical strategy. In Sect. 5, we present the main empirical results. In Sect. 6, we revisit the KM diagram to analyze the Portuguese economy's macroeconomic adjustment since the 1974 Revolution and Sect. 7 concludes.

2 The Krugman–Macedo Diagram

In their proposed analytical framework, Krugman and Macedo (1979) focused on two key strategic variables: the real wage rate and output level. Among the various determinants of employment and balance of payments, the authors argued that these two variables are critically important. A higher level of output is associated with a higher level of employment, ceteris paribus. In turn, real wages are a key relative price in a small open economy, as they affect the incentives to consume and produce tradable and non-tradable goods (and hence, the current account).

Given that economies are constantly being exposed to different types of shocks that affect the levels of both output and real wages consistent with full employment and external balance, the authors focused on the gaps between the actual levels of these two strategic variables and their corresponding reference levels. The diagram's two dimensions, replicated in Fig. 1, are therefore the "output gap" (defined as the actual relative to potential output) and the "real wage gap" (defined as the actual relative to the "warranted" real wage, i.e., the level consistent with internal and external balance).

The strategic variables are determined by both policy (government spending, exchange rate, and laws) and exogenous factors (such as productivity). These factors can have an impact either through the variable's actual levels (actual real output and actual real wages) or through changes in the corresponding reference levels (full

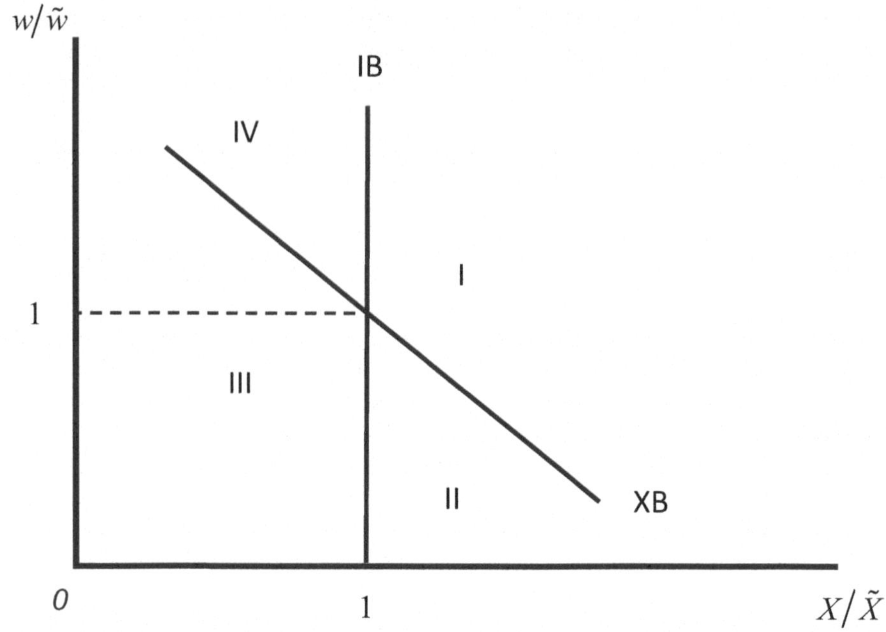

Fig. 1 Krugman–Macedo diagram

employment output or warranted real wage). For example, an increase in oil prices causes the trade balance to deteriorate, thereby requiring a lower real wage to ensure external balance, ceteris paribus. If market failures or legal impediments prevent the actual wage from reaching its "warranted" level, then a positive real wage gap will result.

The strategic variables, in turn, affect the employment level and balance of payments. The KM diagram thus plots the "output gap" and "real wage gap" combinations that are consistent with full employment and external balance. Potential output is assumed to depend only on endowments and technology, and not on real wages.[2] For this reason, the internal balance (IB) locus is vertical. By construction, observations on the right-hand side of IB correspond to situations of macroeconomic overheating, and those of the left-hand side describe situations of unemployment.

The external balance (XB) locus is represented by the negative relationship between the real wage gap and output: Ceteris paribus, an increase in real wages causes a reallocation of resources toward non-tradable goods and a demand shift toward tradable goods, causing the trade balance to deteriorate. Thus, a decrease in domestic demand is required to restore the external balance.[3] As shown in Fig. 1, the

[2]For the sake of simplicity, the model ignores the labor supply response to changes in real wages.

[3]Note that the external balance does not refer to a country's state of intertemporal solvency. It refers instead to the non-accumulation of liabilities vis-à-vis the rest of the world. This is not necessarily a

IB and XB loci split the diagram into four zones of economic unhappiness: Zone I—inflation and deficit; Zone II—inflation and surplus; Zone III—unemployment and surplus; and Zone IV—unemployment and deficit. Internal and external balances occur when $w = \tilde{w}$ and $X = \tilde{X}$.

The KM diagram's advantage, relative to the conventional Swan diagram (Swan 1956), is that it focuses on strategic rather than "raw" policy variables. This makes it more versatile to describe an economy's adjustment path, especially when different policies and other exogenous factors simultaneously affect the same strategic/intermediate variable.

3 The Real Wage Gap and the Real Exchange Rate

To map the Portuguese economy's trajectory using the KM diagram, Krugman and Macedo (1979) made "hypothetical calculations" for the real wage gap, based on estimates of the actual real wage, productivity, terms of trade effects, indirect taxation, and social security contributions. In their calculations, the authors assumed a production function with unit elasticity of substitution between capital and labor.

Under the unit elasticity assumption, the wage rate's departures from the level implied by labor demand can be computed as the deviation of labor's share in national income from a reference level. Formally, let W denote the average compensation per employee, including taxes and employer contributions (the "nominal wage") and let a denote the gross-value-added at constant prices per worker (the "average product of labor"). Letting β denote the elasticity of output with respect to the labor input, profit maximization under perfect competition implies that the real warranted wage rate must be such that:

$$\frac{\tilde{W}}{P} = \beta a \tag{1}$$

Given the actual nominal wage, W, the real wage gap is then implied in the following ratio:

$$\frac{W}{\tilde{W}} = \frac{ULC}{\beta P} \tag{2}$$

where $ULC = W/a$. In light of Eq. 2, the wage gap is zero whenever the share of labor in national income equals β. Krugman and Macedo (1979) assumed the labor share benchmark to be equal to one half.

Estimating the real wage gap using Eq. 2 corresponds to assessing the extent to which real wages deviate from the level implied by the demand for labor. This

policy goal at each moment in time, but rather a reference point for what should happen (on average) in order for a country to remain solvent.

method, however, abstracts from wage developments abroad and is therefore an imperfect measure to capture the external balance. In this chapter, we focus instead on unit labor costs at home versus those abroad (the real exchange rate based on unit labor costs):

$$\theta = \frac{ULC}{ULC^*} = \frac{W/a}{W^*/a^*} \tag{3}$$

Letting $\tilde{\theta}$ denote the real exchange that is consistent with internal and external balance, the "warranted" nominal wage rate is thus given by $\tilde{W} = a\tilde{\theta}ULC^*$. Our measure of "wage gap" is essentially a measure of the real exchange rate gap:

$$\frac{W}{\tilde{W}} = \frac{ULC}{\tilde{\theta}ULC^*} = \frac{\theta}{\tilde{\theta}} \tag{4}$$

In light of Eq. 4, the wage gap is zero when the actual real exchange rate (θ) is equal to the warranted real exchange rate ($\tilde{\theta}$). Abstracting for a moment from the value of $\tilde{\theta}$, in Fig. 2 we compare the time paths of Portugal's labor share ULC/P and θ for the period 1960–2018 (for the data, see Footnote 6). The difference between the two curves is given by the ratio P/ULC^*.

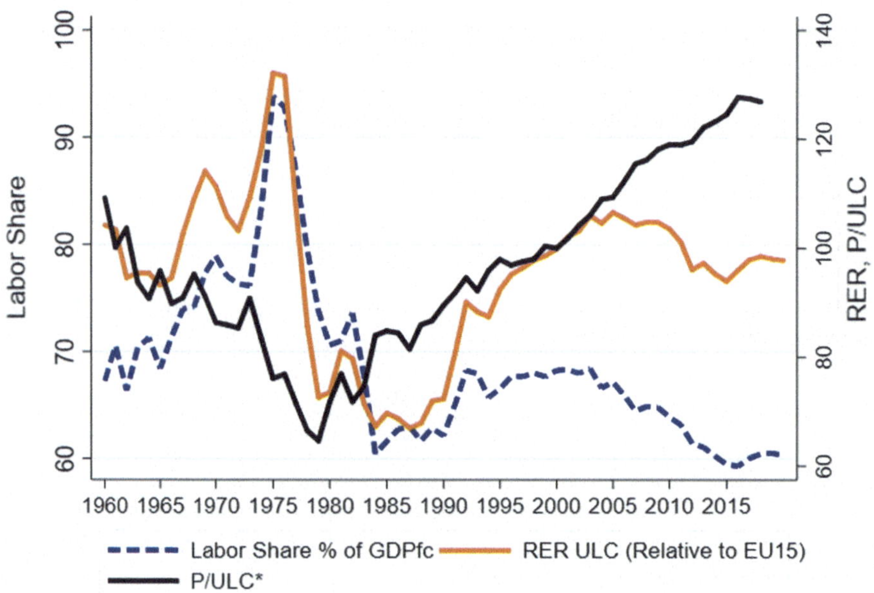

Fig. 2 Unit labor costs, real exchange rate, and labor share, 1960–2017 (*Source* Authors' calculations using AMECO data)

As shown in Fig. 2, the labor share and real exchange rate moved roughly together from the beginning of the sample period until the early 1990s (the 10-year correlation between the two series reaches 93% in 1995). Between the mid-1990s and 2007, however, the real exchange rate is increasing while the labor share remains roughly trendless (the 10-year correlation declines to –0.40%). This observation suggests that the real exchange rate appreciation during this period had more to do with changes in relative prices between tradable and non-tradable goods (caused by imbalances between savings and investment) than with wage–productivity misalignments (Lebre de Freitas and Faria e Castro 2014). This observation motivates our focus on the measure given by Eq. 4.

4 Empirical Approach

Our main methodological challenge is to find the notional warranted real exchange rate (henceforth WRER), against which the observed real exchange rate (RER) can be compared. This WRER must be time-varying since the economy is constantly exposed to real shocks. In this chapter, we use regression analysis to estimate the real exchange rate that would be consistent with full employment and external balance, at each moment in time. We adopt the notion of external balance proposed by Williamson (1983): a situation in which the "fundamental account", *FA*, (defined as the sum of the economy's primary current account deficit with net inflows of foreign direct investment) is equal to zero.

The WRER may, in principle, be influenced by a number of factors that include productivity in the tradable and non-tradable sectors, the composition of government spending, terms of trade, net international investment position, unilateral transfers, among others (Rebelo and Vegh 1995). Let $\mathbf{Y}_t$ be the vector of long-run determinants of WRER, including a constant. Then, a log-linear model of real exchange rate determination can be written as[4]:

$$\theta_t = \boldsymbol{\beta} \boldsymbol{Y}_t + \gamma FA_t + u_t \tag{5}$$

In the short run, deviations of the real exchange rate from WRER are associated with departures of the fundamental account balance from zero (its long-run value). Denoting by x_t and $\tilde{x}_t$ actual and potential output, respectively, we can describe the behavior of short-term fluctuations in the fundamental account as:

$$FA_t = \alpha_0 + a_1(x_t - \tilde{x}_t) + a_2\left(\theta_t - \tilde{\theta}_t\right) + v_t \tag{6}$$

Our baseline approach consists of first estimating Eq. 5 and then using the resulting estimates together with $FA_t = 0$ to obtain a measure of WRER ($\widetilde{\theta}_t = \widehat{\boldsymbol{\beta}} \boldsymbol{Y}_t$). Then,

[4]This approach is adapted from Clark and MacDonald (1998).

we use this measure to estimate Eq. 6. As robustness, we consider a one-step approach that consists of replacing Eq. 5 in Eq. 6 and estimating these relationships in a single step:

$$FA_t = \alpha_0 + a_1\left(x_t - \widetilde{x}_t\right) + a_2\theta_t - \boldsymbol{\delta Y}_t + \varepsilon_t \tag{7}$$

where $\varepsilon_t = \nu_t - a_2 u_t$, and $\boldsymbol{\delta} = a_2\boldsymbol{\beta}$. In the one-step procedure, WRER is computed by first estimating Eq. 7 and then imposing both external balance ($FA_t = 0$) and internal balance ($x_t = \widetilde{x}_t$), i.e., $\widetilde{\theta}_t = \left(-\widehat{\alpha}_0 - \widehat{\boldsymbol{\delta}}\boldsymbol{Y}_t\right)/\widehat{\alpha}_2$. This one-step approach is reminiscent of Dolado and Vinals (1991).[5]

5 Estimation

Our baseline two-step specification consists of first estimating Eq. 5 and then using the resulting WRER estimates to estimate Eq. 6, where we include an autoregressive term to account for potential serial correlation. We do not include any lags of independent variables in order to allow for reverse causality. We experiment with different combinations of variables in the $\mathbf{Y}_t$ vector, guided by the literature: (i) measures of the foreign output gap; (ii) the ratio of government spending to gross domestic product (GDP); (iii) a measure of terms of trade; (iv) a measure of relative total factor productivity vis-à-vis the rest of the world; and (vi) the real price of oil.[6] After some experimentation, our preferred specification is one where the real oil price and its interaction with a linear trend appear as determinants of WRER. The linear trend accounts for structural changes in oil's importance for the Portuguese economy, which has declined over time.[7]

Table 1 presents the two-stage results in columns 1 and 2, respectively. Column 3 shows the single-step specification results from Eq. 7. All coefficients are significant at the 5% level in both stages. Furthermore, all coefficient signs are consistent with the relationships predicted by theory. In the first stage, the real exchange rate depreciates with an increase in the real oil price or with an increase in the fundamental account balance. In the second stage, the fundamental account balance deteriorates either with an increase in the domestic output gap or with an increase in the real exchange rate gap. These relationships are preserved in the single-step specification.

[5]Studies using the Dolado and Vinals (1991) approach that focus on the Portuguese economy include Lebre de Freitas (1992), Costa (1998), and Lebre de Freitas and Faria e Castro (2014). Over the overlapping periods, the corresponding gap estimates are broadly consistent with our own.

[6]Data on fundamental account, output gap, real exchange rate, estimated WRER, and real exchange rate gap are available from the corresponding author upon request. For details on the sources and construction of all data series, see the Annex.

[7]The relevant data series shows that the energy deficit at constant prices, which is interpretable as an indicator of oil dependency, has been decreasing over time (source in previous footnote).

Table 1 Estimation results: two-step and one-step

	(1)	(2)	(3)
	First stage: $\log \theta_t$	Second stage: FA_t	Single-step: FA_t
Constant	4.645*** (142.68)	−0.00102 (−0.27)	0.810*** (4.84)
FA_t	−1.797*** (−4.82)		
Real Oil_t	−0.210*** (−5.39)		−0.0450*** (−3.31)
Real Oil_t *t	0.00327*** (3.60)		0.000768** (2.61)
FA_{t-1}		0.683*** (7.22)	
$\log \theta_t - \log \tilde{\theta}_t$		−0.0789** (−2.67)	
$x_t - \tilde{x}_t$		−0.240** (−2.15)	−0.287* (−1.72)
$\log \theta_t$			−0.174*** (−4.84)
N	54	53	54
Adj. R2	0.457	0.663	0.321

Notes t-statistics in parentheses *$p < 0.10$, **$p < 0.05$, ***$p < 0.01$

In Fig. 3, we plot the data for the fundamental account balance, along with the fitted values from the one- and two-step procedures. As a robustness check, Fig. 4 plots the real exchange rate path together with alternative WRER estimates (using either the two- or one-step procedures or replacing Real Oil by the AMECO terms of trade series).

The corresponding measures of the real exchange rate gap are shown in Fig. 5. The paths for WRER and the corresponding gap estimates are similar across specifications. The estimated path for the equilibrium real exchange rate indicates significant departures from the period average, reflecting large swings in oil prices throughout the 1970s and early 1980s, and again in the 2000s. In this latter episode, however, the impact on WRER was lower, due to the fundamental balance being less sensitive to changes in oil prices.

Figure 6 shows the relative contributions of the output and real exchange rate gaps to the movements in the fundamental account, using the second stage of our two-step procedure (Table 1, column 2). These relative contributions are plotted starting in 1995. The decomposition highlights the fact that most of the fundamental account deficit prior to the recent adjustment program can be accounted for by a positive real exchange rate gap. The RER gap's contribution falls in recent years, disappearing completely by 2012. By 2014, the RER has depreciated sufficiently so that the RER gap contributes positively to the fundamental account balance.

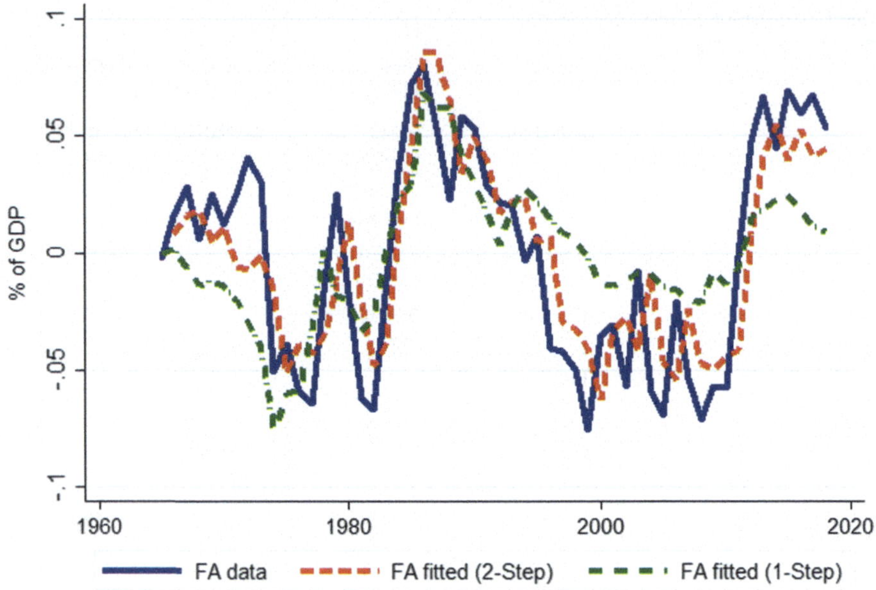

Fig. 3 Fundamental account balance: actual and fitted, 1960–2017

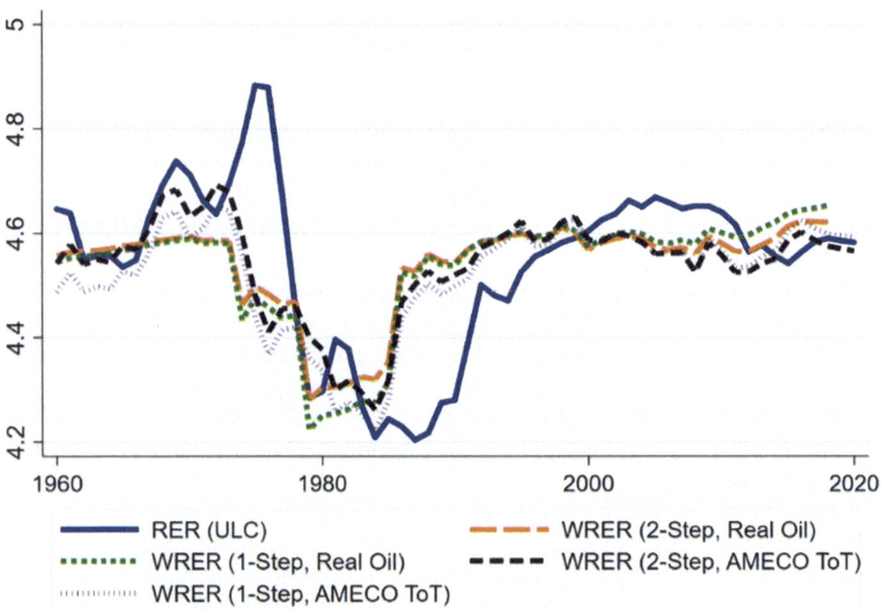

Fig. 4 Real exchange rate and estimated WRER (logs), 1960–2017

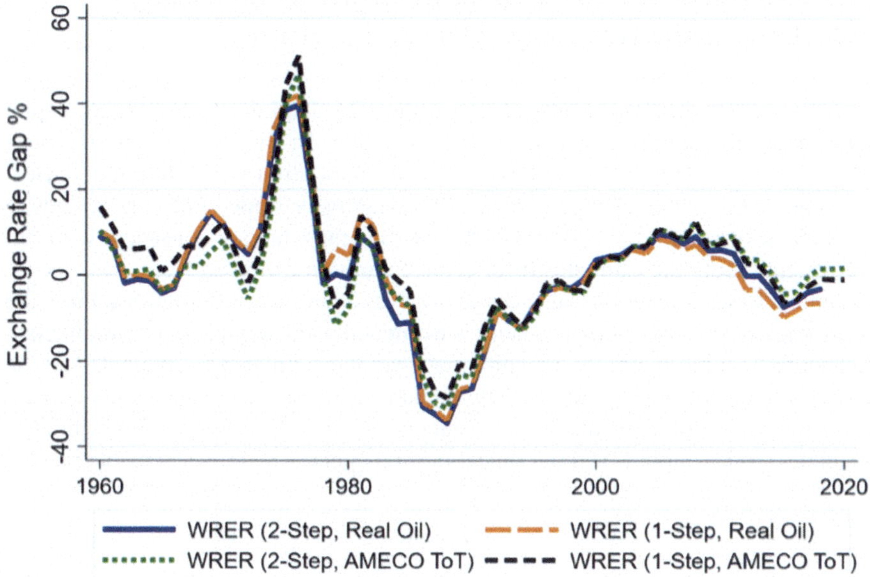

Fig. 5 Exchange rate gap estimates, 1960–2017

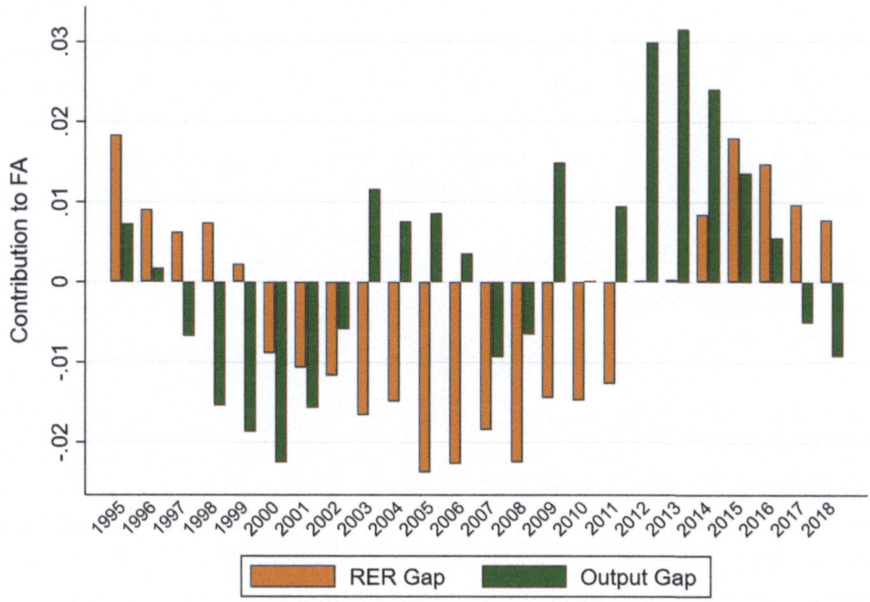

Fig. 6 Fundamental account decomposition, 1995–2018. *Notes* The figure shows the long-run contributions of the output and real exchange rate gaps to movements in the fundamental account based on Eq. 6 and Table 1, column 2 estimates

6 Five Decades of Macroeconomic Adjustment Through the Lens of the Krugman–Macedo Diagram

We now use the estimated results to revisit the KM diagram. In Fig. 7, we depict the Portuguese economy's path from 1971 to 1995. In Fig. 8, we continue until 2017. As in Fig. 1, the horizontal axes measure the output gap, while the vertical axes measure the real exchange rate gap. The negatively sloped line corresponds to the combinations of output and real exchange rate gaps that are consistent with full employment (using the estimates from Table 1, column 2).

Needless to say, the empirical exercise involves a number of limitations. First, the second stage of our two-step procedure is estimated using a dependent variable lag, which slightly complicates the mapping between the estimated coefficients and the external balance locus. Second, the output and real exchange rate gaps only explain around 66% of the fundamental account balance's variation, based on our estimates. Nonetheless, our simple KM diagram calibration appears to deliver sensible results.

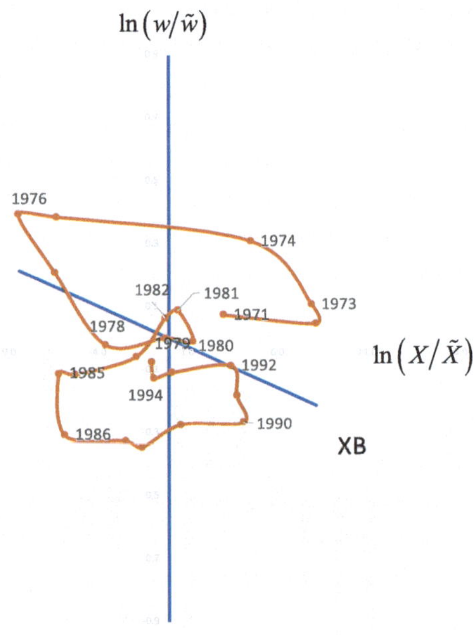

Fig. 7 Krugman–Macedo diagram, 1971–1995

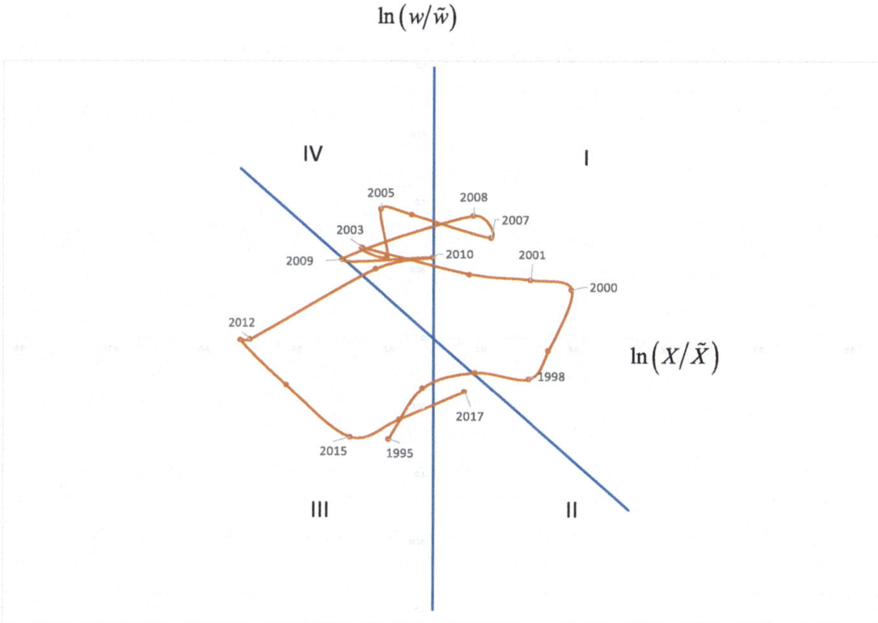

Fig. 8 Krugman–Macedo diagram, 1995–2017

6.1 Stop and Go (1973–1985)

In the early 1970s, unit labor costs were apparently already above equilibrium. At that time, Portugal was engaged in a rapid economic export-led expansion and the labor market was tightening, in part due to high emigration and the ongoing colonial war. Both Krugman and Macedo (1979) and Braga de Macedo (1984, 1990) place the economy close to the origin in 1973. Current data indicate however a positive output gap, and our estimates suggest that the economy would have been located in Zone I (external deficit and inflation). In practice, large emigrant remittances, a positive income balance, and net foreign direct investment (FDI) inflows allowed the fundamental balance to remain positive, in spite of increasing trade deficits.

In line with Krugman and Macedo (1979), we identify a significant impact of the first oil shock on the warranted real wage rate. According to our calculations and data (referred to in Footnote 6 unless otherwise stated), relative unit labor costs should have declined cumulatively by 9.7% between 1973 and 1976. However, both government actions (such as wage setting and price controls) and inactions (passive fixed-exchange-rate policy) helped the actual real exchange rate to move in the opposite direction, at odds with the economy's fundamentals. Between 1974 and 1975, the real exchange rate appreciated 21% and the economy entered in Zone IV (unemployment and external deficit) in the face of a deep recession (Fig. 7).

In 1975, imports declined by 22% largely as a result of the fall in investment, which helped contain the current account deficit. After the 1976 elections, however, Constitutional Government I attempted to expand the economy by stimulating aggregate demand. Although measures were deployed to mitigate the loss of competitiveness (such as limits to nominal wage expansion, the introduction of temporary labor contracts, and nominal exchange rate depreciation), these proved to be insufficient and the current account deficit reached a record high of 7.8% of GDP by year-end. It was only after the exchange rate regime was changed, with the introduction of a crawling peg in August 1977, that competitiveness started to recover. During 1977–1979, the real exchange rate depreciated by as much as 45% and the wage gap was virtually closed by the end of 1979, in spite of the second oil shock. Thanks to a significant surge in exports in the face of a favorable external environment, and also the recovery of emigrant remittances spurred on by renewed confidence, the Portuguese economy managed to approach the internal balance locus even as it implemented the IMF standby stabilization program (April 1978–March 1979).

During 1980–1982, the terms of trade remained stable. However, Constitutional Government VI shifted the policy focus away from external balance and toward disinflation and assigned an anti-inflation role to the exchange rate. Although the crawling peg was maintained, the escudo was revalued by 6% in 1980. Throughout 1980–1982, real exchange rate appreciation was small compared to the previous phase but it occurred in a more unfavorable external environment, which was marked by a world recession, high international interest rates, and an appreciating dollar.[8] On the other hand, the general government deficit had deteriorated significantly, reaching a record high in 1981. In 1982, the trade balance deficit reached 17.3% of GDP and, following the Latin American debt crisis, Portugal turned again to the IMF.

The 1983–1984 stabilization plan was implemented by Constitutional Government IX in a context of decelerating export markets. However, the adjustment of expectations had withered the crawling peg's ability to change relative prices (a phenomenon that Braga de Macedo (1985) labeled "erosion of the crawling peg"). This was particularly evident in 1983–1984 when the policy attempt to move the RER gap into negative territory came at the cost of rising inflation. In addition, government deficits increased above 6% of GDP in 1984 and 1985. Unsurprisingly, the 1983–1985 adjustment relied much more on expenditure reduction through tight monetary policy rather than on expenditure switching, in a marked contrast with the previous stabilization plan.[9] In 1985, a political crisis delayed the recovery and the Portuguese economy moved deep into Zone III, with the unemployment rate reaching a record level of 9.8% and the fundamental balance account registering a surplus.

[8]As pointed out by Braga de Macedo (1985), the real exchange rate based on unit labor costs underestimates the loss in competitiveness in this period because it ignores the cost of capital, which was increasing due to tight credit constraints.

[9]For reviews of this period, see Pinto (1983), Braga de Macedo (2008), and Amaral (2019).

6.2 *Liberalization and Disinflation (1986–1992)*

In 1986, Constitutional Government X took over a recovering economy under quite favorable external conditions. First, the world economy was expanding. Second, as a new member of the then European Economic Community, Portugal became entitled to a net inflow of official transfers, which averaged 1.3% of GDP between 1986 and 1992. Third, Portugal faced a surge in FDI, which peaked at 4% of GDP in 1990. Fourth, and most importantly, oil prices fell sharply and remained low for almost two decades. This meant that external finance constraints were significantly relaxed. According to our estimates, the warranted real exchange rate appreciated by 19.9% between 1985 and 1986. As shown in Fig. 8, the economy expanded with a negative wage gap during 1986–1989 and approached Zone II (inflation and external surplus), which Braga de Macedo (1990) also identified.

In terms of structural reforms, the commitment of Constitutional Government X to fighting inflation (which was 19.5% in 1985) and to the progressive elimination of capital controls challenged the policy practice that had prevailed until then. This policy had relied on the use of credit ceilings as the main tool of monetary policy and both seigniorage and financial repression as sources of government finance (Beleza and Braga de Macedo 1988; Braga de Macedo and Sebastião 1989). The required reforms thus entailed a change in the monetary policy framework and fiscal reform to ensure the sustainability of government debt in a context of financial liberalization.

In the short run, openness to capital flows was likely to cause a real exchange rate appreciation, unless fiscal policy acted in a strongly countercyclical manner (Krugman 1990). Since that was not the case, money supply expanded above its target level causing inflation to surge again in 1988. The central bank responded with higher reserve requirements, barriers to capital inflows, and a movement toward exchange rate-based stabilization. From 1988 onward, the rate of crawl became non-accommodating, and in October 1990, the crawling peg was itself replaced by a managed float (where the exchange rate was allowed to appreciate in an unpredictable manner). Meanwhile, nominal wages were growing at a two-digit rate, reflecting a fall in the unemployment rate to below its natural level.[10] From 1988 until 1992, the real exchange rate appreciated 33%, and the economy approached external balance with a positive output gap (Fig. 7).

In 1992, six months after Jorge Braga de Macedo was appointed Minister of Finance of Constitutional Government XII, the Portuguese escudo joined the exchange rate mechanism (ERM) of the European Monetary System (EMS) and became fully convertible by year-end, completing a regime change that Braga de Macedo (2001) determines to have started with the 1989 Constitutional Amendments. From 1992 to 1995, the escudo's central parity was adjusted three times (6% in November 1992, 6.5% in May 1993, and 3.5% in March 1995) due to speculative attacks on the ERM. Meanwhile, wage growth decelerated, reflecting both adaptation to a low inflation environment and also the emergence of a negative output gap after the 1993 recession. Until 1995, the real exchange rate remained close to its warranted

[10]See Abreu (2001) for a discussion of Portugal's disinflation experience during 1984–1998.

level and the economy approached both internal and external balances (the origin in Fig. 7).

6.3 The Path to the Euro (1993–2000)

Upon the establishment of the single market in 1992, Portugal's main policy goal became eligibility for European Monetary Union (EMU). It was left up to Constitutional Government XIII to establish exchange rate stability, price stability, and fiscal sustainability. Between 1995 and 2000, the economy entered a positive cycle with fast GDP growth (3.8% on average), in a context of easing monetary conditions, marked by free capital movements and policy subordination to the exchange rate. Market perceptions that Portugal would be able to join the EMU as a founding member paved the way to a capital flow bonanza, and government bond yields declined. Bank credit to the private sector expanded rapidly, fueled by capital inflows. Private savings fell and investment surged, both fed by expectations of faster productivity growth (Blanchard and Giavazzi 2002; Fagan and Gaspar, 2007). Private sector debt increased from 81.5% of GDP in 1995 to 124.5% in 1999.

The imbalance between national savings and investment, matched by capital inflows, called for the increase in the relative price of non-tradable goods. During this period, the real exchange rate based on unit labor costs departed from the labor share (Fig. 1). While real wages were basically evolving in line with the average product of labor, the increase in non-tradable good prices made nominal unit labor costs expand faster than abroad (Lebre de Freitas and Faria e Castro 2014). When Portugal joined EMU, the economy was already in Zone I (inflation and external deficit), as depicted in Fig. 8. Blanchard and Giavazzi (2002) contended that the signs of real exchange rate overvaluation were still weak at that time. Our empirical analysis supports this assessment: During 1997–1999, most of the fundamental balance's deterioration is accounted for by the output gap and not the real exchange rate gap (Fig. 6), which was almost zero in 1999. This state of affairs was no longer true after 2000, however: The continuous increase in the relative price of non-tradable goods, together with the terms of trade deterioration, resulted in a positive real exchange rate gap which reached a peak of 10% in 2005.

To be sure, a tighter fiscal policy could have mitigated the pressure on the market for loanable funds and banks' appetite for external borrowing. Unfortunately, this policy never materialized. During 1995–1999, the reductions in both the government deficit (from 5.2 to 3.0% of GDP) and government debt (from 58.3 to 51% of GDP) were largely due to the cyclical component as well as a favorable snowball effect, while the cyclically adjusted primary budget moved from a surplus to a deficit (for the data source, see Footnote 6). It came therefore as no surprise that Portugal failed its commitment to ensure fiscal consolidation after the 2000 downturn. In July 2002, Constitutional Government XV disclosed that the 2001 general deficit had amounted to 4.1% of GDP, exceeding the reference value, which triggered the excessive deficit procedure (EDP). In the words of Braga de Macedo (2019), Portugal was still having a "serious budgetary problem that the change in regime had been unable to solve" (p. 40).

6.4 *The Slump and the Global Crisis (2001–2010)*

The 2001 downturn initiated a period of low economic growth, which coincided with rising oil prices (from 18 US dollars/barrel in 1999 to 97.2 in 2008).[11] The warranted real exchange rate was negatively impacted, even though the Portuguese economy was then less energy-dependent than it had been in the 1970s. Since the actual real exchange rate was still increasing, a positive wage gap emerged.[12] As the growth outlook deteriorated, however, investment and consumption declined, reducing the demand for imports. In 2003, the economy moved toward Zone IV, of deficit and unemployment, approaching external balance (Fig. 8).

As an EMU member, Portugal benefited from an aura of safety among investors, which allowed foreign capital to keep flowing in and thus sustained aggregate demand in spite of rising unemployment and government debt.[13] In a small open economy, capital inflows influence the allocation of resources by changing the relative price of non-tradable goods. Between 1995 and 2010, manufacturing employment declined 27.6%, and employment in services increased by 30%. According to Reis (2013), this reallocation of resources took place in an environment plagued by inappropriate incentives that prevented resources from being invested in the most socially productive uses. With government support and under credit market inneficiencies, resources were invested in low-productivity non-tradable industries and in wasteful infrastructure.

During 2004–2007, the European economy entered a new expansionary cycle. Portugal, however, was falling behind, hindered by fiscal fragility,[14] low productivity, and easy access to foreign capital. Real GDP grew modestly, private investment

---

[11] A simple arithmetic exercise using counterfactual oil prices equal to the 1990s' average points to a direct negative impact on the trade balance ranging from 1.2% of GDP in 2000 to 2.9% of GDP in 2008 (for the data source, see Footnote 6).

[12] Additionally, China's accession to the World Trade Organization in 2001 as well as the EU's enlargement in 2004 led to an increase in competition both in Portugal's traditional export markets and in terms of attracting FDI. Amador and Caldeira Cabral (2014) argue that the exporting sector had already recovered from these shocks by 2005. Reis (2013) doubts that these factors explain the slump.

[13] Lebre de Freitas et al. (2017) provide evidence that EMU membership helped mitigate investors' risk perceptions regarding fiscal unsustainability during the bonanza episodes that affected the EU periphery prior to 2007. Eichenbaum et al. (2016) argue that IMF surveillance of Portugal ignored the possibility of a sudden stop.

[14] EU peer pressure was relaxed following the temporary suspension of the Stability and Growth Pack (SGP) by the EU's Economic and Financial Affairs Council. Despite the government's reliance on sizeable one-off measures to keep the deficit below its reference value (1.4% of GDP in 2002, 2.5% in 2003, and 2.3% in 2004), the European Council considered that Portugal had complied with the Treaty and the corrective procedures ended in May 2004. In June 2005, however, Constitutional

declined, and the unemployment rate kept rising. Nevertheless, the slowdown of potential GDP helped close the output gap. In a context of increasing unemployment, real wages grew less than productivity (Duarte et al. 2019), causing a decline in the labor share that would continue throughout the adjustment period. Wage moderation helped stabilize the real exchange rate, though it remained above the warranted level. Between 2005 and 2007, the real exchange rate gap declined slightly but a new surge in oil prices pushed the warranted real wage further down in 2008. By 2008, the real exchange rate gap was of a magnitude similar to that observed in 1981 (9.5% and 9.4%, respectively).

At the time of the global financial crisis, the Portuguese economy was facing a 12.2% current account deficit, a real exchange rate well above its warranted level, and a slightly positive output gap. This situation contrasted with the high deficit period around 2000, where the income effect is likely to have dominated (Fig. 8).

The subprime crisis did not have a significant direct impact on Portugal's financial system. However, the collapse of world trade in 2009 led to a significant hit to the Portuguese economy with exports declining by 10% and GDP contracting by 3.1%. In Fig. 8, the year of 2009 should be seen as an outlier, since the source of GDP contraction was a decrease in external demand that caused the fundamental balance to deteriorate in the first place. During 2009–2010, Constitutional Government XVIII launched an unprecedented fiscal stimulus delivered a temporary output expansion, driving the Portuguese economy close to internal balance but aggravating the external deficit (Fig. 8). At the same time, the fiscal deficit reached 11.4% of GDP in 2010, and a negative snowball effect impacted heavily on debt dynamics. As international investors' appetite for risk decreased, Portugal was caught in the turmoil of the European debt crisis. After a series of downgrades to its credit rating and hikes in yields, Portugal was shut out of global financial markets. In May 2011, that same government asked the IMF and the EU for financial assistance.

6.5 The Bailout and Beyond (2011–2017)

In contrast to the two previous IMF arrangements, the 2011–2014 bailout package was not primarily intended to address external imbalance. The program's first goal was to achieve fiscal sustainability and the sovereign's return to external funding markets. However, the program combined an ambitious agenda of structural reforms—some of them long overdue—with measures to promote banking sector deleveraging, competition in the product market and a more flexible labour market. External adjustment would be a natural consequence of the narrow financial envelope, banking sector deleveraging, and increased competitiveness.

The resulting economic downturn was much larger than anticipated. The program's implementation by the newly elected Constitutional Government XIX,

Government XVII updated the deficit projections for 2005 and 2006. As a result, Portugal was again placed under the EDP in July (European Commission 2005).

occurred in a context of contracting export markets, limited access to international borrowing, legal setbacks in Portugal's Constitutional Court, and poor political communication.[15] Notwithstanding, Portugal had to pursue a markedly procyclical fiscal adjustment in order to regain access to international financial markets. From 2010 to 2013, the cyclically adjusted government primary balance improved by 10.4 p.p. of GDP. Along this period, GDP contracted cumulatively by 6.7% and the unemployment rate jumped from 12% to 16.4%—quite a painful adjustment after years of fiscal profligacy.

Between 2010 and 2012, the economy moved from Zone IV in Fig. 8 to Zone III (unemployment and external surplus). As suggested by Fig. 6, "import compression" played a significant role in the external adjustment (imports contracted by a total of 12.5% in two years). Notwithstanding, average earnings per worker fell 4.9% in nominal terms, and the real exchange rate depreciated 7.3%, reaching the lowest level since 1996. In a context of deep domestic recession and low external demand, exports expanded significantly (10% cumulatively), jumping 7.7 p.p. to a new record high as a percentage of GDP.

The fall in unit labor costs in 2012 was partly accounted for by the suspension of the thirteenth and fourteenth monthly components of the public sector wage bill. These cuts were ruled illegal by Portugal's Constitutional Court, however, so that average nominal wages and the real exchange rate increased again in 2013. The recovery of wage competitiveness also faced a major setback when the government failed to implement a proposed fiscal devaluation. Nevertheless, nominal earnings decreased again in 2014 and virtually stagnated in 2015, delivering a further depreciation of the real exchange rate.

The rapid adjustment of business sector wages could be somehow unexpected in a context of very low inflation, where nominal wage cuts are ruled out by the Constitution. In the case of workers who kept their jobs, nominal wages did not decline, but wage freezes became widespread during the crisis (Martins and Portugal 2019). This was not, however, enough to avoid an unprecedented increase in separation rates. These, in turn, fed the decline in average nominal wages: According to Felix and Portugal (2019), employment restructuring and labor mobility played an important role in real wage adjustment, with new firms and new hires paying significantly below the average. It seems, though, that creative destruction somehow accelerated the required adjustment in real wages.

Before exiting the program, the economy was already recovering, supported by a more favorable external environment. From 2012 until 2015, Brent oil prices fell 53% as measured in US dollars (USD). This terms of trade improvement led to a 5% fall in WRER, adding to the real exchange rate depreciation that had been achieved

[15]The program's political and economic developments are analyzed in Torres and Lebre de Freitas (2019).

by wage moderation.[16] By 2015, the economy was approaching internal balance with a declining unemployment and a negative wage gap.

After the 2015 elections, the main policy challenge was economic recovery while keeping public finances on track. Although the structure of government expenditure and revenues was adjusted to accommodate the government's political support, Constitutional Government XXI managed to drive the general deficit below the 3% benchmark level in 2016. In June 2017, Portugal exited the EDP. The structural primary balance deteriorated slightly during 2015–2017, but market confidence was restored, and yields approached risk-free levels in a context of unprecedented monetary easing by the European Central Bank. Real wages recovered slowly, allowing the wage gap to remain negative, as had been the case at the outset of the 1983–1984 stabilization program. By 2017, the Portuguese economy already had a positive output gap and returned to Zone 1 (Fig. 1).

7 Conclusion

In this article, we revisit the tool developed by Paul Krugman and Jorge Braga de Macedo to study the Portuguese economy's adjustment in the aftermath of the 1974 Revolution, albeit using a different estimation method. We used their framework and updated their analysis to review the recent crisis and adjustment program.

Overall, our findings support Braga de Macedo's (1990) view that real wages have remained relatively flexible, except during the phase of unrealistic wage setting immediately after the 1974 Revolution. For most of the 1990s and early 2000s, the share of labor in national income displays no trend, and real wages increase on par with productivity (on average). Moreover, when unemployment soared after 2005, the labor share in income started declining, revealing flexibility even in a context of very low inflation. It is true that much of the adjustment in average earnings during the crisis was achieved through worker mobility and creative destruction. Still, the Blanchard (2007) view that Portugal would be doomed to a long process of acquiring competitiveness through disinflation did not materialize.

We do find, however, evidence of departures of the real wage from the level that would be consistent with full employment and external balance. These departures were related to changes in the relative price of non-tradable goods that were accompanied with swings in aggregate demand, as well as with changes in terms of trade. Before the crisis, persistent capital inflows drove the real exchange rate gap to a maximum in 2005, which had a similar magnitude as the one observed in 1981. At the outset of the adjustment program, the terms of trade improved significantly, which created a buffer for real wages to recover in the years to come.

---

[16]Portugal also benefitted from the geopolitical instability generated by the Arab Spring, in 2011. Tourism activity picked up and created the incentives for quality improvements, in a virtuous cycle. All else being equal, the warranted real wage should have improved more during that period.

While recent deviations of real wages from the levels consistent with external and internal balance have been smaller than those observed after the 1974 Revolution, we found the diagram to be extremely useful in interpreting the subsequent path of the Portuguese economy. Indeed, the KM diagram is as useful now to understand the constraints in a small open economy like Portugal and to evaluate possible stabilization policy options, as when it was first created.

8 Annex—Data Sources

Our primary sources of data are the Bank of Portugal (BP) and the European Commission's Annual Macroeconomic Database (AMECO). All bilateral and "foreign" variables are measured with respect to the EU15, including West Germany prior to reunification. In the estimation, the following variables were used:

1. *Fundamental Account*—The fundamental account (FA) balance is defined as the primary current account deficit plus net foreign direct investment inflows and is computed as the sum of the following components: (i) trade balance, (ii) secondary income balance, and (iii) foreign direct investment. Post-1995 data are taken from BPstat (the BP's statistical warehouse). Pre-1995 data are taken from the BP's Historical Time Series (*Series Longas*). All variables are measured at current prices and then divided by GDP at current prices from the same sources.
2. *Output Gap*—Output gap series are taken from AMECO (series: AVGDGDP). Foreign output gap is measured for EU15 (including West Germany) up until 1991 and EU15 (including unified Germany) from 1991 onward.
3. *Real Exchange Rate*—Our benchmark measure of the real exchange rate is taken from AMECO (series: XUNRQ), relative to the rest of the EU15 (with double export weights).
4. *Real Oil Prices*—Historical series for oil prices are taken from BP (crude oil), in USD. Historical EUR-USD and PTE-USD exchange rates are then used to convert these prices to current PTE. Historical series for the Portuguese GDP deflator, obtained from the BP, are then used to compute real oil prices.
5. *Terms of Trade*—Taken from AMECO, index for terms of trade for goods and services (series: APGS).

The data on fundamental account, output gaps, real exchange rate, estimated WRER, and real exchange rate gap are available from the corresponding author upon request, as mentioned before.

Acknowledgements and Disclaimer The authors would like to thank João Amador and the editors for helpful comments on earlier versions of this paper. The views expressed in this article are those of the authors and do not reflect the views of the Federal Reserve Bank of St. Louis or the Federal Reserve System.

References

Abreu M (2001) From EC accession to EMU participation: the portuguese disinflation experience in the period of 1984–1998. Bank of Portugal Economic Bulletin

Amador J, Cabral, MC (2014) A economia Portuguesa no contexto global. In: Alexandre F, Bação F, Lains P, Martins M, Portela M, Simões M (eds) A Economia Portuguesa na União Europeia: 1986–2010. Almedina, Lisboa

Amaral L (2019) The modern Portuguese economy in the twentieth and twenty-first centuries. Palgrave Stud Econ History, Palgrave Macmillan, London

Beleza LM, Braga de Macedo J (1990) Implicit taxes and credit ceilings: the treasury and the banks in Portugal. In: Silva Lopes J, Beleza LM (eds) Portugal and the internal market of the EEC. Banco de Portugal, Lisbon, pp 57–72

Blanchard O (2007) Adjustment within the euro: the difficult case of Portugal. Portuguese Econ J 6(1):1–22

Blanchard O, Giavazzi F (2002) Current account deficits in the Euro area: the end of the Feldstein-Horioka puzzle? Brook Papers Econ Activity 2:147–209

Blanchard O, Portugal P (2017) Boom, slump, sudden stops, recovery, and policy options: Portugal and the Euro. Portuguese Econ J 16(3):149–168

Braga de Macedo J (1984) Portugal and Europe: the dilemmas of integration. In: Bruneau T, da Rosa V, MacLeod A (eds) Portugal in development: emigration, industrialization and the European community. University of Ottawa Press, Ottawa

Braga de Macedo J (1985) Integração Europeia: Fim do princípio ou princípio do fim? Economia IX(3):515–29

Braga de Macedo J (1990) External liberalization with ambiguous public response. In: Bliss C, Braga de Macedo J (eds) Unity with diversity in the European Economy: the community's southern frontier. Cambridge University Press, Cambridge, pp 310–354

Braga de Macedo J (2001) Crises? What crises? escudo from ECU to EMU. In: Griffith-Jones S, Montes M, Nasution A (eds) Short-term capital flows and economic crises. Oxford University Press, pp 253–260

Braga de Macedo J (2008) The role of economic advising. In: Franco F (ed) Challenges ahead for the Portuguese economy. Imprensa de Ciencias Sociais, Lisbon, pp 201–229

Braga de Macedo J (2019) Portugal na Zona Euro. Memórias da Academia das Ciências de Lisboa—Classe de Letras, XL(2), pp 35–46

Braga de Macedo J, Sebastião M (1989) Public debt and implicit taxes: the experience of Portugal. Eur Econ Rev 33:573–579

Campos e Cunha L (2008) Is the Dutch disease pandemic in the South? In: Franco F (ed) Challenges ahead for the Portuguese economy. Imprensa de Ciencias Sociais, Lisbon, pp 147–164

Clark PB, MacDonald R (1998) Exchange rates and economic fundamentals; a methodological comparison of BEERs and FEERs. IMF Working Papers 98/67, International Monetary Fund, Washington

Costa S (1998) Determination of the equilibrium real exchange rate for the Portuguese economy using the FEER. Banco de Portugal, Economic Bulletin, pp 69–77

Dolado JJ, Viñals J (1991) Macroeconomic policy, external targets and constraints: the case of Spain. CEPR discussion papers 505, London

Duarte C, Maria J, Sazedj S (2019) Potential output: how does Portugal compare with the euro area over the last 40 years? Banco de Portugal Econ Stud 5(2):1–18

Eichenbaum M, Rebelo S, Resende C (2016) The Portuguese crisis and the IMF. IEO background paper BP/16–02/05, Independent Evaluation Office of the International Monetary Fund Washington, D.C.

European Commission (2005) Technical document by the commission services accompanying the report on Portugal prepared in accordance with the Article 104(3) of the Treaty, 22 July Brussels

Fagan G, Gaspar V (2007) Adjusting to the euro. Working paper 716. European Central Bank, Frankfurt

Felix S, Portugal P (2019) Qual é o contributo da dinâmica das empresas e da mobilidade laboral para a variação dos salários reais? In: O Crescimento Económico Português: uma visão sobre questões estruturais, bloqueios e reformas. Banco de Portugal, Lisbon, pp 89–96
Krugman P (1990) Macroeconomic adjustment and entry into the EC: a note. In: Bliss C, Braga de Macedo J (eds) Unity with diversity in the european economy: the community's southern frontier. Cambridge University Press, Cambridge, pp 131–140
Krugman P, Braga de Macedo J (1979) The economic consequences of the April 25th revolution. Economia III(3):435–483
Lebre de Freitas M (1992) Sobre o Valor Real do escudo: uma Abordagem Empírica. Economia, XV I(3):325–356
Lebre de Freitas M, Nunes LC, Rodrigues MS (2018) Euro area membership and the probability of a sudden stop: an empirical assessment. J Common Market Stud 56(4):818–836
Lebre de Freitas M, Faria e Castro M (2014) The Portuguese real exchange rate, 1995–2010: competitiveness or price effects? Working Paper 12/2014 NIPE, Braga
Martins F, Portugal P (2019). De que forma a rigidez à baixa dos salários afetou o desemprego durante a crise económica? In: O Crescimento Económico Português: uma visão sobre questões estruturais, bloqueios e reformas. Banco de Portugal, Lisbon, pp 97–106
Pinto M (1983) A Economia Portuguesa e os acordos de estabilização económica com o FMI. Economia, UCP, pp 554–596
Rebelo S, Vegh CA (1995) Real effects of exchange rate-based stabilization: an analysis of competing theories. NBER Macroecon Ann 1995(10):125–128
Reis R (2013) The Portuguese slump and crash and the Euro crisis. Brook Papers Econ Activity Spring 2013:143–193
Reis R (2015) Looking for a success in the euro crisis adjustment programs: the case of Portugal. Brook Papers Econ Activity Fall 2015(2):433–458
Swan T (1956) Economic growth and capital accumulation. Econ Record 32(2):334–361
Torres F, Lebre de Freitas M (2019) Portugal's adjustment programme: the run-up to the sovereign debt crisis, programme design, implementation and legacy. In: Chang M, Steinberg F, Torres F (eds) The political economy of adjustment throughout and beyond Eurozone crisis: what have we learnt? Routledge, Taylor and Francis, pp 122–156
Williamson J (1983) The exchange rate system. Institute for International Economics, Washington D.C.

Notes on a Peripheral Economy

Paul Krugman

Abstract This chapter provides some brief, informal notes about Portugal's modern economic history since the 1974 Revolution, as it looks to an outsider observer. Not to be too coy about it, Portugal has done better than many feared but not quite as well as many hoped. There is, however, an asymmetry between the good news and the bad news. Portugal can claim much of the credit for the gratifying resilience of its late commitment to democracy, avoiding economic catastrophe and generally responsible policies. The disappointments, on the other hand, have had a lot to do with outside forces, such as the euro's structural flaws and, since the 1980s, the underlying forces causing trouble for peripheral regions in all advanced economies. Indeed, Portugal achieved only limited convergence on wealthier European nations and is still vulnerable to macroeconomic crisis. Relative to the grim prospects in 1975, however, Portugal has to be considered a major success story.

Keywords Economic development · Economic growth · Economic history · Macroeconomic crisis · Portugal

1 Introduction

I am, obviously, not Portuguese. I do not even speak Portuguese and I am in no sense an expert on Portugal's economy. As I indicated in the preface, however, I have been at least marginally involved, and more than marginally interested, in Portuguese affairs for a remarkably long time, ever since working for three months at the *Banco de Portugal* in 1976, just two years after the revolution that ended Portugal's dictatorship.

I have also studied a number of issues, ranging from the euro crisis to the fall and rise of regional economic disparities, that seem relevant to Portuguese experience. So, in addition to providing a preface about the man this volume honors, I thought it

P. Krugman (✉)
City University of New York, New York City, NY, USA
e-mail: pkrugman@gc.cuny.edu

L. Brites Pereira et al. (eds.), *Economic Globalization and Governance*,
https://doi.org/10.1007/978-3-030-53265-9_14

might be of some interest if I provided some brief, informal notes about Portugal's modern economic history, as it looks to an outsider.

In these notes, I will start by talking about the way things looked in the near-term aftermath of the 1974 Carnation Revolution—the hopes and fears that prevailed at the time. Then, I will talk about how actual experience has borne out those hopes and fears. Not to be too coy about it, Portugal has done better than many feared but not quite as well as many hoped.

There is, however, an asymmetry between the good news and the bad news. Portugal can, I would suggest, claim much of the credit for what went right. Things could easily have gone much worse, and the fact that they did not has a lot to do with the gratifying resilience of Portugal's late commitment to democracy and its generally responsible policies. The disappointments, on the other hand, have had a lot to do with outside forces. Portugal has suffered from both the structural flaws in the euro and, since the 1980s, from underlying forces that have caused trouble for peripheral regions in all advanced economies, very much including the United States.

Without further ado, then, let me describe Portugal's prospects as they looked in the mid-1970s, then turn to how it actually played out.

2 The View from 1975

It is, I suspect, hard for modern observers to appreciate how fragile Portugal appeared, both politically and economically, in the aftermath of the 1974 Revolution.

On the eve of the revolution Portugal was, in a way, triply peripheral to the European project. It was, of course, geographically peripheral, and still is. It was economically peripheral in the sense that it was not part of the European customs union. And it was politically peripheral as a dictatorship on a democratic continent.

Would it manage to overcome this peripheralization? At the time, there was widespread skepticism about whether Portugal would manage to become a normal European democracy. In 1975, according to a report in The New York Times, Henry Kissinger, the US Secretary of State, told reporters that he expected Portugal to have a Communist government within a year. A year later, there were widespread worries that there might be a Pinochet-style military takeover.

A joke from the time, which stuck in my memory, was that *Avenida Almirante Reis* would be renamed *Avenida Ramalho Eanes.* Why? Because it led to the *Praça do Chile.*[1]

[1]**Editors' Note** António Ramalho Eanes is a Portuguese general and former President of Portugal (1976–1986). He is credited with ordering the military operations against the pro-communist radical faction of the Armed Forces Movement (MFA—*Movimento das Forças Armadas*) on November 25, 1975, ending that year's hot summer (*verão quente*). The MFA was responsible for the military coup of the Carnation Revolution (April 25, 1974) that ended Portugal's corporatist New State (*Estado Novo*) regime. The joke refers to a well-known avenue in Lisbon (*Avenida Almirante Reis*) that leads into the Chile Square (*Praça do Chile*).

There were also widespread fears of a Venezuela-style economic collapse or, less extreme, an Argentina-type cycle of inflation and currency crises. In 1976, when I was there, the country was still suffering a serious shortage of foreign exchange, and a flurry of disruptive measures that tried to conserve hard currency. There was even a period when the power was turned off for a couple of hours each day, to limit electricity imports.

Those were the fears. What about the hopes? Aside from hopes that Portugal would become solidly democratic, everyone hoped that it would become much richer, with incomes converging on those of the wealthy nations of northern Europe. (Yes, I know that in Eurospeak "convergence" means something different, and that the preferred term is "cohesion." Never mind.)

If these hopes had been fulfilled, Lisbon would now look more or less like Lyon, a much richer city with a similar population.

There were also hopes, which became much stronger after Maastricht, that Portugal would achieve enduring financial and economic stability, with no more balance of payments crises.

Obviously, the worst fears did not come to pass. Portugal has in fact remained solidly democratic, an achievement that gains extra luster from the contrast with the hard turn toward illiberalism in much of eastern Europe. The Portuguese economy did not collapse in the 1970s, and although it suffered severely in the Eurozone crisis of 2008–2013, it appears to have weathered the storm and experienced a surprisingly strong recovery.

On the other hand, Lisbon still is not Lyon. Portugal is richer than it was, both absolutely and relatively, but convergence seems to have stopped circa 2000. And weathering a crisis is not the same as achieving enduring stability. What Portugal went through during the years of crisis and austerity was worse than almost anyone imagined possible a few years earlier.

Let us look at this history in a bit more detail.

3 Limited Convergence

Figure 1 shows a quick-and-dirty indicator of Portugal's longer-term economic performance: the ratio of its GDP per capita to that of France, which I use as a stand-in for the wealthier nations of northern Europe. The numbers would look a bit different if I used a wider comparison group, but the basic pattern would be the same.

What we see is significant but modest convergence, from 63 to 73% of French GDP per capita, with just about all of the convergence taking place in the 15 or so years following Portugal's entry into the European Union (EU).

This is not a terrible result, but it clearly falls short of what many hoped. And one might have expected more from EU entry. Not only did Portugal gain unimpeded market access, it received substantial amounts of aid in the form of cohesion funds.

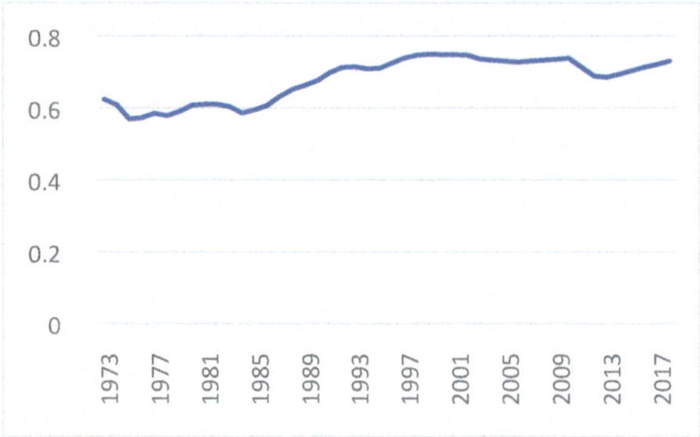

Fig. 1 Relative real GDP per capita, Portugal versus France, 1973–2017 (*Source* OECD and Own Calculations)

The quality of public infrastructure is immensely better than it was a few decades ago. Why has not growth been more impressive?

I would suggest two explanations, both external to Portugal.

First, “hyper-globalization”—the unprecedented expansion in world trade, driven by exports from developing countries, that took place from the 1980s onward—hurt Portugal’s prospects. In the 1970s, Portugal was in large part an exporter of labor-intensive goods, especially textiles and apparel. In 1976, the late José da Silva Lopes, governor of the *Banco de Portugal*, joked that “we are not a banana republic, we are a pajama republic.” These were precisely the kinds of goods hit by surging exports from Asia.

Beyond that, underlying economic forces turned adverse for peripheral regions in advanced economies circa 1980. This is very clear in the USA. From the early twentieth century until the late 1970s, there was a striking process of convergence in US regional incomes, with poor regions growing steadily faster than rich regions. But this process then stopped dead and went into reverse.

Figure 2 shows a US counterpart to the Portugal/France comparison: Mississippi, the poorest state, versus Massachusetts. (There was a break in the series, hence the two lines.) In the 1920s, Mississippi’s income was only around a third of that in its northern counterpart. By the late 70s, that was up to 70%. But it has been in decline since.

The most likely cause of the reversal of regional convergence is the rise of the knowledge economy, which advantaged large metropolitan areas with highly educated work forces. Indeed, within the US metros with high proportions of college graduates have widened their lead over less educated regions. There is every reason to believe that similar dynamics have been at work within Europe.

The point is that while Portugal benefited from the EU membership that democratization made possible, thanks both to market access and to development aid, the timing of that accession meant that the Portuguese economy was in a sense swimming upstream. Changes in the structure of both the global and the European economy

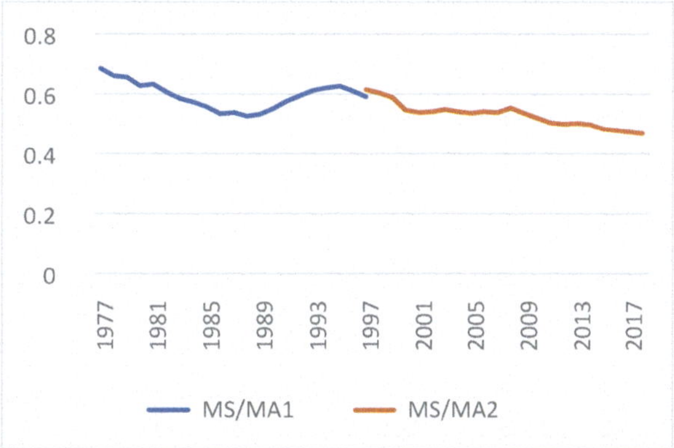

Fig. 2 Relative real GDP per capita, Mississippi versus Massachusetts, 1977–2017 (*Source* FRED and Own Calculations)

were, in effect, trying to widen, rather than narrow, the gap between peripheral economies and the European core. The fact that Portugal nonetheless managed to narrow that gap, even if only modestly, counts as a success story. But, of course, we hoped for more.

4 Portugal in the Euro Crisis

As I said, Portugal faced a moderately severe balance of payments crisis in the aftermath of the 1974 Revolution, and many people feared either that this crisis would deepen or that it would be the first of many. On the other side, there were widespread hopes that deeper integration with the rest of Europe, and especially joining the euro, would put an end to such crises.

In reality, as Fig. 3 shows, Portugal has experienced relative macroeconomic stability, with the exception of the period 2008–2013. On the other hand, that is quite

Fig. 3 Portugal unemployment rate (%), 1983–2016 (*Source* Statistics Portugal)

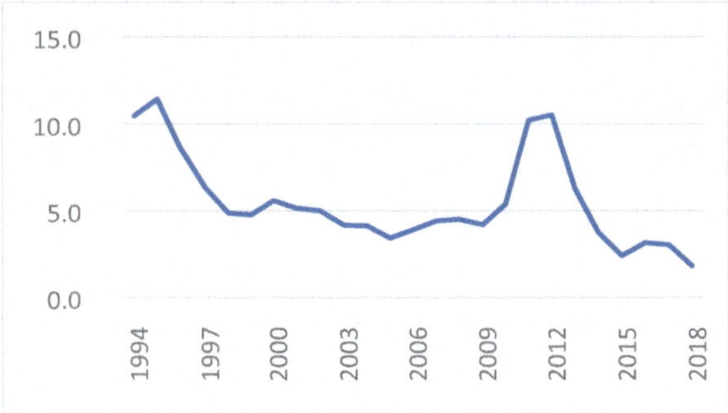

Fig. 4 Portugal 10-year bond rate (%), 1994–2018 (*Source* FRED)

an exception. While not in Greece's league, Portugal was among the countries hit hardest by the euro crisis.

But what was the euro crisis? Although some people, especially in Germany, insist on considering it a fiscal crisis, it is overwhelmingly clear that it was in reality a balance of payments crisis, one that unfolded in three acts. These acts are visible in Fig. 4, which shows the interest rate on 10-year Portuguese bonds.

In the first act, the coming of the euro produced irrational exuberance on the part of investors, who wrongly assumed that the end of devaluation risk had made peripheral-economy bonds safe assets. Interest rates across southern Europe fell sharply, to the point where they were barely higher than borrowing rates in Germany.

This rate cut encouraged huge capital inflows and very large current account deficits as a share of GDP. A few economists warned that these deficits were unsustainable, but they were ignored until the Greek crisis of 2009 produced a dramatic change in sentiment.

At that point southern Europe faced a classic "sudden stop": a cutoff of capital inflows, of the kind that has been the common denominator of financial crises across the developing world.

The crisis was made worse by misdiagnosis of the problem. Key officials, especially in Germany and at the European Commission, took soaring interest rates in peripheral countries as evidence that the crisis was essentially fiscal and demanded harsh austerity as the price of emergency loans. As classic research by Blanchard and Leigh (2013) at the International Monetary Fund (IMF) showed, this austerity greatly deepened the downturn.

In reality, however, with the possible exception of Greece, the underlying fiscal weakness of southern Europe was far less severe than portrayed. As another classic analysis by De Grauwe (2011) pointed out, the actual fiscal position of Spain and other countries facing an interest rate spike was not any worse than that of nations like Belgium or the UK that were not experiencing similar financial pressure.

What was actually happening was a self-fulfilling liquidity panic. Investors feared that governments like Portugal, whose debts were in a currency they could not print, would find themselves unable to come up with the euros needed to pay debt service.

This would force them into default, which might well end up imposing a large haircut on investors, even if such a haircut wasn't necessary to achieve solvency.

This analysis suggested that the crisis could be hugely alleviated simply by assuring investors that debtor nations would not run out of euros. And Mario Draghi did that in 2012, with his famous three words—"whatever it takes"—eventually backed by a promise to engage in bond purchases if necessary. As it turned out, simply saying the words did the trick: interest rates in Portugal and elsewhere dropped rapidly.

I will say that the strength of Portugal's recovery has come as a surprise, even given the success of Draghi's intervention. There is an interesting contrast with Spain, which has also achieved considerable economic recovery. Spain, however, did this through a painful process of "internal devaluation," grinding down wages and labor costs to the point where its manufacturing, especially of autos, became highly competitive. It is much less clear how Portugal achieved an export revival. In any case, however, at this point the crisis has passed.

The conditions that made the crisis possible have not, however, gone away. This is not a Portuguese problem: Portugal's policies were not exceptionally irresponsible, as demonstrated by the strength its recovery once Draghi ended the liquidity panic. Instead, the problem is that the euro is a common currency without the backing institutions that make monetary union safe from crisis. There is no banking union, so failed financial institutions are the responsibility of national governments that may be strapped for cash. There is no fiscal union that would provide automatic transfers to troubled regional economies.

Even the liquidity guarantees that saved the day in 2012 were ad hoc. There is no guarantee that a comparable rescue will come in a future crisis.

The result is that Portugal has not, as so many hoped, achieved durable economic stability. It weathered one big crisis but is vulnerable to future crises. And if anything, closer integration with the rest of Europe has increased that vulnerability.

5 A Qualified Success Story

So how has Portugal done since the 1974 Revolution? It has defied the pessimists, remaining solidly democratic and avoiding economic catastrophe. But it has somewhat disappointed the optimists, achieving only limited convergence on wealthier European nations and finding itself still vulnerable to macroeconomic crisis.

As I said at the beginning, however, it is hard now to capture just how grim Portugal's prospects seemed to many observers in 1975. Relative to that grimness, Portugal has to be considered a major success story.

References

Blanchard OJ, Leigh D (2013) Growth forecast errors and fiscal multipliers. Am Econ Rev 103(3):117–120

De Grauwe P (2011) Managing a fragile eurozone. Vox EU. 10 May. Available online. https://www.voxeu.org/article/managing-fragile-eurozone. Accessed on 28 Mar 2020

International Political Economy

Unlike Part I, devoted almost exclusively to history, and Part II, devoted mostly to European macroeconomic issues, Part III gathers five contributions related to international political economy, ranging from public choice, development economics, industrial, labor and two complementary ones from law and sociology, in keeping with the honoree's interdisciplinary research bent.

There are two papers on international governance, which start and end Part III. In the first, Vítor Gaspar and David Amaglobeli are overarching in scope and set the tone for the others that follow by making the case for global solutions to three global problems: climate change, international corporate taxation and sustainable development. Recalling that collective action was needed to protect the global economy in the context of the global financial crisis and the sovereign debt crisis in the euro area, their paper calls for carbon taxation, a consensus-based solution to revamp the rules-based international tax system and stronger efforts to support developing countries in meeting the Sustainable Development Goals.

Another notable problem requiring collective action, albeit often at a regional level, is that of migratory flows arising either due to economic or security concerns. While inevitable in today's globalized world, such flows are not without their critics, who are increasingly vocal about their negative consequences, either real or perceived. The contribution by Catia Batista, Julia Seither and Pedro Vicente reminds us that there are positive aspects too. Drawing on their published work, the authors show that social network spillovers of political norms exist in the cases of migratory flows from Cape Verde to Portugal, and from Mozambique to South Africa. Being exposed to better democratic political norms and knowledge about electoral processes, via peers, substantially increases the demand for political accountability and electoral participation, which undoubtedly increases the likelihood of improved political governance.

In the context of mitigating climate change, meanwhile, Alfredo Marvão Pereira and Rui Manuel Pereira, father and son, consider the economic and environmental effects of the interaction between regulated early closure of coal-fired power plants and new energy taxation rules on such plants using a dynamic general equilibrium model of the Portuguese economy. They quote many of their previous papers to show the usefulness of the model in examining the economic, budgetary, distributional and environmental impacts of the interaction in question. Here, they ascertain whether there is synergy or rivalry between the two policy instruments mentioned and find no evidence of the former. In fact, their results point to rivalry.

The importance of minding the interactions between policies is also underscored by Pedro Martins, whose study measures the potential interactions between collective bargaining of social partners (trade unions, on one hand, and employer associations, on the other) and wage formation over the business cycle. The study draws on matched data covering all employees in Portugal for the period 1982–2017. Among other results, the study finds evidence of limited realwage cyclicality, which suggests that Portuguese social partners may not yet have fully adjusted to the macroeconomic regime of Eurozone membership. This implies that policy complementarities are conducive to ensuring desired economic outcomes, a topic the honoree has tackled jointly with OECD economist Joaquim Oliveira Martins.

The next two contributions, whose authors are family of the honoree, make important points using two distinct interdisciplinary perspectives that are nonetheless relevant to international governance and economic analysis.

From a sociological perspective, Jorge de La Barre's essay explores some aspects of our new visual experience, which is primarily mediated by technology. Indeed, everyday life is becoming increasingly virtual. Before we even know it, the technological apparatuses become the main relation—the most stable and secured one. More than created by them, we end up interacting with them—and this becomes our world, or the world we live in. Everyday life is also marked by a banal co-existence of the horizontal, vertical, oblique, and virtual, which combine permanently. He notes, for example, that there is a powerful symbol attached to verticality. It is linked to idea of the "vertical entrenchment of the State," and the properties attached—hierarchy, power, surveillance,—which have become all too banal in the cyber, digital and robotic age. Policymakers surely cannot ignore the profound implications these changes have for the economic, political and social fabric of nations.

Next, and true to his legal fascination with "the future of law," Gonçalo Almeida Ribeiro illustrates the shortcomings of constitutional precommitments—mechanical and fiduciary—as means suited to correct short-termist biases in democracies. In short, rules jeopardize constitutional legitimacy as they cannot accommodate reasonable pluralism whereas principles cannot be enforced by judicial review. It goes without saying that the existence of short-termist biases implicitly raise the issue of sustainability in various domains, such as climate change and intergenerational equity, to name but two. Hence, the relevance of the contributor's timely call for a renewal of interest in institutional imagination, design and innovation. This process is underway in some countries and so deserves careful study, especially given that the path is made by walking, as his closing quote reminds us—in Spanish.

Which brings us to the second paper in international governance by Jeffry Frieden, looking afresh at the path of ever-greater collaboration that was being pursued by the principal economic centers of the post-World War II world. In the past decade, however, economic and political trends have called this upward tendency into question. Within both advanced industrial and developing nations, there has been an upsurge in "populist" sentiment with an economically nationalistic tenor and an explicit hostility to "globalist" approaches to economic cooperation. What is the future of international economic cooperation in a world in which domestic political pressures appear to be pushing the major powers apart, rather than together? Without needing to bring in the global threat to health that developed while the book was being finalized. I invite the reader to reflect on this question, as well as the others raised, by now reading into the respective contributions.

Luís Brites Pereira

Tax, Climate Change, and Sustainable Development: Global Problems, Global Solutions?

Vítor Gaspar and David Amaglobeli

Abstract This chapter examines three areas where multilateral cooperation is necessary: climate change, international corporate taxation, and sustainable development. Progress in addressing challenges in all these three areas through global cooperation is crucial. We need to find effective ways to limit the rise in global temperature. Carbon taxation is one of the most effective means. We also need to find a timely, consensus-based solution to revamp the rules-based international tax system. This will help avert a string of unilateral actions by countries to protect their domestic tax base. Finally, the global community should take stronger efforts to support developing countries in meeting the Sustainable Development Goals.

Keywords Climate change · Global challenges · International corporate taxation · Multilateral cooperation · Sustainable development

1 Introduction

One of us worked closely with Jorge Braga de Macedo. But I knew of him before we ever met. I was a student of his father, Jorge Borges de Macedo, who was an Economic Historian. I am passionate about economic history. On one occasion, Professor Borges de Macedo mentioned his son. Once to mention that I should consider a doctorate in law, after graduating in economics. Jorge Braga de Macedo and I met a few years later when I was a graduate student at Nova University of Lisbon. We worked closely together on the Portuguese tax reform in the mid-1980s. Through him, I met Roger Gordon and Joel Slemrod. In the early 1990s, we worked again together when he became Minister of Finance. I was, at the time, Head of Economic Studies and I was the representative of the Minister in the Maastricht

V. Gaspar · D. Amaglobeli (✉)
Fiscal Affairs Department, International Monetary Fund, Washington D.C., USA
e-mail: damaglobeli@imf.org

V. Gaspar
e-mail: vgaspar@imf.org

L. Brites Pereira et al. (eds.), *Economic Globalization and Governance*,
https://doi.org/10.1007/978-3-030-53265-9_15

negotiations. That explains the mix of topics in this tribute: history, institutions, and international economics all come together. As they did in our cooperation.

After the end of World War II, the major world powers agreed on a system of multilateral institutions to foster greater international cooperation, in general, and to facilitate international trade, in particular. For the expansion of international trade to be steady, enduring international monetary cooperation was necessary. For this purpose, the creation of the International Monetary Fund (IMF) was agreed in 1944. At the same time, to support economic development, the IMF's sister institution was also agreed: International Bank for Reconstruction and Development, which later developed into the World Bank Group (WBG). Only later, in 1947, did 23 countries agree on the General Agreement for Tariffs and Trade (GATT). Subsequently, it developed into the World Trade Organization (WTO). This institutional triangle constitutes the core of global multilateral economic cooperation.

The global economic cooperation has ushered in an era of growth and development. Since the middle of the twentieth century, economic growth and international trade have been sustained. The share of world trade as a percentage of GDP more than doubled between 1960 and 2016 (Fig. 1). Subsequently, the real average world GDP per capita more than quadrupled since 1950 (Fig. 1). At the same time, the share of the world population living in extreme poverty declined at an accelerated pace after the 1950s (Fig. 2).

For most of twentieth century the USA was a dominant world economic power (Fig. 3). The share of the US GDP, as a proportion of global GDP, peaked around the middle of the twentieth century. That was precisely when the institutions mentioned above were being shaped. But since then the relative sizes of major economies have changed substantially. The world has become multipolar.

Despite major successes in raising living standards, the popular discontent against global economic cooperation has emerged. One possible explanation is related to

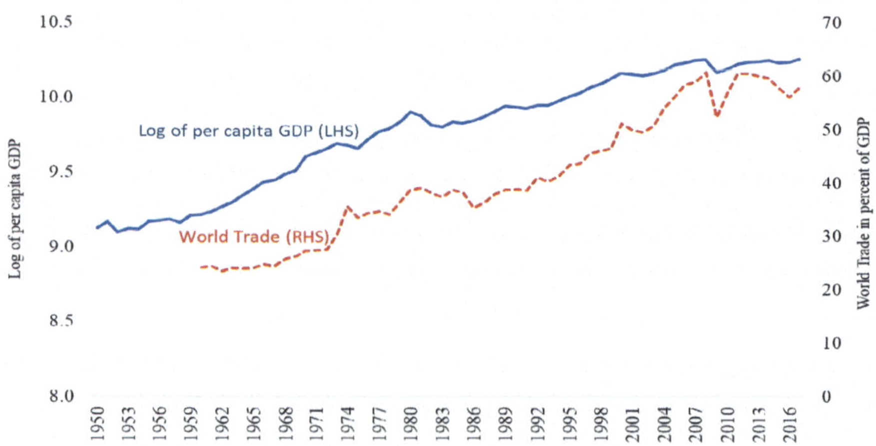

Fig. 1 Real GDP per capita and the world trade (*Source* World Bank)

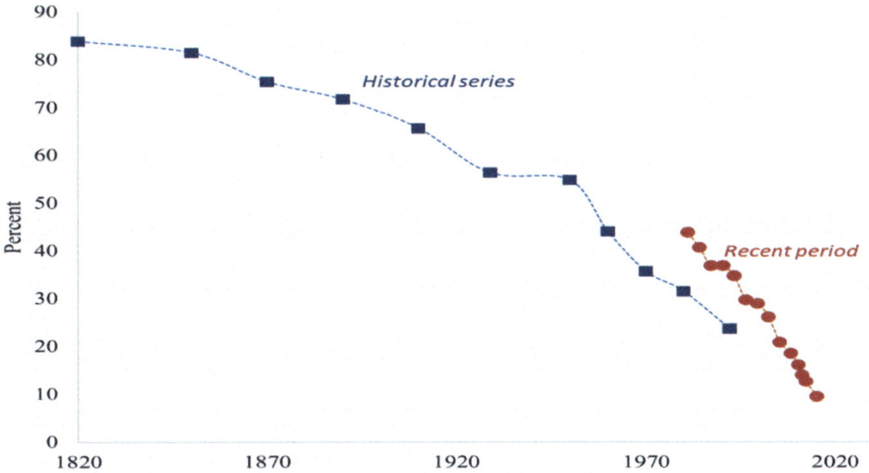

Fig. 2 Global extreme poverty level (*Source* Historical series, Bourguignon and Morrisson 2002; Recent data, PovcalNet, World Bank)

income inequality. While economic integration has helped reduce global inequality over the last three decades (Fig. 4), it has also contributed to greater inequality within many advanced economies (Fig. 5). This led to voter backlash against globalization and the support for populist promises to effectively end globalization (Pastor and Veronesi 2019). Some have argued that globalization was oversold, overstating its benefits, and underestimating its costs (Stiglitz 2017). Another explanation is the cultural backlash against progressive values, such as cosmopolitanism and multiculturalism, and a shift toward national identity encouraging support for populist policies (Norris and Inglehart 2018).

Demographic dynamics is another important factor affecting the attitudes toward global economic cooperation. While total world population will continue to increase, the relative weights of G7 and G20 economies will continue to decline (Fig. 6). These trends, on one hand, primarily reflect continued strong population growth in low-income countries, particularly in sub-Saharan Africa, on the other, the decline in populations in several advanced and emerging market economies.

Another important factor is related to information and communications technologies. It has made an important contribution to strengthening global connectivity. The scale of the ongoing transformation has led to the emergence of the term "the fourth industrial revolution" (Schwab 2016). The implications of this revolution are likely to be profound, creating both important opportunities and challenges.

With digitalization redefining relationships between households, corporations, and governments, new opportunities to increase productivity emerge. At the same time, the digital revolution can have a disruptive power. For example, due to automation 75–375 million workers (3–14% of the global workforce) will need to switch occupational categories while all workers will need to adapt (McKinsey Global Institute 2017). However, there is a fundamental uncertainty as to at what pace and how

Fig. 3 Shares of world powers in the global economy as percentage of global GDP. *Notes* Each data point corresponds to a 10-year average for each country/group in the global economy. The variable used is real GDP per capita in 2011 US dollars (cgdppc). The EU weight reflects the EU integration calendar (*Source* Maddison Database Project 2019; IMF WEO; IMF Staff)

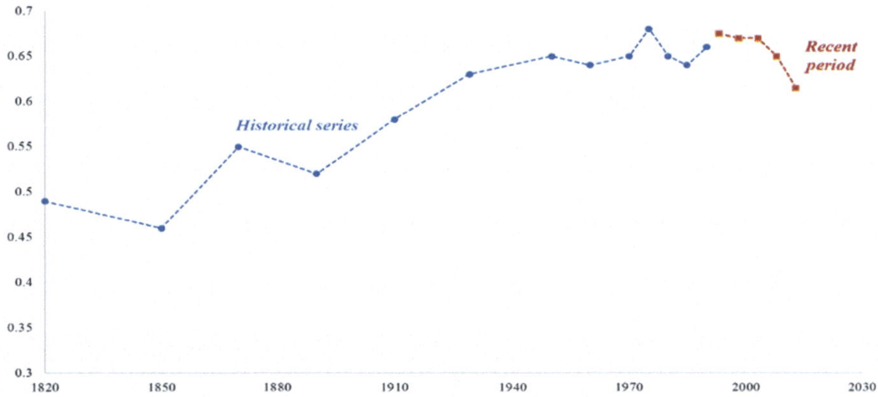

Fig. 4 Global Income Inequality, Gini coefficient. (*Source* Historical series, Van Zanden et al. 2014, building on Bourguignon and Morrisson 2002; Recent data, Lakner and Milanovic 2013)

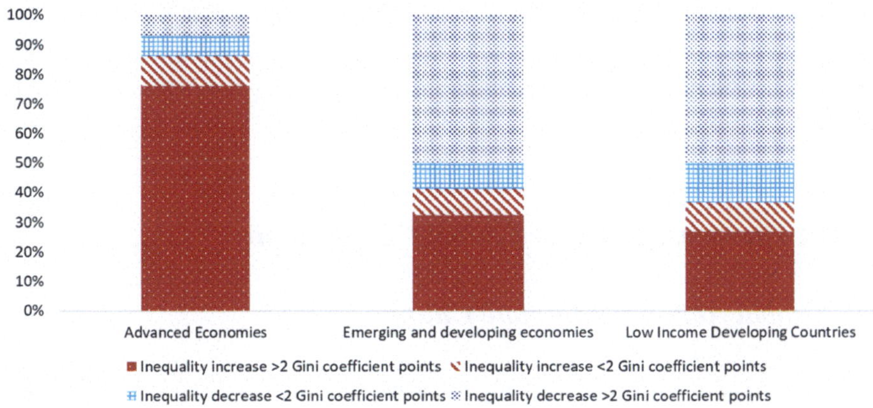

Fig. 5 Change in Income Inequality, percent of countries, 1985–2015 (*Source* IMF, Fiscal Monitor, October 2017)

the transformation will unfold, what will be its distributional consequences and how governments will respond to protect those who will be affected.

Against this challenging backdrop, global economic cooperation is crucial as we argue in this chapter. We specifically illustrate the need for urgent global cooperation in three important areas: climate change, international taxation, and sustainable development. Climate change is an existential threat to humanity and can only be addressed through cooperation at the global level. Climate change is associated with the negative externality, on a global front. Also, the century-old architecture of international taxation has aged and requires common approaches to address rapidly expanding challenges from digitalization and globalization. Finally, many countries,

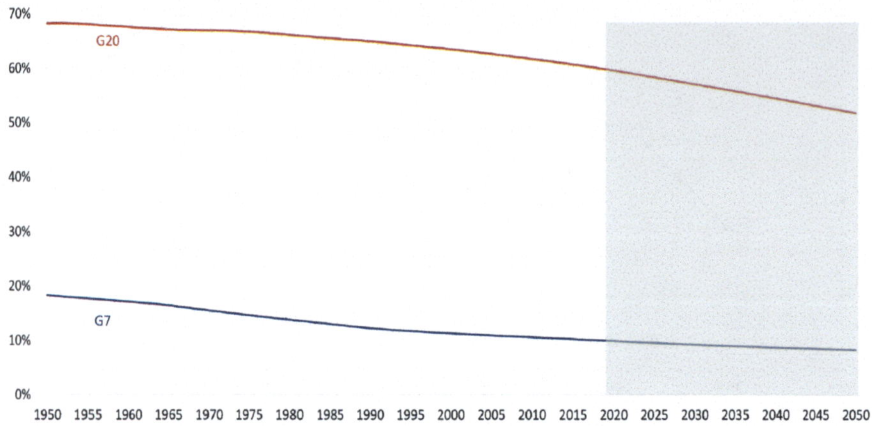

Fig. 6 Population trends, G7 and G20, percent of world population (*Source* UN World Population Prospects 2019)

particularly those with low incomes, will only be able to meet the sustainable development goals (SDG) by raising spending in key sectors, such as education, health, and infrastructure.

2 The Enduring Need for Global Cooperation

2.1 Global Action for Climate Change

Global cooperation is needed not only to ensure the free flow of goods, labor, and capital, but also to seek solutions to such existential problem as the climate change. It offers a great opportunity to unite countries around the common cause, to agree on effective solution mechanisms and to start implementing these policies in a concerted fashion.

Without mitigating actions, global temperatures are projected to rise by 4 °C above pre-industrial levels by the end of the century. This could bring an irreparable damage to the planet and cause massive migrations and huge economic costs. Carbon dioxide (CO_2) emissions from fossil fuel combustion account for a dominant (63%) and growing share of global greenhouse gas emissions. Importantly, the current pledges under the Paris Agreement are not enough. They will limit global warming to 3 °C, which is significantly above the safe level of 2 °C (Fig. 7).

While there are alternative instruments, fiscal policies should be at the heart of climate change mitigation efforts. A carbon tax, which is collected on the carbon content of fossil fuels, is the most powerful and efficient way to reduce domestic fossil fuel CO_2 emissions. It gives people and businesses an incentive to find ways

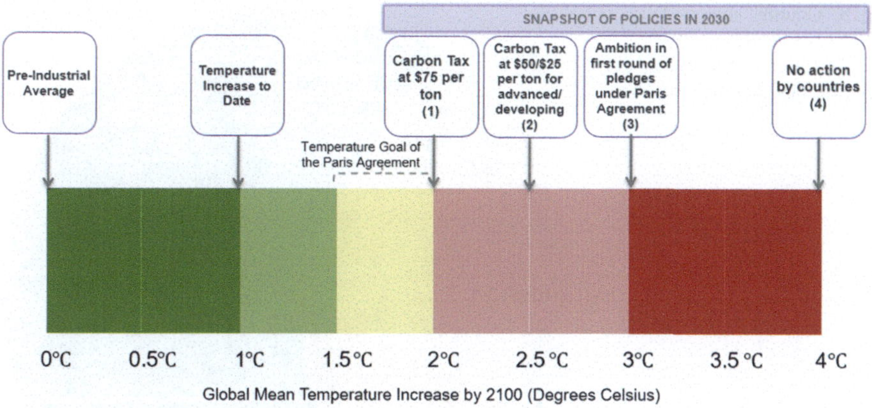

Fig. 7 Climate action and global temperatures. 1. Assumes the explicit carbon-price level of US\$40–80/tCO_2 by 2020 and US\$50–100/tCO_2 by 2030 (*Source* Stiglitz and Stern 2017), 2. (*Source* Fiscal Monitor, October 2019), 3. (*Source* UNEP 2018), 4. (*Source* Nordhaus 2018; Intergovernmental Panel on Climate Change 2014)

to conserve energy and switch to greener sources. Carbon taxes also help mobilize a valuable source of new revenue and are relatively straightforward to administer if it builds on fuel tax systems.

Each country would have to take measures that are as ambitious as a carbon tax rising to $75 per ton of CO_2 by 2030. This is a very tall order given that the current average price per ton is only two US dollars ($). Prices below $75 per ton would fail to limit the temperature rise to below safe levels. If the carbon tax of $75 per ton is implemented globally, the world's largest economies would be the ones making the most contribution to reducing the emissions. Specifically, China will account for more than a half of the reduction in G20 emissions. India and the USA would account for 14% and 13%, respectively (Fig. 8).

Similar to trade liberalization, carbon taxation creates winners and losers within each country. The carbon tax will lead to higher prices for consumers on coal, natural gas, electricity, and gas. Price increases will be particularly large in countries that are most dependent on coal as the source of energy generation. For most countries, such increases, if not accompanied by other measures, will be regressive. Moreover, given that fossil fuel production is often geographically concentrated, implications of carbon taxation are likely to lead to output declines and job losses. On the other hand, fiscal instruments, such as household transfers, public investments, and cuts in labor taxation, can be deployed to reduce the burden on the most vulnerable households and enhance economic efficiency.

Effective combat against the climate change requires building on the early successes of Paris Agreement to achieve a carbon price floor arrangement. The Paris Agreement was a major milestone in finding a globally cooperative solution against climate change. It requires that all parties to the United Nations Framework Convention on Climate Change make efforts to reduce emissions through the nationally

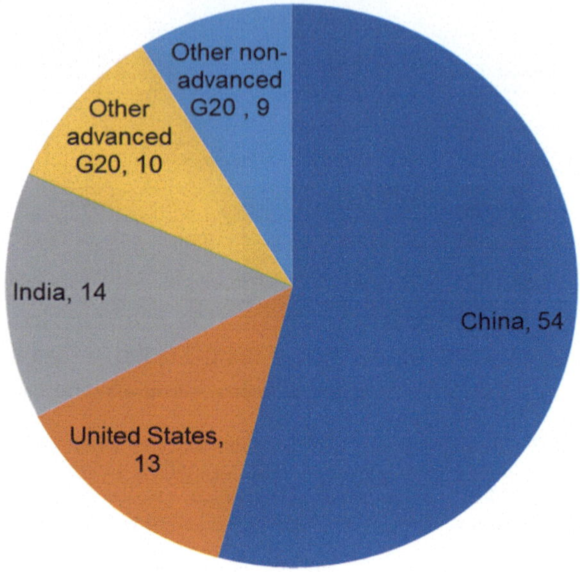

Fig. 8 Country shares of G20 CO_2 reductions, 2030, percent (*Source* IMF Fiscal Monitor, October 2019)

determined contributions. To effectively implement this Agreement, a carbon price floor arrangement could be sought. Such an arrangement should first and foremost involve the largest emitters (China, India, and the USA). For low-income developing and various emerging market economies, a lower carbon price floor could be set.

While the taxation of carbon emissions affects only the polluting companies, corporate taxation, which is discussed in the next section, affects all.

2.2 *Global Solution for International Taxation*

The international corporate tax system is under stress. It has become clear that the century-old tax architecture is no longer adequate for responding to the challenges that have emerged from globalization and digitalization. For example, the golden standard of international taxation—the arm's length principle, which is being applied to intercompany pricing to this day (Ash and Marian 2019) and which was introduced in 1935 by the League of Nations—has been rendered fundamentally inadequate by globalization and digitalization.

The first source of challenge is related to base erosion and profit shifting (BEPS). It is estimated that about 40% of global FDI is directed through special purpose vehicles, which are often set up for tax avoidance purposes (Damgaard and Elkjaer 2017). This results in the loss of large amount of corporate income tax revenue. The Organization for Economic Cooperation and Development (OECD) estimates that annual revenue losses are \$100–240 billion, equivalent to 4–10% of global corporate income tax revenue (OECD 2019a). Developing countries are disproportionally more

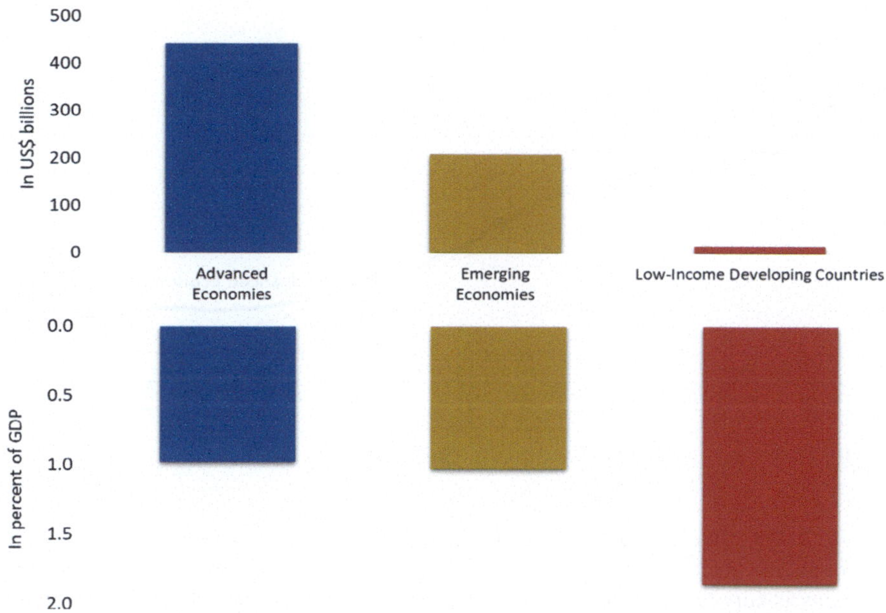

Fig. 9 Estimated revenue losses from profit shifting in 2013 (*Sources* Cobham and Jansky 2018, updating Crivelli et al. 2016; Authors' calculations)

affected. For example, Cobham and Jansky (2018), who update Crivelli et al. (2016), find that revenue losses in low-income developing countries are about 1.8% of GDP, compared with 1% of GDP in advanced and emerging market economies (Fig. 9).

The second source of challenge is tax competition. Globalization encourages countries to compete for productive investments by offering lower corporate income tax rates. Indeed, over the last few decades, corporate income tax rates have been persistently declining across the world. The average tax rate in advanced economies is about 23% down from almost 40% in 1990. Tax rates in low-income developing countries and emerging markets also exhibit similar trend (Fig. 10).

The rapid digitalization of economies, one of the key attendant factors of globalization, has brought about significant implications for the current international tax system. Specifically, three factors have been identified that are characteristic to business models with high degree of digitalization (OECD 2019b). These include, the absence of physical presence to engage in large-scale business in another country, heavy reliance on hard-to-value intangible assets such as software and algorithms, and the generation of value from user participation. All these factors raise questions as to how the taxing rights between jurisdictions should be assigned and how the profit should be allocated within multilateral companies.

Frustrated by the inadequacy of the current international tax rules, some countries have resorted to unilateral actions. In 2015, the UK was among the first to

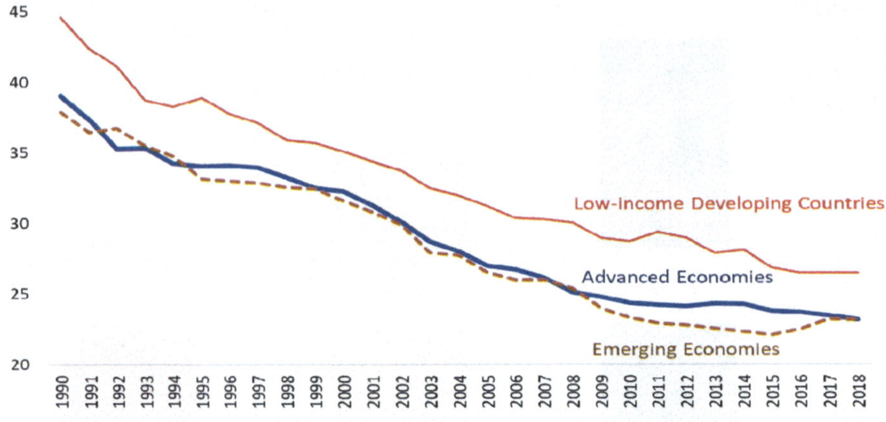

Fig. 10 Statutory corporate income tax rates (*Source* IMF staff compilation)

impose a 25% diverted profit tax (DPT), which targets instances where a multilateral company legitimately avoids a UK taxable presence despite the fact that the company is supplying goods or services to U.K. customers (Grinberg 2019). Other countries (Australia, Argentina, Chile, France, India, Israel, Italy, Japan, Mexico, New Zealand, Poland, Spain, and Uruguay) have followed suit. More recently, some countries started taking unilateral actions to introduce digital services tax that targets turnover from specific activities rather than income. Such uncoordinated actions jeopardize the significant progress that was made under the BEPS project that was possible thanks to a multilateral cooperative approach to international taxation (IMF 2019a, 2019b).

Still-significant revenue losses from profit shifting, tax competition and challenges brought about by the ongoing digital transformation, all point to the need for a cooperative action to find a global solution. The debate around the future international tax architecture is taking place. Various schemes are being considered. The selection of the appropriate scheme should be guided by the principles of limiting profit shifting and competition, the ease of implementation legally and practically, and suitability for low-income country circumstances.[1] The roadmap agreed among members of the OECD/G20 Inclusive Framework on BEPS envisages that the consensus-based long-term solution will be achieved by the end of 2020.[2] The OECD published the relevant proposal to advance international negotiations on October 9, 2019. It remains to be seen whether there is sufficient consensus to lay the foundation for robust cooperation on international corporate taxation that takes into account interests of developing countries.

[1]For the detailed discussion of various proposed schemes, and their pros and cons, please refer to IMF (2019a).

[2]This implies the publication of the final report providing an agreed solution, with the outlines of the architecture agreed in January 2020 (OECD 2019c).

International cooperation is essential to support these developing countries—allowing them to raise their spending envelopes in a sustainable way. This is discussed in the next section.

2.3 International Partnership for Achieving the SDGs

The adoption of the United Nations (UN) resolution on "Transforming our world: the 2030 Agenda for Sustainable Development" in September 2015 is a great example of collective action for the common policy agenda. The resolution introduced a new agenda consisting of 17 SDGs and 169 related targets with the aim to reach them in full by the year of 2030 (UN 2015). These goals range from ending poverty and hunger to ensuring inclusive and equitable quality education and healthy life for all.

The adoption of SDGs follows the millennium development goals (MDGs) that were in effect between 2000 and 2015. The MDGs had set eight different goals ranging from halving extreme poverty rates to halting the spread of HIV/AIDS and providing universal primary education, all by 2015. While causality is difficult to establish, it is clear that significant progress was made across key MDG dimensions during 2000–2015. Most of the progress is accounted for by Asia, due to China and India—the two most populous developing countries. But many low-income countries also managed to record important progress. For example, between 20.9 and 30.3 million additional lives were saved due to accelerated rates of progress, with sub-Saharan Africa accounting for approximately two-thirds of the total, while at least 74 million more children have finished primary school (McArthur and Rasmussen 2018).

Despite important progress, low-income developing countries face the biggest challenge for achieving the SDGs by 2030. This is acknowledged in the 2015 UN resolution that African countries, least developed countries, landlocked developing countries, and small island developing states deserve special attention. In order to reach the SDGs in health, education, and selected sectors of infrastructure (roads, electricity, water, and sanitation), low-income developing countries in aggregate would require raising their annual spending by 15% of GDP by 2030 (see Gaspar et al. 2019 and Fig. 11). For comparison, emerging market economies face additional spending of 4 percentage points of their GDP.

The scale of the challenge facing the low-income developing countries requires strong global partnership. This implies cross-border collaboration between country authorities, international organizations, civil societies, private sectors, and ordinary people. This partnership should aim at supporting the countries to strengthen domestic policies and institutions, to accelerate growth, raise additional tax revenues, achieve greater spending efficiency, mobilize private sector financing, and deliver on existing official development assistance targets. Moreover, the partnership at the country level needs to be anchored in national development strategies.

Boosting tax revenues should take primacy over other potential sources of financing. Despite some progress over the last couple of decades, tax-to-GDP ratios in

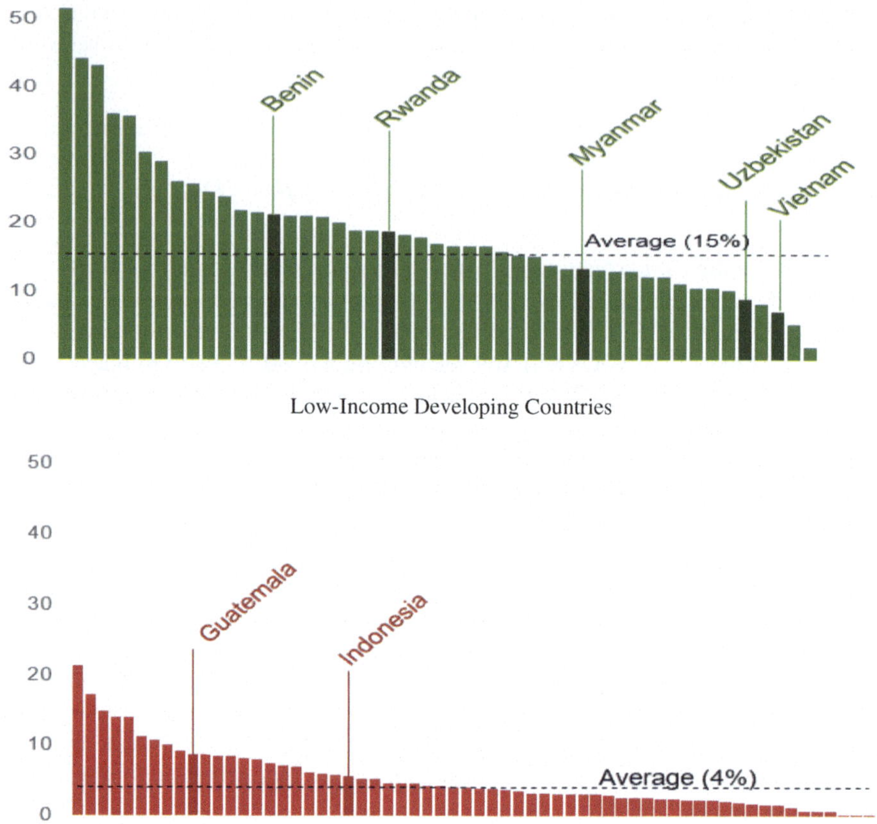

Fig. 11 Additional spending required to meet SDGs by 2030, in percent of 2030 GDP. *Note* Countries identified on the chart are the ones for which country-specific analyses have been done (*Source* Gaspar et al. 2019)

low-income developing countries are very low. About half of low-income developing countries have tax-to-GDP ratios below 13%, a threshold documented as a tipping point for development (Gaspar et al. 2016). Developing tax capacity is crucial if the state is to fulfill its role in sustainable and inclusive growth (Besley and Persson 2009; Gordon 2010). Taxation is necessary to enable the state. Platform for Collaboration on Tax (PCT)—a partnership of the IMF, OECD, UN, and WBG—is supporting countries committed to improving their tax capacity in an enduring way.

Official development assistance is an important but declining source of financing. During the past two decades, net official development assistance inflows to low-income developing countries as a percentage of donor countries' GDP has been relatively stable but they have been falling as a percentage of recipient countries' GDP (Fig. 12). Moreover, in 2018, official development assistance by Development Assistance Committee (DAC) members totaled $153 billion, representing 0.31%

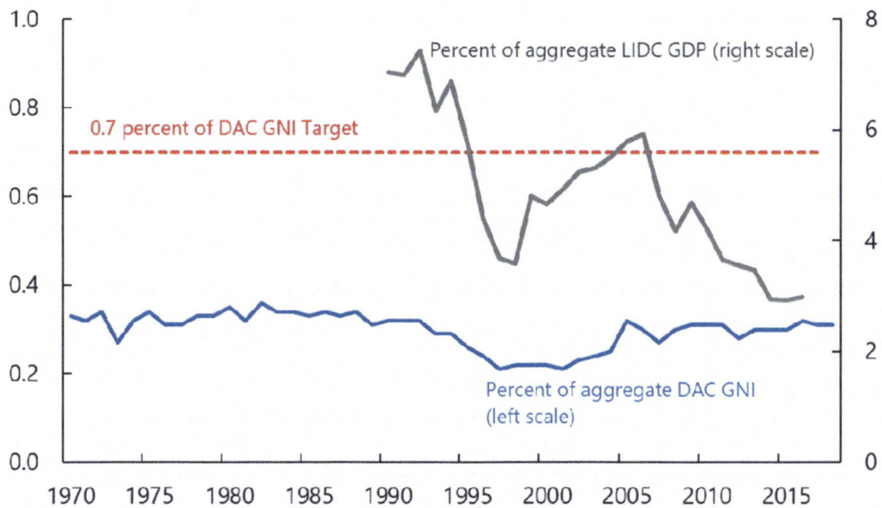

Fig. 12 Official development assistance. *Source* (OECD; Authors' calculations)

of their combined gross national income (GNI), which is well below the donor commitments of 0.7% of GNI.[3]

Decades of development assistance have fallen short of expectations in terms of its impact in lifting the recipient countries firmly out of poverty and putting them onto a sustainable development path. Both donors and recipient countries generally agree that aid is still underperforming in terms of development effectiveness. Various studies have confirmed that the aid effectiveness is low (e.g., Doucouliagos and Paldam 2006) and that higher aid is associated with lower domestic tax capacity (Crivelli et al. 2012). The latter, as mentioned above, is critical for building state capacity in recipient countries.

Therefore, global coordination is needed to increase the effectiveness of aid and create innovative ways and avenues to finance the SDGs. More than 100 bilateral and multilateral donors endorsed the Paris Declaration on Aid Effectiveness in 2005.[4] Given that poorer countries have larger additional financing requirements, some have argued to target the official aid by reallocating funding to those countries least able to finance their own public spending (Manuel et al. 2019). Others have argued for deploying blended finance, which is the strategic use of development finance for the mobilization of additional finance toward sustainable development in developing countries (OECD 2018).

[3]https://www.oecd.org/dac/financing-sustainable-development/development-finance-standards/official-development-assistance.htm.

[4]However, taking the stock on its implementation in 2012, OECD concluded that only one out of the 13 targets established for 2010 had been met (OECD 2012).

3 Conclusions

The global landscape is changing fast. The pace of transformation is accelerating. Demographics, technology, organization of activities, all around us, put into question firmly held perceptions and beliefs. Painful adjustment is pervasive, and that consequently leads to far-reaching political consequences. One important dimension is the weakening of the multilateral cooperative approach that delivered unprecedented peace and prosperity since 1950.

At the same time, the case for multilateral cooperation has never been stronger. Collective action was needed to protect the global economy in the context of the global financial crisis. The need for collective action was also dramatically on display in the euro area during the sovereign debt crisis.

In this paper, we examine briefly three areas where multilateral cooperation is necessary: climate change, international corporate taxation, and sustainable development. Progress in addressing challenges in all these three areas through global cooperation is crucial. We need to find effective ways to limit the rise in global temperature. Carbon taxation is one of the most effective means. We also need to find a timely, consensus-based solution to revamp the rules-based international tax system. This will help avert a string of unilateral actions by countries to protect their domestic tax base. Finally, the global community should take stronger efforts to support developing countries in meeting the SDGs.

Disclaimer The views expressed in this paper are those of the authors and do not necessarily represent the views of the International Monetary Fund, its Executive Board or Management.

References

Ash E, Marian O (2019) The making of international tax law: empirical evidence from natural language processing, UC Irvine School of Law Research Paper No. 2019–02

Besley T, Persson T (2009) The origins of state capacity: property rights, taxation and politics. Am Econ Rev 99:1218–1244

Besley T, Persson T (2011) Pillars of prosperity: the political economics of development clusters. Princeton University Press, Princeton

Bourguignon F, Morrisson C (2002) Inequality among world citizens: 1890–1992. Am Econ Rev 92:727–744

Cobham A, Jansky P (2018) Global distribution of revenue loss from corporate tax avoidance: re-estimation and country results. J Int Dev 30:206–232

Crivelli E, de Mooij R, Keen M (2016) Base erosion, profit shifting and developing countries. IMF working paper 15/118

Crivelli E, Gupta S, Muthoora P et al (2012) Foreign aid and revenue: still a crowding out effect? IMF working paper no. 12/186

Damgaard J, Elkjaer T (2017) The global FDI network: searching for ultimate investors. Danmarks Nationalbank working paper

Doucouliagos H, Paldam M (2008) Aid effectiveness on growth: a meta study. Eur J Polit Econ 24(1):1–24

Gaspar V, Amaglobeli D, Garcia-Escribano M et al (2019) Fiscal policy and development: human, social, and physical investments for the SDG. IMF Staff Discussion Note No. 19/03
Gaspar V, Jaramillo L, Wingender P (2016) Tax capacity and growth: is there a tipping point? Working paper no. 16/234
Gordon R (ed) (2010) Taxation in developing countries. Columbia University Press, New York
Grinberg I (2019) International taxation in an era of digital disruption: analyzing the current debate. Georgetown Law Faculty Publications and Other Works 2145
International Monetary Fund (2017) Fiscal monitor: tackling inequality. IMF, Washington
International Monetary Fund (2018) Macroeconomic developments and prospects in low-income developing countries. IMF, Washington
International Monetary Fund (2019a) Corporate taxation in the global economy. IMF policy paper no. 19/007
International Monetary Fund (2019b) Fiscal monitor: how to mitigate climate change. IMF, Washington
IPCC (2014) Climate Change (2014) Impacts, adaptation, and vulnerability part a: global and sectoral aspects. In: Various (eds) Contribution of working group ii to the fifth assessment report of the intergovernmental panel on climate change. Cambridge University Press, Cambridge, U.K. and New York
Lakner C, Milanovic B (2013) Global income distribution: from the fall of the berlin wall to the great recession. World bank policy research working paper 6719
Manuel M, Manea S, Samman E et al (2019) Financing the end of extreme poverty. Overseas Development Institute Briefing Note
McKinsey Global Institute (2017) Jobs lost, jobs gained: workforce transitions in a time of automation. www.mckinsey.com/global-themes/future-of-organizations-and-work/what-the-future-of-work-will-mean-for-jobs-skills-and-wages. Accessed on 28 Mar 2020
McArthur J, Rasmussen K (2018) Change of pace: accelerations and advances during the millennium development goal era. World Dev 105:132–143
Nordhaus W (2018) Projections and uncertainties about climate change in an era of minimal climate policies. Am Econ J 10(3):333–360
Norris P, Inglehart R (2018) Cultural backlash: Trump, Brexit, and the rise of authoritarian populism. Cambridge University Press, New York
OECD (2012) Aid effectiveness 2011: progress in implementing the Paris declaration. OECD Publishing, Paris, Better Aid
OECD (2018) Making blended finance work for the sustainable development goals. OECD Publishing, Paris
OECD (2019a) OECD/G20 inclusive framework on BEPS: progress report, July 2018-May 2019. OECD, Paris
OECD (2019b) Tax and digitalization. OECD Going Digital Policy Note, OECD, Paris
OECD (2019c) Programme of work to develop a consensus solution to the tax challenges arising from the digitalisation of the economy. OECD/G20 Inclusive framework on BEPS, OECD, Paris
Pastor L, Veronesi P (2019) Inequality aversion, populism, and the backlash against globalization. NBER working paper no. 24900
Schwab K (2016) The fourth industrial revolution. World economic forum
Stiglitz J (2017) The overselling of globalization. Bus Econ 52:129–137
Stiglitz J, Stern N (2017) Report of the high-level commission on carbon prices. Carbon pricing leadership coalition. Available www.carbonpricingleadership.org/report-of-the-highlevel-commission-on-carbon-prices. Accessed on 28 Mar 2020
United Nations (2015) Transforming our world: the 2030 agenda for sustainable development. Resolution adopted by the General Assembly on 25 Sept 2015
United Nations Environment Programme (2018) The emissions gap report 2018. Available www.unenvironment.org/emissionsgap. Accessed 28 on Mar 2020
United Nations Department of Economic and Social Affairs (2017) World economic and social survey 2017: reflecting on seventy years of development policy and analysis

United Nations Environmental Program (2018) Emissions gap report 2018. UNEP, New York
Van Zanden J, Baten J, Foldvari P et al (2014) The changing shape of global inequality: 1820–2000: exploring a new dataset. Rev Income Wealth 60(2):279–297

International Migration and Social Network Spillovers of Political Norms

Cátia Batista, Julia Seither, and Pedro C. Vicente

Abstract International migration flows are shaping world politics in a variety of ways. This chapter summarizes existing evidence on the mechanisms through which these flows affect political attitudes and participation in the countries from where the migrants originate. A comparison is made between the effects of international migration on political institutions in Cape Verde and Mozambique, which both have strong migratory traditions. Emigration from Cape Verde is characterized by relatively high-skilled migration to Portugal and other Organization for Economic Co-operation and Development (OECD) countries, while emigration from Mozambique is mostly driven by unskilled labor flows into South Africa. The results that we describe show that international migration substantially increases political participation in both settings. The demand for political accountability and electoral participation substantially increases after being exposed to better democratic political norms and knowledge about electoral processes. This effect grows with citizens' social proximity, which is characterized as opportunities for personal interaction. Overall, we provide evidence that both South–North as well as South–South international migration strengthen democracy in the poorest countries.

Keywords Cape Verde · Electoral participation · International migration · Mozambique · Political institutions

C. Batista (✉) · P. C. Vicente
Nova School of Business and Economics, Universidade Nova de Lisboa, Carcavelos, Portugal
e-mail: catia.batista@novasbe.pt

P. C. Vicente
e-mail: pedro.vicente@novasbe.pt

J. Seither
Department of Economics, University of Chicago, Chicago, IL, USA
e-mail: jseither@uchicago.edu

L. Brites Pereira et al. (eds.), *Economic Globalization and Governance*,
https://doi.org/10.1007/978-3-030-53265-9_16

1 Introduction

It is increasingly recognized that information, technologies, and social norms spread through social networks—this includes political norms, attitudes, and behaviors such as political participation and the demand for political accountability.[1] The information and norms contained within a social network are thus potentially important to promote better political institutions—which may, in turn, be crucial for economic growth, as shown by Acemoglu et al. (2005). More recently, Batista et al. (2019) show that international migration is an important mechanism for changing the existing norms and information flowing through a social network.

The effects of international migration on the economic development of emigrant source countries have attracted considerable and renewed research interest, particularly in the last two decades. Indeed, a number of studies have emphasized that emigration has a positive impact on the educational attainment of both migrants and non-migrants, on entrepreneurship and new business creation in the home country, as well as on international trade and foreign direct investment (FDI) between the migrants' country of origin and that of destination.[2] However, causal evidence on the relationship between international migration and political participation is relatively scarce.[3]

This chapter presents empirical evidence on international migration's importance for the diffusion of political norms in social network and the relative effectiveness of different types of social networks in facilitating norm transmission. Traditionally, emigration has been regarded as a form of "brain drain" (Baghwati and Hamada 1974; Gruber and Scott 1966) that is detrimental to the supply of better-quality political institutions. This is true if those individuals that leave the country are also the most capable of providing public services. Additionally, Hirschman (1970) regards emigration as an "outside option" that allows citizens to leave the country if they

---

[1]Several studies point to norms about political participation being adopted and passed onto peers. Fafchamps and Vicente (2013) and Fafchamps et al. (2020) show that increasing the political literacy of experiment participants changed perceptions and electoral behavior, respectively, for those participants with more network connections, even if these were not directly targeted by literacy campaign. Closely related to this idea, Giné and Mansuri (2018) find positive spillover effects of an awareness campaign on female voter turnout in Pakistan. Similarly, Nickerson (2008) finds that about 60% of the propensity to vote is passed on to another household member in a randomized controlled trial in the United States.

[2]Evidence of the positive effects of remittances is provided by Edwards and Ureta (2003), Yang (2008), and Batista and Umblijs (2016), among others. The possibility of a "brain gain" as opposed to traditional "brain drain" of human capital was first supported empirically by Beine et al. (2008) and Batista et al. (2012) at the macro and micro levels, respectively. Dustmann and Kirchkamp (2002), Mesnard and Ravallion (2006), and Batista et al. (2017) examine the role of return migration in promoting entrepreneurship and new business formation in the home country. Gould (1994), Rauch and Trindade (2002), and Javorcik et al. (2011) evaluate the relationship between migrant networks, international trade, and foreign investment.

[3]The main recent contributions to this end are Batista and Vicente (2011), Barsbai et al. (2017), and Batista et al. (2019).

are unhappy with their home country's government. In this model, emigration is detrimental to the demand for better political institutions.

International migration may, however, promote better political institutions by creating positive supply effects through return migration and through communication between current migrants and their peers at home, in addition to positive demand effects through the transfer of knowledge and norms. In this chapter, we focus on the effects of international migration on political participation through the demand side, as well as on the channels that are most important in diffusing information and norms in migrant social networks. Specifically, we focus on the cases of Cape Verde and Mozambique, two traditionally large emigration countries with relatively new democracies.

In doing so, we also seek to honor Jorge Braga de Macedo's research contributions to economic development issues over the years. Indeed, one of his more recent studies assessed to what extent Cape Verde and Mozambique may be regarded as relative development successes in West and Southern Africa. This study found that it is possible to ensure positive combinations of institutions and policies that are conducive to successful development outcomes, notwithstanding the impact of history and globalization in these two countries (Braga de Macedo and Brites Pereira 2016). Our present study thus enriches this research focus by addressing the effects of international migration on political attitudes and behavior in these countries.

2 Theoretical Model of Diffusion of Political Norms Through Migration

The effect of international migration on political norms and participation can be modeled by introducing changes in the information set and identity parameters in a simple political economy framework. The general political participation framework (as described in detail in Dhillon and Peralta 2002) considers the decision to participate in politics (such as in elections) as the outcome of a simple cost-benefit analysis. The decision-maker considers the cost of casting a vote and the expected benefit of participating in the elections, given his own decision as well as the collective one of his peers. This optimization is subject to the individual's subjective information set.

Batista et al. (2018) introduce international migration in this model as a driver of political participation in two ways: migration directly affects the decision-making process of return migrants, and indirectly the social network of current and return migrants through spillovers. International migration might thus have positive effects on political participation and the demand for improved political institutions that go beyond changes in individuals with migration experience.

Return migrants might participate more in politics due to two reasons: they might have more knowledge about the importance of democratic processes (information channel), and they might have adopted different political norms from their host country (identity channel). The latter channel requires that political norms in the host country are sufficiently different from those in the migrant's country of origin. The effectiveness of both channels is likely to be increasing in the migrant's level of integration in the host country. Better integrated migrants with stronger social ties to the host country population are potentially more likely to adopt host country norms. Increased integration is further likely to facilitate the transmission of knowledge about the importance of political participation.

In a similar manner, individuals that are influenced by migrants via their social network, learn from them about political participation and are confronted with changed political norms that they bring back home. Current migrants diffuse norms through regular contact with those left behind. Although return migrants can potentially revert to the political participation norms of their home country, they are likely to transmit increased political participation.

The magnitude of the two effects depends on the relative difference in political participation norms and knowledge transmission between origin and host countries. Batista and Vicente (2011) exploit the difference in the two main destination countries of Cape Verdean emigrants to show that emigration to the United States has a greater effect on political participation than emigration to Portugal.

3 Quantifying the Impact of International Migration on Political Norms

Measuring the impact of international migration on political attitudes requires both detailed household data on migration spells and on political attitudes and behavior. However, Batista and Vicente (2011) exploit variation in the proportion of international migrants in Cape Verdean locations, and Batista et al. (2019) analyze the differential effects of different types of migrant networks on the diffusion of political norms. Such analysis requires detailed survey data on the population's migratory experience (as administrative data is rarely available), as well as information about respondent's social proximity.

Furthermore, survey reports on political participation might be informative about changes in political attitudes or knowledge about democratic processes but not necessarily about changes in behavior. Batista and Vicente (2011) and Batista et al. (2019) overcome this challenge by conducting messaging experiments in Cape Verde and Mozambique. Individuals are offered the possibility to send postcards and text messages with policy priorities, respectively. Individuals with a higher demand for political accountability are hypothesized to be more likely to send a message.

4 Controlling for Selection into Migration

The main threat to causal identification of international migration's effect on political participation is that migration might be correlated with political behavior through unobservable factors. These factors cannot be controlled for in an ordinary least squares (OLS) model, and any estimates of a migration effect on political participation would thus be biased.

Most studies tackle this problem with a two-stage least squares (2SLS) estimation approach. The approach requires the existence of an instrumental variable that is strongly correlated with an individual's decision to migrate or the exposure to migrants but is not correlated with the outcome variable of interest. Such instruments are difficult to encounter—especially given the exclusion restriction.

Examples of such instrumental variables include the past migratory history, macroeconomic shocks in the destination country, and variation in the exposure to natural disasters. In the case of Cape Verde, a respondent with stronger links to migrants (current and return) that have emigrated in the past is hypothesized by Batista and Vicente (2011), together with macroeconomic shocks, to be a proxy for the migrant network in the destination country. As Mozambique is prone to natural disasters, the exposure to such shocks around different age bins is highly correlated with emigration in rural Mozambican areas, as shown in Batista et al. (2019). Both papers then use these proxies to instrument for the respondent's social network's self-selection into migration. It can be argued plausibly that these instruments meet the exclusion restriction and are uncorrelated with political participation.

Batista and Vicente (2011) then proceed to estimate the differential treatment effects between current and return migrants, as well as between different destination countries. Batista et al. (2019) complement these findings by also examining different types of social migrant networks and their social proximity. They account for self-selection into social networks with second-degree network links within the respective networks.

5 Related Literature in Economics and Political Science

Empirical contributions on the impact of emigration on political participation in the origin countries of migrants are scarce, but the existing evidence supports the hypothesis that international migrants positively affect the development of local political institutions. Cross-country studies such as Docquier et al. (2016), Spilimbergo (2009), and Mercier (2016) show that migration to democratic countries positively affects democracy in origin countries. Whereas the first study shows that the positive effects of migration to OECD countries on democracy and economic freedom remain in the long-run, and the latter two studies show that education acquired in democratic countries promotes democracy in origin countries.

Barsbai et al. (2017) additionally investigate the underlying mechanisms driving these results. They exploit the variation in migration patterns from Moldova to either democratic or socialist regimes to show that electoral preferences and outcomes are affected primarily by emigration to Western democratic countries. Municipalities with a higher share of migrants are more likely to support democratic ideas in this context. This result suggests that migrants pass on democratic norms and knowledge about improved political institutions.

Further empirical evidence from Mali suggests that a higher stock of migrants positively affects political participation and electoral competitiveness (Chauvet and Mercier 2014). Return migrants from non-African countries, in particular, diffuse political norms to poorly educated peers in their home country. These peers, in turn, increase political participation and thus foster electoral competitiveness.

While the above studies focus on the impact of social remittances, a related literature from political science focuses on the strong correlation between financial remittances and political variables. Migrant remittances increase in election years when the elections are more contested and when the home country is poorer, as shown by O'Mahony (2013). Furthermore, Ahmad (2012, 2013) shows that migrant remittances may deter political change, particularly in autocratic regimes. However, remittances that are being used for the private provision of local public goods may reduce the effectiveness of state patronage and thus promote political change (Adida and Girod 2010; Doyle 2015; Pfutze 2014; Tyburski 2012). Miller and Peters (2018) further show that emigration may increase non-violent demand for political change.

In the remainder of this chapter, we will discuss the mechanisms which might drive the different results.

6 Cape Verde and Mozambique: Two Stories of African Migration

Cape Verde and Mozambique are two African countries that traditionally experienced large international migratory flows. Analyzing the role that migrant networks play in the transmission of political norms is particularly interesting in these two cases, as the nature of international migration is inherently different. However, Cape Verde may be described as experiencing South–North migration, and Mozambique's migration occurs within the continent, i.e., South-South migration.

Cape Verde is composed of nine islands off the West African coast. According to available data from INE (2015), around 44% of the 524.833 inhabitants live in the two major cities, *Praia* and *São Vicente*. A sizable share of Cape Verdeans is living abroad. More than 70% of total emigrants live in the United States and Portugal which are the main outward-bound migratory destinations.

Remittances received by local communities are substantial and close to equaling the level of development aid. In recent years, remittances always surpassed foreign direct investments in Cape Verde.

Mozambique, a country in East Africa, is characterized by a long coastline prone to natural catastrophes. Despite its high growth rates driven by natural resource discoveries, it has been aid-dependent for many years—especially after natural catastrophes that typically displaced many Mozambicans.

Most of the population living in rural areas is dependent on agriculture, so that climate change is a major threat to their livelihoods. Recurring floods and droughts force many Mozambicans to emigrate to neighboring African countries to find low-skill employment opportunities. Formal remittances flows accounted for less than 2% of Gross National Income (GNI) in 2013 and are thus relatively small compared to those of other countries like Cape Verde.

In addition to their legacies of emigration, both countries are recent democracies after having been Portuguese colonies until 1975. However, Cape Verde experienced a stable democracy after its first free elections in 1991, and Mozambique experienced recurring episodes of armed conflict and social unrest. Freedom House considers it to be a "partly-free" country, and the importance of democracy is difficult to grasp for many Mozambicans.

7 Data Description

The datasets and empirical evidence described in this chapter are based on two detailed household surveys that were specifically conducted for the purpose of eliciting the effect of international migrant networks on political participation. The data from Cape Verde was collected between December 2005 and March 2006 and the data from Mozambique in 2009.

For both countries, detailed data on the socio-economic background of migrant and non-migrant households is available. A household is considered a migrant household if at least one household member is currently living abroad or has been for at least six months in the past. Batista and Vicente (2011) additionally collected information about perceived corruption, whereas Batista et al. (2019) exploit detailed data on the relationships between households, specifically differentiating between kinship and friendship relations.

8 Descriptive Statistics

Table 1 summarizes the share of current and return migrants in both samples and illustrates the relevance of international migration in both Cape Verde and Mozambique.

In Cape Verde, almost 15% of all household members were living abroad at the time of data collection, whereas this is the case for only around 7% of sampled household members in Mozambique. Current migrants are more likely to be men compared to the household members that remained in the respective country of

Table 1 Characteristics of individuals in both samples depending on migration status

		Non-migrants	Current migrants	Return migrants
Sample size Cape Verde		4997	907	241
Mozambique		4500	381	473
Male Cape Verde		47.95%	51.99%	64.46%
Mozambique		54.22%	71.92%	43.97%
Education (males aged 15–64) Cape Verde	No education	3.72%	3.6%	5.2%
	Pre-school	1.54%	0.7%	0.0%
	Alphabetized	11.35%	8.2%	14.3%
	Primary	59.69%	62.4%	50.7%
	Intermediate secondary	18.79%	9.9%	19.5%
	Secondary	1.12%	0.4%	3.9%
	Post-secondary	3.78%	14.9%	6.5%
Mozambique	No education	21.79%	31.02%	22.71%
	Pre-school	6.61%	10.58%	14.01%
	Alphabetized	31.19%	32.48%	24.64%
	Primary	14.81%	17.52%	23.19%
	Intermediate secondary	15.72%	5.11%	12.56%
	Secondary	6.85%	2.19%	2.90%
	Post-secondary	3.03%	1.08%	0%

Source Own surveys

origin in both countries. Return migrants in Mozambique, i.e., household members that have lived abroad in the past but are now living there, are more likely to be female. This result only holds for Mozambique but not Cape Verde.

Mozambican migrants differ substantially from Cape Verdean migrants with respect to their educational level. Mozambicans are less educated, and a large proportion of sampled migrants has never received any education. Migrants from Cape Verde, on the contrary, are more likely to have received post-secondary education than Cape Verdeans who never migrated. This disparity is explained by the difference in migration patterns, which is mostly labor driven in Mozambique.

Emigration from both countries also differs substantially with respect to the top destination countries. However, migration from Mozambique is clearly dominated by South Africa as a destination country, and Portugal is the main destination for migrants from Cape Verde, followed by the United States. Table 2 displays the top destinations for both countries in descending order. The table illustrates the inherent difference of migration patterns between the two countries and, hence, the different classification, respectively, North–South and South-South migration.

Table 2 Destination countries of all migrants (%)

Destination countries for Cape Verde		Destination countries for Mozambique	
Portugal	55	South Africa	86.62
United States	20	Tanzania	5.16
France	12	Other African	1.64
Brazil	3	Zimbabwe	1.41
Netherlands	2	Malawi	1.17
Luxembourg	2	Swaziland	1.17
Other	6	Other European	0.94
		Portugal	0.7
		Other	0.47
		Germany	0.47
		Cuba	0.23

Source Own surveys

However, Batista and Vicente (2011) estimate the impact of the total share of migrants within a location on political participation, and Batista et al. (2019) consider the differential impact of different types of migrant networks. Table 3 illustrates the distribution of migrant network links for each of the three network types in Mozambique. In the Mozambican sample, more than 30% of households have a least one household member that is currently living abroad or was doing so for more than six months. At the location level, only 17.5% of households live in a location where no person has migrated ever. The distinction into different types of networks illustrates the relative importance of the same. About 41% have kinship relations to a migrant household, and almost 50% chat with a migrant household on a regular basis. These figures indicate the relative importance migration that may play in the diffusion of political norms and participation.

Table 4 provides summary statistics of the different outcome measures that explain political participation and demand for political accountability in both samples. Batista and Vicente (2011) conduct a simple voting experiment in Cape Verde to estimate a respondent's political participation in the context of corruption and demand for accountability. The sampled survey respondents were asked to mail a pre-stamped postcard if they wanted the survey results on perceived corruption to be made public. In total, around 43% of respondents in the sample mailed the postcard, so that results would be published.

This behavioral measure improves over self-reported measures of political participation, as may be illustrated with data from the Mozambican sample. The dataset contains both self-reports as well as a behavioral measure from a text messaging experiment. The data collection took place during the 2009 presidential elections in Mozambique. After the elections, respondents were asked to send a text message

Table 3 Migration networks in Mozambique. All households (%)

All households		
	Number of links	Migration experience
Households with at least one migrant		32.41
Migrant households in geographical network	0	17.50
	1	15.63
	2	10.48
	3	8.10
	4	11.10
	5	13.02
	6	6.85
	7	5.55
	8	4.25
	9	5.66
	10	1.87
Kinship relations with migrant households	0	58.28
	1	24.28
	2	7.89
	3	4.34
	4	2.34
	5	1.04
	6	1.47
	7	0.09
	8	0.09
	9	0.17
Chatting relations with migrant households	0	51.78
	1	23.59
	2	8.76
	3	5.55
	4	4.42
	5	2.43
	6	1.91
	7	0.69
	8	0.52
	9	0.35

Table 4 Summary statistics. All households

	Variable	Mean	Min	Max
Mozambique	Self-reported voting	0.92	0	1
	Proxy for actual voting	0.29	0	1
	Sending text message	0.18	0	1
Cape Verde	Returned postcards	0.43	0	1

with policy priority suggestions for the mandate of the president-elect. Table 4 illustrates that although around 91% of Mozambican respondents claimed to have voted during the elections, only 18% sent a text message with policy priorities.

Batista et al. (2019) further exploit data from an actual voting measure obtained by enumerators indicating whether a respondent had an inked finger after the elections. Table 4 shows that around 29% of respondents participated in the elections according to this measure. The difference between these measures can be interpreted as a possible "desirability bias" where respondents acknowledge the importance of casting a vote but have not actually acted accordingly.

9 Discussion of Results

In both Cape Verde and Mozambique, the probabilities of political participation increase with each additional migrant in a respondent's social network. In Batista and Vicente (2011), the probability of sending back a postcard increases by 0.94 p.p. for each additional 1 p.p. in the fraction of emigrants in a location. This result is robust to the inclusion of relevant covariates and geographical and local financial controls. This effect is driven by emigration to the United States, which is the main migration destination with best governance indicators in our sample. The results by Batista and Vicente (2011) furthermore suggest that the impact of return migrants is much larger than the impact of current migrants, independent of their migration destination.

Similarly, one additional migrant in a village increase the probability to vote by up to 2.5 p.p. in Mozambique. After controlling for self-selection into migration, this effect increases to up to 3.4 p.p. and seems to be driven, in line with the findings for Cape Verde, by regular contact with migrants via chatting. On the positive effect of one more migrant within a respondent's kinship network, the Mozambican results are not robust to controlling for self-selection into migration.

10 Concluding Remarks

This chapter summarizes and examines existing empirical evidence on the impact of international migration on political participation in migrant origin countries for both North–South and South–South migration. We focused on the cases of two traditionally large but very different migration countries: Cape Verde and Mozambique.

Despite their common history as Portuguese colonies and relatively new democracies, the typical migration flows of both countries are very different. However, emigrants from Cape Verde are typically highly educated and mostly migrate to Portugal and other OECD countries, and emigrants from Mozambique head almost exclusively to South Africa to work as low-skilled migrants in mines and commercial farms.

The results presented in this chapter show that not only may South-South migration be effective in promoting political participation, but also that this effect is mostly driven by direct, regular contact with migrants. This result is in line with a positive effect of migration on political institutions in Cape Verde that is mostly driven by return migrants—and thus direct personal contact rather than indirect interaction with current migrants.

The empirical evidence suggests that the more an individual is exposed to better social norms regarding political participation, the more likely she is to act accordingly. It follows that the relative difference in the quality of democratic structures is relevant, so that even migration within the African continent is important for the promotion of democracy.

References

Acemoglu D, Johnson S, Robinson JA (2005) Institutions as a fundamental cause of long-run growth. In: Aghion P, Durlauff S (eds) Handbook of economic growth, chap 6. North-Holland, Amsterdam

Adida CL, Girod DM (2010) Do migrants improve their hometowns? Remittances and access to public services in Mexico, 1995–2000. Comp Polit Stud 44(1):3–27

Ahmad FZ (2012) The perils of unearned foreign income: aid, remittances and government survival. Am Polit Sci Rev 106(1):146–165

Ahmad FZ (2013) Remittances deteriorate governance. Rev Econ Stat 95(4):1166–1182

Barsbai T, Rapoport H, Steinmayr A, Trebesch C (2017) The effect of labor migration on the diffusion of democracy: evidence from a former Soviet Republic. Am Econ J Appl Econ 9(3):36–69

Batista C, Umblijs J (2016) Do migrants send remittances as a way of self-insurance? Oxford Econ Pap 68(1):108–130

Batista C, Vicente PC (2011) Do migrants improve governance at home? evidence from a voting experiment. World Bank Econ Rev 25(1):77–104

Batista C, Lacuesta A, Vicente P (2012) Testing the "brain drain" hypothesis: micro evidence from Cape Verde. J Dev Econ 97(1):32–45

Batista C, McIndoe-Calder Vicente T (2017) Return migration, self-selection and entrepreneurship. Oxford Bull Econ Stat 79(5):797–821

Batista C, Seither J, Vicente PC (2018) Migration, political institutions, and social networks. CReAM discussion paper CPD N.13/18, August

Batista C, Seither J, Vicente PC (2019) Do migrant social networks shape political attitudes and behavior at home? World Dev 117:328–343

Beine M, Docquier F, Rapoport H (2008) Brain drain and LDCs' growth: winners and losers. Econ J 118:631–652

Bhagwati J, Hamada K (1974) The brain drain, international integration of markets for professionals and unemployment: a theoretical analysis. J Dev Econ 1(1):19–42

Braga de Macedo J, Brites Pereira L (2016) Cape Verde and Mozambique as development successes in West and Southern Africa. In: Edwards S, Johnson S, Weil DN (eds) African successes sustainable growth, vol IV. University of Chicago Press, Chicago, pp 203–293

Chauvet L, Mercier M (2014) Do return migrants transfer political norms to their origin country? evidence from mali. J Comp Econ 42(3):630–651

Dhillon A, Peralta S (2002) Economic theories of voter turnout. Econ J 112:F332–F352

Docquier F, Lodigiani E, Rapoport H, Schiff M (2016) Emigration and democracy. J Devel Econ 120(C):209–223

Doyle D (2015) Remittances and social spending. Am Polit Sci Rev 109(4):785–802

Dustmann C, Kirchkamp O (2002) The optimal migration duration and activity choice after re-migration. J Dev Econ 67(2):351–372

Edwards AC, Ureta M (2003) International migration, remittances, and schooling: evidence from El Salvador. J Dev Econ 72(2):429–461

Fafchamps M, Vicente P (2013) Political violence and social networks: experimental evidence from a Nigerian election. J Dev Econ 101:27–48

Fafchamps M, Vaz A, Vicente P (2020) Voting and peer effects: experimental evidence from Mozambique. Econ Dev Cult Change 68(2):567–605

Giné X, Mansuri G (2018) Together we will: experimental evidence on female voting behavior in Pakistan. Am Econ J Appl Econ 10(1):207–235

Gould DM (1994) Immigrant links to the home country: empirical implications for U.S. Bilateral trade flows. Rev Econ Stat 76(2):302–316

Gruber H, Scott A (1966) The international flow of human capital. Am Econ Rev 56(1/2):268–274

Hirschman A (1970) Exit, voice and loyalty: responses to decline in firms. Harvard University Press, Cambridge, Mass, Organizations and States

Instituto Nacional de Estatística (2015) Cabo Verde statistical yearbook 2015. INE, Praia

Javorcik B, Özden Ç, Spatareanu M, Neagu M (2011) Migrant networks and foreign direct investment. J Dev Econ 94(2):231–241

Mercier M (2016) The return of the prodigy son: do return migrants make better leaders? J Dev Econ 122:76–91

Mesnard A, Ravallion M (2006) The wealth effect on new business startups in a developing economy. Economica 73(291):367–392

Miller MK, Peters ME (2018) Restraining the huddled masses: migration policy and autocratic survival. Brit J Polit Sci 1–31

Nickerson DW (2008) Is voting contagious? Evidence from two field experiments. Am Polit Sci Rev 102(1):49–57

O'Mahony A (2013) Political investment: remittances and elections. Brit J Polit Sci 43(4):799–820

Pfutze T (2014) Clientelism versus social learning: the electoral effects of international migration. Int Stud Quart 58(2):295–307

Rauch J, Trindade V (2002) Ethnic Chinese networks in international trade. Rev Econ Stat 84(1):116–130

Spilimbergo A (2009) Democracy and foreign education. Am Econ Rev 99(1):528–543

Tyburski MD (2012) The resource curse reversed? Remittances and corruption in Mexico. Int Stud Quart 56(2):339–350

United Nations (2015) Trends in international migrant stock: migrants by destination and origin. United Nations, Department of Economic and Social Affairs, Population Division, New York
Yang (2008) International migration, remittances and household investment: evidence from Philippine migrants' exchange rate shocks. Econ J Royal Econ Soc 118(528):591–630

Regulated Early Closures of Coal-Fired Power Plants and Tougher Energy Taxation on Electricity Production: Synergy or Rivalry?

Alfredo Marvão Pereira and Rui Manuel Pereira

Abstract This chapter examines the economic and environmental effects of the interaction between regulated early closure of coal-fired power plants and new energy taxation rules on such plants using a dynamic general equilibrium model of the Portuguese economy. Simulation results show that regulated early closures lead to meaningful emission reductions but induce significant detrimental macroeconomic and distributional effects. Upon application of the new energy taxation rules, no significant environmental gains or macroeconomic and distributional losses are observed beyond those already induced by the forced closures. The public sector also seems to benefit from additional tax revenues. If the coal-fired power plants operators react by unilaterally decommissioning their installations, however, the adverse macroeconomic and distributional effects will substantially deteriorate even though the environmental ones improve. Moreover, the adverse budgetary effects will be substantially larger. Overall, we find no synergies between the two policies and, in fact, the opposite is potentially true.

Keywords Coal-operated power plants · Dynamic general equilibrium · Energy taxation · Economic and environmental effects · Portugal

1 Introduction

In November 2017, the Portuguese Government announced its commitment to retire all coal-fired power plants by 2030. In addition, in the context of the 2018 State Budget, the tax on energy products (*Impostos sobre Produtos Petrolíferos e Energéticos*, ISP hereafter) was extended to include the taxation of coal used in electricity generation. This extension has a fixed component of 4.26 euros per ton of coal used and a variable component, which depends on the carbon content of the coal and is indexed to the carbon price in the European Union Emissions Trading System (EU-ETS hereafter).

A. Marvão Pereira (✉) · R. M. Pereira
Department of Economics, Williams & Mary, Williamsburg, VA, USA
e-mail: ampere@wm.edu

L. Brites Pereira et al. (eds.), *Economic Globalization and Governance*,
https://doi.org/10.1007/978-3-030-53265-9_17

Portugal has two large coal-fired power plants, one in Sines and the other in Pego. The Sines plant was commissioned in 1985, has a capacity of 1192 MW, and is operated by *Energias de Portugal* (EDP). The Pego plant was commissioned in 1993; it has a capacity of 628 MW and is operated by *Tejo Energia* a joint venture between TrustEnergy and Endesa Generation. These two plants play a major role in the Portuguese energy system. Thermal production of electricity from coal accounted for 26% of the electricity generated in Portugal in 2017: 18% from Sines and 8% from Pego (DGEG 2018). These power plants account for more than half of thermal production of electricity in Portugal with natural gas accounting for the remainder. In addition, coal-fired units are a substantial component of electric power operators generating portfolios. In 2017, the production of electricity from coal in Sines accounted for about 12.5% of the electricity produced by EDP and the production of electricity from coal in Pego accounted for about 42.7% of the electricity produced by Endesa (EDP 2018).

The environmental impact of these coal-fired power plants is very substantial. In 2017, Sines and Pego accounted for 19.1% of carbon dioxide emissions in Portugal. In fact, they were the two largest individual contributors to greenhouse gases emissions in the country (APA 2018). Therefore, it is not surprising that increasing efforts of environmental groups and increasing awareness by policymakers ultimately translated into the regulated early closure of the two power plants by 2030.

In this chapter, we consider three research questions. First, we want to identify the effects of closing coal-fired power plants in 2030 in the absence of any changes in ISP taxation. Second, we want to determine the effects of the changes in ISP tax rules if the coal-fired power plants close by 2030 as scheduled. Third, we want to establish the effects of the changes in ISP tax rules in an environment in which operators decide to close the plants ahead of the scheduled closure dates, as a response to the increases in operation costs implied by the new ISP rules.

We address these questions in the context of a multi-sector, multi-household dynamic computable general equilibrium model of the Portuguese economy that builds upon the aggregate dynamic general equilibrium model (known as DGEP). Previous versions of this model are documented in Pereira and Pereira (2014c) and have been used recently to address energy and climate policy issues (see Pereira and Pereira 2014a, b, 2017a, b, 2019a, b and Pereira et al. 2016). The current version of the model has a detailed description of the tax system. On the production side, it features a fine differentiation of consumer and producer goods, particularly those with a focus on energy products. On the household side, it captures the heterogeneity in income and consumption patterns by considering five differentiated household groups.

General equilibrium models have been used extensively in energy and environmental studies. For general surveys, see Ballard et al. (2009), Bergman (2005), and Bhattacharyya (1996). For a discussion of the merits and concerns with this approach, see Blanchard (2016) and Sbordone et al. (2010). In general terms, our model follows in the tradition of the early models developed by Ballard et al. (2009) and Borges and

Goulder (1984). In its specifics, however, it is more directly linked to the recent contributions of Annicchiarico et al. (2017), Bhattarai et al. (2016), Fullerton et al. (2012), Goulder and Hafstead (2013), and Tran and Wende (2017), by way of example.

The remainder of the chapter proceeds as follows. Section 2 provides a brief description of the disaggregated dynamic general equilibrium model. Section 3 presents the effect of closing the coal-fired power plants by 2030. Section 4 discusses the impact of the extension of the tax on energy products to coal used in electricity generation and the effects of accelerated plant closures. Finally, Sect. 5 provides a summary, policy implications, and concluding thoughts.

2 The Dynamic General Equilibrium Model and Simulation Design

What follows is necessarily a very brief and general description of the design and implementation of the new multi-sector, multi-household dynamic general equilibrium model of the Portuguese economy. See Pereira and Pereira (2017c) for further details.

2.1 The General Features

The dynamic multi-sector general equilibrium model of the Portuguese economy incorporates fully dynamic optimization behavior, detailed household accounts, detailed industry accounts, a comprehensive modeling of public sector activities, and an elaborate description of energy sectors. We consider a decentralized economy where there are four types of economic agents: households, firms, the public sector, and a foreign sector. All agents, and the economy in general, face financial constraints that frame their economic choices. All agents are price takers and are assumed to have perfect foresight. With money absent, the model is framed in real terms.

Households and firms implement optimal choices, as appropriate, to maximize their objective functions. Households maximize their intertemporal utilities subject to an equation of motion for financial wealth, thereby generating optimal consumption, labor supply, and savings behaviors. We consider five household income groups per quintile. While the general structure of household behavior is the same for all household groups, preferences, income, wealth, and taxes are household-specific, as are consumption demands, savings, and labor supply.

Firms maximize the net present value of their cash flow, subject to the equation of motion for capital stock to yield optimal output, labor demand, and investment demand. We consider thirteen production sectors covering the whole spectrum of economic activity in the country. These include energy producing sectors, such as electricity and petroleum refining, other EU-ETS sectors, such as transportation, textiles, wood pulp and paper, chemicals, and pharmaceuticals, rubber, plastic and ceramics and primary metals, as well as sectors not in the EU-ETS such as agriculture, basic manufacturing and construction. While the general structure of production behavior is the same for all sectors, technologies, capital endowments, and taxes are sector-specific, as are output supply, labor demand, energy demand, and investment demand. The public sector and the foreign sector evolve in a way that is determined by the economic conditions and their respective financial constraints.

All economic agents interact through demand and supply mechanisms in different markets. The general market equilibrium is defined by market clearing in product markets, labor markets, financial markets, and the market for investment goods. The equilibrium of the product market reflects the national income accounting identity and the different expenditure allocations of output by sector of economic activity. The total amount of a commodity supplied to the economy, be it produced domestically, or imported from abroad, must equal the total end-user demand for the product, including the demand by households, by the public sector, its use as an intermediate demand, and its application as an investment good.

The total labor supplied by the different households, adjusted by an unemployment rate that is assumed exogenous and constant, must equal total labor demanded by the different sectors of economic activity. There is only one equilibrium wage rate, although this translates into different household-specific effective wage rates, based on household-specific levels of human capital which obviously differ by quartile of income. Different firms buy shares of the same aggregate labor supply. Implicitly, this means that we do not consider differences in the composition of labor demand among the different sectors of economic activity, in terms of the incorporated human capital levels. Saving by households and the foreign sector equals the value of domestic investment plus the budget deficit.

The evolution of the economy is described by the optimal change in stock variables—household-specific financial wealth and sector-specific private capital stock, as well as their respective shadow prices. In addition, the evolution of the stocks of public and foreign debt acts as resource constraints in the overall economy. The endogenous and optimal changes in these stock variables—investment, saving, the budget deficit, and current account deficit—provide the link between subsequent time periods. Accordingly, the model can be conceptualized as a large set of nonlinear difference equations, where flow variables are determined through optimal control rules.

The intertemporal path for the economy is described by the behavioral equations, the equations of motion of stock and shadow price variables, and the market equilibrium conditions. We define the steady-state growth path as an intertemporal equilibrium trajectory in which all the flow and stock variables grow at the same rate while market prices and shadow prices are constant.

2.2 Calibration

The model is calibrated with data for the period 2005–2014 and stock values for 2015. The calibration of the model is designed to allow the model to replicate as its most fundamental base case, a stylized steady state of the economy, as defined by the trends and information contained in the data set. In the absence of any policy changes, or any other exogenous changes, the model's implementation will just replicate into the future such stylized economic trends. Counterfactual simulations thus allow us to identify marginal effects of any policy or exogenous change, as deviations from the base case.

There are three types of calibration restrictions imposed by the existence of a steady state. First, it determines the value of critical production parameters, such as adjustment costs and depreciation rates, given the initial capital stocks. These stocks, in turn, are determined by assuming that the observed levels of investment of the respective type are such that the ratios of capital to GDP do not change in the steady state. Second, the need for constant public debt and foreign debt to GDP ratios implies that the steady-state budget deficit and the current account deficit are a fraction of the respective stocks of debt equal to the steady-state growth rate. Finally, the exogenous variables, such as public or international transfers, have to grow at the steady-state growth rate.

2.3 Numerical Implementation

The dynamic general equilibrium model is fully described by the behavioral equations and accounting definitions, and thus constitutes a system of nonlinear equations and nonlinear first-order difference equations. No objective function is explicitly specified, on account that each of the individual problems (the household, firm and public sector) is set as first order and Hamiltonian conditions. These are implemented and solved using the General Algebraic Modeling System (GAMS) software and the MINOS nonlinear programming solver.

MINOS uses a reduced gradient algorithm generalized by means of a projected Lagrangian approach to solve mathematical programs with nonlinear constraints. The projected Lagrangian approach employs linear approximations for the nonlinear constraints and adds a Lagrangian and penalty term to the objective to compensate for approximation error. This series of sub-problems is then solved using a quasi-Newton algorithm to select a search direction and step length.

3 Reference Case, Counterfactual Scenarios, and Simulation Design

3.1 Reference Case

The model's numerical implementation and calibration are consistent with the economy being in a long-term steady-state trajectory. The reference case for our simulations is obtained from this steady-state trajectory by incorporating the international fossil fuel price, as projected by the International Energy Agency, and carbon dioxide prices, as forecasted by the Bloomberg News Energy Finance Group. Our reference case assumes that coal-fired power plants are operational indefinitely, and that the ISP tax rules on such activities in effect in 2017 apply for the time horizon of the model.

3.2 Counterfactual Scenarios and Simulation Design

The counterfactual scenarios are designed around two issues: first, the scheduled closure of Sines and Pego in 2030, as announced by the Government on November 2017; second, the changes to the ISP tax after 2018 to include coal used in the generation of electricity, which will impact the competitiveness of these power plants in the short term. In CF1, we consider the effects of the regulated early closure of the two coal-operated power plants in the presence of the old ISP tax rules.

There are two sets of additional ISP rules. The first is an energy component, a unit tax which consists of a fixed amount depending directly on the volume of coal used. The second is an additional component, a tax that reflects the carbon content of coal and which is indexed to the price of carbon in the EU-ETS. Specifically, the unit tax rate applying to the purchases of a ton of coal is:

$$\tau_{isp,fuel,t} = \tau_{unit,fuel,t} + \tau_{carbon,c,t} \times \varepsilon_{carbon,c}$$

where $\varepsilon_{carbon,c}$ is the conversion factor between physical units of coal and its carbon content.

The effect of the additional tax burden depends on how long the coal-operated plants will remain active. At the same time, the increase in fuel costs associated with the expanded ISP tax is expected to move up the closure dates for the two power plants. The policy, as designed, will make the plants unprofitable and lead to their closure years earlier than the date determined by the plant's functional life expectancy. In this case, operators in the electric power industry will react to the additional tax burden with an accelerated closure schedule.

Accordingly, we consider four counterfactual scenarios (Table 1). We consider first a set of scenarios, CF2 and CF3, in which the extension to the ISP includes only

Table 1 List of simulation scenarios

Reference	No closure for Sines and Pego No changes to the ISP rules
CF1	Current closure schedule of 2030 for Sines and Pego No changes to the ISP rules
CF2	Current closure schedule of 2030 for Sines and Pego New ISP tax rules—fixed amount for energy component alone
CF3	Modified closure schedule of 2025 for Sines and Pego New ISP tax rules—fixed amount for energy component alone
CF4	Current closure schedule of 2030 for Sines and Pego New ISP tax rules—fixed amount as well as on carbon content
CF5	Modified closure schedule of 2020 for Sines and 2021 for Pego New ISP tax rules—fixed amount as well as on carbon content

the fixed unit tax on energy, and then a second set of scenarios, CF4 and CF5, in which both the energy and carbon tax components are in place. In CF2 and CF4, there is no reaction by operators in the electric power industry and the plant closure will be as scheduled in 2030. In turn, in CF3 and CF5, the industry responds to the additional tax burden by closing the plants ahead of schedule. Specifically, we consider that the increase in fuel costs associated with the energy component of the tax moves up the plant closure by five years (from 2030 to 2025). In addition, the increase in fuel costs driven by both the base fixed energy tax and the fuel's carbon content is large enough to justify the closure of these plants ten years earlier than expected based on operational considerations.

3.3 On the Presentation of the Simulation Results

In this section, we present the simulation results as percent deviations from the reference scenario, thereby allowing for a direct comparison across counterfactual scenarios. In Tables 2, 3, 4 and 5, we focus on the effects of the different policy scenarios as simulated for 2040, which we refer to as long-term effects.

While the coal-operated power plants remain active, the higher costs associated with the production of electricity from coal due to the increase in the ISP tax burden will increase the cost of generating electricity relative to the status quo. Naturally, such price effects disappear in the long term as both power plants eventually close.

Accordingly, the main differences among the five scenarios are going to be short-term transitional effects. We would not expect significant differences in the long-run trajectories for the flow variables. The same is not true, naturally, for the stock variables, such as public and foreign deficits or accumulated reduction in emissions.

Accordingly, we focus in the differences in the transitional effects of the different policies in most of our discussion of the results, as well as their cumulative effects by 2040. See Tables 6, 7, 8, 9, 10, 11 and 12. Finally, Table 13 presents a snapshot of the policies' main effects relative to CF1, which is the simple case of the regulated early closure in 2030.

Table 2 Long-run energy and environmental effects (2040)

Percent change from baseline

		Energy tax		Energy and carbon taxes	
	Current CF1	Current CF2	Early CF3	Current CF4	Early CF5
Electricity price	7.21	7.20	7.15	7.19	7.13
Electricity production	−5.60	−5.60	−5.56	−5.59	−5.55
Natural gas	2.12	2.12	2.10	2.11	2.09
Renewable energy	1.50	1.51	1.61	1.53	1.65
Net electricity imports	34.55	34.53	34.28	34.49	34.16
Energy demand	−2.08	−2.08	−2.07	−2.08	−2.07
Electricity share	−3.58	−3.58	−3.57	−3.58	−3.56
CO_2 emissions	−22.01	−22.02	−22.02	−22.02	−22.02

Table 3 Long-run macroeconomic effects (2040)

Percent change from baseline

		Energy tax		Energy and carbon taxes	
	Current CF1	Current CF2	Early CF3	Current CF4	Early CF5
GDP	−0.57	−0.57	−0.58	−0.57	−0.59
Consumption	−0.14	−0.14	−0.14	−0.14	−0.15
Investment	−0.12	−0.12	−0.12	−0.13	−0.12
Employment	−0.19	−0.19	−0.20	−0.19	−0.20
Public debt	1.89	1.86	2.98	1.82	4.22
Foreign debt	0.74	0.73	1.16	0.75	1.66

Table 4 Long-run effects on industry output (2040)

Percent change from baseline

		Energy tax		Energy and carbon taxes	
	Current CF1	Current CF2	Early CF3	Current CF4	Early CF5
Total	−0.572	−0.571	−0.582	−0.569	−0.591
Petroleum refining	−0.026	−0.030	−0.028	−0.036	−0.028
Electricity Production	−5.599	−5.595	−5.562	−5.589	−5.546
Biomass	1.281	1.286	1.349	1.297	1.380
Agriculture	−0.374	−0.372	−0.388	−0.369	−0.400
Equipment manufacturing	−1.435	−1.432	−1.527	−1.427	−1.594
Construction	−0.132	−0.133	−0.132	−0.134	−0.130
Transportation	−0.326	−0.325	−0.339	−0.324	−0.351
Textiles	−0.699	−0.697	−0.707	−0.692	−0.718
Wood, pulp, and paper	−1.499	−1.493	−1.541	−1.482	−1.575
Chemicals and pharmaceuticals	−0.944	−0.943	−0.957	−0.939	−0.970
Rubber, plastic, and ceramics	−1.226	−1.224	−1.256	−1.221	−1.279
Primary metals	−1.473	−1.470	−1.520	−1.465	−1.558
Other	−0.167	−0.166	−0.176	−0.165	−0.183

Table 5 Long-run welfare effects (2040)

Percent change from baseline

		Energy tax		Energy and carbon taxes	
	Current CF1	Current CF2	Early CF3	Current CF4	Early CF5
All households	−0.143	−0.142	−0.145	−0.141	−0.147
First quintile (lowest income)	−0.317	−0.316	−0.319	−0.315	−0.321
Second quintile	−0.198	−0.198	−0.199	−0.197	−0.200
Third quintile	−0.146	−0.146	−0.147	−0.145	−0.148
Fourth quintile	−0.130	−0.130	−0.133	−0.129	−0.135
Fifth quintile (highest income)	−0.081	−0.081	−0.084	−0.080	−0.086

Table 6 Effects on electricity prices (intertemporal) percent change from baseline

Percent change from baseline

	2020	2021	2022	2023	2024	2025	2026	2027	2028	2029	2030	2040
CF1	-0.11	−0.13	−0.15	−0.18	−0.21	−0.24	−0.27	−0.31	−0.35	−0.39	7.12	7.21
CF2	0.17	0.13	0.10	0.06	0.03	−0.01	−0.05	−0.09	−0.13	−0.17	7.11	7.20
CF3	0.11	0.06	0.01	−0.04	−0.09	6.99	6.97	6.97	6.98	6.98	6.99	7.15
CF4	0.77	0.71	0.65	0.60	0.55	0.50	0.45	0.40	0.36	0.32	7.10	7.19
CF5	6.97	6.94	6.91	6.90	6.89	6.89	6.88	6.89	6.90	6.91	6.93	7.13

Table 7 Cumulative effects on CO_2 emissions

2015 = 100

	2020	2021	2022	2023	2024	2025	2026	2027	2028	2029	2030	2040
CF1	−0.01	−0.02	−0.02	−0.03	−0.03	−0.04	−0.05	−0.06	−0.08	−0.09	−20.32	−233.55
CF2	0.07	0.08	0.09	0.09	0.10	0.10	0.10	0.10	0.10	0.10	−20.13	−233.38
CF3	0.07	0.07	0.08	0.08	0.08	−19.20	−38.67	−58.33	−78.18	−98.22	−118.45	−331.73
CF4	0.26	0.30	0.33	0.37	0.40	0.43	0.45	0.48	0.50	0.53	−19.71	−232.98
CF5	−18.12	−36.64	−55.36	−74.26	−93.36	−112.64	−132.11	−151.78	−171.63	−191.68	−211.92	−425.22

Table 8 Cumulative effects on GDP

2015 = 100

	2020	2021	2022	2023	2024	2025	2026	2027	2028	2029	2030	2040
CF1	0.01	0.02	0.03	0.04	0.05	0.07	0.08	0.10	0.12	0.14	−0.41	−6.41
CF2	0.00	0.00	0.01	0.02	0.02	0.03	0.04	0.06	0.07	0.09	−0.45	−6.44
CF3	0.01	0.01	0.02	0.04	0.05	−0.46	−0.99	−1.52	−2.06	−2.62	−3.18	−9.32
CF4	−0.02	−0.03	−0.04	−0.05	−0.06	−0.06	−0.06	−0.06	−0.06	−0.05	−0.60	−6.56
CF5	−0.50	−1.01	−1.52	−2.04	−2.56	−3.10	−3.64	−4.18	−4.74	−5.31	−5.88	−12.14

Table 9 Cumulative effects on employment

2015 = 100

	2020	2021	2022	2023	2024	2025	2026	2027	2028	2029	2030	2040
CF1	0.04	0.05	0.05	0.06	0.07	0.08	0.10	0.11	0.12	0.14	−0.05	−2.11
CF2	0.03	0.04	0.05	0.06	0.07	0.08	0.09	0.10	0.12	0.13	−0.05	−2.11
CF3	0.05	0.07	0.08	0.09	0.11	−0.07	−0.24	−0.42	−0.61	−0.79	−0.99	−3.12
CF4	0.02	0.02	0.03	0.03	0.04	0.05	0.06	0.07	0.08	0.10	−0.08	−2.14
CF5	−0.11	−0.28	−0.45	−0.62	−0.80	−0.98	−1.17	−1.35	−1.54	−1.74	−1.94	−4.12

Table 10 Cumulative effects on public debt

2015 = 100

	2020	2021	2022	2023	2024	2025	2026	2027	2028	2029	2030	2040
CF1	0.00	0.00	−0.01	−0.01	−0.02	−0.02	−0.03	−0.04	−0.06	−0.07	−0.09	6.99
CF2	−0.01	−0.01	−0.02	−0.03	−0.05	−0.06	−0.08	−0.11	−0.13	−0.16	−0.20	6.68
CF3	−0.01	−0.01	−0.03	−0.04	−0.06	−0.08	0.02	0.22	0.55	1.01	1.59	15.69
CF4	−0.01	−0.02	−0.04	−0.06	−0.08	−0.10	−0.14	−0.17	−0.21	−0.26	−0.31	6.34
CF5	−0.01	0.09	0.30	0.63	1.08	1.65	2.36	3.20	4.17	5.29	6.56	28.68

Table 11 Cumulative effects on foreign debt

2015 = 100

	2020	2021	2022	2023	2024	2025	2026	2027	2028	2029	2030	2040
CF1	0.01	0.02	0.03	0.05	0.07	0.09	0.12	0.15	0.18	0.22	0.26	6.44
CF2	0.01	0.02	0.03	0.05	0.07	0.09	0.12	0.15	0.19	0.23	0.27	6.40
CF3	0.01	0.03	0.05	0.07	0.10	0.13	0.25	0.45	0.75	1.14	1.63	13.44
CF4	0.02	0.04	0.06	0.10	0.13	0.17	0.22	0.27	0.33	0.40	0.47	6.84
CF5	0.03	0.14	0.33	0.61	0.99	1.46	2.04	2.72	3.52	4.43	5.47	24.04

Table 12 Cumulative effects on welfare

2015 = 100

	2020	2021	2022	2023	2024	2025	2026	2027	2028	2029	2030	2040
CF1	−0.03	−0.03	−0.04	−0.04	−0.04	−0.04	−0.04	−0.04	−0.04	−0.04	−0.18	−1.75
CF2	−0.04	−0.05	−0.05	−0.06	−0.06	−0.06	−0.07	−0.07	−0.07	−0.07	−0.21	−1.77
CF3	−0.06	−0.07	−0.07	−0.08	−0.08	−0.22	−0.36	−0.50	−0.64	−0.79	−0.93	−2.52
CF4	−0.07	−0.08	−0.09	−0.10	−0.11	−0.12	−0.12	−0.13	−0.14	−0.14	−0.28	−1.83
CF5	−0.22	−0.35	−0.49	−0.63	−0.76	−0.91	−1.05	−1.19	−1.34	−1.49	−1.64	−3.26

Table 13 Comparative results: cumulative effects by 2040

Effects of CF1 = 100.0

		Energy tax		Energy and carbon taxes	
	Current CF1	Current CF2	Early CF3	Current CF4	Early CF5
CO_2	100.0	100.0	142.0	99.8	182.0
GDP	100.0	100.5	145.4	103.9	189.4
Employment	100.0	100.0	147.9	101.4	195.3
Public debt	100.0	95.6	224.5	90.7	410.3
Foreign debt	100.0	99.4	208.7	106.2	373.3
Welfare loss	100.0	101.1	144.0	104.5	186.5

3.4 A Note on Electricity Prices in General Equilibrium

Lastly, as the price of electricity plays such a critical role in our analysis (and given the different notions prevalent in the literature as to what they represent), it is important to clarify the exact meaning of electricity prices in general equilibrium. In our model, electricity prices are market-clearing prices under general competitive market assumptions.

Electricity prices reflect equilibrium conditions and therefore a balance between supply and demand conditions. Ultimately, they can be conceptualized as average production prices for the amounts of electricity produced under the prevailing market demand conditions.

On the supply side, prices reflect all costs of production: capital, labor, energy, and materials. Because of the model's dynamic nature, all stocks have fixed costs in the short term but are variable in the long term. On the demand side, prices reflect fuel substitution effects by households and businesses as well as higher production costs by businesses across all sectors of economic activity. They reflect income effects and losses in purchasing power by households due to higher prices across sectors of economic activity and feedbacks that affect consumers' budget constraints.

4 Simulation Results

4.1 Regulated Early Closures (CF1)

Overall, closures and limits to the Portuguese coal generating capacity result in an increase in electricity prices. The electric power system adjusts to the plant closures by partially replacing coal-operated generation with natural gas. Where possible, further expansionary investment in renewable energy, including hydroelectric facilities, wind turbines, and solar energy systems will provide for a cost-effective way to address the capacity shortfall associated with discontinuing coal-operated electricity generating units. Finally, an increase in electricity imports partially compensates the decline in domestic electric production.

The closure of coal-operated power plants has a significant and positive effect on environmental performance. At the same time, this effect is very narrow in scope, as it comes exclusively, and by design, from the electric power system. These reductions do not reflect an overall change in the patterns of energy use in the economy. This leads to a residual concern on the pedagogical value of this measure of early closure vis-à-vis system wide measures aimed at reducing the country's emissions across the board.

The increase in electricity prices due to the early closure of coal-operated power plants reverberates throughout the economy, leading to detrimental macroeconomic effects, as well as adverse distributional effects. The negative macroeconomic effects are widespread and notable across sectors of economic activity. The distributional effects are pronounced and highly regressive. These effects also raise concerns with respect to international competitiveness and social justice.

4.2 ISP Extension: Fixed Energy Component (CF2 and CF3)

It is informative to compare the transitional effects associated with the extension to the ISP tax on energy products under the scheduled 2030 closure date (CF2) and with an accelerated plant closure date (CF3) with our previous counterfactual scenario (CF1), which has the same scheduled 2030 closure date and old ISP rules.

Under CF2, we see a short-run and temporary increase in the price of electricity that ripples throughout the economy when closure of power plants remains scheduled for 2030. Ultimately, cumulative economic effects by 2040 are only marginally more adverse than in CF1, in terms of GDP, employment, and welfare losses, and marginally less adverse in terms of public debt and foreign debt positions. Should the coal-operated power plants remain operational through 2030, we would observe a marginal improvement in the public sector account, reflected in lower levels of public indebtedness, which is due to the additional tax revenues.

The accelerated plant closure by 2025 induced by additional operating costs (as under CF3), yields more substantial differences relative to the counterfactual scenario (CF1). With the earlier closure, we observe an additional cumulative reduction in CO_2 emissions of 42.1%. These additional reductions in emissions reflect the additional five years during which the coal-operated power plants will be inactive and thus not contributing toward atmospheric emissions.

The accelerated closures also move forward the reduction in economic activity and weaker economic conditions associated with higher electricity costs. The cumulative effect of these additional years of weaker economic conditions is that the cumulative indicators of economic performance deteriorate, as accumulated GDP losses increase by 45.4% and accumulated employment-years increase by 47.5% vis-à-vis CF1. Noticeably, the intertemporal welfare indicator is 32.0% lower than under CF1.

Importantly, public debt now deteriorates by 124.5% relative to CF1 under CF3. The larger increase in public debt is due to the combination of two effects: first, the fact that additional tax revenues from extending the tax on energy products will arise for a shorter period of time due to the accelerated plant closures: and, second, the negative contractionary effects last longer with an accelerated closure schedule.

Overall, if the plant operators do not respond to the new ISP rules, the effects of these rules will be, in general, marginal for emissions, macroeconomic performance and welfare while being significant only as a new source of public revenues. If, however, the plant operators respond to the new ISP rules by deciding to close down the coal-operated power plants earlier than scheduled, the environmental impact will be much greater but so will the adverse macroeconomic, budgetary and welfare effects.

4.3 ISP Extension: Energy and Carbon Components (CF4 and CF5)

Finally, we consider the effects of the additional costs associated with both the energy and the carbon tax component of the ISP tax extension. In both CF4 and CF5, electric power producers face the additional tax on energy content, as well as the indexed tax on carbon, in the cost of coal used to produce electricity. In the first case (CF4), the scheduled closure in 2030 applies, while in the second case (CF5), operators react by anticipating the closure by ten years. In both cases, the patterns of results are similar to the previous subsection's cases which only consider the new rules on the ISP's energy component. The differences in the cumulative environmental, macroeconomic, and distributional effects are substantially more pronounced, however.

Under the scheduled closures (CF4), the new ISP rules applying to both energy and carbon content have relatively small effects. There is a marginal reduction in emissions, which goes hand in hand with small deteriorations in economic performance and household welfare relative to CF1. The effects on the public sector account are more favorable when extending the tax on energy products, only under the assumption that the plants remain operational through 2030. In this case, we would observe a 9.3% gain in the public debt position under CF4 when compared to CF1.

The situation is fundamentally different if plant operators accelerate the closure schedule due to operational considerations, so that plants cease to operate in 2020. It is important to note that these changes are due exclusively to the early closure itself as the extensions to the ISP tax will barely be felt before the closure of the two facilities. The accumulated gain in CO_2 emissions reductions relative to CF1 increases by 82.2%, which reflects the additional decade without coal-operated power plants.

In turn, the negative effects on economic performance also occur concomitantly for an additional decade. The accumulated detrimental effects on GDP increase by 89.4% and the accumulated loss in employment-years increases by 95.1% relative to CF1. The intertemporal effects on household welfare increase by 61.3%. The effects on public debt are quite severe under CF5, showing an 310.3% increase in the public debt in CF5 relative to CF1, as the early closure substantially decreases the tax bases as it deepens the contractionary effects and eliminates the tax revenues benefits of the ISP changes.

5 Summary and Policy Implications

This chapter examines the environmental, economic, budgetary, and distributional effects of the scheduled closure of coal-fired power plants in Portugal, as well as the extension of ISP taxation to coal used in power generation. Specifically, we consider three research questions. First, what are the effects of closing coal-fired power plants in Portugal in 2030, in the absence of any changes to ISP taxation? Second, what are the effects of changes in ISP tax rules when coal-fired power plants close as scheduled? Third, what are the effects of changes in ISP tax rules when operators decide to close coal-fired power plants ahead of schedule?

The five policy scenarios we consider have similar long-term effects. Over time, once the plants have closed, extending the tax on energy products to these facilities has no effect, as the new ISP rules disappear when the power plants are effectively closed. The differences in short-term transitional effects, however, are very significant, as the new ISP rules are relevant while the plants are still operational, and an accelerated closures' schedule extends the duration of the adverse effects on economic performance and household welfare.

More specifically, and in answer to the first research question, we find that the closure of coal-operated power plants has a significant and positive effect on the environmental performance. The increase in electricity prices due to the early closure of coal-operated power plants reverberates throughout the economy, leading to detrimental macroeconomic effects, as well as adverse distributional effects. The negative macroeconomic effects are widespread and notable across sectors of economic activity. The distributional effects are pronounced and highly regressive. These effects also raise concerns with respect to international competitiveness and to social justice.

In turn, and responding to the second question, extending the tax on energy products to coal used in electricity generation provides little to no additional environmental gains, as long as private sector agents do not react to these facilities' changing profitability and maintain the scheduled closure dates at 2030. The economic and distributional effects, however, are marginally worse than the old energy tax rules due to a small increase in production costs and its effect on electricity prices. Naturally, there is a small gain in the public debt position.

Regarding the third research question, an important result emerges in the case of accelerated closures by electric power industry operators. Indeed, if operators react to the new ISP rules by accelerating the closure of coal-operated power plants, the situation changes substantially. The environmental gains are much more pronounced but so too are the negative economic and distributional effects. More importantly from the public sector's perspective, the public debt position clear deteriorates due to contracting tax bases in the face of weaker economic conditions.

These results lead to several important policy recommendations. First, the regulated early closure of coal-fired power plants may be very effective in reducing emissions but it is not innocuous from a macroeconomic or a distributional perspective. The domestic authorities, therefore, should undertake the proper efforts to mitigate such adverse effects.

Second, the new ISP rules are at best irrelevant in the presence of forced closures. Regardless of whether or not the scheduled closures are enforced, there are no environmental advantages from the new ISP rules although they will certainly produce economic and distributional costs. Emissions reductions would only result from the accelerated closures of coal generating units, in which case the adverse macroeconomic, distributional, and budgetary effects would be substantially larger. From both macroeconomic and social justice perspectives, the least detrimental of the five policy scenarios we consider is the basic central scenario of scheduled closures in 2030 without changes to the ISP tax.

A final note: In 2016, Portugal introduced a tax on carbon dioxide emissions due to fossil fuel combustion activities. This tax was implemented as an additional component to ISP, based on the carbon content of each type of fossil fuel (with a level indexed to the EU-ETS). The tax expanded the policy efforts' scope to reduce emissions beyond the large energy-intensive industrial emitters participating in the EU-ETS—which were exempted from this add-on to ISP—to include the many households and businesses that together can make a substantial contribution toward domestic emissions reductions efforts. The additional component to the ISP for coal based on the carbon content of the fuel effectively doubles the price on carbon in electricity generation from coal and raises both legal and equity concerns. This is because the coal-fired power plants already participated in EU-ETS and were therefore already subject to carbon pricing mechanisms.

Acknowledgements The authors want to thank Ana Quelhas, Maria Pedroso Ferreira, and Ana Cristina Nunes for very useful discussions and suggestions. This is the second of two twin papers dealing with the regulated early closures of the two Portuguese coal-fired power plants. The other chapter focuses on the detailed effects of the regulated early closure and how they compare with alternative ways of achieving the same environmental effects (see Pereira and Pereira 2019a, b).

References

Annicchiarico B, Battles S, Di Dio F, Molina P, Zoppoli P (2017) GHG mitigation schemes and energy policies: a model-based assessment for the Italian economy. Econ Model 61:495–509

Ballard CL, Fullerton D, Shoven JB, Whalley J (2009) A General Equilibrium Model for Tax Policy Evaluation. University of Chicago Press, Chicago, National Bureau of Economic Research

Bergman L (2005) CGE modeling of environmental policy and resource management. In: Mäler KG, Vincent JR (eds) Handbook of environmental economics, vol 3, chap 3. Elsevier, Holland, pp 1273–1306

Bhattacharyya SB (1996) Applied general equilibrium models for energy studies: a survey. Energy Econ 18(3):145–164

Bhattarai K, Haughton J, Tuerck D (2016) The economic effects of the fair tax: analysis of results of a dynamic CGE model of the US economy. IEEP 13(3):451–466

Blanchard O (2016) Do DSGE models have a future? Peterson Institute for International Economics, Number PB16-11, pp 1–4

Borges AM, Goulder LH (1984) Decomposing the impact of higher energy prices on long-term growth. In: Scarf HE, Shoven JB (eds) Applied general equilibrium analysis, chap 8. Cambridge University Press, Cambridge

Fullerton D, Heutel G, Metcalf GE (2012) Does the indexing of government transfers make carbon pricing progressive? Am J Agr Econ 94(2):347–353

Goulder LH, Hafstead MAC (2013) A numerical general equilibrium model for evaluating U.S. energy and environmental policies. Working paper, Stanford University, Stanford, CA

Pereira A, Pereira R (2014a) Environmental fiscal reform and fiscal consolidation: the quest for the third dividend in Portugal. Publ Fin Rev 42(2):222–253

Pereira A, Pereira R (2014b) On the environmental, economic and budgetary impacts of fossil fuel prices: a dynamic general equilibrium analysis of the Portuguese case. Energy Econ 42(C):248–261

Pereira A, Pereira R (2014c) DGEP—a dynamic general equilibrium model of the Portuguese economy: model documentation. Working paper 127, The College of William and Mary

Pereira A, Pereira R (2017a) The economic and budgetary impact of climate policy in Portugal: carbon taxation in a dynamic general equilibrium model with endogenous public sector behavior. Environ Resource Econ 67(2):231–259

Pereira A, Pereira R (2017b) On the relative roles of fossil fuel prices, energy efficiency, and carbon taxation in reducing carbon dioxide emissions. J Environ Plan Manage 60(10):1825–1852

Pereira A, Pereira R (2017c) The role of electricity for the decarbonization of the Portuguese economy—DGEP technical report. Available online https://www.mpra.ub.uni-muenchen.de/id/eprint/84782. Accessed on 28 Mar 2020

Pereira A, Pereira R (2019a) Achieving the triple dividend in Portugal: a dynamic general-equilibrium evaluation of a carbon tax indexed to emissions trading. J Econ Pol Reform 22(2):148–163

Pereira A, Pereira R (2019b) On the macroeconomic and distributional effects of the regulated closure of coal-operated power plants. Working paper GEE, Ministério da Economia, Lisboa, Portugal

Pereira A, Pereira R, Rodrigues P (2016) A new carbon tax in Portugal: a missed opportunity to achieve the triple dividend? Energy Pol 93:110–118

Sbordone AM, Tambalotti A, Rao K, Walsh K (2010) Policy analysis using DSGE models: an introduction. FRBNY Econ Pol Rev 16(2):23–43

Tran C, Wende S (2017) On the marginal excess burden of taxation in an overlapping generations model. ANU working papers in economics and econometrics 2017-652, Australian National University, College of Business and Economics, School of Economics

Measuring What Social Partners Do About Wages Over the Business Cycle

Pedro S. Martins

Abstract Collective bargaining (CB) conducted by trade unions and employer associations (the social partners) plays a key role in the formation of wages in many countries. This paper investigates the potential interactions of CB with the macroeconomy by estimating the business cycle sensitivity of the many thousands of CB minimum wages. Drawing on matched worker and CB data covering all employees in Portugal, we find that, over the 1982–2017 period, CB real wages are no more than 0.7% lower when the unemployment rate increases by one percentage point. This is less than half the equivalent entry-level effect (1.8) documented in (Martins et al., Am Econ J Macroecon 4:36–55, 2012). Moreover, much of the sensitivity of CB wages is driven by the high-inflation period until 1992, with effects as large as 5.2. Overall, our findings of limited CB real wage cyclicality suggest that, in Portugal (and possibly also in other countries in Southern Europe), the social partners may not yet have fully adjusted to the macroeconomic regime of Eurozone membership.

Keywords Collective bargaining · Euro · Inflation · Unemployment · Wage rigidity

1 Introduction

In many countries around the world, large shares of workforces have their wages shaped at the firm, sectoral, or national level, in the context of collective bargaining between firms and their representatives (employers' associations) and workers and their representatives (trade unions).[1] These two types of representatives or economic

[1]According to OECD (2019), on average, across OECD member countries, 32% of all workers were covered by collective agreements in 2017. In Southwestern Europe (France, Italy, Spain, and Portugal), this share increases to over 85%.

P. S. Martins (✉)
School of Business and Management, Queen Mary University of London, London, UK
e-mail: p.martins@qmul.ac.uk

L. Brites Pereira et al. (eds.), *Economic Globalization and Governance*,
https://doi.org/10.1007/978-3-030-53265-9_18

agents, sometimes referred to as "social partners," can therefore play an important role in shaping the economic performance of their countries.

This form of wage determination involving social partners may also represent an important departure from the context of search and matching models (Mortensen and Pissarides 1994) in which wages are determined in an individualized manner, within worker/employer matches, and through Nash bargaining. In contrast, the collective bargaining process, particularly at the sectoral or national level, involves a collective form of wage determination, stemming from some form of aggregation of heterogenous outside options and bargaining power levels. Moreover, the Nash bargaining assumption tends to generate significant procyclicality in real wages and much smaller cyclical fluctuations in unemployment than actually occur (Shimer 2005).[2]

In contrast, in a collective bargaining context, while individual wages can surpass (and, in some specific cases, undercut) collective bargaining (minimum) wages, the latter can be critical forces in shaping overall wage developments over the business cycle. More specifically, collective bargaining (and its implicit contracts and insurance mechanisms) can introduce substantial rigidity in the wage determination process at all job levels, including entry positions, in contrast to the potential volatility driven by Nash bargaining in individualized bargaining.

This paper contributes empirical evidence to this macroeconomic debate, ongoing at least since Keynes (2019) and including Barro (1977) and many other contributions. Here, we focus on the potentially limited cyclical variability of collective bargaining wages and its role in the cyclical volatility of employment and unemployment. Specifically, we investigate the extent to which collective bargaining real wages respond to the business cycle, as proxied by the unemployment rate. Our approach thus complements the existing literature focused on hiring wages (Hall and Milgrom 2008; Pissarides 2009) which tends to find that these are quite procyclical (Carneiro et al. 2012; Martins et al. 2012).[3] To the best of our knowledge, this is the first paper that examines what we label here as "collective bargaining real wage cyclicality."[4]

A second motivation for our study complementary to the macroeconomic debate above concerns the specific case of Southern Europe. The relatively weak economic performance over the last 20 years of countries such as Greece, Italy, and Portugal

---

[2] Indeed, a number of studies including Gertler and Trigari (2009) and Kennan (2010) have suggested including stickiness in real hiring wages as a way of modifying the Mortensen–Pissarides model to generate realistically large quantity fluctuations.

[3] There is also a great deal of evidence on real wage cyclicality in general. For example, using 1967–1987 data, Solon et al. (1994) estimated that a one percentage point increase in the unemployment rate is associated with a 1.2% reduction in real wages. Several other studies using longitudinal microdata from the United States and elsewhere have produced similar results (e.g., Beaudry and DiNardo 1991; Bils 1985; Devereux and Hart 2006; Martins 2007).

[4] See Gartner et al. (2013) for an analysis of real wage cyclicality under different collective bargaining settings in Germany. In contrast to our approach, Gartner et al. (2013) consider individuals' total wages and not the collective bargaining wages per se. See also Björklund et al. (2019) for an analysis of the duration and renewal of collective agreements in Sweden.

(as well as France and Spain to a lesser extent) may be related to an incomplete modernization of political and economic institutions in these countries toward the new macroeconomic regime of low inflation, a fixed exchange rate, and low interest rates that followed from Eurozone membership.[5]

A potentially important component of these institutions is precisely collective bargaining and, more broadly, "social dialog" or even "tripartite dialog," the latter involving both trade union and employer confederations and the government. In this context, examining collective bargaining real wage cyclicality across the Eurozone, both before and after the adoption of its regime, as we do in this study, can offer important, policy-relevant insights.

The lack of evidence on collective bargaining real wage cyclicality is related to the limited availability of data on collective bargaining wages, in particular over long periods of time. We overcome this constraint by considering the case of Portugal, for which we use matched worker and collective agreement data covering all (private-sector) individual employees between 1982 and 2017. Using this large data set, corresponding to over 67 million individual-year observations, we compute modal wages per each collective-agreement/job-category/year combination as our proxy for collective bargaining minimum wages, following Cardoso and Portugal (2005). We then regress the real values of these minimum wages (about 30,000 different values per year, see Martins 2020) on the unemployment rate of the year in which they were in force to estimate our measure of collective bargaining real wage cyclicality.

We find that, on average, over the 1982–2017 period, collective bargaining real wages are non-cyclical in several specifications. Moreover, in general, these real wages are no more than 0.7% lower when the unemployment rate increases by one percentage point. This is less than half the effect (1.8) documented in Martins et al. (2012) when focusing on entry-level jobs in Portugal using the same data set. We also find that much of the limited sensitivity of collective bargaining wages that we find is driven by the high-inflation period until 1992 (when the macroeconomic regime change began), with effects as high as 5.2. Overall, our findings suggest that collective bargaining in Portugal has not yet adjusted fully to Eurozone membership, in the sense that collective bargaining minimum wages exhibit a very limited degree of responsiveness to the business cycle, potentially exacerbating employment fluctuations during downturns.

Section 2 discusses the role of collective bargaining upon wage formation, with a focus on the case of Portugal. In Sect. 3, we present the data set that we use and several descriptive statistics. Section 4 presents our main findings about collective bargaining real wage cyclicality. Finally, in Sect. 5, we briefly summarize our findings and discuss some of their implications.

---

[5] See Braga de Macedo (2001) for an informed discussion of the steps toward Eurozone membership in Portugal.

2 Collective Bargaining and Wage Formation

Collective bargaining concerns the dialog and discussions established between firms and their representatives, on the one hand, and multiple workers and their representatives, on the other hand, regarding wages and other working conditions (holidays, overtime premia, health and safety, training, etc.). When employment relationships are longer-lasting and firm-specific skills more relevant, the premises of spot markets do no longer apply, as gaps or wedges will emerge between the outside options of each party and their productivity and wages. Bargaining will therefore become more relevant. It can also be conducted individually (between one firm and one worker) and or in groups.

The latter case, of collective bargaining, is seen in many countries, in particular in Continental Europe, as a way to promote social dialog, leading to more harmonious industrial relations, economies, and even societies, with higher levels of productivity (Martins 2019) and wages and fewer instances of industrial conflict. The distribution of income between labor and capital, and within labor itself, may become more balanced as well. Those countries have thus introduced several regulations and procedures to shape collective bargaining in particular directions, with potentially significant effects on wage formation, including over the business cycle.

In the particular case of Portugal (and similarly to several Southern European countries), a number of CB or related regulations should be taken into account in this context (see also Hijzen et al. 2019). First, employment protection law is relatively restrictive as far as open-ended contracts are concerned. Nominal base wages also cannot legally be cut in ongoing employment contracts except in exceptional circumstances. This strengthens the bargaining power of employees under open-ended contracts and may increase downward nominal wage rigidity.[6]

Second, sectoral collective agreements (by far the most common type of collective agreement) are virtually automatically extended to all workers in the relevant sector (and region, if applicable) through administrative decisions (Martins 2020). This practice creates an important wedge between trade union density and CB coverage, sometimes of 80% or more of total employment, as in the case of France, and of about 50% of total employment in the case of Portugal (OECD 2019), except in the period 2011–2015 (Hijzen and Martins 2020).

Third, similarly to the case of statutory minimum wages, CB wages function as wage floors, with employers commonly paying wages above those levels (Cardoso and Portugal 2005). However, such CB wages can function as reference or even focal points in the hiring of new workers or upon the promotion of existing workers to a higher job category. Moreover, while collective agreements include many other clauses than those specifically about (minimum) wages, the former tend to add relatively little value compared to the already applicable regulations stemming from statutory employment law (Martins and Saraiva 2020).

[6]Moreover, until 2004, according to employment law, collective agreements could not be terminated unilaterally in a number of cases. This may have further strengthened the bargaining power of employees.

3 Data and Descriptive Statistics

Our data come from Personnel Records (*Quadros de Pessoal*), an annual mandatory census of all employers in Portugal (except most of the public sector) and all their employees. Employee information is available for every year between 1982 and 2017 (except 1990 and 2001). Employee information includes monthly nominal wages (base and total), hours of work (base and overtime), collective agreement and its job category that applies to each worker, and several other variables (age, gender, schooling, occupation, job level, hiring date, etc.). The census takes March of each year as the reference month through 1993 and October from 1994 onward. The data base suits our purposes very well: By tracking each collective-agreement/job-category (simply agreement/job, henceforth) pair longitudinally, we can study how their wages vary over the business cycle.[7]

Our main measure of the collective bargaining minimum wage in each agreement/job/year combination is its modal value across all firms and workers. This approach was first adopted in Cardoso and Portugal (2005), which show a good correspondence between these modes and the actual collective bargaining minimum wages in a sample of agreements that they examine in greater detail. Our computation of the mode was also based on the real monthly wage of each worker (drawing on Statistics Portugal's monthly consumer price index) rounded to nearest 2017 Euro. If a tie occurred, we selected the lowest modal value. The only restriction imposed in the construction of the sample was that the number of base hours worked in the reference month be at least 140, so to ensure that we examine full-time employees, the focus of collective bargaining minimum wages.

Table 1 describes the workers considered in each year and their average and modal wages. In the first column, we find that the annual number of employees ranges between 1.3 million in 1984 and 2.5 million in 2008. Average real wages peak in 2010 at 956 Euros and have their lowest value in 1988 (706 Euros). As to our modal (real) wages, they exhibit much less fluctuation over the period covered, ranging between 813 and 634 Euros, in 1982 and 1989, respectively. Only in three years (other than 1982) are modal wages higher than 700 Euros (1983, 2010, and 2017). All yearly wages, including the modes, are computed using as weights the number of workers in each agreement/job pair.

Even before taking into account the business cycle—as shown in Fig. 1, Portugal's annual unemployment rate varied widely over the period, with peaks in the mid 1980s, mid 1990s, and mid 2010s—this time series can already be regarded as indirect evidence of non-cyclical collective bargaining real wages. Note that the high real modal wages in the very first years of the series will be driven partially by

[7]In contrast, Martins et al. (2012) focused exclusively on entry-level jobs (Baker et al. 1994; Doeringer and Piore 1971), defined as specific five-digit occupation codes at the same job level (hierarchy level) in each firm. To ensure their "port-of-entry" nature, the job must also account for at least three new hires (with up to four months of tenure) and at least 10% of the firm's new hires in at least half the years the firm is present in the data. None of restrictions above apply in the present paper, which is not focused on entry-level wages.

Table 1 Sample sizes and average weighted salaries by year

Years	Number of workers	Nominal salary	Real salary	Modal real salary
1982	1,538,917	85.1	864.9	812.9
1983	1,550,507	101.0	780.1	739.9
1984	1,334,338	123.6	682.6	645.2
1986	1,506,146	176.1	684.5	641.5
1987	1,543,241	203.3	713.2	671.8
1988	1,597,997	223.4	706.3	657.5
1989	1,737,154	252.5	698.5	634.0
1991	1,760,303	346.1	729.7	649.2
1992	1,796,795	396.0	754.7	664.6
1993	1,757,991	439.5	780.6	671.9
1994	1,753,774	473.9	796.2	671.1
1995	1,779,220	489.2	787.6	665.6
1996	1,777,333	518.7	809.1	678.1
1997	1,908,168	529.4	806.8	664.0
1998	1,935,118	559.5	830.5	687.9
1999	2,035,372	579.8	840.8	681.5
2000	2,105,047	604.0	850.5	687.4
2002	2,199,269	668.7	867.8	693.8
2003	2,239,089	689.3	865.9	685.0
2004	2,285,091	714.7	876.2	681.4
2005	2,407,842	741.4	888.1	668.5
2006	2,440,077	762.4	885.0	666.3
2007	2,498,262	780.9	883.8	661.1
2008	2,541,942	816.0	899.5	671.4
2009	2,412,114	843.8	937.5	699.2
2010	2,307,517	872.5	955.8	716.5
2011	2,267,542	880.7	929.2	697.1
2012	2,114,102	891.9	914.6	682.7
2013	2,262,414	873.1	892.6	675.0
2014	2,315,508	876.8	899.1	677.9
2015	2,206,253	890.5	908.5	686.9
2016	2,283,859	901.6	914.5	694.7

(continued)

Table 1 (continued)

Years	Number of workers	Nominal salary	Real salary	Modal real salary
2017	2,379,251	918.4	918.4	703.2

Notes The number of workers indicates the number of individuals (full-time workers) considered in the analysis of each year; Nominal salary is the value in Euros of each year of the mean base salary paid in the country; Real salary is the real version of the previous column (considering 2017 prices); Modal real salary is our measure of the (real) minimum wages set by collective agreement/job level pairs (weighted by the number of workers under each agreement/job pair). Source: Author's analysis based on the *Quadros de Pessoal* data set

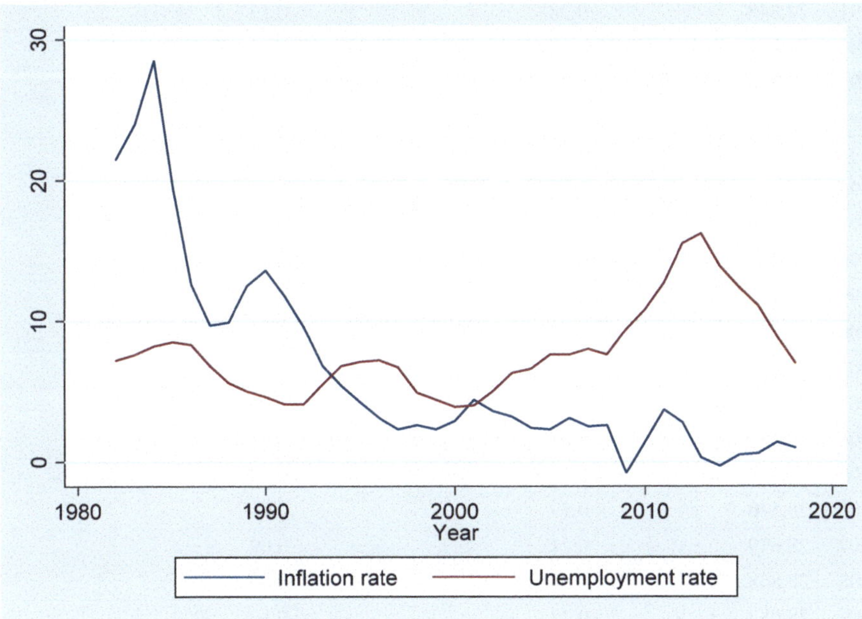

Fig. 1 Annual unemployment and inflation rates in Portugal, 1982–2018. (*Source* INE—Statistics Portugal and Pordata)

composition effects stemming from higher levels of informality in the early 1980s and possibly imperfect compliance with the census at the time, particularly among firms in low-wage sectors. Another complementary explanation is that of the very steep increases in collective bargaining wages in the mid and late 1970s, following the 1974 Revolution and the strong increase in trade union bargaining power that it generated. This bargaining power was, however, eventually eroded by the high levels of inflation (and, to a lesser extent, unemployment) in the early 1980s.

Table 2 examines the modal wages in different ways. Column 1 presents a count of the number of agreement/job pairs per year, showing that this number varies between around 26,000 in 1982 and 36,000 in 2016 (Martins 2020, 2019). Columns 2 and

Table 2 Number of agreement/jobs by year and their fit

Years	Agreements/job-titles	% (salary) base equal to mode	% (salary) total equal to mode
1982	26,532	0.31	0.14
1983	27,367	0.31	0.14
1984	26,288	0.32	0.14
1986	28,248	0.33	0.16
1987	28,696	0.32	0.16
1988	28,543	0.29	0.15
1989	29,969	0.28	0.15
1991	29,848	0.28	0.13
1992	29,681	0.25	0.11
1993	29,390	0.23	0.10
1994	30,146	0.25	0.12
1995	30,886	0.29	0.13
1996	30,561	0.28	0.13
1997	30,519	0.27	0.12
1998	30,519	0.27	0.12
1999	29,730	0.27	0.12
2000	29,285	0.25	0.11
2002	28,456	0.21	0.09
2003	29,072	0.22	0.09
2004	29,559	0.21	0.09
2005	29,178	0.21	0.09
2006	28,570	0.19	0.08
2007	28,679	0.21	0.09
2008	28,868	0.21	0.09
2009	28,082	0.23	0.10
2010	28,156	0.23	0.08
2011	28,088	0.30	0.15
2012	33,947	0.30	0.16
2013	34,654	0.22	0.08
2014	34,963	0.26	0.09
2015	35,196	0.32	0.16
2016	35,640	0.34	0.16

(continued)

Table 2 (continued)

Years	Agreements/job-titles	% (salary) base equal to mode	% (salary) total equal to mode
2017	35,262	0.34	0.16

Notes The number of agreements/job-titles indicates the number of different job titles across agreements available in the collective agreements applicable in each year; % base equal to mode indicates the percentage of workers that are paid a base wage equal to the model base wage of their agreement/job-title pair; % total equal to mode indicates the percentage of workers that are paid a total wage equal to the model total wage of their agreement/job-title pair (weighted statistics). Source: Author's analysis based on the *Quadros de Pessoal* data set

3 present an indication of the fit between such modal wages and the corresponding base or total wages of the corresponding workers (in the same agreement/job pair), averaged by year, using again the number of workers in each pair as weights. In the case of base wages, we find that the percentage of workers that are paid exactly the same (real) modal wage ranges between 19% in 2006 and 34% in both 2016 and 2017.

The latter cases may pick up the role of a very steeply increasing statutory minimum wage in those two years (which by law overrides the "minimum minimorum" of the collective agreements if the latter is lower). However, the overall distribution of modal "bites" across the 36-year period covered may be broadly consistent with the view that collective bargaining wages that tend to be more pressing at times of higher unemployment.

An important exception to this pattern is 2013, when unemployment was particularly high but the collective bargaining bite dropped significantly. This outcome may have been influenced by the significant slowdown in the renewal of agreements and their non-automatic extension (Hijzen and Martins 2020), implying that collective bargaining wages froze in a large percentage of cases. Automatic wage growth determined by tenure-related increments and dismissals or non-renewals of employment contracts of younger or less experienced workers (typically on lower wages) would also drive the drop in collective bargaining bite over that year.

If considering instead the mode of the total wage, we find that its fit with the total wages of workers in each agreement/job pair is much lower than in the case of base wages. This indicates that total wages (base wages plus additional wage components such as overtime pay or bonuses) exhibit much greater dispersion within agreement/job cells.

Finally, we mention that the version of the data set used in our estimations described below has nearly one million observations (992,277), each corresponding to a particular agreement/job/year combination and representing an average of 68 workers. There is a total of 213,770 different agreement/job pairs and 2,186 different agreements. The number of different agreements per year increases from little above 400 in the early 1980s to over 800 in the late 2010s. We also find that each specific agreement/job pair is observed over ten years (weighted average).[8]

[8]This possibly relatively low number (in contrast to the 34 years covered in our data) may reflect several factors including the emergence of entire novel agreements (including at the firm level,

4 Results

Let w_{jt} denote the collective bargaining real minimum wage applicable to workers in collective agreement and job-level pair j in period t, corresponding to the modal base wages described above. Our empirical analysis is then based on the following statistical model for w_{jt}:

$$\log w_{jt} = \alpha_j + \beta U R_t + \varepsilon_{jt} \quad (1)$$

where α_j is a set of fixed effects for each agreement/job pair, $U R_t$ is the unemployment rate of year t, and ε_{jt} indicates the zero-mean error term. Given the log-level specification adopted, β indicates the percentage change in a collective bargaining real minimum wage following a one percentage point increase in the unemployment rate.

We estimate this or adjusted versions of our model in the agreement/job/year data set described above (covering the entire period or different subsets) and present the coefficient (and standard error) of β in the different rows of Table 3. The first row shows the estimated coefficient of the unemployment rate when controlling for a linear time trend and using weighted least squares to weight for the number of workers in each agreement/job/year observation. In this benchmark estimate, we find a coefficient estimate of −0.15 (with an estimated standard error 0.13), indicating that there is not a significant relationship between the business cycle and CB wages. However, despite the lack of precision of the estimate, its confidence interval is not wide enough to reach cases of highly procyclical real wages, in contrast to the literature on entry-level (not necessarily CB-based) wages.

This result of limited procyclicality is also consistent with our original eyeballing of the data in Table 1, by comparing mean modal wages over the 36-year period covered. However, this contrasts with the micro-literature on real wage cyclicality, which finds significant evidence of procyclicality, including in the case of Portugal (Carneiro et al. 2012; Martins et al. 2012). Next, we investigate further this finding, regarding the specific and novel case of CB real wage cyclicality, by conducting several robustness checks and extensions.

In the next row of Table 2, we use ordinary least squares instead of weighted least squares. The resulting coefficient estimate, −0.44 (with estimated standard error 0.10), is larger and more precise than the weighted result. However, the implied procyclicality in this specification is still much lower than that found in other longitudinal studies.

---

complementing the more dominant sectoral agreements), the demise of old agreements, and also some degree of churning in ongoing collective agreements, for instance through the addition or exclusion of signatories which may lead to a new collective agreement code. According to our analysis, agreement turnover was particularly high in 2004, when employment law allowed for the unilateral revocation of collective agreements, and in 2012, when the administrative extensions of agreements were restricted (Hijzen and Martins 2019a, b).

Table 3 Estimates of the cyclicality of log collective bargaining wages

Estimation method and sample	Estimated unemployment rate coefficient and (standard error)
1. Log modal monthly wage weighted regression, including linear trend, 1982–2017	−0.15 (0.13)
2. Same as (1) but (unweighted) ordinary least squares	−0.44 (0.10)
3. Same as (1) for low-wage (below annual median) job levels	0.03 (0.24)
4. Same as (1) with log average base wage	−0.53 (0.16)
5. Same as (1) with log average total wage	−0.67 (0.22)
6. Same as (1) with log modal hourly wage	−0.70 (0.27)
7. Same as (1) with weights corresponding to the number of workers paid the modal value	−0.07 (0.19)
8. Closest specification to (1) in Martins et al (2012) [row 1 in Table 2, p. 46]	−1.81 (0.38)
9. Same as (1) for 1982–2008	−0.74 (0.31)
10. Same as (1) for 2009–2017	−0.72 (0.14)
11. Same as (1) for 1982–1992	−5.17 (2.73)
12. Same as (1) for 1993–2017	−0.23 (0.10)

Notes Each coefficient corresponds to a different wage regression, based on a different specification and or a different sample. Weights correspond to the number of workers in each agreement/job-title (regardless of whether they are paid at the modal level). All specifications except 3 and 8–12 draw on 937,397 observations, each corresponds to an agreement/job-title pair in a given year over the period 1982–2017. All specifications control for up to 158,872 agreement/job-title fixed effects. Clustering of standard errors by year. All coefficients are significant at the 5% level except those of specifications 1, 7, and 11. Specification 11 is significant at the 10% level. Source: Author's analysis based on the *Quadros de Pessoal* data set

In the third row, we consider only those agreement/job pairs that pay below median wages, in which the reference median is computed across all modal wages in each year. This represents a subset of CB that may be closer to the entry wages in "ports of entry" that are more relevant from the perspective of the macroeconomic debate discussed in the Introduction. We find again, as in the first row, a very small and statistically insignificant coefficient (0.03, with a standard error of 0.24).

In the next three rows, we redo the regression from row 1 except that we consider alternative wage measures: the average base wage, the average total wage, and the modal hourly wage. We find in all cases statistically significant coefficients, ranging between −0.53 and −0.70. These point estimates are all higher (in absolute terms) than the previous cases with significant estimates but still lower (by half or more) than the existing cyclicality estimates using longitudinal data.

In row 7, we consider a different approach toward the weighting of the data, not based on the total number of workers in each agreement/job pair but considering instead the number of workers that is actually paid the modal wage in each observation. Again, we find an insignificant coefficient of 0.07 (standard error of 0.19).

All the figures above contrast considerably with those of Martins et al. (2012), in which real wage cyclicality was found to be at around −1.8 (row 8). In order to compare as closely as possible that figure under the present methodology focused on CB wages, we redo our analysis of row 1 but considering only the same time period as in Martins et al. (2012). Row 9 presents a coefficient of 0.74 (standard error 0.31), indicating that our focus on CB wages, as opposed to the more specific subset of job entry wages, cuts the degree of cyclicality in half.[9]

Of course, "cyclical upgrading" may underestimate procyclicality: If, in a recession, employers recruit a higher quality of workers at any given wage, the effective wage they pay per efficiency unit of labor is lower. This process is likely to apply in CB as well, and we see no reason why it could be strong or differentiated enough to explain the big difference in cyclicality that we present here.

Finally, we revisit the macroeconomic regime change mentioned in the Introduction. Portugal and other Southern European countries underwent a significant change in their macroeconomic context in the run up to Eurozone membership, involving a steep decrease in inflation and increasingly more stable exchange rates. To what extent did CB cyclicality evolve and adjust as this macroeconomic regime adapted? We shed light on this question by running our main specification separately for the period before and after this regime change. We choose 1992 as the threshold year, based on Braga de Macedo (2001).

Our findings are striking: When considering the 1982–1992 period (row 11), we estimate a very high degree of procyclicality, with a coefficient of −5.17. Given that the standard error is 2.73, the coefficient is not extremely precise even if still significant at the 10% level. On the other hand, when considering the remaining period (1993–2017, row 12), we find again very small and insignificant cyclicality effects, in this case with a coefficient of −0.23 (standard error 0.10). These results indicate that CB real wage cyclicality decreased dramatically as the macroeconomic regime of Portugal changed from high inflation, high interest rates, and high government deficits, under the frequent devaluation of the then national currency (the "crawling-peg" system), as described in Braga de Macedo (1990), toward the very opposite context, along all these dimensions, in the run up to the Euro and during Eurozone membership.

5 Summary and Discussion

Collective bargaining conducted by trade unions and employer associations (the social partners) can play a key role in the formation of wages in many countries, with potentially significant interactions with the macroeconomy. In this study, we

[9]For the sake of completeness, we also estimate CB cyclicality for the remaining period of 2009–2017, in which we find nearly the same estimates as in the earlier period (row 10 of Table 3).

quantified for the first time the business cycle sensitivity of the many minimum wages set in collective bargaining in a country. Our analysis is based on matched worker and collective agreement data covering all private-sector employees in Portugal over the 1982–2017 period.

Our first main result is that, in contrast to the literature focused on the longitudinal analysis of individual wages, CB real wages appear to be largely non-cyclical. Indeed, we find that, on average, CB wages are no more than 0.7% lower when the unemployment rate increases by one percentage point. This is less than half the entry-level effect (1.8) documented in Martins et al. (2012). The same comparison result also applies when restricting our CB sample period to match that of Martins et al. (2012), 1982–2008, and in several robustness checks.

We also find that much of the sensitivity of collective bargaining wages is driven by the high-inflation period in Portugal, until 1992, in which CB real wage effects are as high as 5.2. As the economy changed its regime to prepare for and then join the Eurozone, with radically lower inflation rates, CB real wage cyclicality diminished dramatically. In other words, the ability of CB wages to adjust to the business cycle nearly disappeared, which may have increased the sensitivity and volatility of employment and unemployment. In particular, this may explain, at least in part, the large response of unemployment to the 2011–2014 crisis, at least up to 2013, when the unemployment rate exceeded 16%.

These findings suggest that collective bargaining in Portugal (and perhaps also in other Southern European countries) has not adjusted to the macroeconomic regime change associated to Eurozone membership. As soon as inflation stopped "greasing the wheels" of the labor market, CB real wages stopped or nearly stopped responding to the business cycle, which may have aggravated the employment consequences of that same business cycle. Of course, not all workers are paid the CB wages (on average, in our data, around 25% are paid the modal value), something which will restrict the relevance of CB wages. On the other hand, these workers that are paid CB wages will typically be less skilled individuals who have joined their firms more recently and who are employed under fixed-term contracts, all of which will already make them more vulnerable to the business cycle.

As stated in Martins et al. (2012), "[the literature] requires not a theory of wage *rigidity*, but a theory of why wages are not even more variable than they are." Our results suggest that collective bargaining may be part of such theory. Most of the procyclicality documented earlier will be driven by the "wage cushion" between actual wages and CB wages, while CB wages are largely non-cyclical, at least in periods of low inflation. We hope that the methodology presented in this paper will be applied to additional countries, in particular those in which social partners have operated under a low-inflation environment for a longer period of time.

Acknowledgements The author thanks Gary Solon for comments, Joana Saraiva for research assistance, the Ministry of Employment of Portugal for data access, and the European Commission (CoBExt action, grant VS/2016/0340) for financial support. The usual disclaimer applies.

References

Baker G, Gibbs M, Holmstrom B (1994) The internal economics of the firm: evidence from personnel data. Quart J Econ 109(4):881–919
Barro RJ (1977) Long-term contracting, sticky prices, and monetary policy. J Monetary Econ 3(3):305–316
Beaudry P, DiNardo J (1991) The effect of implicit contracts on the movement of wages over the business cycle: evidence from micro data. J Polit Econ 99(4):665–688
Bils MJ (1985) Real wages over the business cycle: evidence from panel data. J Polit Econ 93(4):66–89
Björklund M, Carlsson M, Nordström Skans O (2019) Fixed-wage contracts and monetary non-neutrality. Am Econ J Macroecon 11(2):171–192
Braga de Macedo, J (1990) External liberalization with ambiguous public response: the experience of Portugal. CEPR Discussion Paper 378, London
Braga de Macedo, J (2001) Crises? What crises? Escudo from ECU to EMU. In: Griffith-Jones S, Montes MF, Nasution A (eds) Short-term capital flows and economic crises. Oxford University Press, Oxford
Cardoso AR, Portugal P (2005) Contractual wages and the wage cushion under different bargaining settings. J Lab Econ 23(4):875–902
Carneiro A, Guimarães P, Portugal P (2012) Real wages and the business cycle: accounting for worker, firm and job title heterogeneity. Am Econ J Macroecon 4(2):133–152
Devereux PJ, Hart RA (2006) Real wage cyclicality of job stayers, within-company job movers, and between-company job movers. Indus Lab Relat Rev 60(1):105–119
Doeringer P, Piore M (1971) Internal labor markets and manpower analysis. Lexington, Lexington, Mass
Gartner H, Schank T, Schnabel C (2013) Wage cyclicality under different regimes of industrial relations. Indus Relat 52(2):516–540
Gertler M, Trigari A (2009) Unemployment fluctuations with staggered nash wage bargaining. J Polit Econ 117(1):38–86
Hall RE, Milgrom PR (2008) The limited influence of unemployment on the wage bargain. Am Econ Rev 98(4):1653–1674
Hijzen A, Martins PS (2020) No extension without representation? Evidence from a natural experiment in collective bargaining. IZA J Lab Econ, forthcoming
Hijzen A, Martins PS, Parlevliet J (2019) Frontal assault versus incremental change: a comparison of collective bargaining in Portugal and the Netherlands. IZA J Lab Policy 9(1):1–26
Kennan J (2010) Private information, wage bargaining and employment fluctuations. Rev Econ Stud 77(2):633–664
Keynes JM (2019) The general theory of employment, interest, and money. Macmillan, London
Martins PS (2007) Heterogeneity in real wage cyclicality. Scottish J Polit Econ 54(5):684–698
Martins PS (2020) 30,000 minimum wages: the economic effects of collective bargaining extensions. Brit J Ind Rel, forthcoming
Martins PS (2019) The microeconomic impact of employee representatives: evidence from membership thresholds. Indus Relat 58(4):591–622
Martins PS, Solon G, Thomas J (2012) Measuring what employers do about entry wages over the business cycle: a new approach. Am Econ J: Macroecon 4(4):36–55
Martins PS, Saraiva J (2020) Assessing the legal value added of collective bargaining agreements. Int Rev Law Econ 62(C): 1–13
Mortensen DT, Pissarides CA (1994) Job creation and job destruction in the theory of unemployment. Rev Econ Stud 61(3):397–415
OECD (2019) Negotiating Our Way Up Collective Bargaining in a Changing World of Work. OECD, Paris
Pissarides CA (2009) The unemployment volatility puzzle: is wage stickiness the answer? Econometrica 77(5):1339–1369

Shimer R (2005) The cyclical behavior of equilibrium unemployment and vacancies. Am Econ Rev 95(1):25–49

Solon G, Barsky R, Parker JA (1994) Measuring the cyclicality of real wages: how important is composition bias? Quart J Econ 109(1):1–25

Selling the View

Jorge De La Barre

Abstract As an attempt to critically engage with the contemporary visual experience, this chapter explores the horizontal, vertical, and virtual viewpoints. Its main purpose is to question the virtual realm as a place where technology allows for various visual experiences including new, digital, and oblique perspectives on both horizontality and verticality.

Keywords Contemporary visual experience · Horizontal and vertical viewpoints · Surveillance · Urbanism · Technology

Our contemporary visual experience may be defined by a permanent, endless combination of the horizontal, vertical, oblique, and virtual viewpoints.[1] Technology has orchestrated our escape from the way we see the world when we are standing and looking around—the anthropological, horizontal viewpoint. From mountain to satellite views, we have experienced verticality; the god's or bird's eye views are in fact tightly connected with questions of power and surveillance. Powerful indeed whoever gets to look at others without being noticed; empowered indeed whoever gains a standpoint above the horizon. If verticality has amplified our field of vision, then virtuality has multiplied it, virally. Now that Jeremy Bentham's oblique *Panopticon* has fractally expanded through satellite views and surveillance data, and the virtual is evermore the definitive domain of power and control.

[1] This contribution, in the format of a short essay, draws on a longer piece titled "On the Contemporary Visual Experience," originally published in the 2019 Streetnotes issue (vol. 26): "From Above: The Practice of Verticality," which I co-edited with Blagovesta Momchedjikova. On a personal note, I completed my Ph.D. at the *École des Hautes Études en Sciences Sociales* (Paris) in 2004 under the supervision of Dominique Schnapper. As it turns out, her father Raymond Aron directly influenced my grandfather, Jorge Borges de Macedo.

J. De La Barre (✉)
Department of Sociology and Methodology of Social Sciences, Universidade Federal Fluminense, São Domingos, Niterói, RJ, Brazil
e-mail: jorgelabarre@id.uff.br

L. Brites Pereira et al. (eds.), *Economic Globalization and Governance*,
https://doi.org/10.1007/978-3-030-53265-9_19

It seems worthwhile to explore some aspects of our new visual experience, primarily mediated by technology. As everyday life becomes increasingly virtual (in the sense that our daily activities are routinely mediated by technological devices such as smartphones and computers), it is also marked by an equally banal co-existence of the horizontal, vertical, oblique, and virtual plans—all viewpoints combining in fact permanently. As an attempt to critically engage with such kaleidoscopic visual experience, one should aim at decomposing its various plans and trace back, if possible, some basic regimes of visuality: the elementary forms of horizontality and verticality, so to speak. One should also engage with the virtual realm, a place where technology allows for various visual experiences including new, digital, and oblique perspectives on both horizontality and verticality.

In common language, "top-down" usually refers to some official authority coming "from above" (the state or else); while "bottom-up" is considered grassroots, organic, "from the people." "From below" indicates usually some kind of underground activity—a form of resistance perhaps—certainly not something official, approved by the government or the state. While verticality may represent the authority of god, the state, or the father, it is highly symbolic; horizontality on the contrary refers to flow, movement, and imagination. The flag, the church, and the state are all things considered "to stand for," opposed to the somewhat ambiguous, flexible horizontal fraternity.

There is a practice of viewing that is specific to verticality. Almost immediately, the practice of verticality translates in an esthetics of verticality; there is a form of vertical fascination: literally, vertigo is a vertical high. Vertical wonders have been aestheticized, branded, and streamlined. Here again, the New York skyline immediately comes to mind. Panoramic views—natural or built—are always powerful; they should remind us that the production of visuality has relied immensely on verticality.

In urbanism and architecture, the production of space translates horizontally and vertically; there is a higher value—all puns intended—attached to the production of vertical space, and then, there is to the so-called urban sprawl. Horizontal expansion implies that the value of land is accessible, while urban verticalization refers to the centralization of power and money. Obviously, when "the visual" is highly valued, verticality becomes a source of speculation: Real-estate promoters are indeed "selling the view." There is a specific imaginary attached to living in a penthouse: whoever can afford a penthouse separates from the mob and lives closer to heaven—or god perhaps.

There is a form of aestheticized "solutionism" (Morozov 2014) attached to the construction of cable-cars above slums (La Barre 2015). In Medellin or Rio de Janeiro, public transportation has been "solved from above:" While the inextricable labyrinths of tiny streets and alleys could never be destroyed entirely, they have been dealt with the flyover approach and a form of vertical "aestheticization of poverty" (Harvey 1990). Now that the famed "favela tours" have also expanded vertically, territories of survival long abandoned by the state are somehow being mapped and controlled through vertical visuality. The attractiveness of seeing the world from above has been applied to flying over the immense favelas by cable-car, which is another way of claiming that "view sells."

When horizontality applies to displacement and speed (the bullet train), verticality is immediacy and permanence—a permanent immanence, perhaps. There is a powerful symbol attached to verticality: It is the idea of the "vertical entrenchment of the state" (Kurtz 2001), and the properties attached—hierarchy, power, surveillance. In the drones age, these features have become all too banal.

The expansion from horizontality-to-verticality-to-virtuality may inform a recent history of visuality; it certainly helps to define a contemporary visual experience that has been marked increasingly by a virtually endless patchwork of the horizontal, the vertical, and the virtual.

While horizontality has been the name for geographical mobility, social imitation, and fraternal imagination, verticality has proven an enduring force of territoriality, exteriority, and coercion: the vertical entrenchment of the state remains a powerful narrative and reality, against all indistinctive dreams claiming that "the world is flat" (Friedman 2005). As Gilles Deleuze once said, it is important to first learn how to paint a landscape, before you can draw a portrait. He implied that landscaping is randomly generic, while portrayal is eminently personal.

Verticalization, virtualization, and estheticization are walking hand in hand along a process that has visually translated as follows: There is a solutionist folly about some vertical surveillance that calls for pacification, in the midst of a short to mid-term process of diversification and renewal. Here again, the politics of verticality has been doubled by an immersive experience that is now almost impossible to escape—as it is itself the utmost escapist experience. If surveillance implies the colonization of private life by technological devices (it certainly does!), then the image of the *Panopticon* is now complete; We have achieved an almost perfect blurring of horizontality and verticality, and now they have both merged into a permanent, virtual connectedness.

There was a specific, anthropological way of seeing horizontally. Now with both vertical and virtual viewings, we have reached a point beyond the infinite, precisely because we are being told—and telling ourselves—the same stories about the eye of the beholder, or the technique that allows us to actually view the world and understand ourselves. Horizontality was about direct (eye and other) contact, here and now, and memory also. Verticality was always about (the visual and other pleasures of) symbolic control and allegiance. Now with the virtual multiplication of both verticality and virtuality combined, we get the permanent immanence of an eternal present, of which the selfie is a perfect symbol, and symptom: the viral and horizontal spread on the social networks, of a vertical entrenchment of self's hyper-identity.

What will be left when the whole world has been "shot?". As we see, going back to the natural, anthropological horizontal gaze might prove impossible: It is now filled with ups and downs, vertical hick-ups, pitfalls, and downfalls. Before we even know it, the technological apparatuses become the main relation—the most stable and secured one. More than created by them, we end up interacting with them—this becomes our world, or the world we live in. Without even knowing, we give everything that we got to surveillance capitalism (Zuboff 2019), and all of its techno-visual wonders. That is what I call *selling the view*.

References

Friedman TL (2005) The world is flat: a brief history of the twenty-first century. Farrar, Strauss & Giroux, New York

Harvey D (1990) The condition of postmodernity: an enquiry into the origins of cultural change. Blackwell Publishers, Oxford

Kurtz DV (2001) Anthropology and the study of the state. Political anthropology. Power and paradigms. Westview Press, Oxford

La Barre JD (2015) Future shock: mega-events in Rio de Janeiro. Leisure Studies 35(3):352–368

Morozov E (2014) To save everything, click here: the folly of technological solutionism. PublicAffairs, New York

Zuboff S (2019) The age of surveillance capitalism. The fight for a human future at the new frontier of power. PublicAffairs, New York

A Constitutional Theory of Intergenerational Equity

Gonçalo de Almeida Ribeiro

Abstract Taking cue from the honoree's lifelong interest in constitutional issues, interdisciplinary research, and intergenerational equity, this chapter presents and assesses the case for constitutional precommitments as means to correct the short-termist bias of democracy. It discusses two different forms that rationality-securing precommitment can take—mechanical and fiduciary—and argues that the former (rules) cannot accommodate reasonable pluralism with respect to intergenerational justice, hence jeopardizing constitutional legitimacy. As to the latter (principles), while it may be able to reconcile rationality and pluralism, the standard method for its enforcement—judicial review—is unfit for the task within the realm of intergenerational issues. That calls for a different type of constitutional arrangement, and therefore a renewal of interest in institutional imagination and design.

Keywords Constitutional precommitments · Financial freedom · Institutional design · Intergenerational equity · Political economy

1 Introduction

Jorge Braga de Macedo has had a lifelong interest in constitutional issues, documented in a rich array of publications spanning across his outstanding career in the academia and in public service.[1] Indeed, such an interest is the most prominent

[1] This essay is my tribute to someone whom I counted elsewhere as one among a handful of people "that played, in one way or another, a decisive role in my academic career." I could have added on that occasion that, unlike almost all others in that treasured list of benefactors, my debt to "Uncle George" is immeasurable and intangible. Indeed, the man whose legacy his students and colleagues celebrate with this Festschrift opened the doors of my mind to three mainstays of what has become my scholarly constitution—the excitement and fecundity of interdisciplinary inquiry, a solid bond with the academia on the other side of the ocean, and the commitment to reconcile the universal and the particular dimensions of political community. Apart from reflecting that shared heritage, this essay is my attempt to fulfill an old promise of mature interdisciplinary collaboration on the constitutional issues that we are both passionate about.

G. de Almeida Ribeiro (✉)
Católica School of Law, Universidade Católica Portuguesa, Lisbon, Portugal
e-mail: gmvaribeiro@gmail.com

L. Brites Pereira et al. (eds.), *Economic Globalization and Governance*,
https://doi.org/10.1007/978-3-030-53265-9_20

manifestation of a forceful passion for interdisciplinary studies. It is one of a few traits—perhaps the most notorious among them—that set him apart from the bulk of his brethren in the economics department.

That shows in his peculiarly diverse education. It started with the *baccalauréat* in experimental sciences followed by a year of *dilettantisme* in the Paris of the 1960s reading Althusser, Bachelard, Levi-Strauss, Piaget, among other fancy theorists,[2] and doubtlessly engaging in other forms of leisure and recreation alluring to an adventurous young man thrown into a garden of novel delights. Then, came a five-year undergraduate degree obtained with an exceptionally high grade point average (GPA) at that cradle of the ruling elite of the ancien régime that was the Law School of the University of Lisbon. At last, Jorge crossed the enormous pond to pursue graduate studies in economics at Yale, toil and pain in the sweatshop of the mind for an aspiring card-carrying member of the dominant neoclassical party in the universal brotherhood of the dismal science—a transformative experience that earned him a M.A. in 1973 and a Ph.D. in 1979, with the dreadful interregnum of military service in the colonial war sandwiched between the crowning achievement of the two degrees.

It is difficult to establish the direction of causation here—it could be that the uniquely diverse education ignited the interdisciplinary passion or that an innate passion prompted an unusual educational journey. One suspects that other factors played a significant role: the son of a remarkable historian who pioneered the field of economic history in Portugal and later achieved prominence for his original contributions within the established domain of political history, Jorge's precocious intellect flourished in a polymathic atmosphere. As it often happens in human affairs, causation in this case was probably a two-way street, if not a meeting point of multiple independent roads. Although it has inspired some of the best literary fiction, that kind of fuzzy causation presents a catch-22 for a discipline that migrated in the transition from the nineteenth to the twentieth centuries from the old realm of the moral sciences, where it was recognized among its peers as *political* economy, to a brave new world of hard social science keen on emulating and earning the approval of the folk doing physics and mathematics, and—befitting to a spiritual conversion of such magnitude—rebranding itself as econom*ics*. The first convert was Alfred Marshall, as pointed out in Braga de Macedo (2000b, p. 105).

In this regard as well, Jorge enjoys the advantages of a broad education and a broadminded intellect, treasuring the achievements of economics while keeping the profession honest about its origins as household governance writ large. He adheres impeccably to Aristotle's wise maxim: "[i]t is the mark of an educated man to look for precision in each class of things just so far as the nature of the subject admits [...]" (Aristotle 2001, p. 936).

[2]See Braga de Macedo (1976) for evidence of this.

2 From Political Economy to Constitutional Theory

The association between political economy and constitutional theory is fairly obvious. It is well displayed in the work of two of the most accomplished economists of the twentieth century, both Nobel Prize laureates, von Hayek (1960), Buchanan and Tullock (1962). It is equally well displayed in Jorge's work on what he calls the fiscal constitution—the constitutional arrangements that shape the economy and constrain its management by the government (Braga de Macedo 2003a).

In the earliest stages of his career, Jorge was mostly preoccupied with the economic dimension of the transition to democracy in Portugal following the Revolution of April 25, 1974 (Braga de Macedo 1977, 1983, 1989). The original version of the constitution, which came into force in 1976 following a troubled process (Miranda 2015), embodied an ideological compromise, purporting to reconcile the constitutional ideals of pluralist democracy and socialist transformation. The eclectic language of the document betrayed its political origins. Article 1 proclaimed that, "Portugal is a sovereign Republic, based in human dignity and popular will, *and committed to building a classless society*." Article 2 declared that, "The Portuguese Republic is a democratic state, based on popular sovereignty, the fundamental rights and freedoms as well as democratic pluralism of political opinion and organization, *with the goal of enabling the transition to socialism* through the creation of the conditions required for the exercise of democratic authority by the working classes."

It seemed to Jorge—as it did to some constitutional theorists of the day (Pires 1988)—that the socialist teleology was hard to square with majority rule (Braga de Macedo 1977, pp. 193, 203–5, and Braga de Macedo 1983, pp. 217–18). You can have a socialist dictatorship or a pluralist democracy; and within the latter, there might be at any point in time a majority that supports collective ownership of the means of production. But "socialist democracy" is bananas.

More significantly, the programmatic language with overtones of vulgar Marxism of the "transition to socialism" and "building a classless society" concealed the dirty little secret that what was most revolutionary about the fiscal constitution was the provision (Article 83-1 of the original version) that proscribed the reversion of the nationalizations carried out in 1975 (Braga de Macedo 1989, pp. 808–11). As ironic as it may sound, the transformative agenda was ultimately backward-looking, *conservative* at heart: To entrench in the relatively rigid form of constitutional law, under the guardianship of then existing Council of the Revolution, the "revolutionary conquests" that the electorate in its petty-bourgeois shortsightedness could be tempted to do away with. It took three amendment processes—in 1982, 1989, and 1992—to purge the constitution of the bulk of this comically *démodé* revolutionary baggage, and thus to complete, nearly two decades after the overthrow of an equally outdated dictatorship, the transition to liberal democracy (Braga de Macedo 1989, pp. 809–10). Jorge warned both early and later on about the astronomic economic costs of this protracted course of political maturing (Braga de Macedo 1989, p. 809).

The price to be paid for political immaturity was charged in the currency of financial freedom. This is Jorge's rough equivalent of what Benjamin Constant famously called "the liberties of the moderns": the security of property endowments that enable our lives in the private sphere—as consumers, workers, investors, students, and parents—a requirement for individuals to draw life plans that they can reasonably expect to fulfill. The contrast is with political freedom, what Constant called "the liberties of the ancients": popular participation in the affairs of government, the identity (mediated by the representative nexus and electoral arrangements) between those who rule and those who are ruled, as well as those liberties—such as freedom of speech, freedom of the press, freedom of association, and the right to protest—indispensable to democratic self-determination (Constant 1997).

It has been one of Jorge's highest ambitions as both scholar and public servant to strive for what he calls a virtuous cycle combining financial and political freedom. He challenges the "myth" that what the modern history of the country documents is for the most part the collective failure to do so. In "our fiscal and monetary experience prior to 1910," he writes, "the compatibility of political and financial independence has been the norm, not the exception" (Braga de Macedo 2000a, p. 307). It is only the twentieth century that displays alternating periods of financial stability with dictatorship and democracy with financial instability.

To overcome that vicious cycle, his recipe has never been to delve into the depths of utopian political philosophy. Instead, it has been to find in the European and Lusophone elements of the historical fabric of collective identity the resources to remedy domestic institutional deficiencies and to furnish a distinctively national way of operating in the global economy (Braga de Macedo 2000b). That is most obviously the case of the country's membership in the European Union—although Jorge is ever hopeful and passionate about the prospects of an ever-closer community among the Portuguese-speaking countries—which has, by any honest account, contributed enormously to strengthen our democracy and bring about prosperity, notwithstanding the dark clouds hanging nowadays over the Eurozone and Schengen.

Jorge's account of the fiscal constitution and what should be done in the way of reforming it is quite elaborate. Moreover, his thought on the subject remains incomplete and appears to have changed perhaps more than just a tad over time. It is not my goal to put the whole package together, the way Friedrich Engels put together the second and third volumes of *Das Kapital* from the notes left by Karl Marx. There is plenty of time for Jorge to prepare a *magnum opus*—one hopes a single parsimonious tome—if that really is what his mind and heart are set on. What I mean to do is to explore an important aspect of the delicate balance between financial and political freedom continuously stressed in Jorge's writings on the fiscal constitution: intergenerational equity.[3]

According to his account, financial freedom depends on the fair treatment of future generations in at least two closely related ways. First, the present generation may use its political freedom to deprive the next generations of financial freedom by passing on to future taxpayers the burdens of chronic public deficit and balance of payment problems: This might be construed as an abuse to the extent that those who are most affected by a fiscal policy have no say in the process that led to its

[3] I shall use "equity" and "justice" interchangeably throughout this essay.

adoption. Second, the unfair treatment of future taxpayers turns out to affect the financial freedom of even the current generation, because shifting the burden of debt to the future generates an atmosphere of negative expectations that distort the incentives to save and invest, contributing to economic stagnation; these subtle effects may nonetheless be muddled by the fiscal anesthesia administered by irresponsible governments on voters through a combination of stealth taxation—e.g., indirect taxes, financial engineering, currency devaluation—and populist spending—e.g., subsidies for interest groups, unproductive public investment, unsustainable social security (Braga de Macedo 2000a).

It seems rather straightforward to propose constitutional arrangements to cope with these democratic failures. Indeed, regional integration—operating as an "insurance against (domestic fiscal) voracity" (Braga de Macedo 2003b)—might be taken as part of the fiscal constitution in a broad sense; a case in point is the stability and growth pact. The more basic problem, however, is how to accommodate within a domestic constitutional framework *both* the political freedom of the present generation *and* the financial freedom of the future generation (which turns out to be at least in part that of the present generation as well). Other remedies, such as supranational laws and peer pressure, are extensions of that problem, intimations of the ever more present phenomenon of "constitutionalism beyond the state" (Weiler and Wind 2003).

The gauntlet is thrown at the feet of the constitutional theorist. The challenge will take us deep into the woods of a different discipline, honoring Jorge's passion for interdisciplinary collaboration.

3 Constitutions and Precommitment

What does the constitutional protection of future generations bring to the table of intergenerational equity? The assumption underlying the elevation of an individual right or a policy choice to the constitutional level is that constitutions are endowed with extraordinary normative force: normative in the sense that their prescriptions, to the extent that they are justiciable, are not proclamations serving a rhetorical or expressive function, but standards against which the validity of ordinary laws and other decisions of public authority is measured; extraordinary in the sense that constitutional laws cannot be altered through the ordinary legislative process, but only through a qualified procedure of constitutional amendment, which comprises the requirement of a super-majority. It follows that the constitutional elevation of a particular decision—say, to define a public debt ceiling—limits the political freedom of ordinary lawmaking agencies empowered by the electorate. The constitution plays an inhibiting or constraining role (Holmes 1995).

That suggests an immediate analogy with individual precommitment (Elster 1984). The classical paradigm is the episode in Book XII of the Odyssey in which Ulysses, knowing the siren's chant to be irresistible, has the sailors bind him tightly to the ship's mast (Homer 2018). Everyday life furnishes a rich harvest of less pedantic examples. Take the case of the sleepyhead disabling the snooze function of the alarm clock in order to prevent him from staying in bed in the morning of a workday. Consider the glutton on a weight loss regimen who eats a large bowl of vegetable soup to reduce his appetite before a feast of greasy and sugary food.

These situations seem to embody a paradox: a free and rational individual—an agent—deliberately limits his freedom of choice. But the paradox is only apparent. For the agent is aware that he is afflicted by the deliberative pathology that Aristotle called *akrasia*—weakness of the will—whose effect is to prevent action upon grounds that the agent himself acknowledges as reasonable or correct (Aristotle 2001, Book VII). Precommitment is hence a warrant of freedom because it enables *self*-control, the ability of the agent to affirm reason against passions, impulses, inclinations, and the like. Indeed, it is an indispensable precaution in those typically akratic states—such as intoxication, addiction, lust, hysteria, laziness, depression, and jealousy—in which rationality loses its way. In spite of its inhibiting or constraining nature, then, precommitment turns out to be an assurance of autonomy.

Here is what the constitutional appropriation of individual precommitment looks like. Taking stock of the multiple prejudices and distortions that may pollute popular deliberation in the ordinary political process—such as racism, misogyny, homophobia, xenophobia, fundamentalism, populism, and alarmism—we must acknowledge the wisdom of the people binding itself to the mast of constitutional precommitments endowed with extraordinary normative force. Hence, there is a good reason to raise a decision to the constitutional level—say, proscribing discrimination on grounds of race and gender, requiring just compensation for takings of property, or protecting the freedom to worship of religious minorities—if a solid case can be made that ordinary democratic deliberation is pathological in that regard. The particular deliberative pathology that vindicates the constitutional protection of future generations is what we may call short-termism—the predisposition of the current generation, which controls the ordinary political process, to disregard the impact of its decisions on future generations (MacKenzie 2016).

Cultural factors may go a long way into explaining the short-termism of contemporary politics. Maybe in our societies dominated by individualism and materialism—as opposed to notions of personal excellence and the common good—there is no room for any serious concern with the future. If that is all there is to say, the honorable thing to do is to enlist in the old-fashioned but surprisingly ever-renewed jeremiad about the moral bankruptcy and apocalyptic fate of modernity, liberalism, and capitalism.

Yet there is quite a bit more to be said. For short-termism is built into the structure of representative democracy as we know it. It is a pervasive institutional bias of our regimes. It stems from four characteristic features (Silva 2015, pp. 418–21). The first is representativeness: Since future individuals cannot participate in current elections, they are not represented in any meaningful sense by elected officials. The second is accountability: Since they cannot vote, future individuals cannot hold current officials accountable for any decisions that have a negative impact on them. The third is majoritarianism: The *intra*generational legitimating force of majority rule, which is based on political equality, does not hold *inter*generationally, as a majority of the current generation could very well turn out to be a minority in a hypothetical intergenerational vote. The fourth is temporality: There are no intergenerational surrogates for the mechanisms that mitigate the power of temporary majorities—such as periodic renewal of mandates, limits on renewability, and lame duck restrictions—for the obvious reason that it falls necessarily on the current generation to rule.

Therefore, skepticism about the ability of the ordinary political process to dispense fair treatment to future generations seems to be vindicated by an analysis of the structure of representative democracy. Moreover, this a priori judgement—a priori because it is based on conceptual analysis—resonates with the casual observation of the weakest democratic systems, afflicted by chronic fiscal imbalances, excessive consumption of non-renewable energy, high levels of carbon dioxide emissions, unsustainable social security systems, and labor policies that hurt the competitiveness of the economy. It seems to follow that existing constitutional arrangements ought to be interpreted as incorporating clauses of environmental protection, financial sustainability, fiscal moderation, and the like (Häberle 2006).

4 Two Forms of Precommitment

Before we take a closer look at the seemingly strong case for the constitutional protection of future generations, it is worth examining the different forms of precommitment. One must distinguish in this regard between mechanical and fiduciary arrangements.

In the literature on individual precommitment, it is common to distinguish between causal and non-causal devices (Elster 1984, pp. 42–3). Take the following hypothetical example. It is prom night for George. Anticipating the excesses to come and the dangers of driving under the influence, he undertakes precautionary measures. He may do one of two things: either leave the car keys at home and take a cab to the party or entrust the keys to his fiancée Louise whom he knows to be a paragon of moderation. The first option involves the creation of a barrier against action in the akratic circumstances; it is a causal device, since it removes the physical possibility of a particular course of action. The second option involves the empowerment of a third-party to whom the agent submits in the akratic circumstances; it is a non-causal device, since the possibility of a particular course of action is made dependent on another agent's decision (Waldron 1999, pp. 260–66).

In a loose sense, both causal and non-causal devices are forms of precommitment. But only the former are forms of precommitment in the proper sense of the term, since through them the agent makes a thoughtful decision and prevents its revocation in a future moment of presumable thoughtlessness; they are mechanical arrangements. The latter, on the contrary, involve an abdication of the power to decide on the issue and a submission to the independent judgement of a third-party; these are hence fiduciary arrangements.

The pros and cons of each of the two types of arrangement are obvious. The main virtue of mechanical arrangements is that they prevent the possibility, inevitable with the fiduciary alternative, of third-party error or abuse: In our example, imagine that Louise refuses to return the car keys to George on the next day because she is incensed about the fact that he got so intoxicated at the party that he could not get the dancing act together and collapsed on a chair. Conversely, the advantage of fiduciary arrangements is that they are flexible, enabling decisions responsive to the actual circumstances. Suppose that George gets a phone call from his little sister crying that she twisted her ankle and begging him to drive her to the hospital.

There is a rough parallel to that distinction in the realm of constitutional precommitment. Indeed, constitutional norms may be either rules or principles.[4] Boiled to its bare bones, the distinction comes to the following. If a norm is a rule, it applies mechanically or in an all-or-nothing fashion. As long as the conditions that are included in the antecedent clause of the rule obtain, it provides a definitive outcome to the case at hand. If a norm is a principle, it is a consideration to be balanced in proportion to its strength. As long as it is applicable to the case at hand, a principle furnishes a *pro tanto* reason to be weighed against countervailing reasons before an all-things-considered judgment is reached. As an illustration of the distinction in the domain of the constitutional protection of future generations, consider two interpretations of a constitutional provision to the effect that "the public deficit on the government budget cannot exceed 3 p.p. of the GDP." According to one possible interpretation, the provision simply rules out a deficit higher than 3 p.p. of GDP. According to an alternative interpretation, whether a deficit above that threshold is tolerated in a given context depends on the strength of the underlying reasons.

The distinction should not be overstated. On the one hand, notwithstanding their categorical semblance, rules are not absolute, even if their scope of application is not explicitly limited by exceptions. In abnormal circumstances, when the reasons not to apply a rule are evident and massive, so as to make its application self-defeating or plainly absurd, it may be cast aside. The provision against an excessive deficit, for instance, could presumably be cast aside in the event of a war or public calamity. On the other hand, principles are not symbolic or programmatic expressions but genuine norms binding on their addressees, such that they ought to be observed, subject to a balancing constraint, to all cases that fall within their scope of application. The principle that the budget deficit should not exceed 3 p.p. places the government under a duty to keep that limit unless it can offer a plausible argument that countervailing reasons justify discarding it, and even then the sacrifice ought to be kept at the minimum required by such reasons.

In spite of these relativizing remarks, there is an obvious affinity between rules and mechanical arrangements, on the one hand, and principles and fiduciary arrangements, on the other. Within a model of rules, the constitutional lawmaker decides on certain issues in advance. The people in its presumably thoughtful constitutional moment makes decisions that cannot be revoked in the akratic circumstances of the ordinary political process, decisions that are to be mechanically enforced by an

[4]On the distinction, see Alexy (1994, pp. 71–103), Atienza and Manero (2012, pp. 23–50), and Dworkin (1977, pp. 22–31, 71–80).

institution such as a constitutional court. Within a model of principles, the constitutional lawmaker entrusts the decision to a third-party—typically a constitutional court. The people in its presumably thoughtful constitutional moment delegates to an institution insulated from the akratic circumstances that tarnish the ordinary political process the authority to balance the competing reasons at stake and to issue a final all-things-considered decision.

The pros and cons of rules and principles are likewise the ones we encountered earlier with respect to the distinction between mechanical and fiduciary arrangements. Rules have the advantage of preventing errors and abuses carried out by the guardian of the constitution. Principles have the advantage of flexibility, preventing outcomes that are unreasonable in the actual circumstances.

5 Irrationality and Pluralism

As we have seen, the idea of precommitment—whether individual or collective—is premised on the contrast between two first-person agents: 'The Rational I' and 'The Akratic I,' The former knows what is best and has the will to do it. The latter might or might not know what is best, but in any case, lacks the will to do it. Rational-Ulysses knows that it is best not to respond to the chant of the sirens and wills to avoid it; Rational-George knows that he should not drive under the influence and wills to avoid it. The problem they face, in that thoughtful moment, is how to secure the right course of action in akratic circumstances in which freedom of choice is likely to lead to a bad outcome. The problem is technical or instrumental in nature: It concerns the selection of the means suitable to keep the effects of akrasia under control.

The problem is quite different and more complex if instead of a conflict between 'The Rational I' and 'The Akratic I' that the agent experiences a conflict within the former—not a conflict between reason and inclination but within reason itself (Waldron 1999, pp. 266–70). Take another illustration. Imagine a student named Avellino who decides to write a dissertation on the issue of whether non-human animals have moral rights. Following a great many hours of careful research and study, he is torn between two opposing views. On the one hand, it seems to him that moral rights presuppose self-consciousness, the ability to not only feel pain or face disappointment but also to experience suffering and understand disappointment, which rules out non-human animals as we know them. He tests this proposition by considering an interesting example: While it would be morally repugnant for a surgeon to kill a healthy person to harvest the organs needed to save the lives of five patients, it seems permissible, perhaps even a good thing, for a non-human animal to be, ceteris paribus, sacrificed for the sake of a human being or a larger number of non-human animals. On the other hand, he fears that the former conception of rights is so restrictive that it rules out not only non-human animals but newborns and toddlers, the profoundly disabled, and individuals in a deep coma—and that strikes him as morally repugnant as well. Moreover, any conception of rights capacious enough to include those persons, such as, for instance, the notion of a right as a protected interest makes it very hard to exclude non-human sentient animals from its scope.

Consumed by the flames of doubt and pressed by the deadline, Avellino commits to the negative view, according to which non-human animals have no moral rights. To seal the commitment, he informs his supervisor about the central thesis of the dissertation. The reasons to do so are intelligible and compelling. Yet they have nothing to do with a conflict between Rational-Avellino and Akratic-Avellino, that is to say, with limiting the possibility of irrational choices. On the contrary, the whole point of Avellino's precommitment is to inhibit the continuing exercise of his rational powers because the more he delves into the problem, the more aware of its complexity he becomes, making it even harder to take a stance on it (Waldron 1999, pp. 269–70). In other words, Avellino takes steps to control the rational affluence, as opposed to the indigence, of his future self. That is the only way of making sure that his dissertation will see the light of day.

Now, with respect to a broad range of issues, the people in a constitutional moment finds itself in a situation at least as close to that of Avellino's as that of George or Ulysses. That is so because of the reasonable pluralism characteristic of our liberal and democratic societies (Rawls 2005). People disagree reasonably and obdurately not only about religious, metaphysical, and ethical issues that modern social arrangements largely confine to the private realm but also about matters of unavoidably public concern, such as the scope of basic liberties, the demands of social justice, the direction of economic policy, the design of collective institutions, and the like (Waldron 1999). Library bookshelves, academic seminars, public debates, social networks, and other fora of discussion provide an eloquent testimony of a loud and interminable cacophony. The disagreement comes in all shapes and sizes, from more or less articulated conceptions of justice to the relatively mundane realm of public policy in areas such as taxation, health, education, culture, social security, and environmental protection. Moreover, the diversity of views is headquartered everywhere in civil society, from the dinner table to the lecture room, such that it cannot be explained away as a symptom of thoughtlessness: It is the "normal result of the exercise of human reason within the framework of the free institutions of a constitutional democratic regime" (Rawls 2005, xvi).

In the constitutional realm, reasonable pluralism manifests itself in the following way: There is a broad consensus over a small set of basic principles—equal protection, due process, legal certainty, the separation of powers, etc.—and over human rights—civil and political rights, surely, but to a large extent over so-called second-, third-, and fourth-generation rights as well—accompanied by persistent controversy over the concrete implications of those principles and the scope and relative weight of these rights. In other words, a shared core of foundational platitudes supports a wildly diverse repertoire of rival political agendas more or less explicitly informed by disputed moral, economic, psychological, and historical assumptions. To give but a few examples, consider the controversies over the legalization of surrogate motherhood, the criminalization of abortion, the role of the market in the provision of social goods such as health and education, the correct macroeconomic policies in the wake of a sovereign debt crisis, the sustainability of pay-as-you-go social security in aging societies, and affirmative action in the access to higher education, the labor market, and public office.

In these vast and convoluted matters, "the people" in a thoughtful moment is no agent confident about the right course of action: It is a deeply conflicted soul. Bringing one of the views in contention to the constitutional level is hence not simply a technique to inhibit the akratic degeneration of the political process, i.e., an effective means against collective irrationality, but a way of foreclosing the democratic management of our political differences, an alienation of the reasonable pluralism characteristic of an open society. Just as Avellino commits to a particular thesis, not out of conviction but out of expedience, suspending along the way the exercise of his intellectual powers, the people in its constitution-making capacity ties the whole of society to the mast of a controversial decision, preventing its revocation as a result of public debate and democratic deliberation.

It goes without saying that this raises the question of legitimacy. Before we turn to it, however, let us examine just how complex and controversial intergenerational equity or the protection of future generations can be.

6 The Complexity of Intergenerational Equity

Although we disagree about social justice, at both the levels of conception and implementation, most of us do not question the category of social justice itself.[5] It is not the case of intergenerational equity. Apart from the extended controversy over the right conception of intergenerational equity and the correct policies to implement a particular conception, the very idea that we owe anything in the way of duties, in fact politically significant duties, to future individuals is itself quite controversial (Beckerman 2006).

Surely, no one denies that there are innumerable actions and omissions in the present moment that are likely to have an impact on the future, such as the consumption of non-renewable resources, technological innovation, the anticipation of future gains, and investment with an extended time-frame. The controversy is over the moral and political implications of that fact. Notice that this is *not* a normative question, concerning the fairness of sacrificing interests or limiting the rights of the current generation for the sake of future generations. It is a conceptual question. The problem is whether the very notion of intergenerational equity does not involve a category mistake, the type of mistake one makes when complaining about the cruelty of a pack of lions feeding on a baby gazelle. This sort of skeptical assault on intergenerational equity takes two main forms.

The first questions whether we can speak meaningfully about future individuals holding rights or possessing interests that create duties for us at the present moment.[6]

[5] Two notable dissenters are Hayek (1982) and Nozick (1974).

[6] Although rights and interests are not the same, I shall not elaborate on the distinction on this occasion.

Sometimes the issue is subsumed under the old legal problem of "rights without a subject" (Sequeira 2017). There are increasing levels of complexity to that problem. The first level concerns rights that are temporarily without a holder, such as an estate in the moment between the death of the deceased and the acceptance of the inheritance by the heirs. The second level concerns the rights whose future holder does not yet exist but is individuated, such as a bequest to a child in her mother's womb. The third level involves those situations in which the holder of the right neither exists nor is individuated, such as a bequest to a future child that is yet to be conceived. The fourth level involves those cases in which neither the holder nor the object of the right exist, such as the right to life of future babies in a nursery where a terrorist set a bomb that will go off in a decade.

Most problems of intergenerational equity would seem to be of the latter type. Alas, they are *even more* complex than that. For they typically involve situations in which not only is it the case that both the holder and the object of the right or interest do not yet exist, but it is also the case that the violation of the right or interest comes to be retrospectively ascertained as a *necessary* condition for the very existence of its holder. Let us suppose that nuclear waste buried by the current generation will contaminate the planet in about a century from now to such an extent that it will have dramatically negative effects on the health of human beings. At the same time, the waste is created by the use of nuclear energy, which enabled all sorts of comforts and benefits that in one way or another shape the lives, including of course the reproductive life, of the current generation. Given the radical contingency of each instance of human fertilization, it is practically certain that not a single of those future individuals whose health is harmed by radioactivity would come to be if society had not used nuclear energy. If they were to claim that their rights were violated by their ancestors, they would run into a performative contradiction—they would be effectively questioning their own existence and arguing, in self-defeating fashion, that individuals other than themselves ought to exist.

This is the paradox of nonidentity (Parfit 1984, pp. 351–79). It is a formidable problem for a theory of intergenerational justice. One way of overcoming it is to argue for rights not of individuals belonging to future generations but of future generations themselves; not individual rights, then, but corporate or group rights, identical in nature to the rights of "cultures" or "minorities" (Campos 2018). Yet, even if we are willing to accept that entities other than individuals can have *moral* rights, it is doubtful whether an entity so undefined as a generation, moreover an entity that does not yet exist, can have any such rights or interests.

Another way of overcoming the nonidentity paradox is to argue that we do not need rights or interests of future individuals to create a general duty incumbent on us to nurture the future (Tremmel 2009, pp. 46–47). This argument has weaknesses of its own. It is true that not all moral duties are correlated with rights—think about duties of charity (to assist those in dire straits) and duties to ourselves (e.g., to cultivate moderation). But such duties are not a matter of justice, enforceable by nature (Kant 1996), as intergenerational duties are said to be. Furthermore, it is doubtful whether we can speak meaningfully about duties of any sort if we cannot affirm an underlying interest—say, the interest of an individual in being relieved from dire straits or the interest of a person in avoiding harmful excesses—and the notion of the interests of future individuals hostage to the non-identity paradox runs into difficulties largely akin to those that afflict the notion of such individuals having rights.

A second line of assault on the very idea of intergenerational equity explores the "circumstances of justice," meaning the background conditions for the problem of justice to arise in the first place (Hume 1969, pp. 536–52) and (Rawls 1971, pp. 126–30). They fall into three main categories: physical, psychological, and epistemological. Among the first are geographic proximity, scarcity of resources, comparable strength, and vulnerability to harm. The psychological condition is the limited altruism of human beings, the fact that they are biased toward their interests and the interests of the people dearest to them, but nonetheless take an interest in fair terms of social cooperation. Finally, the epistemological conditions have to do with our capacity to ascertain harmful conduct and to estimate damages, knowledge required to single out instances of wrongful conduct and administer mechanisms of redress.

It is doubtful whether any of these conditions obtains in the case of intergenerational effects. First, the current generation neither lives in geographic proximity with future generations, nor is exposed to the harmful effects of the behavior of future individuals. Second, social intercourse between generations is meager, limited to those whose existence overlaps in time. Third, and perhaps most importantly, it is difficult to predict the long-term consequences of present day conduct, all the more so if we wish to incorporate in the prediction not only harmful effects but also the positive impact of future technology and collective behavior directed toward avoiding harm. Indeed, intergenerational concerns might be afflicted by a neo-Malthusian bias, pessimistic about the future of the species and optimistic about our ability to foresee it (Beckerman 1999).

It is true that these forms of skepticism about intergenerational equity—the nonidentity paradox and the circumstances of justice—are less menacing when the current and future generations are not very far removed in time. It is even more manageable when *inter*generational and *intra*generational equity are not at odds with each other but run closely together. That is precisely case of financial freedom, as Jorge understands it, given his insistence that fiscal unsustainability is a problem not only for future taxpayers, workers, consumers, and investors but also for current ones. Yet even that has its limits. Recall the words of David Stockman, the former Director of the Office of Management and Budget in the Reagan Administration, when asked about social security reform: "I'm just not going to spend a lot of political capital solving some other guy's problem in 2010" (Glenn and Teles 2009, p. 187).

Moreover, skepticism about the very idea of intergenerational equity is just the tip of the iceberg. Assuming we move on from the daunting abstraction of the conceptual inquiry, there are plenty of normative and technical controversies ahead. The seemingly endless abundance of theories of intergenerational justice and policy proposals informed by each such theory stand as compelling evidence of reasonable pluralism in this domain.[7]

---

[7]For a survey of the theories, see Gosseries (2004) and Campos (2017).

7 Constitutional Legitimacy

Reasonable pluralism all the way down removes intergenerational equity from the table of issues in relation to which constitutional protection might be understood solely by analogy with the model of individual precommitment. It does not follow immediately that it would be illegitimate for the constitutional lawmaker to tie ordinary lawmakers to the mast of some decisions in this area, such as a public debt ceiling or the proscription of nuclear energy. For although such decisions limit the political freedom of future majorities, one might argue that the apparent democratic difficulty dissolves in the face of a dualist account of lawmaking (Ackerman 1991, pp. 3–33).

The theoretical foundations of the doctrine lie in the familiar distinction established by Sieyès in the wake of the French Revolution between *pouvoir constituant* and *pouvoir constitué* (Sieyès 2013, p. 136). Political authority lies originally with "the people," which has the foundational right to organize itself politically in whatever form it sees fit; this is its *pouvoir constituant*. The authority of the various branches of government instituted by the people in its constitution-making capacity, on the other hand, is derivative and precarious, and they are mere *pouvoirs constitués*. Therefore, we must be careful to distinguish between two senses of "democracy" in constitutional discourse: There is democracy as a form of government enabled by constitutional norms, meaning essentially the process of legislative decision making; and there is democracy as popular sovereignty, the supreme power of the people to establish a constitution. It is in the very nature of constituent power, as the primeval embodiment of democracy, that it can do as it pleases, and that includes the entrenchment of policy choices aimed at the protection of future generations.

The argument makes much of the notion that the constitution is a law made by "the people" and that popular sovereignty is the ultimate source of political legitimacy (Schmitt 1928, pp. 91–99). Yet this account of constitutional law faces insurmountable theoretical obstacles. If we conceive the constitution as "jumped up" legislation—as a reinforced statute enacted by a supreme legislator—there is no way out of a long list of unresolved constitutional paradoxes: namely, the intergenerational paradox (How can it be legitimate for a constitution-making generation to bind future generations to its political will?); the democratic paradox (How can it be legitimate for a present-day minority favorable to the policy enshrined in the constitution to prevail over the majority?); and the amendment paradox (How can it be legitimate for a simple majority in the constituent assembly to require a qualified majority to amend the constitution it enacted?). These and similar paradoxes boil down to one simple idea: Any voluntarist or decisionist account of constitutional law is bound to fail, because it renders the binding force of the constitution arbitrary.

The alternative conception is substantive. It tells us that the constitution is legitimate on account of the values it embodies as opposed to the political power behind it. Hence, popular will is not identified with the constitution-making majority—it reveals itself in a particular type of constitution. It is not an empirical but an a priori concept. Indeed, to think of "the people" as an empirical legislator is to incur in the naturalistic fallacy; for "the people" is no agent, no acting entity in the realm of observable or measurable reality; it is a regulative idea of political agency.

It should not surprise us, then, that appeals to a latent popular will have served so many different and incompatible ideologies. Each such ideology embraces a distinctive conception of the people. There is a charismatic conception, according to which the people manifests itself in the agency of a leader sanctioned by spontaneous popular acclamation. There is a romantic conception, which defines the people in terms of a national culture whose custodians are the academic elite. There is a revolutionary conception, which identifies the people with the vanguard of the social class that bears at that historical moment the universal aspirations of humankind. Yet another conception is populist and sees the people in the workings of social movements, street protests, revolutionary struggles, and other inorganic phenomena. So varied and contradictory are these invocations of popular will that we might feel tempted to say, paraphrasing Proudhon's quibble about humanity, that "whoever invokes the people wants to cheat" (*apud* Schmitt 1963, p. 51).

Therefore, any conception of popular will is embedded in—it is actually *identified with*—certain a priori values. Prominent among such conceptions is the liberal-democratic, in the view of which "we the people" is a community of free and equal individuals living in close proximity under a common system of laws. It is the conception of popular sovereignty that underlies both classical social contract theory and the tradition of modern constitutionalism. This conception furnishes a criterion to determine whether a given constitutional document expresses the will of the people or merely the contingent will of whoever claims to act on its behalf. The criterion is the consent of free and equal individuals, imagined for such purposes as the denizens of a state of nature, or of an original position, or of an ideal speech situation, or of some other "purely hypothetical situation characterized so as to lead to a certain conception of justice" (Rawls 1971, p. 12). In other words, it is not the will of the constitution-maker that determines constitutional content but the other way around: certain values identified a priori with the will of the people communicate constitutional dignity to the document or practice that is the formal source of constitutional law.

That is the deep meaning of article 16 of the Declaration of Rights of Man and Citizen of 1789: "a society in which neither the guarantee of rights is assured nor the separation of powers established is deprived of a constitution." Only a constitutional law that contains those elements can be ascribed to "the people" as liberal democracy conceives it—only then can it be regarded as a genuine constitutional foundation of a collective order among free and equal individuals. It follows that it is illegitimate for the constitutional lawmaker, acting as an agent of "the people" of liberal democracy, to bind ordinary lawmakers to particular decisions on intergenerational issues. That is because "the people," understood as a plurality of free and equal individuals, is ineradicably divided on such issues, such that no particular choice can be traced back to its will. A constitutional lawmaker that brings a particular policy to the constitutional level—say, a public debt ceiling—is no longer acting as an agent of its sovereign principal but as a usurper of the *pouvoir constituant*, seeking to entrench in the constitution particular choices on issues that belong in the ordinary track of lawmaking. For when the individuals that make up "the people" are divided at the policy level, their united will can only be to manage their differences democratically, that is, devolving the decision to institutions and procedures through which they are consulted periodically as political equals.

Does the argument prove too much? If constitutional decisions are legitimate only insofar as they can be traced back to the consent of "the people," understood as a community of free and equal individuals, it would seem that it is impossible to establish a legitimate constitution in a pluralist society. Surely, the constitution cannot devolve to ordinary political institutions, procedures, and forms the decision to create the very institutions, procedures, and forms of ordinary decision making. These presuppose constitutional norms, and yet political disagreement extends to those choices as well, as evidenced by longstanding controversies over the best political system (parliamentary versus presidential), the best electoral system (proportional versus majoritarian), the best system of representation (free mandate versus imperative mandate), as well over many more choices essential to the architecture of collective deliberation. It would be plainly absurd and self-defeating to conclude that these disagreements render any constitutional frame of government illegitimate.

There is in any case a decisive difference between issues concerning the organization of collective deliberation and issues pertaining to the substance of collective choices. The former is a necessary condition of democracy itself: Parliaments, cabinets, courts, elections, statutes, decrees etc.—these are not natural facts but creatures of the law, without which "the people" cannot sort out democratically its internal divisions. Notwithstanding the importance of finding common ground in these matters, the legitimacy of constitutional choices in this domain is fundamentally a matter of necessity and expediency: Democracy cannot be left to decide its own constitution. There is a clear analogy with Avellino's decision to commit to a thesis not because he is confident in its truth but because he needs to make sure that he will meet the deadline to submit the dissertation. The argument does not work, however, with respect to choices that do not have to be made at the constitutional level—choices that no practical or logical reason removes from the purview of ordinary politics. That is precisely the case of intergenerational equity.

8 Intergenerational Principles

We face a dilemma. On the one hand, we are right to think that representative democracy has a systematic short-termist bias that leads to collective choices that disregard or at least underestimate the interests of future individuals affected by them. On the other hand, intergenerational equity is a controversial subject, reasonably dividing public opinion, which makes it an appropriate object for democratic deliberation. In other words, we have good *prima facie* reasons to accept and to reject the democratic management of intergenerational problems. The challenge when it comes to the constitution of intergenerational equity is thus how to address the worry of short-termism without usurping democratic authority.

I introduced earlier the distinction between rules and principles: These are, roughly speaking, the mechanical and fiduciary arrangements of constitutional law. The distinction furnishes a promising starting point to work ourselves out of the dilemma between collective akrasia and democratic illegitimacy. Recall that, contrary to rules, which tend to operate in an all-or-nothing fashion, principles embody *pro tanto* reasons, to be balanced against competing reasons relevant in the actual circumstances. Therefore, the democratic objection against the constitutional protection of future generations is on a much stronger footing when the latter takes the form of rules. This is because principles may be balanced in different ways by ordinary lawmakers, reflecting their divergent political judgments, perhaps even the skeptical judgment that future generations are only worthy of protection as long as we are talking about already existing individuals, notably persons under the age to vote. In fact, it is plausible to argue that the constitutional entrenchment of intergenerational principles—say, a principle of sustainability—is justified along the exact same lines of other constitutional principles and fundamental rights: Consent only breaks down once we move from the principle to its application. Insofar as it remains a matter of principle, then, the constitutional protection of future generations is seemingly unproblematic.

The application of principles is subject to a balancing proviso. The technical expression of that notion is the doctrine of proportionality in the broad sense of the term, also known as the "prohibition of excess." It establishes that the sacrifice of a principle cannot be excessive. When the principle embodies a reason to act instead of a limitation to action—a positive rather than a negative duty—proportionality takes the form of a "prohibition of deficit," meaning that the legislature cannot fall below a threshold of sufficient protection or promotion of the principle at stake.

Proportionality entails the requirement that any law that infringes upon a principle fulfills four conditions. The first condition is legitimacy: The goal pursued must be some other principle to which the legislature is bound, such that the sacrifice may be justified. The second condition is suitability: The sacrifice must be a suitable means to promote a legitimate goal, or it would be incurred in vain. The third condition is necessity: The sacrifice must be the least costly of the means suitable to attain the goal, or it would be wasteful. The fourth condition is the balancing test properly so called, proportionality in the narrow sense of the term: The sacrifice must be worth having in light of the goals or reasons underlying the law, that is to say, the overall benefits must outweigh the costs (Klatt and Meister 2012, pp. 8–10).

Now, with respect to each of these conditions, and particularly the last two, there is a question concerning the proper degree of judicial scrutiny of legislative choices. Judicial scrutiny is a variable, ranging from a perfunctory "rational basis" test on the lower end of the spectrum, which merely determines whether the law subject to review is not manifestly disproportional, to full-blown judicial second-guessing of the legislature on the higher end of the spectrum.

If we are serious about democratic rule, we must be supportive of the notion that judicial scrutiny should remain as close as possible to the lower end of the spectrum, and repudiate any suggestion that the normal procedure to settle political disagreements is to subject the matter to voting by a handful of non-elected and unaccountable judges. A democracy is a self-governing community of equals, meaning that the decisions by public authorities should ultimately be traced back to the authorship of the very people to whom they are addressed. On the many issues of principle that divide the citizenry that translates into a requirement that each citizen's opinion, either about the issue itself or about who should decide it, be given the exact same weight as that of any other. Hence, the political branches representative of and directly accountable before the electorate enjoy a presumption of legitimacy when they take a side in the ongoing dispute within society about matters of common concern.

Thus, special circumstances must obtain for the opinion of a majority of judges to prevail over that of a majority of elected officials—circumstances that evince a failure in the political process. Accordingly, courts may only deploy heightened scrutiny when reviewing laws that draw on suspect classifications of race, gender, sexual orientation, age, and others that may serve to oppress political minorities or disenfranchised social groups (Ely 1980, pp. 135–80). The discrimination against future generations is another instance where tighter control is warranted. In these domains of collective akrasia, a public authority that is electorally unaccountable yet bound to offer arguments for its decisions, such as a constitutional court, is more representative of reasonable pluralism than the rule of little more than "Aye!" and "Nye." It embodies a form of "argumentative representation," a virtuous synthesis of pluralism and thoughtfulness (Alexy 2005, pp. 578–81). How plural and thoughtful that type of representation actually is depends on the particular features of judicial arrangements in a society—for instance, one might argue that a specialized constitutional court staffed by judges appointed by a robust parliamentary majority or by a mix of political institutions for a non-renewable term in office offers better assurances of pluralism than an ordinary supreme court staffed by judges appointed for life (Kumm 2017). In any case, these institutional worries should not distract us from the basic point that under conditions of collective akrasia strict judicial review of legislative choices serves the vital task of preventing democratic government from degenerating into a tyranny of the many—the rule of majority deliberation from decaying into the rule of majority prejudice.

9 Conclusion

Just as George entrusts the car keys to Louise because he knows that she is more trustworthy than his akratic self, the citizens of a liberal democracy may entrust intergenerational equity to the few among them who serve as judges because judicial deliberation is a more trustworthy method of securing a fair treatment of future individuals than casting ballots in general elections and voting in the parliamentary process of legislation. Following many twists and turns, the way out of the dilemma between collective akrasia and democratic illegitimacy seems finally straightforward: protect future generations under the form of constitutional principles and subject the laws that infringe upon them to strict judicial control within the framework of proportionality analysis.

Alas, it is not as simple as that. The problems of intergenerational equity implicate quite a bit more than the balancing of rights and interests that is the bread and butter of constitutional justice. They involve complex empirical prognoses and technical judgments regarding the future impact of current decisions. Judges are not cut out for these tasks. Imagine a constitutional court scrutinizing, on account of the principle of sustainability, the macroeconomic assumptions of the overall state budget. We would not just have a variety of constitutional philosophies represented at the apex of the judicial system but also a variety of half-baked economic ideas. That sounds crazy. The same applies to decisions in areas such as environmental protection, social security, and energy policy. It seems highly unlikely that pushing the courts into the thick of the woods of public policy will create much added value in the collective deliberation in those domains. Indeed, things usually take a turn for the worse when the agent selected to execute a fiduciary arrangement is incompetent to decide in the relevant domain.

These worries reintroduce and reshape our dilemma. On the one hand, short-termism debases the democratic authority of ordinary political actors in areas where their decisions have a significant impact on the future. On the other hand, the traditional checks and balances of constitutional democracies are ill-suited to protect future generations. We need different institutions to police the sustainability of government choices. Courts are not the answer. That requires both the careful study of the experience with institutional innovations in this domain that took place in some countries—e.g., the Hungarian Parliamentary Commissioner for Future Generations or Israel's Commission for Future Generations—and a renewal of interest in institutional imagination and design, a discipline to which great political thinkers of the past such as Condorcet and Madison devoted considerable intellectual energy but which has since sunk into near complete oblivion.

More twists and turns. I bet Jorge is already on the move, looking forward to the extra leg of interdisciplinary collaboration. *Se hace camino al andar* (the path is made by walking).

References

Ackerman B (1991) We the people: foundations. Harvard University Press, Cambridge, Mass

Alexy R (1994) Theorie der Grundrechte. Suhrkamp, Berlin

Alexy R (2005) Balancing, constitutional review, and representation. Int J Constit Law 3(4):572–581

Aristotle (2001) Ethica Nichomachea. In: McKeon R (ed) The basic works of Aristotle (trans: Ross WD). The Modern Library, New York, pp 927–1112

Atienza M, Manero J-R (2012) Las Piezas del Derecho: Teoría de los Enunciados Jurídicos. Ariel, Barcelona

Beckerman W (1999) Sustainable development and our obligations to future generations. In: Dobson A (ed) Fairness and futurity: essays on environmental sustainability. Oxford University Press, Oxford, pp 71–92

Beckerman W (2006) The impossibility of a theory of intergenerational justice. In: Tremmel JC (ed) Handbook of intergenerational justice. Edward Elgar Publishing, Cheltenham, Chap. 3

Braga de Macedo J (1976) O Socialismo como Ideologia. Nação e Defesa 2:3–19

Braga de Macedo J (1977) Princípios Gerais de Organização Económica. In: Miranda J (ed) Estudos sobre a Constituição, 1.º volume. Petrony, Lisboa, pp 189–205

Braga de Macedo J (1983) A Ilógica do Sistema Constitucional Português. In: Estudos, vol 1. Direcção-Geral das Contribuições e Impostos, Lisboa, pp 216–237

Braga de Macedo J (1989) A Constituição como Bloqueio da Sociedade Portuguesa. In: Coelho MB (ed) Portugal – O Sistema Político e Constitucional 1974–1987. ICS, Lisboa, pp 801–811

Braga de Macedo J (2000a) Liberdades Futuras dos Portugueses. In: Estudos Jurídicos e Económicos em Homenagem ao Professor João Lumbrales. Coimbra Editora, Coimbra, pp 305–344

Braga de Macedo J (2000b) Pertenças dos Portugueses numa Economia Global. In: Estudos em Homenagem ao Professor Doutor Pedro Soares Martínez, vol II. Almedina, Coimbra, pp 95–134

Braga de Macedo J (2003) Portugal's European integration: the good student with a bad fiscal constitution. South Eur Soc Polit 8(1–2):169–194

Braga de Macedo J (2003b) Europa Seguro Contra a Voracidade. In: Portugal e a Construção Europeia. Almedina, Coimbra, pp 217–234

Buchanan JM, Tullock G (1962) The calculus of consent: logical foundations of constitutional democracy. Liberty Fund, Indianapolis

Campos AS (2017) Teorias da Justiça Intergeracional. In: Silva JP, Almeida Ribeiro G (eds) Justiça Entre Gerações – Perspectivas Interdisciplinares. Universidade Católica Editora, Lisboa, pp 41–69

Campos AS (2018) The rights of future persons under attack. Philosophia 47(3):625–648

Constant B (1997) De La Liberté des Anciens Comparée à Celle des Modernes. In: Gauchet M (ed) Écrits Politiques. Gallimard, pp 589–619

Dworkin R (1977) Taking rights seriously. Oxford University Press, Oxford

Elster J (1984) Ulysses and the Syrens: studies in rationality and irrationality. Cambridge University Press, Cambridge

Ely JH (1980) Democracy and distrust: a theory of judicial review. Harvard University Press, Cambridge, Mass

Glenn BJ, Teles SM (2009) Conservatism and American Political Development. Oxford University Press, Oxford

Gosseries A (2004) Penser la Justice entre les Générations. Flammarion, Paris

Häberle P (2006) A constitutional law for future generations—the 'other' form of the social contract: the generational contract. In: Tremmel J (ed) Handbook of intergenerational justice. Edward Elgar, Cheltenham, pp 215–229

Holmes S (1995) Passions and constraint: on the theory of liberal democracy. The University of Chicago Press, Chicago, London

Homer (2018) The Odyssey (trans: Wilson E). W. W. Norton & Company, New York, London

Hume D (1969) A treatise of human nature. Penguin, London

Kant I (1996) The metaphysics of morals. Cambridge University Press, Cambridge

Klatt M, Meister M (2012) The constitutional structure of proportionality. Oxford University Press, Oxford

Kumm M (2017) Constitutional courts and legislatures: institutional terms of engagement. Católica Law Review 1(1):55–66

MacKenzie MK (2016) Institutional design and sources of short-termism. In: González-Ricoy I, Gosseries A (eds) Institutions for Future Generations. Oxford University Press, Oxford, pp 24–45

Miranda J (2015) Da Revolução à Constituição – Memórias da Assembleia Constituinte. Principia, Cascais

Nozick R (1974) Anarchy, State, and Utopia. Harper and Row, New York

Parfit D (1984) Reasons and persons. Oxford University Press, Oxford

Pires FL (1988) Teoria da Constituição de 1976—A Transição Dualista. Dissertation, University of Coimbra

Rawls J (1971) A theory of justice. Harvard University Press, Cambridge, Mass

Rawls J (2005) Political liberalism. Columbia University Press, New York

Schmitt C (1928) Verfassungslehre. Duncker & Humblot, Berlin

Schmitt C (1963) Der Begriff des Politischen. Duncker & Humblot, Berlin

Sequeira EV (2017) Direitos Sem Sujeito? In: Silva JP, Almeida Ribeiro G (eds) Justiça Entre Gerações – Perspectivas Interdisciplinares. UCE, Lisboa, pp 19–40
Sieyès (2013) What is the third estate? In: Sonenscher M (ed) Political writings. Hackett, Indianapolis, pp 92–162
Silva JP (2015) Deveres do Estado de Protecção de Direitos Fundamentais. Universidade Católica Editora, Lisboa
Tremmel J (2009) A theory of intergenerational justice. Routledge, London
von Hayek FA (1960) The constitution of liberty. Routledge, London, New York
von Hayek FA (1982) Law, legislation and liberty: a new statement of the liberal principles of justice and political economy. Routledge, London and New York
Waldron J (1999) Law and disagreement. Oxford University Press, Oxford
Weiler JHH, Wind M (2003) European constitutionalism beyond the state. Cambridge University Press, Cambridge

International Cooperation in the Age of Populism

Jeffry Frieden

Abstract For much of the post-World War Two period, the world seemed on a path of ever-greater collaboration among the principal economic centers. In the past decade, economic and political trends have called this upward tendency into question. Within both advanced industrial and developing nations, there has been an upsurge in "populist" sentiment with an economically nationalistic tenor and an explicit hostility to "globalist" approaches to economic cooperation. What is the future of international economic cooperation in a world in which domestic political pressures appear to be pushing the major powers apart, rather than together?

Keywords Global governance · Globalization · International cooperation · Nationalism · Populism

1 Global Governance, Found and Lost

A couple of decades ago, at the turn of the twenty-first century, the age of global governance seemed to have dawned—or at least appeared on the horizon. Logic supported it: global markets, global problems, and global externalities all demanded global solutions. Policymakers seemed increasingly committed to an unprecedented level of inter-state economic integration and policy coordination. An ever more expansive class of globalists—cosmopolitan, educated, energetic—was coalescing. The future of the world was presaged by the galloping pace of economic and political integration in Europe, now joined in a single market heading toward the free movement of goods, capital, and people, and mostly sharing a common currency. The most dramatic experiment in integration since the Roman Empire seemed well on its way to prove that global governance was feasible—even necessary.

The crisis that erupted late in 2007, troubling as it was, seemed only to demonstrate the promise of the new globalizing reality. Elected policymakers faced many obstacles to an adequate response to the crisis, and there was a notable lack of

J. Frieden (✉)
Department of Government, Harvard University, Cambridge, MA, USA
e-mail: jfrieden@harvard.edu

L. Brites Pereira et al. (eds.), *Economic Globalization and Governance*,
https://doi.org/10.1007/978-3-030-53265-9_21

appropriate, or appropriately coordinated, fiscal policies. However, the monetary and financial authorities of the major economic powers did in fact work closely together to engineer coordinated policies to address the frightening prospect of a crisis that might well have been longer and deeper than the Great Depression of the 1930s. This hardly amounted to the existence of a global lender of last resort and a global financial regulatory agency to provide the global public goods of monetary and financial stability. Nonetheless, the cooperative measures among policymakers came close enough to fill this bill that there was speculation that the next step would in fact be to create such a global institution—or to transform the International Monetary Fund (IMF) into one. Difficult as the crisis was, the early returns suggested guarded optimism about the possibility of global governance provided by far-seeing policymakers.

It was not to be. Stirrings of discontent surfaced almost as soon as countries began to emerge from the depths of the crisis. In the USA, a rebellious right-wing reaction took the form of the Tea Party movement, which helped the Republican Party sweep the midterm election of 2010. Europe's governments collapsed into bitter disputes over how best to address accumulated debts, and the region fell into a second recession, as leftist movements and parties opposed to austerity shot to prominence in the debtor nations.

Even after the purely economic impact of the crisis began to fade, its political effects matured and grew. In almost all the developed world, and much of the developing one, movements arose and proliferated that varied on many dimensions but were similar on several. They rejected most existing political institutions, parties, and politicians. They couched their rejection in absolutist terms, pitting "the people" against a spent and corrupt elite. They were hostile to globalism and the stateless cosmopolitanism of the new global ruling class. These "populist" movements of right and left grew almost everywhere—and were able to win elections in some cases, most prominently in the USA.

What explains the emergence of this rejection of global economic and political integration? What is its significance? Has it put a definitive stop to efforts to create and extend global governance? What might slow or stop the march of populism? This essay suggests some answers to these questions.

2 The Sources and Meaning of the Populist Upsurge

The 2016 presidential election in the USA was both a symbol of the new political reality and a watershed in American political history. For the first time in over 80 years, candidates for the presidential nomination of *both* political parties ran on platforms of explicit hostility to international trade, international finance, and international investment. The rhetoric of Bernie Sanders and Donald Trump was, indeed, strikingly similar. Donald Trump said:

> Our politicians have aggressively pursued a policy of globalization, moving our jobs, our wealth and our factories to Mexico and overseas. Globalization has made the financial elite very, very wealthy.[…] But it has left millions of our workers with nothing but poverty and heartache.

For his part, Bernie Sanders argued:

> [T]rade is […] a significant reason why Americans are working longer hours for low wages and why we are seeing our jobs go to China and other low-wage countries.[…] [W]e should have a trade policy which represents the working families of this country, that rebuilds our manufacturing base, not that just represents the CEOs of large multinational corporations.

By the same token, Trump claimed:

> NAFTA was the worst trade deal in history.[…] And China's entrance into the World Trade Organization has enabled the greatest job theft in the history of our country.[1]

While Sanders was only slightly less bombastic:

> NAFTA, CAFTA, PNTR with China […] have been a disaster for the American worker.[…] Working people understand that after NAFTA, CAFTA, PNTR with China we have lost millions of decent paying jobs.[2]

Of course, one of those candidates won the nomination of his party and went on to win the presidency. And this brought to the most powerful office in the world, again for the first time in 80 years, a policymaker who was avowedly hostile to international trade, finance, investment, and immigration, as well as to what he called "globalism," and to multilateralism.

The root causes of this striking turn in American politics, and in American foreign economic policy, go back at least forty years. The country's income distribution has deteriorated almost continually—with a pause in the 1990s—since the early 1970s. Almost from the start, many Americans connected this trend with the position of the USA in the international economy. In the 1970s and 1980s, there were those who blamed the stagnation and decline in the wages of unskilled workers on a dramatic increase in imports from developing countries. It is worth noting that this had little to do with China and referred primarily to what were then called the Newly Industrializing Countries (NICs): South Korea, Taiwan, Hong Kong, Singapore, Mexico, and Brazil. As late at 1990, China ranked fourth among developing-country exporters to the USA, after South Korea, Taiwan, and Mexico. The connection was based on good Heckscher-Ohlin logic: greater trade with countries rich in unskilled labor would put downward pressure on unskilled wages in the USA.

This logic led to the original "trade and wages" debate, about the relative importance of trade and skill-biased technological change respectively to the deterioration of the return to unskilled labor in the USA. It is useful to recall that this debate raged in the late 1980s and early 1990s, long before China was a major force (Freeman

---

[1]For the Trump quotes, see David Jackson, "Donald Trump targets globalization and free trade as job-killers," U.S.A Today, 28 June 2016.

[2]For the Sanders quotes, see "Bernie Sanders on Free Trade," On The Issues, available at: https://www.ontheissues.org/International/Bernie_Sanders_Free_Trade.htm.

1995). The consensus was that technological change was far more important than trade, although more recent reevaluations tend to find a greater impact of trade than had previously been expected (Autor et al. 2013; Krugman 2008).

In the 1990s and early 2000s, as unskilled wages largely stabilized—at a lower level—much of the attention shifted to the increasing separation between the middle class and the top registers of the income distribution. Whether the target was the top 1 percent or the top 10 percent, activists and others pointed to the emergence of "headquarters cities" and "superstar firms" collecting in prosperous urban agglomerations, pushing out the middle class and leaving them behind. Again, many made a connection to globalization and regarded the problem as result of an alliance among internationalist firms and banks, globalist governments, and international organizations that privileged markets over social goals. This perspective, largely from the Left, was especially prominent in the late 1990s, culminating in the so-called Battle for Seattle in 1999, on the occasion of a World Trade Organization (WTO) Ministerial Conference.

The American middle class had reason to complain. Over the 1980s and into the early 1990s, median household income was largely stagnant in real terms. Rapid economic growth in the 1990s served to paper over some of the discontent. But into the 2000s, real median household income again stagnated. Some of this middle-class stagnation was masked by the 2001–2007 boom in housing and asset prices, which helped increase middle-class wealth. But even during those go-go years, the gains from economic growth were not distributed evenly. During the expansion, two-thirds of the country's income growth went to the top one percent of the population. These American families, each earning more than US$ 400,000 a year, saw their incomes rise by more than 60% between 2002 and 2007, while the income of the rest of the country's households rose by 6%.[3] And even that meager growth was taken back by the Great Financial Crisis (GFC) that began late in 2007.

The impact of the GFC is hard to over-estimate. We see it easily in Europe, where the crisis in the Eurozone was so severe that it took almost ten years for GDP per capita to recover to its pre-crisis levels. Moreover, the unequal distribution of the burden of adjustment is clear in the European context, where the heavily indebted countries suffered depression-like economic collapses. In Spain and Greece, GDP per capita fell by 10 and 25%, respectively, while unemployment peaked at over 25%—and over 15% in Portugal and Ireland.[4]

The crisis in the USA was almost as severe and almost as unequally distributed. It took six years for American GDP per capita to recover, nine years for median household income. As in Europe, the aggregate numbers mask substantial regional variation. Median household income in prosperous states like Massachusetts and New York has risen by 10 or 15% since the crisis, while troubled states like Michigan, Wisconsin, and Florida are still below pre-crisis levels. The regional contrast was

[3]For more details, see Chinn and Frieden (2011).

[4]All data are from Eurostat.

also clear in differential rates of unemployment. The unemployment rate in Michigan peaked at 15%, while it never reached 9% in New York and Massachusetts.[5]

The disparities in the impact of the American crisis among social groups were even greater. At the height of the GFC, the national unemployment rate was 10%. Among the poorest third of American households, however, unemployment was 18%; if the underemployed (including discouraged and involuntary part-time workers) are included, the rate rises to 35%. Meanwhile, in the richest third of American households, unemployment peaked at 4% and, including the underemployed, at 9% (Chinn and Frieden 2011, pp 148–149). Perhaps most striking has been the collapse of middle-class wealth: median household wealth in 2016 was 34% *below* where it had been in 2007—this while the household wealth of the top 20% of the population *grew* by 33%. Indeed, by 2016, the richest 20% of American households owned 77% of the country's wealth—more than three times that owned by the entire middle class (the middle 60% of households). Even more striking, the richest 1% of American households owned substantially more than the middle class combined (Sawhill and Pulliam 2019; Wolff 2017). The most striking imbalances in the American crisis and recovery were—as in the expansion that preceded it—among groups in the population. Not only had the rich gotten richer during the boom, they continued to get richer during the crisis and the recovery.

In both Europe and the USA, the crisis and its aftermath highlighted the failures of existing elites to address their societies' problems. In Europe, the member states of the Eurozone were completely unable to arrive at a reasonable resolution of the Eurozone debt crisis. The catastrophic mess that enveloped the Eurozone was entirely avoidable, and yet the region's political leaders could not avoid it (Frieden and Walter 2017). In the USA, politicians and pundits emphasized the general recovery of the economy—and of the stock market—and focused on the booming prosperity of the big cities. They ignored the fact that vast swaths of the population, including much of the middle class, were worse off than they had been before the crisis.

Existing political institutions, parties, and leaders had failed on two dimensions. There was a *failure of compensation*: an unwillingness or inability to safeguard the interests of those harmed by international and domestic economic events, while catering to and celebrating the beneficiaries. There was a *failure of representation*: an unwillingness or inability to accurately reflect and address the needs of large portions of the population.[6] For decades since World War Two, in Europe and North America, a centrist consensus had reigned. The center-left and the center-right, for all their differences, agreed on the broad contours of domestic and international economic policies. As large portions of these economies fell farther behind, those left out of the consensus had nowhere to turn—until they did.

The political reaction to these failures was swift. Over the course of 2009, the Tea Party movement swept the USA and the Republican Party, culminating in major successes in primary and general elections in 2010. The movement lay the groundwork for Donald Trump's populist campaign of 2016 and played a major role in

---

[5]All data are from the St. Louis Fed's FRED.

[6]For more details, see Frieden (2019).

remaking the Republican Party in its, and Trump's, images. On the democratic side, Senator Bernie Sanders led the "progressive" wing in attacking Democratic Party moderates. In Europe, populists of the left quickly rose in Greece and Spain, soon taking power in the former and becoming a major political force in the latter. Within a few years, almost every western European country had a powerful populist movement, whether of the right or of the left.

Although there were substantial differences among the various populist movements, some things tied them together. They all, to one extent or another, rejected existing political institutions, parties, and leaders. And they all harbored a basic hostility toward economic and political integration. In Europe, the European Union was the principal target; in the USA, the target was globalization, "globalism" and multilateralism in general.

There is not always a direct connection between this sort of populism—especially of the right—and opposition to globalization. In Europe, it often takes the form of opposition to European integration or of aspects of integration that they see as impinging upon national sovereignty. The target of the hostility might be EU-imposed austerity, in the debtor nations, or EU policies toward regulation or immigration, in other countries. Some in the Trump administration, like some British supporters of Brexit, might argue that their economic nationalism is in pursuit of the ultimate goal of a *more* open economy. Nonetheless, virtually all these movements share an aversion to "globalism" and to the kind of international collaboration and integration that has been the norm since the 1940s.

Donald Trump was explicit in speaking to the United Nations in September 2018. "We reject the ideology of globalism," he said, and promised to "defend against threats to sovereignty [...] from global governance."[7] In this context, the future of international cooperation on economic problems—or any problems, for that matter—is in serious doubt.

3 Nationalist Populism and International Cooperation

Populists of the modern variety have made abundantly clear that they are uninterested in—and often hostile to—the previous elites' quest for global cooperation. The Trump Administration has eschewed multilateralism in favor of bilateral, or unilateral, action on trade. It is hostile to the WTO, ignoring it in most of its actions and actively impeding the work of the Dispute Settlement System. Such central European populists as Hungarian prime minister Viktor Orban boast about building "a

[7]"Remarks by President Trump to the 73rd Session of the United Nations General Assembly," United Nations, New York, 25 September 2018. Available at https://www.whitehouse.gov/briefings-statements/remarks-president-trump-73rd-session-united-nations-general-assembly-new-york-ny/. Accessed 2 January 2020.

new state built on illiberal and national foundations."[8] They reject EU oversight of their domestic policies, and EU attempts to allocate refugees and asylum-seekers among member states. They may welcome the openness of European markets to their goods and people, but they resist the attempts of other EU member states to harmonize and coordinate policies and principles.

This is not to take a position on the correctness or less of the populists' positions. In most instances, there is a logic to their arguments. There is a great diversity of socio-economic realities and political views among the member states of the European Union and attempts to create common policies may well be unrealistic in many arenas. Supporters of the populist nationalists in Europe often argue that integration has gone too far, too fast, and that the EU needs to correct its course and set its integrationist sights lower. This view is also held by some decidedly non-populist observers (such as Mody 2018).

The American populist variant shares with its European counterparts a bitter disdain for elite internationalism, which it blames for inflicting hardship on "the people" and for steering the country away from its traditions. Donald Trump's 2016 presidential campaign, and his rhetoric in office afterward, emphasized his dedication to the middle class, and to the country's industrial base. Trump on campaign, and Trump in office, have been explicitly hostile to globalization. More specifically, the Trump Administration has moved sharply away from the country's post-war commitment to multilateralism. The Administration's trade policy, in particular, has been a notable departure from that of past administrations. It has undertaken a series of unilateral measures and bilateral negotiations, most of which are clearly inconsistent with reigning WTO principles. Trade is only one foreign-policy arena in which America's nationalist populists have largely jettisoned previous patterns of multilateral engagement.

While the specific policies pursued by populists in power are important—especially in the case of the United States—their policy principles are less important than the underlying political realities they reflect. For if it were simply a matter of one political party of two, or among many in the European cases, one might expect an eventual reversion to the strategies of the past. However, there is substantial evidence that the populists—in or out of office—are a political reflection of powerful socio-economic trends that affect most industrial societies. The power of these trends is indicated by the fact that the democrats have moved in a decidedly more protectionist direction—something evident in the 2016 presidential campaign, when Hillary Clinton felt constrained to disavow the Trans-Pacific Partnership she had helped design. Similar pressures have led many European center-right (and even center-left) parties to move closer to the positions of their populist challengers.

The new economic nationalists in western Europe and the USA find their principal bases of support in regions of their respective countries that are economically

[8]"Prime Minister Viktor Orbán's Speech at the 25th Bálványos Summer Free University and Student Camp," 26 July 2014, available at: https://www.kormany.hu/en/the-prime-minister/the-prime-minister-s-speeches/prime-minister-viktor-orban-s-speech-at-the-25th-balvanyos-summer-free-university-and-student-camp. Accessed 2 January 2020.

distressed—and, in particular, in regions that have experienced deindustrialization.[9] While, as previously noted, there are many reasons for the loss of manufacturing jobs in rich countries, foreign competition and the relocation of production offshore are prominent causes, and causes that—unlike automation—suggest potential policy responses.

The problems of formerly industrial regions in decline are complex and of long standing, and they are not amenable to quick fixes. Their recovery will require some combination of adjustment policies to soften the blows from technological change and globalization, and structural policies whose impact is likely to be felt only over decades. These regions need substantial improvements in education, in workforce development, and in the economic and social infrastructure. They also need good jobs for their residents, although we have little clear guidance as to the measures best suited to ensure a steady supply of such good jobs.[10]

There are substantial, long-term, structural sources of the discontent that has rippled—or torn—through advanced industrial societies over the past decade. It was probably not preordained that the discontent would be captured and channeled by nationalist populists, largely of the right but also of the left. However, that is how the politics developed, and they are unlikely to recede any time soon.

The underlying politics of the present day—and of the present-day backlash against globalization and integration—must be the foundation for any sensible projection of the prospects for international economic cooperation. Current trends would not seem promising even for a maintenance of current levels of cooperation, let alone for their deepening into some meaningful forms of global governance.

4 Global Governance: Past Imperfect, Present Tense, Future Conditional[11]

The battle for international economic cooperation will be won or lost on the field of domestic politics. This much seems clear from current trends, and how they have affected international economic relations in the past few years. A look at the history of the successes and failures of global economic integration—and there is a long history to draw upon—is equally instructive.

The central problem of an integrated international economy is to manage the delicate relationship between the demands of international economic collaboration, on the one hand, and the demands of domestic social and political realities, on the other. The first era of globalization, in the nineteenth and early twentieth centuries, solved this problem by excluding most domestic groups from meaningful participation in

[9]For examples of evidence along these lines, see Broz et al. (forthcoming), Colantone and Stanig (2018, 2019) and Dal Bó et al. (2018).

[10]Rodrik and Sable (2019) provide one perspective.

[11]With apologies to Frieden et al. (2012), from which some of this section is adapted.

political and social life. This proved untenable in the interwar years and led to catastrophe. During the first decades of the post-World War Two order, which we may call the Bretton Woods period, the balancing act was managed with a series of important compromises. As the world transitioned to the "high globalization" of the 1990s and after, that balancing act became increasingly difficult—and its difficulties are central to the problems of today. A short sketch of this trajectory is illustrative.

For decades before 1914, the international economy was roughly as integrated as it is today. That first era of globalization was remarkably successful by the standards of the time. The world economy grew more in the 75 years before 1914 than it had in the previous 750, and there was substantial convergence among countries of the core and lands of recent settlement. Macroeconomic conditions were relatively stable, despite periodic crises and "panics." None of this is to ignore the uglier sides of the period—colonialism, authoritarian governments, agrarian crises and grinding urban poverty were all parts of the 19th and early twentieth-century world order. Nonetheless, compared to what had come before—and what came immediately after—this was a flourishing global economy.

And yet that globalized economy came to a grinding halt in 1914. After WWI was over, the world's political and economic leaders attempted to restore the classical order that had prevailed for so long—and failed. It was not for lack of trying, as conferences, meetings, treaties and international organizations proliferated as never before. But nothing worked. The global economy fragmented and eventually, after the 1929 downturn hit, broke up into trade and currency wars, and eventually shooting wars.[12]

There are some interesting parallels between the interwar period and the present day. Apart from the superficial similarities between some of the current populist movements and interwar ones—such as the re-use of the America First label by the Trump Administration—there are deeper connections. One is that the regional political base of the Trump Administration, and in particular of its more protectionist trade policies, is to be found in the regions of the country that were the principal sources of isolationist sentiment in the 1920s and 1930s, especially the industrial belt in the midwest along with states in the Great Plains and the Rocky Mountains. Another parallel has to do with the rejection of multilateralism: the isolationists, along with many Americans, felt that existing international organizations did not accurately reflect the role of the USA in the world and were indeed intended to constrain US influence.

There are two principal lessons of the first era of globalization and its collapse after 1918. First, an open international economy requires collaboration among the major economic powers, especially during periods of economic stress. The nineteenth-century fiction of self-equilibrating international markets may have applied to particular markets but it did not apply to the world economy as a whole. For a globalized economy to persist, especially in the face of periodic crises, the principal financial centers need to cooperate to stabilize markets and safeguard openness.

[12]Eichengreen (1992) is the classic account.

The second lesson of the collapse of the classical version of globalization is that national governments cannot undertake the measures needed to sustain an open economy if they do not have the support of their constituents. Policymakers must answer to their constituents, and if constituents are hostile to the world economy, policymakers who ignore this hostility will cease to be making policy.

The stability of the classical gold-standard era in the nineteenth century and early twentieth century was due in part to the fact that the major member states gave few political rights, and little political power, to the middle and working classes and poor farmers. The failures of the interwar period were largely due to the inability of political leaders to sustain classical policies in newly democratic nations. Indeed, by the 1920s, almost every industrial country was democratic, and attempts to subject these political economies to gold-standard austerity measures led to a powerful backlash—both against the government, and often against the rest of the world.

The post-World War Two international economic order, planned in broad outlines at Bretton Woods, attempted to find a middle ground between classical gold-standard stability and interwar confusion, while allowing room for more flexible national macroeconomic and social policies. Trade was liberalized, but gradually and with exceptions and escape clauses where liberalization would have been politically difficult. Exchange rates were stabilized but capital controls limited the degree of financial integration. Social safety nets and the welfare state were accepted as part of the post-war compromise (Lamoreaux and Shapiro 2019). This system worked well for 25 years. However, economic integration eventually caught up with some of the contradictions in the Bretton Woods order, symbolized by the extent to which the gradual rebirth of international finance undermined the Bretton Woods monetary system.

The march toward globalization started in earnest in the early 1980s, as the Reagan and Thatcher administrations led the developed countries toward greater engagement with global markets. Over the late 1980s and early 1990s, many developing countries jettisoned their previous economic nationalism. When the Soviet Union collapsed and it, and most of its former allies, embraced economic integration—as China and Vietnam had done long before—it seemed that globalization had triumphed for good.

However, the second age of globalization faced problems parallel to those of the first: international economic forces increasingly bumped up against domestic political pressures. As we have seen, the crisis of 2007–2009 and its aftermath brought these tensions to the fore, as political movements rejected past patterns of economic and political integration—and, in some cases, took power on anti-integrationist platforms. It remains to be seen whether this reflects the end of the second era of globalization, or merely a pause in its onward march.

5 Ways Forward

The future of global cooperation, let along global governance, is in doubt. The principal doubts are about the extent of domestic political opposition to the measures necessary to secure cooperative international economic and political relations. The roots of this opposition are broad and deep, and they cannot be wished or persuaded away. Progress in addressing global problems depends on progress in addressing the *domestic* problems that underlie the current upsurge of pessimism about, and hostility to, globalization.

A first step in this direction requires *recognizing* the legitimacy of many of the concerns that populist nationalists have seized upon. Major regions of our economies, and major segments of our population, have faced and continue to face serious economic difficulties. What started with the decline of manufacturing industries in these areas typically has led to broader economic distress, and eventually to grim social problems (Feler and Senses 2017). In the USA, social mobility has declined to alarmingly low levels, especially in the distressed regions (Chetty et al. 2014). Inter-regional mobility has also fallen dramatically, largely due to rapidly rising housing prices in prosperous areas, which makes it difficult or impossible for people to move from areas where good jobs are scarce to areas with more opportunities (Ganong and Shoag 2017).

Both short-term and long-term measures are needed to address the problems of those left out of globalization's prosperity. In the short run, troubled regions need help in pulling themselves out of what is often a downward spiral. Central governments need to consider "place-based policies" that can address immediate problems effectively (Shambaugh and Ryan 2018). In the longer run, more structural policies to address regional differences will be important, especially those aimed at improving the economic and social infrastructure, and the educational institutions, in regions that have been struggling.

The contours of effective short- and long-term policies are not necessarily clear. Regions differ, as do countries, and what works in one may not work in another. Nonetheless, if the needs of troubled regions, sectors, and people are not addressed, we can reliably expect a continuation and deepening of the current skepticism about international economic and political integration. Those with the most at stake in globalization need to find ways to address the valid concerns of those who regard it with skepticism and fear.

Theory and history demonstrate that an open international economy requires cooperation among the major economic centers. That cooperation in turn requires domestic political support for the measures necessary to help keep the world economy functioning smoothly. Support for globalization and integration has eroded continually over the course of the twenty-first century. A reversal of this erosion depends on the willingness and ability of supporters of international economic and political integration to demonstrate to their compatriots, with deeds rather than words, that its benefits can be distributed much more broadly than they have been to date.

References

Autor DH, Dorn D, Hanson GH (2013) The China syndrome: local labor market effects of import competition in the United States. Am Econo Rev 103(2)

Broz JL, Frieden J, Weymouth S (forthcoming) Populism in place: the economic geography of the globalization backlash. International Organization
Chetty R, Hendren N, Kline P, Saez E (2014) Where is the land of opportunity? The geography of intergenerational mobility in the United States. Q J Econ 129(4)
Chinn M, Frieden J (2011) Lost decades: the making of America's debt crisis and the long recovery. Norton, New York, W.W
Colantone I, Stanig P (2018) The trade origins of economic nationalism: import competition and voting behavior in Western Europe. Am J Political Sci 62(4):936–953
Colantone I, Stanig P (2019) The surge of economic nationalism in Western Europe. J Econ Persp 33(4). Fall
Dal Bó E, Finan F, Folke O, Persson T, Rickne J (2018) Economic losers and political winners: Sweden's Radical Right. Working paper
Eichengreen B (1992) Golden fetters: the gold standard and the great depression, 1919–1939. Oxford University Press, New York
Feler L, Senses MZ (2017) Trade shocks and the provision of local public goods. Am Econ J Econ Policy 9(4):10–43
Freeman RB (1995) Are your wages set in Beijing? J Econ Perspecti 9(3). Summer
Frieden J (2019) The political economy of the globalization backlash: sources and implications. In: Obstfeld M, Catão L (eds) Meeting globalization's challenges. Princeton University Press, Princeton
Frieden J, Pettis M, Rodrik D, Zedillo E (2012) After the fall: the future of global cooperation. Geneva Report 14, Center for Economic Policy Research, London
Frieden J, Walter S (2017) Understanding the political economy of the eurozone crisis. Annual Review of Political Science
Ganong P, Shoag D (2017) Why has regional income convergence in the US declined? J Urban Econ 102:76–90
Krugman P (2008) Trade and wages, reconsidered. Brookings Papers on Economic Activity 1, Spring
Lamoreaux N, Shapiro I (eds) (2019) The bretton woods agreements. Yale University Press, New Haven
Mody A (2018) EuroTragedy: a drama in nine acts. Oxford University Press, Oxford
Rodrik D, Sable C (2019). Building a good jobs economy. Working paper
Sawhill IV, Pulliam C (2019). Six facts about wealth in the United States. Brookings blog Up Front. Available at www.brookings.edu/blog/up-front/2019/06/25/six-facts-about-wealth-in-the-united-states. Accessed 3 Jany 2020
Shambaugh J, Nunn R (eds) (2018) Place-based policies for shared economic growth. Brookings Institution, Washington
Wolff EN (2017) Household wealth trends in the United States 1962 to 2016: has middle class wealth recovered? NBER Working Paper 24085, November

Postface

The last quarter of the twentieth century was transformative for Portugal. The country's opening following the revolutionary upheaval led not only to economic convergence, but notably, to an intellectual convergence with liberal Europe. The events that comprised the transformation are largely known and are now part of history. Less well known, however, is the generation of young minds that brought the world to Portugal and that propelled its transformation. This was a group of young mavericks, endowed with a new openness to the world, a singular intellectual potential and the courage to lead the country out of Plato's cave.

Jorge Braga de Macedo was one of the great exponents of this tribe of visionaries. His experience in the USA, and his success in what remains the most competitive academic market in the world, demonstrated the potential of Portuguese minds in the international academic landscape. His return to Portugal was instrumental in opening Portuguese academia to the world. In this regard, the Faculty of Economics of the *Universidade Nova de Lisboa*, now the Nova School of Business and Economics (Nova SBE), was the perennial stage for his sprawling influence. His generation's effect inspired dozens of Portuguese academics currently leading research around the world. It also helped shape Nova SBE's culture of research, rigour and academic excellence—elevating it to become one of the top schools of business and economics in Europe. As his student in the past, and now as Dean, I believe he leaves an indelible mark on our institution, from the energy of his academic persona and the brilliance of his rebellious mind.

Above all else, Jorge Braga de Macedo was keenly aware of the responsibility of academics to contribute towards the public interest and to shape the world by transforming knowledge and theory into practice and reality. On this score, a historic contribution as the Portuguese Finance Minister, a lifetime's dedication to Portugal's relationship with African countries and their economic development, and a successful career in international institutions like the Organization for Economic Cooperation and Development and the European Commission, stand out as part of his professional impact and personal journey.

His commitment to impact is a lesson for the academics of our day. To be sure, the challenges now facing the world, not unlike the ones that motivated the generation

L. Brites Pereira et al. (eds.), *Economic Globalization and Governance*,
https://doi.org/10.1007/978-3-030-53265-9

that renewed Portugal, require open-minded, innovative and courageous academics, who bring about effective new ideas to renovate our liberal society. Jorge's dedication to the public cause and to disruptive ideas stands out to inspire academics in Portugal and around the world.

Daniel Traça, Dean of Nova School of Business and Economics.

Appendix

A.1 Curriculum

Fortunately for the editors, Jorge Braga de Macedo launched a professional website more than 23 years ago.[1] Unfortunately, the information provided is so vast in scope that we doubt the author himself can navigate it without occasional irritation, except perhaps in a few instances, such as the following biographical note[2]:

> Jorge Braga de Macedo is Jubilee Professor of Economics at Nova School of Business and Economics in Carcavelos; member of Lisbon Academy of Science, Royal Academy of Belgium; Euro50 Group and Trilateral Commission (honorary); Distinguished Fellow at Centre for International Governance Innovation (CIGI, Waterloo, Ont.); Research Associate at National Bureau of Economic Research (NBER, Cambridge, Mass.); Research Fellow at Centre for Economic Policy Research (CEPR, London). At Nova since 1976, he founded and

[1]The website domain www.jbmacedo.com was registered on 12 August 2008 and includes detailed information about Jorge Braga de Macedo's career, especially research and teaching. It also contains interesting items that give us a glimpse into his interests, memories and hobbies (e.g. photos of Atlantic beaches neighbouring his home to successive canine running companions and opinions about sushi restaurants around the world), among other items. As Nova's professional websites were discontinued in February 2020, he updated his CV and publication record in Working Paper # 634 (http://hdl.handle.net/10362/98815), which was posted on the SSRN website on 1 July 2020. In particular, it incorporates his experience as the personal representative of the Prime Minister Pedro Passos Coelho at the Strategic Council for an Open Economy (2011-15), activities undertaken after the merger of the Tropical Research Institute into the University of Lisbon (2015), as well as including a list of membership in boards of corporations, journals and non-profit organizations.

[2]By way of personal information Jorge Braga de Macedo was born on 1 December 1946 in Lisbon, where he married Luiza Almeida Ribeiro in 1972, and has children João (born 1977) and Ana (born 1984) as well as Jorge de la Barre (born to Geneviève in 1965). Interestingly, our source states that he "inherited the well-known bad temper" of his father (Jorge Borges de Macedo) before providing full names and places of birth for the nuclear family (though the daughter was born in New Jersey rather than Connecticut). It also specifies the first name of his sister Branca Maria (1948–2020), her widower and their elder son (who contributed to Part I) but not of their younger sister Ana Irene, who died shortly after their mother, Branca Rosa (See pt.wikipedia.org/wiki/Jorge_Braga_de_Macedo. Accessed 24 March 2020). More personal information is available in the footnotes to Working Paper #634, partly drawing on the website.

L. Brites Pereira et al. (eds.), *Economic Globalization and Governance*,
https://doi.org/10.1007/978-3-030-53265-9

> directed the Centre for Globalization and Governance (CG&G) and the Doctoral Program on Tropical Knowledge and Management (TropiKMan), having taught at Yale, Princeton, Sciences-Po and served as Director for National Economies at the European Commission in Brussels, Minister of Finance for Portugal and chair of the Parliamentary Committee for European Affairs. The last President of the OECD Development Centre and of the Tropical Research Institute (1998–2015), he is on the supervisory board of EDP *Energias de Portugal* since 2013. (www.jbmacedo.com/bio20.pdf).

Before we list the publications, the online introduction to his very detailed curriculum vitae provides not only a quotable narrative but also a good frame his research interests:

> After an early interest in psychology and medicine, I obtained a law degree and then pursued a professional career in economics. My foremost objective was mastering economic analysis so as to apply it to international and development issues. After thirty years of economic theory and practice, though, interdisciplinary research continues to attract me. Similarly, my interest in European economic and financial issues goes along with a commitment to research in transition and international development, prompted by the economic, political and social experience of Portugal during my lifetime. My father (1921–1996) taught history at the University of Lisbon and his father (1876–1948) wrote on international and colonial issues while my mother (1918–1981) worked at the National Development Bank. I attended the *Lycée Français* Charles Lepierre in Lisbon from 1958 until July 1964, when the University of Toulouse, France, granted me a *Baccalauréat* in Experimental Sciences. After a year spent in Paris working in different jobs (mostly hotel receptions), I decided to apply to the Faculty of Law at the University of Lisbon and consequently attended a preparatory high school, *O Académico*.
>
> I was first exposed to economics in 1967/68 and decided to pursue it at the graduate level. To do so, I applied to a Fulbright scholarship in 1969 and, a few months after obtaining a LL.B. in July 1971, I enrolled in the Yale Graduate School. I obtained an M.A. in International Relations (Economics) in September 1973 and transferred into the PhD program in economics but, before taking my comprehensive examinations in economic theory, I was drafted into the army. As my military service began, I was teaching the principles of economics course at the law school I had graduated from. My interest in processes of economic and social development was reinforced while stationed in Angola as a junior lieutenant: from August 1974 to September 1975, I offered three courses at the Faculty of Economics, University of Luanda […].
>
> Upon returning to Nova, on 23 October 1985, I was appointed director of the Centre for Social Economics at the Tropical Research Institute (IICT). In early 1986, I led a mission to Guinea Bissau sponsored by UNDP, and another to São Tome, joint with the Bank of Portugal. As a follow up, the possibility of fixed exchange rate agreements with Guinea Bissau and São Tome was also studied under sponsorship of what is now the Portuguese Development Aid Institute (IPAD). I also participated in the first World Bank mission to Angola in 1987, and CSE contributed the chapter on the colonial economy to the accession report. In December 1986, I was invited to the first Presidential visit of Mario Soares to São Tome and Cape Verde. Following up on this visit, I convened at IICT a series of meetings of Portuguese entrepreneurs interested in Africa which culminated in the creation of ELO—Portuguese association for development and cooperation. In the 2003 by-laws, ELO and IPAD became members of the steering committee and monitoring unit of IICT, joined by CPLP, OECD, Ministry of Economy, Ministry of Finance, European Commission, World Bank, etc. In 2015, IICT was moved to the new University of Lisbon and eventually led to the creation of its Tropical College, whereas ELO became part of the Confederation of Entrepreneurs in 2016.

Table A1 Publications of Braga de Macedo J (by type)

B	BC	CMT	JR	OJ	POL	PREF	REV	WP	TOT
23	99	18	17	67	26	18	4	20	292

Notes TOT denotes total and see text for the other abbreviations. (*Source* Tables A2–A5)

The introduction continues with evidence of the other ongoing interest, which was leveraged by a specific research project and in time helped political and even business activities, though he would be decorated for his teaching:

> My interest on international finance began in preparing a term paper a term paper on the Portuguese external debt for the public finance course in the spring of 1969. I arranged to visit London, Paris and New York where I gathered material on the private placements and public loans to the Republic of Portugal. Interviews with market participants in Europe and the USA gave me opportunities to work in financial markets. This experience helped in 1993, when Portugal returned to the international bond market after the currency had become fully convertible: the Republic received the Euromoney Borrower of the Year Award and I won a special commendation in the Award for Best Finance Minister, which was given to India [...].
>
> My political experience had begun with a public statement of support to Prime Minister Cavaco Silva during the electoral campaign of 1987, and I joined the Social Democratic Party (PSD) in late 1988. I supported the second candidacy of Mario Soares to the Presidency of the Republic, was included in the PSD lists of the Porto constituency to parliament and participated in the electoral campaign in September 1991, during my annual leave from the European Commission.[...] In November 2005, I made another public statement of support to Cavaco Silva's successful bid for the Presidency of the Republic. At the end of his second term, President Jorge Sampaio awarded me the Great Cross of Henry the Navigator for my commitment to teaching economics. (www.jbmacedo.com/currieng09).

A.2 Publications

The website lists 534 (mostly) professional publications from 1970 to 2019, including published working papers, translations, chapters in edited books, presentations, etc.[3] There are also another 228 other entries from newspapers, radio and television.[4] This section includes 292 entries, divided as in the table below: books (B); book chapters (BC); comments (CMT); refereed journals (JR); other journals (OJ); policy documents (POL); prefaces to books (PREF); book reviews (REV) and unpublished working papers (WP). The number of publications by type is provided in Table A1.

The publications are provided below in Tables A2, A3, A4 and A5, whose three columns are self-explanatory: number, type (as per Table A1), year and title. The first three subsections correspond to the three parts in this volume: Economic History (and lifes of economists) with 14% of the entries, European Macroeconomics (and

[3]See www.jbmacedo.com/research. Though most contributions are not in IDEAS or RePEc, the author is in the top 5% of world economists. Working Paper #634 lists his writings and media presence (558 academic and 489 professional/popular), spanning over five decades.

[4]See www.jbmacedo.com/pt/escritos and the previous footnote.

other open-economy) with 32% and International Political Economy (and beyond) with 34%, reflecting the tilt towards international and African development issues, especially among the Community of Portuguese-speaking Countries.

The fourth subsection lists those publications absent from the 534 count mentioned above, as these were not easily subsumed into the topics of the previous three: Doctrine, policy, politics (and other issues) which includes theoretical papers in international finance and macro in addition to doctrinal material and contributions to policy documents that are deemed relevant for this volume.

Table A2 Economic History (and Lifes of Economists)

#	Type	Year	Title
1	B	(2017)	Alfredo de Sousa Evolução Recente da Economia Portuguesa 1945–1985 Estudos inéditos. (ed) with Cardoso JL, Mata ME. Imprensa das Ciências Sociais, Lisboa
2	B	(2009)	Nove Ensaios na tradição de Jorge Borges de Macedo. (ed) with Amaral L, Ferreira da Silva A, Castro Henriques A. Tribuna da História in collaboration with CG&G and IICT, Lisboa
3	B	(2005)	Jorge Borges de Macedo: Saber Continuar. (ed) Instituto Diplomático, colecção Biblioteca Diplomática série A nº 1, Lisboa
4	B	(1999)	Bem Comum dos Portugueses. with Maltez JA, Castro Henriques M. Vega, 2nd edition, Lisboa
5	B	(1996)	Currency Convertibility: The Gold Standard and Beyond. (ed) with Eichengreen B, Reis J. Routledge, London (Portuguese version available)
6	B	(1989)	Nova Economia em Portugal, Estudos em Homenagem a António Manuel Pinto Barbosa. (ed) with de Sousa A, Pereira de Moura F et al. Faculdade de Economia, UNL, Lisboa
7	B	(1970)	A Dívida Externa Portuguesa. Centro de Estudos Fiscais, Ministério das Finanças, Lisboa
8	BC	(2015)	Globalização e Governação: uma perspetiva portuguesa. In: Contente Domingues F, da Silva Horta J, David Vicente P (eds) D'aquém, d'além e d'ultramar Homenagem a António Dias Farinha. Faculdade de Letras, II (V) Lisboa, p 1771–1804
9	BC	(2008)	Duzentos anos de Europa e lusofonia em memória de Francisco Lucas Pires. In: A Revolução Europeia por Francisco Lucas Pires, Antologia de textos. Parlamento Europeu Gabinete em Portugal, Lisboa, p 113–115
10	BC	(2008)	Economic Advice and Regime Change in Portugal. In: Franco F (ed) Challenges Ahead for the Portuguese Economy. ICS, Lisboa, p 201–229
11	BC	(2001)	War, taxes and gold: the inheritance of the real. (with Ferreira da Silva A, Martins de Sousa R) In: Bordo M, Cortes-Conde R (eds) Transferring Wealth and Power from the Old to the New World. Cambridge University Press, Cambridge, p 187–228
12	BC	(2000)	Globalização: uma perspectiva nacional. In: Severiano Teixeira N, Cervaens Rodrigues J, Ferreira Nunes I (eds) O Interesse Nacional e a Globalização. Edições Cosmos Instituto de Defesa Nacional, Lisboa, p 167–178
13	BC	(2000)	Liberdades Futuras dos Portugueses. In: Estudos Jurídicos e Económicos em homenagem ao Professor João Lumbrales. Edição da Faculdade de Direito da Universidade de Lisboa, Coimbra Editora, Coimbra, p 305–344
14	BC	(2000)	Pertenças dos portugueses numa economia global. In: Estudos em homenagem ao Professor Doutor Pedro Soares Martínez. Livraria Almedina, II Ciências Jurídico-Económicas, Coimbra, p 97–134

(continued)

Table A2 (continued)

#	Type	Year	Title
15	BC	(1995)	Convertibility and Stability 1834–1994: Portuguese Currency Experience Revisited. In: Ensaios de Homenagem a Francisco Pereira de Moura. Instituto Superior de Economia e Gestão, Lisboa, p 421–438
16	BC	(1980)	Portuguese Currency Experience: An Historical Perspective. In: Estudos em Homenagem a J. J. Teixeira Ribeiro. vol. IV, Coimbra: Boletim da Faculdade de Direito, reprint, Coimbra, 46 pp
17	CMT	(1986)	Francisco Pereira de Moura, O ensino da Teoria Geral no ISCEF/ISE. Cinquentenário da Teoria Geral de Keynes. Instituto Superior de Economia, Lisboa, p 86–90
18	OJ	(2013)	Krugman's tridoc, Texts prepared for delivery at Paul Krugman's honorary doctorate by three Lisbon universities on 27 Feb. Notas Económicas, Faculdade de Economia, Coimbra
19	OJ	(2007)	Diferencialidade Portuguesa na Globalização. (with Brites Pereira L) Negócios Estrangeiros, 11(2):223–236
20	OJ	(2007)	Diferencialidade revisitada: a propósito dos lançamentos da 2ª edição revista e ilustrada de História Diplomática Portuguesa. Negócios Estrangeiros, 10 (Feb): 26–37
21	OJ	(2007)	Jorge Borges de Macedo dez anos depois (1996–2006). Special issue of Negócios Estrangeiros, 11(3): Agradecimento, 14–16: Comentário a Luís Aguiar Santos: 27–29, Depoimento Final: 92–99
22	OJ	(2006)	Por onde vai a diferencialidade portuguesa? Negócios Estrangeiros, 9(1): 38–53
23	OJ	(2005)	Dez citações de Jorge Borges de Macedo. Nova Cidadania, 25:33–36
24	OJ	(1988)	Os Prémios Nobel em Economia. Economia I (1), Jan
25	OJ	(1987)	Interdependência e Política Económica Externa. Prelo, Oct-Dec
26	OJ	(1985)	Carlos F. Diaz-Alejandro (18/7/37–17/7/85) In Memoriam. Economia IX (2) May: 381–388
27	OJ	(1982)	Tobin: Prémio Nobel. (with Barbosa M, Coutinho R) Economia VI (3), Oct
28	OJ	(1980)	Prémio Nobel: A Segunda Geração. Economia, IV (3), Oct
29	OJ	(1979)	Introdução: Grandeza e Misérias dos Estudos Portugueses, in Proceedings of a panel on the Portuguese Economy. Economia III (3):421–426 Oct
30	OJ	(1979)	Prémio Nobel do Desenvolvimento ou Desenvolvimento do Prémio Nobel. Economia III, Oct
31	OJ	(1978)	Prémio Nobel em Economia Para Herbert Simon: O "Homo Interdisciplinaris". Economia II (3), Oct
32	OJ	(1977)	Prémio Nobel para Ohlin e Meade. Economia I (3), Oct
33	PREF	(2019)	Salazar e o Saneamento Financeiro by de Sousa da Câmara J. Lisboa: Almedina, p 9–45; annex, p 237–261
34	PREF	(2006)	História Diplomática Portuguesa Constantes e Linhas de Força: Estudo de geopolítica by Borges de Macedo J 1987. 2nd edition, Lisboa: Tribuna da História, p 17–24

(continued)

Table A2 (continued)

#	Type	Year	Title
35	PREF	(2005)	A Aventura das Plantas e os Descobrimentos Portugueses by Mendes Ferrão JE. 1992, 3rd edition, IICT; Lisboa
36	PREF	(2001)	Marilu Hurt McCarty, Como os grandes economistas deram forma ao pensamento moderno os laureados do Nobel de Economia. Lisboa, p 15–22
37	WP	(2019)	Cem Anos de Crédito Externo da República, Nova SBE Working Paper nº 631 (Abstract in English)
38	WP	(2017)	Elogios e Memórias de economistas—e não só parte 1 depois da crise, Nova SBE Working Paper nº 612, 3 Jul (Abstract in English)
39	WP	(2017)	Elogios e Memórias de economistas—e não só parte 2 antes da crise, Nova SBE Working Paper nº 613, 3 Jul (Abstract in English)
40	WP	(2013)	António Manuel Pinto Barbosa, Economista e Governante, (with Soares Martínez P, Jacinto Nunes M), Nova Economics Working Paper nº 577 ver.2, Dec

Table A3 European Macroeconomics (and Other Open Economy)

#	Type	Year	
1	B	(2018)	Macro de Economia Aberta: Ensino e Prática depois de Abril. (ed) LeYa para Academia das Ciências de Lisboa, Lisboa
2	B	(2011)	Open economy dynamics: selected papers by Pentti Kouri. (ed) with Lempinen U, Taloustieto, Helsinki
3	B	(2001)	Don't fix don't float. (ed) with Cohen D, Reisen H, OECD Development Centre Study, September, preface, p 7–10 (French version available)
4	B	(1999)	Unity with Diversity in the European Economy. The Community´s Southern Frontier. (ed) with Bliss C, Cambridge University Press, Cambridge
5	B	(1986)	Custos Certos, Benefícios Incertos: Políticas Públicas Portuguesas na CEE. (ed) Associação Portuguesa de Relações Internacionais, Lisboa
.6	B	(1984)	Economic Policy in the Enlarged European Community. (ed) with de Pitta e Cunha P, Economia, Lisboa
7	B	(1982)	Portfolio Diversification and Currency Inconvertibility Three Essays in International Monetary Economics. Serviços Gráficos da Universidade Nova de Lisboa, Lisboa
8	B	(1982)	The International Monetary System Under Flexible Exchange Rates: Global, Regional and National. (ed) with Cooper R, Kenen P, and Van Ypersele J, Ballinger, Cambridge, Mass
9	B	(1981)	Portugal since the Revolution: Economic and Political Perspectives. (ed) with Serfaty S, Westview Press, Boulder, Colorado

(continued)

Table A3 (continued)

#	Type	Year	
10	B	(1977)	Interdependência Económica, Sistema Monetário Internacional e Integração Portuguesa. Banco de Fomento Nacional, Lisboa
11	BC	(2013)	A estratégia de Portugal para a economia aberta. In: As Conferências da FEP-UP com os Ministros das Finanças desde o 25 de Abril de 1974. fevereiro-maio 2012. Assumir a responsabilidade pelo passado-projetar o futuro. Fronteira do Caos Editores, Porto, p 69–81
12	BC	(2012)	Actualité de Robert Triffin. In: Koeune JC, Lamfalussy A (dir./eds) A la recherche d'un nouvel ordre monétaire mondial/In Search of a New World Monetary Order. PIE Peter Lang pour Fondation Internationale Robert Triffin, Brussels, p 125–128
13	BC	(2011)	Nem Estabilidade nem Crescimento? In: Paz Ferreira E, Lobo C, Palma CC (eds) PEC: Programa de Estabilidade ou Crescimento? Colóquios IDEFF, nº 4, Jan, Lisboa, p 77–92
14	BC	(2010)	Saudades do bom aluno. In: Miranda J, Menezes Cordeiro A, Paz Ferreira E, Duarte Nogueira J (eds) Estudos em homenagem ao Professor Doutor Paulo de Pitta e Cunha. vol II Economia, Finanças Públicas e Direito Fiscal, Almedina, Coimbra, p 319–348
15	BC	(2007)	A mudança do regime cambial português: Um balanço 15 anos depois de Maastricht. In: Andersen Leitão N (ed) Vinte anos de integração europeia (1986–2006)—o testemunho português. Edições Cosmos, Lisboa. p 91–137
16	BC	(2007)	As reformas não podem parar: regresso ao contributo português para a convergência europeia. In: Laíns P, Costa Lobo M (eds) Em nome da Europa Portugal em Mudança (1986–2006). Principia, Lisboa, p 59–75
17	BC	(2007)	Competitividade portuguesa na economia global. In: Porto M, Silva B (ed) Uma Sociedade Criadora de Emprego. Almedina. Lisboa, p 123–156
18	BC	(2005)	A economia portuguesa dentro de trinta anos. In: 25 de Abril: Os desafios para Portugal nos próximos trinta anos. Presidência do Conselho de Ministros, Comissão das Comemorações dos 30 anos do 25 de Abril. Imprensa Nacional, Lisboa, p 15–25
19	BC	(2004)	Float in order to fix? Lessons from emerging markets for new EU member countries. (with Reisen H) In: Szapary G, von Hagen J (eds) Monetary strategies for joining the euro. Edgar Elgar: National Bank of Hungary, Budapest, p 109–133
20	BC	(2004)	Moving the escudo into the euro. (with Catela Nunes L, Covas F), In: Landersmann M, Rosati D (eds) Shaping the New Europe: Economic Policy Challenges of EU Enlargement. Palgrave Macmillan, New York, p 246–264
21	BC	(2003)	Europa seguro contra a voracidade. In: Tavares Ribeiro MM, Barbosa de Melo, Porto M (eds) Portugal e a Construção Europeia. Livraria Almedi na, Coimbra, p 217–234
22	BC	(2003)	Portugal's European Integration: the good student with a bad fiscal constitution. In: Royo S, Manuel PPC (eds) Spain and Portugal in the European Union The first fifteen years. Frank Cass, London

(continued)

Table A3 (continued)

#	Type	Year	
23	BC	(2003)	Portugal's European Integration: the limits of external pressure. In: Monteiro F, Tavares J, Glatzer M, Cardoso A (eds) Portugal: Strategic Options in a European Context. Lexington Books, Landham, Md, p 61–97
24	BC	(2001)	Crises? What Crises? Escudo from ECU to EMU. In: Griffith-Jones S, Montes M, Nasution A (eds), Short-Term Capital Flows and Economic Crises. Study prepared for UNU/WIDER, Oxford University Press, Oxford, p 253–260
25	BC	(2001)	Financial Crises: a Eurocentric perception. In: Abreu M, and Mendes V (eds) What financial system for the year 2000? ISEG, Lisboa, p 109–126
26	BC	(2001)	The European Payments Union and its Implications for the Evolution of the International Financial Architecture (with Eichengreen B), In: Lamfalussy A, Snoy B, Wilson J (eds) Fragility of the International Financial System—How can we prevent new crises in emerging markets? PIE Peter Lang pour Fondation Internationale Robert Triffin, Brussels, p 25–42
27	BC	(2000)	Convergence, démocratie et cohésion: existe-t-il une approche européenne du développement? In: Rapport Moral sur l´Argent dans le Monde. Montchrétien, Paris, p 203–217
28	BC	(2000)	Portugal's European Integration: lessons for enlargement. In Tang H(ed) Winners and Losers of EU Integration - Policy Issues for Central and Eastern Europe. The World Bank: Washington DC, p 290–310
29	BC	(2000)	Portugal's European Integration. In: Bara Z, Csaba L(eds) Small Economies Adjustment to Global Tendencies. Aula Publishing Co. Ltd, Budapest, p 115–128
30	BC	(1999)	Converging European Transitions. In: Dimitrov M, Andreff W, Csaba L(eds) Economies in Transition and the Variety of Capitalisms: Features, Changes, Convergence. Gorex Press, Sofia, p 13–41
31	BC	(1998)	Generational Accounting in Portugal. (with Auerbach A, Kotlikoff L, Braz J, Walliser J). In: Auerbach A, Kotlikoff L, Leibfritz W (eds) Generational Accounting around the World. University of Chicago Press, Chicago, p 471–488
32	BC	(1998)	Portugal. In: Fukasaku K, Hausmann R (eds) Democracy, Decentralisation and Deficits in Latin America. OECD, Inter-American Development Bank, Paris, p 191–200
33	BC	(1996)	Portugal and European Monetary Union: Selling Stability at Home, Earning Credibility Abroad. In: Torres F (ed) Monetary Reform in Europe. Universidade Católica Portuguesa, Lisboa, p 23–58
34	BC	(1995)	Credibilidade da Mudança em Portugal 1989–1992. In: Loureiro J (ed) Portugal e a Integração Monetária Europeia. UP, Porto, p 143–151
35	BC	(1994)	European Union and Cohesion. In: Europaische Antagonismen. Swiss Institute of International Affairs, Zurich, p 33–57
36	BC	(1992)	Labour Mobility, Fiscal Solidarity and the Exchange Rate Regime: a Parable of European Union and Cohesion. In: Fair DE, Boissieu C (eds) Fiscal Policy, Taxation and the Financial System in an Increasingly Integrated Europe. Ruswes Academic Publishers, Dordrecht, p 263–280

(continued)

Table A3 (continued)

#	Type	Year	
37	BC	(1992)	The Path of Reform in the Soviet Union. (with Pisani-Ferry J) In: Clesse A, Tokes R (eds) Preventing a New East–West Divide: The Economic and Social Imperatives of the Future Europe. Nomos, Baden-Baden, p 292–301
38	BC	(1991)	Economic Reform in Central and Eastern Europe, The Next Steps. (with Pearce J) In: Clark D, Mandelbaum M (eds) Politics, Economics and Western Policy in the Post-Communist Era. Aspen Institute, Boulder
39	BC	(1991)	Política Externa Portuguesa: Uma Abordagem Económica. In: Portugal em Mudança, Ensaios sobre a Actividade do XI Governo Constitucional. Imprensa Nacional Casa da Moeda, Lisboa, p 157–238
40	BC	(1991)	Unidade com Diversidade na Economia Europeia. In: Portugal e a Transição para a União Económica e Monetária. Ministério das Finanças, Lisboa, p 17–28
41	BC	(1990)	Financial Liberalization and Exchange Rate Policy in the Newly Integrating Countries of the European Community. In: Ferri P (ed) Prospects for the European Monetary System. Macmillan, London, p 178–194
42	BC	(1990)	Implicit Taxes and Credit Ceilings: The Treasury and the Banks in Portugal. (with Beleza LM), in Silva Lopes J, Beleza LM (eds) Portugal and the Internal Market of the EEC. Banco de Portugal, Lisboa, p 57–72
43	BC	(1990)	Interest Differentials, Financial Integration and EMS Shadowing: A Note on Portugal with a Comparison to Spain. (with Torres F) In: Silva Lopes J,, Beleza LM (eds) Portugal and the Internal Market of the EEC. Banco de Portugal, Lisboa, p 173–180
44	BC	(1990)	Portugal's Twenty-Five EFTA Years. In: EFTA Countries in a Changing Europe: 30th Anniversary Round Table. EFTA, Geneva
45	BC	(1989)	Le Portugal et l'Europe: La Transition la Plus Longue. In: d'Haenens A (ed) L'Europe d'Aujours'hui, Artis-Historia. Brussels, p 123–135 (English version available)
46	BC	(1988)	Perspectives on Financial Liberalization in the Newly Integrating Countries of the European Community. In: European Economy (French version available)
47	BC	(1987)	Portugal and Europe: the longest transition. In: Erkenntnis und Entscheidung die Weltproblematike in Wissenschaft und Praxis. Europaisches Forum Alpbach, Austrian College, Vienna
48	BC	(1985)	Experiências de liberalização do Mercado de capitais: relevância para o caso português. In: Reforma do Mercado de Capitais, Instituto Francisco Sá Carneiro. Lisboa, p 37–65
49	BC	(1984)	International Portfolio Diversification: Short-Term Financial Assets and Gold. (with Goldstein J, Meerschwam D) In: Bilson J, Marston R (eds) Exchange Rate Theory and Practice. University of Chicago Press, Chicago, p 192–232 (NBER Reprint 593)

(continued)

Table A3 (continued)

#	Type	Year	
50	BC	(1984)	Portugal and Europe: The Dilemmas of Integration. In: Bruneau T, da Rosa V, MacLeod A (eds) Portugal in Development: Emigration, Industrialization and the European Community. University of Ottawa Press, Ottawa
51	BC	(1983)	A Portfolio Model of an Inconvertible Currency: The Recent Experience of Portugal. In: de Cecco M(ed) International Economic Adjustment. Basil Blackwell. Oxford
52	BC	(1981)	Perspectives on the Stagflation of the 1970's. (with Kouri P) In: Giersch H(ed) Macroeconomic Policies for Growth: The European Perspective. J.C.B. Mohr, Tubingen
53	BC	(1981)	Portugal e a Europa: Deslizar ou Flutuar? In: Intereuropa and Trade Policy Research Center, Portugal e o Alargamento das Comunidades Europeias. Lisboa, p 171–200
54	CMT	(2012)	Eichengreen B, Rose A Flexing your Muscles: Abandoning Fixed Exchange Rates for Greater Flexibility. International Seminar on Macroeconomics 2011, Frankel JF, Pissarides C (eds) University of Chicago Press for NBER, Chicago, p 392–399
55	CMT	(1990)	Borges A Portuguese Banking in the Single European Market. European Banking in the 1990s. Dermine J (ed), Basil Blackwell, Oxford, p 328–334
56	CMT	(1989)	Bruni F, Penati A, Porta A Implicit Taxes and Fiscal Adjustment in Italy. In Monti M (ed) Fiscal Policy Economic Adjustment and Financial Markets. IMF, Washington, p 235–243
57	CMT	(1983)	Mateus A Crescimento Económico e Dívida Externa - O Caso de Portugal. In: Seminário sobre Crescimento Económico e Dívida Externa - O Caso de Portugal. Instituto de Estudos para o Desenvolvimento, Caderno 8, Lisboa
58	CMT	(1981)	Dornbusch R Portugal's Crawling Peg In: Williamson (ed) Exchange Rate Rules: The Theory, Performance and Prospects of the Crawling Peg. Macmillan, London, p 272–278
59	JR	(2001)	The euro in the international financial architecture. Acta Oeconomica, 51 (3):287–314
60	JR	(2000)	Converging European Transitions. The World Economy, 23 (10):1335–1365
61	JR	(1989)	Public Debt and Implicit Taxes: The Experience of Portugal. (with Sebastião M), European Economic Review, 33(2–3):573–579
62	JR	(1979)	The Economic Consequences of the April 25th Revolution. (with Krugman P), Economia, III (3):435–483 (Economic Growth Center Paper 299)
63	JR	(1978)	Exchange Rates and the International Adjustment Process. (with Kouri P), Brookings Papers on Economic Activity, Sep (Cowles Foundation Paper 464)
64	OJ	(2019)	Portugal na Zona Euro. Memórias da Academia das Ciências de Lisboa - Classe de Letras, tomo XL, volume 2, Sep:35–46

(continued)

Table A3 (continued)

#	Type	Year	
65	OJ	(2007)	A comparative view on reform complementarities. Revue d'Économie Politique 117(4) July–August:601–605
66	OJ	(2002)	Uma dinâmica para o bem comum europeu, Euro para além da moeda número especial da revista do IEEI. Estratégia, nº 17 2º semestre: 39–45
67	OJ	(1999)	Relações monetárias entre a zona do euro e os Estados-membros. In: Aspectos Jurídicos e Económicos da Introdução do Euro. Revista da Faculdade de Direito, Lisboa:55–62
68	OJ	(1997)	Mercados Financeiros Internacionais e Cidadania Portuguesa In: Direito dos Valores Mobiliários. Lex, Lisboa, 1997:15–25
69	OJ	(1996)	Portugal e a União Monetária Europeu: ganhar credibilidade externa vender estabilidade internamente. Análise Social,138, vol. XXI,4:895–924
70	OJ	(1993)	Les Leçons de la Crise des Changes. De Pecunia, Agosto:29–32
71	OJ	(1992)	Convergência Europeia: O Contributo Português. Análise Social nº 118/119, número especial dedicado a Portugal e a Integração Europeia: Balanço e Perspectivas:623–654
72	OJ	(1989)	Consequências Económicas de 1992 para os Sindicatos. Revista dos Quadros Técnicos do Estado, IV (3),Maio/Julho
73	OJ	(1989)	Perspectives sur la Libéralisation Financière: Grèce, Espagne, Portugal. Revue d' Economie Financière nº 8/9, Março-Junho:112–123
74	OJ	(1987)	Aproveitar o Ambiente Macroeconómico Estável. Cadernos de Economia, APEC,Nov
75	OJ	(1987)	Finança e Confiança. Cadernos do IEP, Nov
76	OJ	(1986)	Integração Europeia: Fim do Princípio ou Princípio do Fim? Factos e Ideias, CERI, Universidade do Minho II nº 3
77	OJ	(1986)	Multinacionais, Estado e Empresas Nacionais: Códigos ou Estratégias? Nação e Defesa nº 40, Oct-Dec
78	OJ	(1985)	Integração Europeia: Fim do Princípio ou Princípio do Fim? Economia, IX (3), Oct
79	OJ	(1985)	Sobre a Liberalização Económica em Portugal. Risco, I(2)
80	OJ	(1984)	Portugal e a Comunidade Europeia: Transição Socialista para o Livre-Câmbio? Indústria em Revista, March
81	OJ	(1981)	O Sistema Monetário Europeu: Comentário. Economia, V(3), Outubro
82	OJ	(1981)	Dilemas da Integração Europeia. Nação e Defesa, 18, Apr-Jun:69–104
83	OJ	(1976)	Entrevista ao grupo do MIT. Nação e Defesa, ano 1, Nov:185–195
84	OJ	(1970)	O Mercado das Euro-emissões. Revista Bancária, Jan
85	POL	(1995)	Multiple allegiances as fate: The Portuguese idea of Europe presented at FLAD. November, Available online www.jbmacedo.com/papers/fate.html. Accessed 29 March 2020
86	POL	(1990)	One Market One Money: An evaluation of the benefits and costs of forming an economic and monetary union. European Economy, nº 44, Oct. (Ch 9)

(continued)

Table A3 (continued)

#	Type	Year	
87	POL	(1990)	Stabilization Liberalization and Devolution: Assessment of the economic situation and reform process in the Soviet Union. European Economy, n°45, Oct
88	REV	(1981)	Portugal: Revolutionary Change in an Open Economy. Morrison R, The World Economy 4, Dec
89	REV	(1981)	The Economic Transformation of Spain and Portugal. Baklanoff E, Journal of Comparative Economics, Dec
90	WP	(2017)	Reform complementarity and policy coordination in Europe: a view from Portugal. CIGI Paper n° 132, Jun 6
91	WP	(1989)	The Timing and Sequencing of Trade Liberalization Policies: Portugal 1948–86. (with Corado C, Porto M) Nova Economics Working Paper n° 114, Mar

Table A4 International Political Economy (and Beyond)

#	Type	Year	Title
1	B	(2015)	Writing to Queens while Crises Proceed In memory of Manuel Jacinto Nunes. (ed) Instituto de Investigação Científica Tropical and Center for Globalization & Governance, 2nd edition, enlarged, Lisboa
2	B	(2005)	Parcerias Público-Privadas e Integração Económica na África austral. (ed) with Feijó C, 2nd edition, IICT and Universidade Católica de Angola, Lisboa
3	B	(2002)	Development is Back. (ed) with Foy C, Oman CP, Paris: OECD De-velopment Centre (French version available)
4	B	(1989)	Debt, Stabilization and Development, Essays in Memory of Carlos Diaz Alejandro. (ed) with Calvo G, Findlay R, Kouri P, Blackwell for WIDER, Oxford
5	BC	(2016)	Cape Verde and Mozambique as Development Successes in Sub Saharan Africa. (with Brites Pereira L) In: Edwards S, Johnson S. Weil DN (eds) African successes. Volume IV, University of Chicago Press for NBER, Chicago, p 203–294
6	BC	(2015)	A globalização liberta aproximando. 3° Encontro Presente no Futuro À procura da liberdade. Fundação Francisco Manuel dos Santos, Lisboa, p 115–119
7	BC	(2015)	Lisbon meetings and global lusophonia rising, 25 years of Cooperation among Central Banks. Banco de Portugal, Lisbon: 82–84 (Portuguese edition available)

(continued)

Table A4 (continued)

#	Type	Year	Title
8	BC	(2014)	Cape Verde's Foreign Policy: an economic perspective. (with Brites Pereira L) In: Pina Delgado J, Barros Varela O, Costa S (editors) As Relações Externas de Cabo Verde: (Re) Leituras Contemporâneas. Edições ISCJ, Praia, p 229–266
9	BC	(2013)	Globalisation et Gouvernance tous azimuts In: Actes du colloque "La démocratie, enrayée? Académie Royale de Belgique, Brussels, p 75–96
10	BC	(2013)	Writing to Queens while Crises Proceed. (with Santos JFP, Malhó R) In: Rodrigues V, Martins AC, Duarte MC, Carvalho MO, Antunes LF (eds) Science in the Tropics: Glimpsing at the past, projecting the future. IICT, April, bilingual brochure with DVD, Lisbon, p 1–33
11	BC	(2012)	A Língua Portuguesa e o seu valor económico no contexto da lusofonia e da economia global. In: Livro de Actas Formando Conhecimento Diálogos de Internacionalização. AICEP: Lisboa, p 41—46
12	BC	(2011)	Global crisis and national policy responses: together alone? In: Renaud M, Marcelo G (eds) Ética, Crise e Sociedade. Húmus, V.N. Famalicão, p 91–159
13	BC	(2011)	Peer pressure to meet G20 commitments. A promising innovation? In: Brem M (ed) The G20 Agenda and Process: Analysis and Insight by CIGI Experts, p 30–31
14	BC	(2009)	How globalisation improves governance. (with Bonaglia F, Bussolo M) In: Yueh L (ed) The Law and Economics of Globalisation. Edward Elgar, London, p 193–224
15	BC	(2007)	Financial Reputation and Foreign Exchange Markets: The Pataca in comparison with the Cabo Verde Escudo and other Exotic Currencies. (with Brites Pereira L) In: Foreign Trade Law in the context of China relations with Portuguese Speaking Countries. University of Macau, Macau p 1–32
16	BC	(2006)	Comparative development and institutional change. In: Stathakis G, Vaggi G (eds) Economic development and social change. Routledge Studies in the History of Economics, Routledge, Milton Park, UK p 74–96
17	BC	(2005)	Argentina and Brazil Risk: a Eurocentric tale. (with Grandes M) In: Langhammer R, Vinhas de Souza L (eds) Monetary policy and macroeconomic stabilization in Latin America. Springer, Berlin, p 153–172
18	BC	(2003)	Development, Peer Pressure and Democracy. (with Foy C) in Chung CS, Park J (eds) National Visions and Strategies. KDI School of Public Policy and Management, OECD and World Bank, Paris, p xvii–xxxv
19	BC	(2003)	Globalisation and Governance: Main Results of the OECD Development Centre Programme of Work 2001/2002. OECD, Paris, May (preface), 68 pp (French version available)
20	BC	(2002)	La Chine et sa séquence de modernisation. (with Burgeat E) In: La Mondialisation et la Chine—Actes du Colloque présidé par M. Olivier Giscard d' Estaing. Fondation Singer-Polignac, Paris, p 85–96

(continued)

Table A4 (continued)

#	Type	Year	Title
21	BC	(2002)	Reducing Poverty under Global Finance. (with Blommestein H) In: Borghi M, Postiglione Blommestein L (eds) For an Effective Right to Food. University Press Fribourg, Switzerland, p 167–183
22	BC	(2002)	Sécurité internationale, démocratie et développement. In: Boniface P (ed) Le 11 Septembre un an après. IRIS, Presses Universitaires de France, Paris, p 153–158
23	BC	(2002)	Sustainable development and social protection in East Asia. (with Fukasaku K, Hiemenz U) In: Towards Asia's Sustainable development: the role of social protection. OECD, Paris, p 415–430
24	BC	(2002)	Armadilhas do determinismo histórico e geográfico. In: Pinho M(ed) Produtividade e Crescimento em Portugal. Economia Pura, Lisboa, p 17–26
25	BC	(2001)	Globalisation and Institutional Change: a development perspective. In: Malinvaud E, Sabourin L (eds) Globalisation, Ethical and Institutional Concerns. Pontifical Academy for Social Sciences, Vatican, p 223–268
26	BC	(2000)	Um relacionamento económico e financeiro mais durável entre Portugal e Brasil. In: Cavalcanti de Albuquerque R, Romão A (eds) O diálogo dos 500 anos Brasil*Portugal desenvolvimento e cooperação. EMC Edições, Rio de Janeiro, p 459–476
27	BC	(1996)	Europa e Lusofonia, Política e Financeira: Uma Interpretação. In: Ensaios de Homenagem a Manuel Jacinto Nunes. Instituto Superior de Economia e Gestão, Lisboa, p 53–72
28	BC	(1992)	Economia, Ética e suas Implicações de Política. In: Estudos em Homenagem a Jorge Borges de Macedo. Instituto Nacional de Investigação Cientifica, Lisboa, p 613–622
29	BC	(1990)	The Constitution and the Economy. In: Maxwell K, Monje S (eds) Portugal: The Constitution and the Consolidation of Democracy, 1976–1989. Camões Center Special Report nº 2, Columbia University, New York
30	BC	(1989)	A Constituição como Bloqueio da Sociedade Portuguesa. In: Baptista Coelho M (ed) Portugal—O Sistema Político e Constitucional 1974–1987. Instituto de Ciências Sociais, Lisboa, p 801–812
31	BC	(1987)	Currency Inconvertibility, Trade Taxes and Smuggling. In: Bardhan P, Behrman J, Fishlow A (eds) International Trade Investment, Macro Policies and History. Amsterdam
32	BC	(1987)	Small Countries in Monetary Unions: The Choice of Senegal. In: Gersovitz M, Waterbury J (eds) The Political Economy of Risk and Choice in Senegal. Frank Cass, London
33	BC	(1986)	Collective Pegging to a Single Currency: The West African Monetary Union. In: Edwards S, Ahamed L (eds) The Real Exchange Rate and Adjustment in Developing Countries. The University of Chicago Press, Chicago, p 333–362 (NBER Reprint 999)

(continued)

Table A4 (continued)

#	Type	Year	Title
34	BC	(1986)	Trade and Financial Interdependence under Flexible Exchange Rates. The Pacific Area. In: Tan A, Kapur B(eds) Pacific Trade and Financial Interdependence. Brian and Unwin Australia, Sydney, p 277–284 (Princeton Reprint in International Finance 25, NBER Reprint 700)
35	BC	(1985)	Exchange Rate Volatility in an Interdependent World Economy. In: Supplement to Word Economic Survey 1984. United Nations, New York (Spanish and French version available)
36	BC	(1985)	Macroeconomic Policy Under Currency Inconvertibility. In: Connolly M, McDermott J (eds) The Economics of the Caribbean Basin. Praeger Publishers, New York, p 336–355
37	BC	(1985)	O Estado nas Nações Pobres. In: César Neves J (ed) Pobreza, Perspectivas de Análise Pluri-Disciplinar. Universidade Católica Portuguesa, Lisboa
38	BC	(1985)	Políticas Anti-Inflacionistas no Processo de Ajustamento. In: Silva Lopes J (ed) Ajustamento e Crescimento na Actual Conjuntura Económica Mundial. IMF, Washington
39	BC	(1985)	Princípios Gerais da Organização Económica. In: Estudos sobre a Constituição. vol. I, Petrony, Lisboa, p 189–206
40	BC	(1985)	Profitability, Employment and Structural Adjustment in France. (with Kouri P, Viscio A) In: Melitz J, Wyplosz C (eds) The French Economy: Theory and Policy. Westview Press, Boulder
41	BC	(1983)	A Ilógica do Sistema Constitucional Português. In: Centro de Estudos Fiscais, Estudos, vol. I, Comemoração do XX aniversário. Imprensa Nacional-Casa da Moeda, Lisboa, p 213–237
42	CMT	(2002)	Krueger A, Yoo J, Chaebol Capitalism and the Currency-Financial Crisis in Korea. In: Edwards S, Frankel J (eds) Preventing Currency Crises in Emerging Markets. The University of Chicago Press for NBER, Chicago, p 649–658
43	CMT	(2001)	Kaminski A, Kaminski B Convergence in transition: the challenge of subverting corruption. In: Economic Survey of Europe. nº 2, UN Economic Comission for Europe, Geneva, p 145–147
44	CMT	(1999)	Global Financial Turmoil and Reform: A United Nations Perspective. Herman B (ed), The United Nations University Press, Tokyo, p 438–447
45	CMT	(1997)	Berthélemy JC, Valousdakis A Financial Development, Savings and Growth Convergence: a Panel Data Approach. In: Hausmann R, Reisen H (eds) Promoting Savings in Latin America. OECD and Inter-American Development Bank, Paris, p 71–76
46	CMT	(1991)	Calvo G, Frenkel J The Transformation of Centrally Planned Economies. In: Winckler G (ed) Enduring Reform in Eastern Europe. Central and Eastern Europe: Roads to Growth. International Monetary Fund and Austrian National Bank, Vienna
47	CMT	(1989)	Powell A, Gilbert C The Use of Commodity Contracts for the Management of Developing Country Commodity Risks. In: Currie D, Vines D (eds) Macroeconomic Interactions Between North and South. Cambridge University Press, Cambridge p 180–184

(continued)

Table A4 (continued)

#	Type	Year	Title
48	CMT	(1988)	McKinnon R, Financial Liberalization and Economic Development: Interest Rate Policies in LDCs. In: Ranis G, Schultz TP (eds) The State of Development Economics. Basil Blackwell, Oxford, p 411–415
49	CMT	(1984)	Kouri P, A Europa na Economia Mundial. In: de Pitta e Cunha P (ed) Política Económica na Comunidade Europeia Alargada. Intereuropa, Lisboa
50	CMT	(1983)	Oudiz G, Sachs J International Policy Coordination in Dynamic Macroeconomic Models. In: Buiter W, Marston R (eds) International Coordination of Economic Policy. Cambridge University Press; Cambridge
51	CMT	(1983)	Mairesse J, Dormont B Labour and Investment Demand at the Firm Level: A Comparison of French, German and U.S. Manufacturing. ISOM. European Economic Review
52	CMT	(1993)	Minc A, Lucena D. Sociedade de Valores Culturais e Desenvolvimento. In: Patrício Gouveia T (ed), Dom Quixote, Lisboa, p175-181
53	JR	(2013)	Are complementary reforms a "luxury" in developing countries? (with Oliveira Martins, Rocha B) Journal of Comparative Economics 42(2):417–435
54	JR	(2009)	Comparing Exchange Market Pressure across Five African Countries. (with Brites Pereira L, Mendonça Reis A) Open Economies Review: 20(5):645–682
55	JR	(2008)	Growth, Reform indicators and Policy complementarities. (with Joaquim Oliveira Martins) Economics of Transition 16(2):141–164
56	JR	(1982)	Currency Diversification and Export Competitiveness: A Model of the "Dutch Disease" in Egypt. Journal of Development Economics, 11 (NBER Reprint 378)
57	JR	(1982)	Profitability, Employment and Structural Adjustment in France. (with Kouri P, Viscio A). Annales de I' INSEE, n°s 47–48:85–112 (French version available)
58	OJ	(2019)	Sobre a Lusofonia Global. Memórias da Academia das Ciências de Lisboa—Classe de Letras, tomo XL, volume 1, Sep:273–88
59	OJ	(2014)	A globalização liberta ou apavora? Lucere, special issue UCAN, Luanda, Setembro: 147–165
60	OJ	(2014)	Mutual knowledge and global lusofonia. Capital, Maputo, October (available in Portuguese)
61	OJ	(2006)	Liberdade financeira e cooperação inter temporal. Cadernos de Economia n° 74:80–89
62	OJ	(2006)	Segurança, desenvolvimento e o "espírito de Bissau". Revista de Segurança e Defesa, ano 1 n° 1, Nov:56–61
63	OJ	(2005)	Vinte e cinco anos económicos. O Mundo em Português, special 25th anniversary issue, Oct: 19–20
64	OJ	(2004)	Melhorar o conhecimento mútuo dos países da CPLP através de parcerias público-privadas. Estratégia, n° 20 1° semestre, Instituto de Estudos Estratégicos e Internacionais:183–195

(continued)

Table A4 (continued)

#	Type	Year	Title
65	OJ	(2003)	Public Private Partnerships for Development. (with Braz J, Mantero F), OrienteOcidente EastWest, Number 11 May–August, Instituto Internacional de Macau, 15 pp
66	OJ	(2002)	Constituição fiscal e voracidade. Nova Cidadania, October:18–22
67	OJ	(2000)	Mercado monetário e de valores mobiliários: relações de dependência à escala mundial. Direito dos Valores Mobiliários, vol. II, Coimbra Editora:9–29
68	OJ	(1999)	Governo, Pertenças e Liberdades. Brotéria, vol. 149 nº 1 Jul: 7–28 e nº 2/3 Aug/Sep pp. 149–184 reprinted in Economia e Prospectiva, vol. II nº3/4, Oct/Mar:75–122
69	OJ	(1997)	Liberdades e Pertenças dos Portugueses: Lições para Sul e para Leste. Revista Luso-Africana de Direito, vol 1:327–338
70	OJ	(1995)	Acompanhamento e Apreciação Parlamentar dos Assuntos Europeus. LEGISLAÇÃO, Cadernos de Ciência de Legislação, INA, nº 13/14 Apr/Dec, Lisboa
71	OJ	(1991)	Coesão e União Europeias: O Exemplo de Portugal. Revista da Banca, Jun/Sep
72	OJ	(1990)	Ajuda Externa e Ajustamento Estrutural: Uma Perspectiva Luso-Comunitária. (with Abreu O), Nova Economia
73	OJ	(1990)	As Grandes Mudanças a Sul e a Leste ou Três Ds da África do Sul à União Soviética. Revista ELO, nº 1, Set/Oct
74	OJ	(1989)	Nota Prévia do Relator do Bloco II, Políticas e Processos de Desenvolvimento e Subdesenvolvimento, Conferência internacional "Desenvolvimento e Subdesenvolvimento em África: Teorias, Ideologias, Políticas e Processos". Revista Internacional de Estudos Africanos, nº 10–11:133–140
75	OJ	(1987)	Currency Inconvertibility, Trade Taxes and Smuggling. Journal of Development Economics, vol 27:109–125; special issue Essays in Memory of Carlos F. Diaz Alejandro
76	OJ	(1985)	A Vintage Model of Supply Applied to French Manufacturing (with Kouri P, Viscio A), Economia, IX (1):159–193 (NBER Reprint 657)
77	OJ	(1984)	Portugal, Spain and the World Economy: Challenge and Response? (with Sebastião M), Assuntos Europeus, (3), Oct:141–154
78	POL	(2007)	Cumprir Bissau. Nova Cidadania, ano IX nº 34 Oct-Dec: 48–49
79	POL	(2004)	Moçambique: Melhor Estado Melhor Ambiente de Negócios. organizer (with Cardosos A), conference of África Hoje magazine with the support of IICT, Mar
80	POL	(2003)	Angola: Melhor Estado Melhor Ambiente de Negócios. organizer (with Cardosos A), conference of África Hoje magazine with the support of IICT, Aug
81	POL	(1980)	Portugal and Africa since the Revolution, in Hearing Before the Subcommittee on Africa of the Committee on Foreign Affairs, U.S. Interests in Africa. U.S. Government Printing Office, Washington, D.C. (Portuguese version Nação e Defesa, 14)

(continued)

Table A4 (continued)

#	Type	Year	Title
82	PREF	(2018)	O Último Ultramarino by Xavier de Figueiredo.Ulisseia, Lisboa p 5–13.3
83	PREF	(2017)	"Sabre, silêncio e saudades", Pearl Harbor Lisboa Tóquio by Morito M. Portuguese translation, Ad Litteram, Lisboa, p 9–17
84	PREF	(2015)	131 anos em imagem. IICT, Lisboa 31 Jul
85	PREF	(2008)	Futuro e história da lusofonia global. Rodrigues MJ (ed), Lisboa: IICT (11 contributions listed in pt/escritos)
86	PREF	(2008)	Autonomia de Angola by José de Macedo, 1910. 3rd edition, IICT; Lisboa
87	PREF	(2005)	Empresas portuguesas e mercados lusófonos. 2nd edition, IICT; Lisboa
88	PREF	(1997)	Roque FM, Construir o Futuro em Angola. CELTA editora, Lisboa; xi-xv
89	PREF	(1997)	Crespo A, Empresas e Emprego na Moeda Única. "Introdução: Macroeconomia para as pessoas", Edições Sílabo, Lisboa: 9–29
90	PREF	(1995)	Crespo A, Portugal Economia Aberta, Sílabo; Lisboa
91	PREF	(1991)	Roque FM et al., Economia de Angola. Bertrand, Lisboa: 7–11
92	PREF	(1990)	César das Neves J, Equilíbrio da Pobreza. Lisboa: Ciência e Técnica Fiscal: 11–14
93	REV	(2014)	Maria Costa A, The Checkmate Pendulum: from fiction to reality. Available on-line. www.the-checkmate-pendulum.com. Accessed 29 March 2020
94	WP	(2018)	Antevendo mais lusofonia e outras memórias lusófilas. Nova SBE Working Paper nº 622 (Abstract in English)
95	WP	(2017)	Carta à Rainha Lusófona: Esboço e Interpretação. Nova SBE Working Paper nº 611 (Abstract in English)
96	WP	(2017)	Science for development and EU-Africa advanced training partnerships: the case of TropiKMan PhD (with Melo AP) In: African Higher Ed-ucation Week and RUFORUM, Fifth Biennial Conference 2016″, Cape Town
97	WP	(2014)	Interdépendance, liberté et développement international. Fondation pour les études et recherches sur le développement international (FERDI), document de travail politiques de développement nº 86, Feb
98	WP	(2013)	Globalization, Democracy and Development. (with Oliveira Martins J, Jalles J, Brites Pereira L), NBER Working Paper nº 19,575, Oct
99	WP	(2009)	Drivers of China's Foreign Direct Investment into Africa: How Specific? (with Brites Pereira L, Lopes JM), Nova Economics Working Paper nº 544, Aug
100	WP	(2006)	Exchange market pressure and the credibility of Macau's currency board (with Braz J, Brites Pereira L, Catela Nunes L), Nova Economics Working Paper nº 492, Sep
101	WP	(2006)	The Credibility of Cabo Verde's Currency Peg. (with Brites Pereira L) Nova Economics Working Paper nº 494, Sep

(continued)

Table A4 (continued)

#	Type	Year	Title
102	WP	(2002)	Development Redux: Reflections for a new paradigm. Presented at a conference promoted by CzechAid, Prague 12 Sep, OECD Development Working Paper n°215
103	WP	(1987)	"Locomotive" and Other Channels of Transmission Under Flexible Exchange Rates. (with Meerschwam D), CEPR Discussion Paper n° 165, Mar
104	WP	1983	Policy Interdependence Under Flexible Exchange Rates. Woodrow Wilson School Discussion Paper in Economics 64, Oct

Table A5 Doctrine, Policy, Politics (and Other Issues)

#	Type	Year	Title
1	B	(1999)	Sustaining Social Security. guest editor and contributor. United Nations; New York
2	B	(1977)	Fundamentos da Microeconomia. Lisboa (collection of entries from Verbo- Enciclopédia Luso-Brasileira de Cultura)
3	B	(1976)	Noções de Análise Económica. 2nd edition, Textos Defesa Nacional; Lisboa
4	BC	(2017)	Diversidade da Lusofonia, no Espaço e no Tempo. In: Baptista FP (ed) Homenagem ao Papa Francisco por ocasião da sua vinda a Fátima. Edições Piaget, Lisboa, p 487–8
5	BC	(2014)	Programa Doutoral em Saber Tropical e Gestão—Lusofonia Global no Ensino Superior. (with Capece B, Abernathy D, Melo A), A importância da Difusão das Línguas Portuguesa e Chinesa para a Colaboração Académica no Ensino Superior e Promoção do Turismo. XXIV Encontro da AULP, Macau, p 285–290
6	BC	(2011)	Use (less) value and MDGs. (with de Macedo A) USELESS. babel, Lisboa: 191–210 (available in Portuguese)
7	BC	(2004)	Partnerships: the essential role of the state. In: Feinstein O, Ingram GK, Liebenthal A (eds) Evaluation and Development—The Partnership Dimension. Transaction, London and New Brunswick, NJ, p 121–128
8	BC	(1985)	A Mão Invisível. (with Barbosa A, Barbosa M, Beleza M, Borges A and Lucena D), Semanário, Lisboa
9	BC	(1983)	Newspaper and Democracy in Portugal: The Role of Market Structure. In: Maxwell K (ed) The Press and the Rebirth of Iberian Democracy. Greenwood Press, Westport, CT

(continued)

Table A5 (continued)

#	Type	Year	Title
10	JR	(1986)	Small Countries in Monetary Unions: A Two-Tier Model. Journal of Economic Dynamics and Control 10(1–2):275–280. Also Mondes en Developpement 56: 41–63
11	JR	(1983)	Optimal Currency Diversification for a Class of Risk-Averse International Investors. Journal of Economics Dynamics and Control 5:173–185 (NBER Reprint 408)
12	JR	(1982)	Exchange Rate Behaviour Under Currency Inconvertibility. Journal of International Economics 12(1–2):65–81 (Princeton Reprint in International Finance 22)
13	JR	(1982)	The Optimal Weighting of Indicators for a Crawling Peg. (with Branson W) Journal of International Money and Finance 1:165–178 (NBER Reprint 365)
14	JR	(1978)	De Chicago ao FMI: A Abordagem Monetária da Balança de Pagamentos. Economia II (3)
15	JR	(1977)	Teoria da Desvalorização Cambial: A Abordagem Keynesiana. Economia, I (2)
16	JR	(1977)	Emigration and Remittances in Neoclassical Steady-State. Economia, I (1)
17	OJ	(2018)	Annex to Jean-Pierre Contzen. Memórias da Academia das Ciências de Lisboa - Classe de Ciências, tomo 45, Oct:251
18	OJ	(2016)	Memória de Gago para além das suas políticas. Nova Cidadania 59, Summer
19	OJ	(2015)	De Mariano Gago a Damião de Góis via Borges de Macedo. Nova Cidadania 57, Fall:57–73
20	OJ	(2002)	Economia em três tempos (=3 × 3 × 3 pontos). Boletim de Ciências Económicas da Faculdade de Direito de Coimbra, XLV-A: 499–536 (special 50th anniversary issue, dedicated to Teixeira Ribeiro)
21	OJ	(2001)	Da cultura económica. Tradição do Futuro, nº 6, Summer:65–66
22	OJ	(2001)	From Transformation to Development: Globalisation and Perspectives for Economic Policy. Emergo, Journal of Transforming Economies and Societies, vol. 8 nº 2, Spring
23	OJ	(1994)	Bancos não são Talhos. Nova Economia
24	OJ	(1991)	Ajuda à Europa do Leste numa Perspectiva Luso-Comunitária. Risco, nº 16:43–54
25	OJ	(1987)	Bancos, Desenvolvimento Financeiro e Perspectivas Macroeconómicas. Revista da Banca, vol. 1
26	OJ	(1985)	Exchange Rate Flexibility and the Transmission of Business Cycles. (with Meerschwam D) NBER Working Paper nº 1573, Mar
27	OJ	(1984)	Currency Inconvertibility, Portfolio Balance and Relative Prices, Dynamic Modelling and Control of National Economies. (ed) Basar T, Pau L, IFAC Proceedings Series, 7, Oxford:401–408 (NBER Reprint 630)

(continued)

Table A5 (continued)

#	Type	Year	Title
28	OJ	(1976)	Economia Política da Defesa. Nação e Defesa, ano 1, Jul:75–83
29	OJ	(1976)	O que é o Socialismo, Democracia e Liberdade. Boletim da IDL, nº 1, Oct, adapted in Nação e Defesa, ano 1, Nov:3–19
30	POL	(2016)	Afirmar o Diálogo Global num Fórum Político, ou Estoril ao Quadrado. presentation at Estoril Political Forum 2016, available in Nova Cidadania
31	POL	(2016)	Política externa portuguesa, africana e social: Madiba e TropiK-Man Ph. D., Povo Livre nº 1949 21 Dec:15
32	POL	(2006)	Plano de Desenvolvimento Estratégico Sintra 2015. Final Report (with Luís Azevedo Coutinho, Regina Salvador and Paulo Trigo Pereira), GANEC, March (unpublished)
33	POL	(2005)	Comment to Marcos 1, 12–15, Os Evangelhos 2006 Comentados. Firmamento, Lisboa: 66–69
34	POL	(2001)	Financing Cities and Regions. (with Rui Nuno Baleiras) final report of a project financed by Fundação Luso-Americana para o Desenvolvimento, Sep
35	POL	(1997)	Depoimento à Comissão Parlamentar de Inquérito ao Acordo estabelecido entre o Estado e o Senhor António Champalimaud. Parliament, Lisboa, Feb
36	POL	(1995)	Acompanhamento e Apreciação da Revisão do Tratado da União Europeia na Conferência Inter-Governamental de 1996. vol 1, Parliament, Lisboa, Apr
37	POL	(1995)	Acompanhamento e Apreciação da Revisão do Tratado da União Europeia na Conferência Inter-Governamental de 1996. vol 2 (Resolution nº 21/95, 8 Apr), Parliament, Lisboa, Sep
38	POL	(1994)	Depoimento à Comissão Eventual de Inquérito Parlamentar para a Apreciação do Processo de Privatização do Banco Totta & Açores. Parliament, Lisboa, Sep
39	POL	(1994)	Portugal na União Europeia, lei de acompanhamento e apreciação. Parliament, Lisboa, Jun
40	POL	(1994)	Transparência, Alargamento e Emprego, Teses Portuguesas na X COSAC. Parliament, Jul
41	POL	(1994)	Portugal na União Europeia em 1993: Apreciação Parlamentar. Parliament, Lisboa, Aug
42	POL	(1993)	A Política Económica Global em 1993. Ministry of Finance, Lisboa, Jan
43	POL	(1993)	Orçamento Suplementar para 1993; Programa de Convergência Revisto; Orçamento do Estado para 1994: Apresentação Publica, Relatório e Proposta de Lei. Ministry of Finance, Lisboa, Oct
44	POL	(1992)	Sustained structural reform in Portugal, Trilogue. Trilateral Commission World Meeting in Lisbon, Paris, Apr
45	POL	(1992)	Orçamento do Estado para 1992: Apresentação Publica, Relatório e Proposta de Lei. Ministry of Finance, Lisboa, Feb

(continued)

Table A5 (continued)

#	Type	Year	Title
46	POL	(1992)	Política Económica Global - Os Primeiros Seis Meses. Ministry of Finance, Lisboa, May
47	POL	(1992)	Orçamento do Estado para 1993: Apresentação Publica, Relatório e Proposta de Lei. Ministry of Finance, Lisboa, Oct
48	POL	(1991)	Assegurar a Convergencia com a Comunidade Europeia: um Objectivo da Política Económica do XII Governo, Ministry of Finance, Lisboa, Dec
49	PREF	(2012)	Lencastre A. Evolução Cristo o alfa e o ómega—o princípio e o fim. Leya, Lisboa: 13–16
50	PREF	(2009)	Mendes Ferrão JE. O Café: a bebida negra dos sonhos claros. Chaves Ferreira Edições; Lisboa
51	PREF	(2007)	Mendes Ferrão JE. Plants in the first globalization. IICT, Lisboa (available in Portuguese)
52	WP	(2013)	Exchange rate dynamics revisited (with Lempinen U), NBER Working Paper nº 19,718 Dec

The manufacturer's authorised representative in the EU is Springer Nature Customer Service Centre GmbH, Europaplatz 3, 69115 Heidelberg, Germany. If you have any concerns regarding our products, please contact ProductSafety@springernature.com

Printed and bound by CPI Group (UK) Ltd, Croydon, CR0 4YY
30/09/2026
02225699-0012